WIDE RIVERS CROSSED

WIDE RIVERS CROSSED

The South Platte and the Illinois of the American Prairie

Ellen Wohl

UNIVERSITY PRESS OF COLORADO
Boulder

© 2013 by University Press of Colorado

Published by University Press of Colorado
5589 Arapahoe Avenue, Suite 206C
Boulder, Colorado 80303

Printed in the United States of America

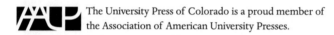 The University Press of Colorado is a proud member of
the Association of American University Presses.

The University Press of Colorado is a cooperative publishing enterprise supported, in part,
by Adams State University, Colorado State University, Fort Lewis College, Metropolitan State
University of Denver, Regis University, University of Colorado, University of Northern Colorado,
Utah State University, and Western State Colorado University.

∞ This paper meets the requirements of the ANSI/NISO Z39.48-1992 (Permanence of Paper).

Library of Congress Cataloging-in-Publication Data

Wohl, Ellen E., 1962–
  Wide rivers crossed : the South Platte and the Illinois of the American prairie / Ellen Wohl.
    pages cm
  Includes bibliographical references and index.
  ISBN 978-1-60732-230-6 (hardcover : alk. paper) — ISBN 978-1-60732-231-3 (ebook)
  1. South Platte River (Colo. and Neb.)—Environmental conditions. 2. Illinois River (Ill.)—
Environmental conditions. 3. Streamflow—South Platte River (Colo. and Neb.) 4. Streamflow—
Illinois—Illinois River. 5. Water use—South Platte River Watershed (Colo. and Neb.) 6. Water
use—Illinois—Illinois River. 7. Natural history—South Platte River (Colo. and Neb.) 8. Natural
history—Illinois—Illinois River. I. Title.
  GB1225.C6W65 2013
  917.73'509693—dc23

                        2013006729

Design by Daniel Pratt

22   21   20   19   18   17   16   15   14   13   10   9   8   7   6   5   4   3   2   1

Contents

WIDE RIVERS CROSSED

Prologue

The North American prairie—the portion of the continent bounded on the east by forest and on the west by forested mountains—is a landscape of distances. When one
is traveling across the western prairie, the periodic mountain ranges rimming the grasslands seem unnatural, as
though Earth's interior had been extruded and exposed
for reasons not apparent. Piñon pines and juniper trees
appear at the slightest increase in elevation and the landscape becomes more cryptic, hiding breaks in slope from
view. The big mountains have forced the aridity of the
prairie, shielding the lowlands to the east from moisture-
bearing winds off the Pacific Ocean. The aridity of the
prairie has in turn shaped the biological and cultural evolution of central North America. Plants adapted to periodic droughts and to continual high rates of evaporation
and desiccating winds. Animals of all kinds, including the
first humans to occupy the landscape, adapted migratory habits by following the seasonal and year-to-year
variations in moisture and the plant food the moisture
supported. Only people of European descent squat heavily on this landscape, attempting to alter it to meet our
expectations of trees, crops, and three-season greenery
within cities, not to mention recreational lakes.

Come spring, a flush of bright green spreads among
the wild grasses and the cottonwoods lining the stream

The shortgrass prairie at Pawnee National Grassland in the South Platte River basin, northeastern Colorado, in autumn. The cottonwood trees in the foreground grow next to a spring and were likely planted by settlers creating shade for their cattle; otherwise, trees are absent from the landscape.

courses of the western prairie. By midsummer the grasses are fading toward the golden brown color they will hold through the remainder of the year, and only the wildflowers and the trees along the streams provide more vivid hues. Patches of pale gray or brown reveal exposed soil or outcrops of soft, crumbling bedrock. Subtle shadings across the landscape come with changes in the angle of light or differences between vegetation in the swales and on the steeper hill slopes. Grasses bend in the ever-present wind. Clouds of blue, gray, and white form individual puffs that change from moment to moment. During summer afternoons, virga hangs in a gray smudge over the horizon.

The big streams head in the mountains, and their eastward flow of cold, fresh water seems like a miracle among the white patches of salt-encrusted depressions and ground-hugging grasses and cacti. Other streams depend on a slow but steady excess overflow from springs and seeps in this landscape that appears to have no excess of water. The least reliable streams depend on the exuberance of

Blue grama at Pawnee National Grassland; the darker clumps at the rear of this view are small shrubs. These bunchgrasses of the shortgrass prairie are mostly about 10 cm tall; seedheads may rise to 30 cm. Where heavily grazed by cows, the blue grama forms a continuous lawn-like cover. In the absence of such grazing, the plants grow as distinctly separate bunches with bare ground between.

a thunderstorm that transmits the excess of the atmosphere—the generosity of the oceans—to the land. All the streams flow sinuously east, the larger channels interrupted by reservoirs contrary to climate and geography, like clots along their arteries.

Because any vantage point reveals such a vast extent at once and maps suggest that the prairie goes on and on beyond sight, it can be difficult to realize that the native plant and animal communities of this landscape can be endangered. Those who see the western prairie with the eyes of a botanist speak of vanished landscapes. Close scrutiny reveals subtle changes in vegetation. Some of the grasses moving so gracefully beneath the wind are crested wheatgrass (*Agropuron cristatum*) from Asia or introduced cheatgrass (*Anisantha tectorum*) and foxtail barley (*Hordeum jubatum*). Russian olive trees (*Elaeagnus angustifolia*) from Eurasia grow thickly along many of the stream courses. To an ecologist, each of these non-native species is like an exclamation point on the landscape, an emphatic indicator that changes are in fact cascading through the apparently timeless landscape as the invasive plants alter the cycling of nutrients and the biological communities of the soil or the cohesion of the stream banks and the erosive effects of floods.

Although the plants and animals of the western prairie are adapted to periodic drought, mobility is one of the keys to their survival. If conditions are bad in one area, fish migrate downstream to a larger pool or antelope travel across a watershed to better pastures. Mobility becomes a less effective strategy when only isolated remnants of native habitat remain or when barriers restrict movement. The stresses appear everywhere during the dry years at the start of the twenty-first century. Native cottonwood trees show the effects of several years of drought; many have died back at the top. Stream courses are drying, too, where water is diverted to irrigate crops. The drying streams and the absence of floods now stored in reservoirs appear indirectly in the riverside forests of aging and dying trees that are not being replaced by new saplings germinating in freshly deposited flood sediments.

Much of the landscape is overgrazed. In places, fenced rights-of-way along highways form the greenest parts of the landscape. Prairie dogs stand like sentinels at their burrows even in overgrazed patches, but many animals are missing, from the invertebrates of soil and streams to the prairie wolves, grizzly bears, and bison described by the first Europeans to visit the western prairie.

The landscape of the prairie evolved with grazing animals, and we know the history of changes in the landscape in part from the fossil record of changes in these animals. Horses evolved in North America, although the animals present today are the descendants of imports from Europe. Horse fossils cover 60 million years of geologic history in North America. About 25 million years ago horses developed high-crowned teeth especially adapted for eating grass, as did the camels and rhinoceros living in North America at that time. Grazers need high-crowned teeth because they must eat a great deal of grass that is less nutritious than other plant parts, and the grass abrades their teeth. These animals' dietary shift to grasses indirectly records uplift of the Rocky Mountains and the development of interior grasslands in the rain shadow of the range. Grasses responded to increasing aridity by evolving a broad network of roots to soak up the limited precipitation. Grazing favors grasses that are shorter and reproduce with underground roots and runners rather than seeds, allowing these plants to become more widespread. Grasses also moved much of their biomass belowground, where it was safer from wildfires, grazing, and dessicating wind and sun.[1]

Wildfires rather than drought probably acted as the invisible fences limiting the spread of trees into the grasslands of the eastern prairie. The underground

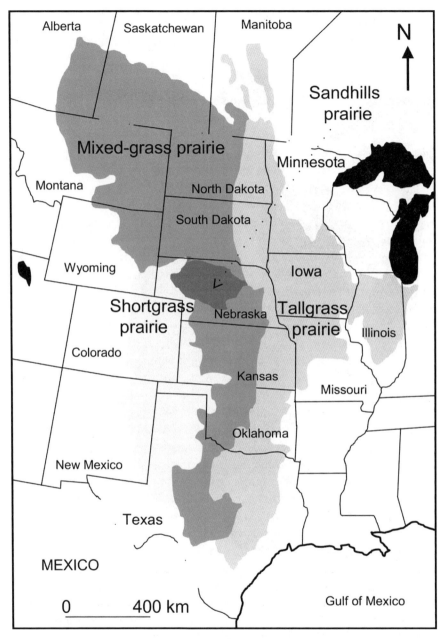

Distribution of the different types of prairie across North America. The 100th meridian is the dashed line running north-south through the center of the map. This line roughly marks the transition to semiarid climate and the western limit of the tallgrass prairie.

growth points of grasses remain relatively safe during fires that can readily injure growth points on the branches of trees. Before Europeans settled the eastern prairie, fires probably recurred every three to ten years as lightning strikes ignited the dry grasses of late summer or Native Americans set fires to improve the grazing for animals they hunted.

Unlike the western prairie, water is not noticeably absent on the eastern prairie. Diverse grasses and forbs grow waist- or chest-high in vivid hues of green topped by white, yellow, purple, blue, and red flowers. The air lies heavy with humidity beneath the flat white sky of late summer and loud with the shrilling of insects and the calls of songbirds. The big rivers here do not rise in snow-covered mountains but rather collect their waters from hundreds of small tributaries that start in shallow springs and seeps. Groundwater is close to the surface in every depression, and the gently sloping rivers overflow their banks regularly to spread across broad floodplains. Wetlands are abundant compared to the shortgrass prairie.

You have to work to find tiny patches of native grasses among the vast fields of corn, soybeans, and other crops that cover the eastern prairie. The once limitless horizons are in many places hemmed in by trees that fire suppression has allowed to flourish. Unlike the relatively open grazing lands of the western prairie, the densely planted crops of the eastern prairie give no impression of natural grasslands.

When Europeans first reached North America, prairies covered approximately 40 percent of the contiguous United States, more land than any other ecosystem on the continent. Now, an estimated 98 percent of the tallgrass prairies are gone, replaced by croplands or urbanization or altered in obvious and subtle ways by introduced plants. One-fifth to one-third of the plant species currently in North America—as many as 6,600 species—are introduced, and the grasslands have the greatest number of introduced species of any ecosystem on the continent.[2]

These changes have affected the shortgrass, mixed-grass, and tallgrass prairies, albeit to different degrees. Shortgrasses growing in tight little bunches separated by bare ground gradually transition eastward to the mixed-grass prairie, where the grasses grow progressively taller. Shortgrass prairie—also referred to in this book as the western prairie—is predominantly west of the 100th meridian. This ecosystem largely overlaps the Great Plains, a north-south band of the western interior of North America that stretches from the base of the Rocky Mountains on the west to the central lowlands east of the 100th meridian and averages about 600 kilometers in width. An estimated 20 percent to 40 percent of the shortgrass prairie remains, whereas at least half of the mixed-grass prairie is gone; some estimates place the loss as high as 85 percent.[3]

Approximately every thirty years, drought cycles shift the border between the mixed-grass and adjacent tallgrass prairie as much as a few hundred kilometers

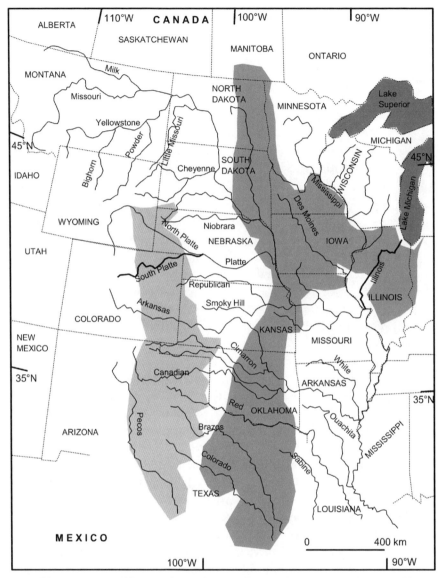

Map of the major rivers of the central United States, showing the approximate location of the shortgrass prairie (pale gray shaded area to west) and tallgrass prairie (darker gray shaded area to the east). Mixed-grass prairie lies between. The western boundary of the Great Plains coincides with the western boundary of the shortgrass prairie, and the eastern boundary with the boundary between the mixed-grass and tallgrass prairies. The South Platte and Illinois Rivers are bold lines.

east. The tallgrass prairie occupies the eastern portion of the grasslands—referred to in this book as the eastern prairie. This is where grasses, including big bluestem and Indiangrass, once grew taller than a horse. The tallgrass prairie once contained at least 200 species of forbs, shrubs, trees, and, above all, grasses. Fire and grazing kept the woodlands at bay except along stream courses. With only 2 percent of the tallgrass prairie remaining, the native grasses and plant communities are now mostly gone, but they inspired admiring descriptions of the land's fertility and the beauty of the flowering plants from the first Europeans to visit the eastern prairie.[4]

Many of the physical changes in the landscape at first seem subtle but become readily apparent once you are aware of them and know what to look for. Yet even changes that appear subtle can have extensive implications for the web of life spread through this landscape, from tiny microbes to relatively large humans, bison, or eagles. Changes that have occurred in the streams of the American prairie during the past century are particularly important because streams are much more vital to plants and animals than is suggested by the thin blue lines on a map. If we mapped surface area proportional to ecological importance, thick strands of blue would bind the grasslands in a close mesh that reflected the abundance and diversity of species in the rivers and floodplains.

This book examines the historical environmental changes that have occurred along streams of the American prairie and their implications for sustaining native plant and animal communities, as well as human communities, in the region. As with rivers across the United States, prairie rivers have changed dramatically during the past two centuries. As people replaced native vegetation with crops, snowmelt and rainfall draining into the rivers carried increasing amounts of soil, as well as excess fertilizers and pesticides. The distribution of water was not always convenient; and levees, dams, diversions, and drainage altered that distribution on a massive scale. These changes in river form and process cascaded through river networks, from the smallest headwater tributaries to the Mississippi, reducing the rivers' ability to provide some of the "ecosystem services" on which people rely—clean water, soil fertility, habitat for diverse forms of life. The rapidly increasing cost of trying to provide these services artificially through water treatment plants or heavy applications of fertilizers raises awareness of the value of what we have lost and encourages innovative approaches to restoring rivers as ecosystems that provide services. Innovation and appreciation, however, rely on understanding of how rivers function and of how these functions have altered during the past two centuries. Such understanding is the focus of this book.

The Mississippi is the preeminent prairie river. Flowing southward, slightly east of center, the great river collects what flows from the continental interior and its fringes—water, sediment, nutrients, and contaminants. The Mississippi integrates the disparate prairies. The largest rivers of the western prairie head among the glaciers and snowfields near the Continental Divide, but they pick up large quantities of sediment as they flow for hundreds of kilometers across the dry plains, and they contribute most of the sediment that moves down the Mississippi toward the Gulf of Mexico. Rivers of the eastern prairie head among the lakes the retreating Pleistocene ice sheet left scattered thickly across the lowlands, or they head almost imperceptibly among the seeps and springs of a thousand small sloughs. These rivers historically flowed clear and contributed most of the water that courses down the Mississippi. Imagine the interior of the United States as an open book. The Mississippi forms its depressed spine with lines of text flowing into it from both sides. Eastern lines are blue for the water they bring; western lines are brown for their sediment. West and east, the prairie rivers have constructed much of the landscape of the continental interior, rearranging sediment left by wind and glacial ice and draping thick mantles of river sediment across the underlying bedrock.

Rivers of the dry western prairie and the wet eastern prairie are two sides of the same coin. The history of environmental change in each region reflects our relentless efforts to control the distribution of water: in the west, to enhance surface water with groundwater pumping and diversion from rivers outside the region and to make the streams flow more evenly throughout the year by using water storage; and in the east, to limit the spread of floods and drain the wetlands along the rivers. The first half of this book explores the characteristics and historical changes of rivers of the arid western prairie. Although the South Platte River basin of eastern Colorado and western Nebraska represents the shortgrass prairie, the text includes information from other rivers in the region where specific features of the riverine community—fish or birds, for example—have received more scientific study than their analogs on the South Platte River. Rivers across the western prairie have undergone a metamorphosis during the past century, largely in response to alteration of the natural flow regime through dams, diversions, and groundwater pumping. Scarcity of water defines the landscape of the western prairie and the history of environmental change on the region's rivers. In this context the headwater mountains—the Rockies—and their life-sustaining snowmelt are crucial. The first half of the book is thus organized around both a downstream progression from the mountainous headwaters, through the foothills transition zone, and on to the arid plains, and around a temporal progression from the first written descriptions of the region in the mid-nineteenth century to the present.

A key point is that the environmental changes described for the South Platte River are not unique. The South Platte is neither the most nor the least altered river of the western prairie but rather represents the type and extent of changes experienced by rivers throughout the region. I chose the South Platte because these historical changes have been well documented by numerous studies and because I live within the drainage basin and am particularly familiar with it.

The second half of the book explores the Illinois River basin of Illinois as representative of the tallgrass prairie and the more humid eastern grasslands. As with the western prairie, I also draw on knowledge of other rivers in the region as appropriate. Rivers across the eastern prairie have also been dramatically altered during the last hundred years through the combined effects of land drainage, channelization, dams, and levees. Abundance of water defines the landscape of the eastern prairie, and attempts to control the spread of water define the history of environmental change on rivers of the eastern prairie. The second half of the book is organized around the historical progression of river engineering and responses by the river ecosystem to this engineering. As with the South Platte, environmental changes on the Illinois River reflect those occurring on rivers throughout the eastern prairie: I chose this river because numerous scientific studies have chronicled environmental change within the drainage basin.

In writing and reading the details of environmental change, it is easy to lose track of the forest for the trees or perhaps the prairie for the grasses, so the discussion of each century starts or ends with a "historical snapshot" that provides a brief but comprehensive summary of the river environment at a point in time. Rivers and groundwater throughout the American prairies have in some areas been heavily contaminated by a variety of pollutants. Both sections of the book explore the causes and implications of this pollution, which is among the environmental changes that are hardest to control and ameliorate.

Despite the contrasts in climate and river flow between different portions of the prairie, rivers of the continental interior share some important characteristics. Unlike the steeper rivers confined by forested ridges or walls of rock in the lands to the east and west, the prairie rivers flow through open landscapes, free to meander widely or shift course when floodwaters surge down the channel. The simple landscape gives rise to complex rivers with backwaters and secondary channels, sloughs and wetlands. During seasons of high flow, the rivers spread and nourish plants and animals across their broad lowlands, shrinking back to narrower, defined courses as the flow diminishes. A river of the Appalachians or the Rockies tears away the forest and the boulders along its course when in flood, scouring its narrow valley and somewhere downstream dumping a lot of wood and sediment. A prairie river in flood can be an awesome force, too, but some of its energy dissipates as the floodwaters spread across the extensive bottoms, swirling into an old, dry channel here and leaving a layer of silt in a wetland there.

The commonality in the changes of rivers in the western and eastern prairie is a narrowing and simplification. The title of this volume reflects these changes. Both the South Platte and the Illinois were once wide rivers. The South Platte spread shallowly across a channel hundreds of meters wide during the annual snowmelt flood, and each year the Illinois spread across floodplain wetlands thousands of meters wide. In each case, the broad river channel served as a corridor for human migration but also as a challenge to movement and settlement. One of the first tasks of European settlers moving west was to physically cross these rivers. The word *cross* has many meanings. In addition to physically passing across something, the word signifies to encounter; to thwart, oppose, contradict, or betray; and a burden or responsibility. People of European descent who first encountered and then physically crossed over these rivers also in a sense opposed and contradicted the rivers by systematically altering their physical nature and ecological communities. More recently, people are assuming responsibility for restoring some of the lost physical and ecological characteristics of the prairie rivers.

Human uses of land, water, and other resources in the western and eastern prairie created differences in historical changes to the rivers of each region, as well as changes shared by rivers in the two regions, yet the prairie rivers still provide life to a wealth of unique plants and animals. An examination of the South Platte River and the Illinois River illustrates how contemporary rivers in the central portion of North America differ from the prairie rivers described during the eighteenth and nineteenth centuries by people of European descent. This information also provides the starting point from which we can work to restore and protect these most endangered of American rivers.

This book is not an environmental history because I am not an environmental historian. I am a river scientist, and I focus on the physical and ecological characteristics of the rivers and how those characteristics changed in response to human resource use. Although this necessitates some mention of changes in resource use through time, I do not explore in detail the societal, economic, and political forces that drove changing resource use. I tell stories in this book, but they are stories of rivers rather than of people. These stories rely on the careful, inspired research of hundreds of scientists from diverse disciplines, and the references footnoted for each paragraph list the original scientific publications summarizing their research.

As someone who studies physical changes in rivers, I have a recurring daydream of being able to travel back in time, with a camera and some simple equipment for making measurements, and thoroughly documenting a particular river in a manner that would be useful to twenty-first-century scientists. It is only a daydream, but much of the work of river scientists—geologists, ecologists, geographers, hydrologists—trying to understand historical changes along rivers involves using proxy historical records to infer how the river looked and functioned at various times in the past. Proxy records can be the measurements, photographs, or plant and animal collections made by the first scientists to study a river. Or the proxies can be less direct: fossil pollen recovered from cores of lake sediments; relict channels scattered across a floodplain as a river meandered back and forth over millennia; variations in the width of tree rings that reflect wet and dry years. Each of these records is somehow incomplete, with gaps in space or time when we use them to infer historical conditions across broad regions. But in the absence of time travel, they are all we have, and individual scientists continue to exhibit great ingenuity in developing new types of proxy historical records. Because of these records we are not ignorant of the history of prairie rivers, particularly the relatively recent history of the past two centuries. Careful attention to the environmental changes occurring during this period can help us avoid repeating some of the most unfortunate episodes of loss and change as we make resource decisions for our future.

NOTES

1. R. Manning, *Grassland: The History, Biology, Politics, and Promise of the American Prairie* (New York: Viking, 1995).

2. Ibid.; D. B. Botkin, *Beyond the Stony Mountains: Nature in the American West from Lewis and Clark to Today* (Oxford: Oxford University Press, 2004).

3. Manning, *Grassland*; Botkin, *Beyond the Stony Mountains*.

4. Manning, *Grassland*; Botkin, *Beyond the Stony Mountains*.

I. STREAMS OF THE SHORTGRASS PRAIRIE: THE SOUTH PLATTE RIVER BASIN

ONE

At the Headwaters

Crossing the summit of an elevated and
continuous range of rolling hills, on the
afternoon of the 30th of June we found
ourselves overlooking a broad and misty valley,
where, about ten miles distant, and 1,000 feet
below us, the South fork of the Platte was
rolling magnificently along, swollen with the
waters of the melting snows. It was in strong
and refreshing contrast with the parched
country from which we had just issued; and
when, at night, the broad expanse of water grew
indistinct, it almost seemed that we had pitched
our tents on the shore of the sea.

—*John Charles Frémont, on reaching the base of
the Colorado Rockies after traveling westward
across the Great Plains, June 1843*

SNOWFALL

In much of the world, a flowing river represents the
excess water that cannot be held by the plants and soil
along the river's course. The adjacent landscape over-
flows into the river, each tributary swelling the flow of
the mainstem. In contrast, the stream flow that sustains
the largest rivers of the western prairie begins far from
the dry lowlands, and tributaries heading on the prairie

DOI: 10.5876/9781607322313.c01

contribute little to the mainstem. This is one of the paradoxes of rivers of the western prairie: flowing for hundreds of kilometers across some of the continent's driest and most open country, the rivers begin in, and are sustained by, abundant winter snows falling in deep, narrow valleys of the topographic exclamation point that is the Rocky Mountains.

Snow starts to fall on the Rockies west of the prairie during September. In most years, the early snowfalls barely persist. A warm air mass moves eastward from the Pacific Ocean, and the thin skin of new snow melts into the soil or sublimates into the cold, dry air of 4,000 meters elevation. Air temperature in the drier central and southern parts of the Rockies can resemble a yo-yo, fluctuating rapidly up and down by 20°C or more from day to day. Within a month, however, at least a portion of each new snowfall remains on the ground. Great rivers and oceans of moist air flowing steadily inland from the Pacific collide with cold, dry Arctic air flowing down the spine of the Rockies. The tumultuous collisions create wind-driven snow granules and feathery powder snowflakes. What began as a light dusting of snow in September quickly deepens to a continuous covering of white as each new storm gradually builds the snowpack. The prairie remains a desiccated landscape of cured tan grasses, but in the mountains the snow can reach depths of 5 meters.

A year of abundant snowfall in the Colorado Rockies reflects the transfer of immense amounts of energy across half the planet. Equatorial and tropical latitudes receive the bulk of the solar radiation reaching Earth. Much of this intense low-latitude sunlight falls upon the broad expanse of the Pacific Ocean, creating a wide band of warm surface waters about the equator. The sun in a sense cooks the tropical oceans, warming the surface water and creating much higher rates of evaporation than occur over colder portions of the oceans. As water vaporizes and crosses the boundary from sea to air, warm, moist air billows up toward the sky. Some of this moisture cools, condenses, and falls back to the sea as torrential rains. Some of the moisture remains aloft and flows out from the equator toward each pole. Below these massive currents of air, warm water floats on the cooler, denser water beneath, flowing across the ocean surface toward higher latitudes until the water gradually cools and sinks to greater depths. These surface currents transfer heat to the atmosphere before sinking into the cold darkness of the deep ocean and returning at depth toward the equator. This is part of the aptly named Great Ocean Conveyor Belt, an endless cycling between the Pacific and the Atlantic that carries heat up into the North Atlantic. Only because of this pattern is northwestern Europe warmer and more suited for agriculture and habitation than equivalent latitudes in Canada and Siberia.[1]

By late January the upper elevations of the South Platte River drainage basin already have a thick snowpack that completely buries headwater creeks, as here in the Poudre River drainage tributary to the South Platte River. Melt water from the snowpack is vital to the ecological health of the rivers in the basin and to the existence of human communities.

Most of the water vapor carried by air moving toward the poles from the equatorial oceans falls as precipitation before the air reaches 30° North and South. This is where the spent, dry air descends back toward Earth's surface before continuing at low elevations within the atmosphere back to the equator. The complete cycle is known as the Hadley Cell after the eighteenth-century gentleman who first described it. Unless another moisture source such as an ocean with warm surface water is nearby, drylands—prairie, pampas, veld, steppe, savanna, and desert—occupy continental interiors at 30°–40° latitude.[2]

This latitudinal belt accounts for a big chunk of the Southern Rocky Mountains within the United States. Every other mountain range between the Pacific and the Rockies only exacerbates the dryness. The ocean of moist air flowing eastward from the Pacific rides a topographic roller coaster, rising and cooling over each mountain range and dropping more of its precious moisture with each rise. By the time the air reaches the eastern half of the Rockies, there often isn't much water vapor left. These mountains receive snowfall each year only because of their great height. Most winds that flow eastward down the mountain front in winter come as warm, dry chinooks that rearrange anything portable in the landscape but do nothing to increase precipitation on the plains. This is a second paradox of the rivers of the western prairie. The Rockies make the prairie drier than it might otherwise be, but they also supply the major rivers of the prairie. These rivers are able to flow through much, if not all, of the year only because of the snow that falls and then gradually melts off the Rockies.

Air does not flow through the Hadley Cell as regularly as the hands of a clock making a circuit, however, and blips in the circulation pattern can create years of heavy snowfall in the Colorado Rockies. While warm surface waters flow toward the poles and cold water flows back toward the equator at depth, water also moves across the Pacific in east-west currents. Cold water wells up from the great depths off the west coast of South America and then flows west across the surface of the tropical and equatorial Pacific, warming as it moves and creating a persistent pool of warm water around Indonesia and northern Australia. Warm water means evaporation and heavy rainfall. Monsoon rains fall on the lands around the western Pacific from December to February during most years, supporting lush rainforests, while the Atacama and Sechin Deserts lie at the other end of the Pacific.

Every few years, for reasons still unknown, the entire pattern reverses. Sea level pressure, which is normally low over the western Pacific and high over the eastern Pacific, flips in a pattern known as the Southern Oscillation. Warm surface waters slosh back toward the eastern Pacific. Indonesia goes into drought, and western South America receives torrential El Niño rains during the Christmas season. The effects of the combined El Niño–Southern Oscillation (ENSO) spread from the

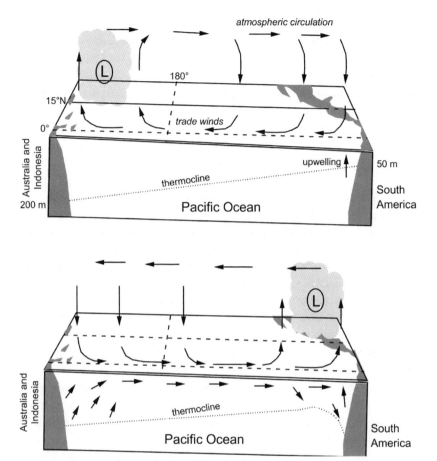

Schematic diagrams of atmospheric circulation patterns over the Pacific Ocean during normal conditions (top) and El Nino–Southern Oscillation (bottom). Under normal conditions, the difference in atmospheric pressure between a high-pressure center in the southeastern Pacific and a low-pressure center (L in diagrams) over Indonesia and northern Australia drives easterly trade winds along the equator. This circulation depresses the thermocline, the boundary between warm surface water and underlying cool layers, to a depth of almost 200 meters in the western Pacific Ocean. Because the trade winds drive surface water offshore along the western coast of South America, the thermocline is shallow, and cool water wells up to the ocean's surface. The trade winds converge with westerly winds near Indonesia, and the moist, rising air brings heavy rain. The air flows eastward at high altitudes before sinking over the central and eastern Pacific, where the weather is dry. During El Niño, the east-west pressure difference decreases, and the trade winds cease or weaken in the western Pacific. Warm surface water flows back toward the east, and the thermocline is depressed off South America, so that upwelling water is warm. The warming of the sea surface leads to convective activity and heavy rains over the eastern Pacific and adjacent land masses. After Ramage (1986, 76).

tropical Pacific like a rock thrown into a still pond. Normal rainfall and snow patterns change from southern Australia to India, and more abundant winter and spring precipitation delights skiers and water managers in the Colorado Rockies.[3]

Year-to-year variations in snowfall across the Rockies also reflect the Pacific Decadal Oscillation (PDO). The northern Pacific Ocean oscillates between warmer and cooler conditions at time spans of twenty to thirty years. Cool phases of the oscillation correspond to drought in Colorado as the surface of the Pacific cools off western North America. The cooling ocean reduces evaporation and inland transport of moisture. The jet stream is the express freight bringing much of this moisture inland, and changes in sea level pressure occurring during the PDO act like a giant switch, sending the jet stream further north. The last warm phase of the PDO persisted from 1977 to 1999, but during the past decade the PDO has alternated at shorter intervals between warm and cool phases.

Between the ENSO, the PDO, and other, less regular fluctuations, snowfall in the Rockies can bury the mountain meadows so deep that not a slight dimple reveals the little headwater creeks, or it can be so miserly that in midwinter the creeks still flow freely between whitened banks. These fluctuations in snowfall translate all the way downstream to the dry plains.

SNOWMELT

A lot happens between a winter storm over the Rockies and stream flow in the rivers of the western prairie. First there is the snow itself, a much more complex entity than delicate little six-pointed flakes drifting quietly down. As a result of variations in the moisture content of the cloud in which the snowflake formed, air temperature when the snow fell, and wind speed at the surface on which the snow landed, not all snowflakes are created equal. Snow falling during the first part of the winter in the Rockies tends to be the light, fluffy "powder" snow that delights skiers. This is the low-density snow that seems bottomless when you fall into it and punch your ski pole down looking for support to get back up. As air temperatures grow warmer during March and April and strong winds buffeting the mountains break snowflakes into fragments that can pack together tightly, falling snow compacts into a dense, wet mass detested by homeowners shoveling their driveways.

The density of the snowpack exerts a vital control on how much water will actually melt out of the pack, as does the depth of snow. Depth is easy to measure, except that it varies quite a lot across the steep, wind-blasted topography of the Rockies. Density is more difficult to measure because it continues to alter once the snow has fallen. As the snow keeps coming—1 meter, 2 meters, 3 meters,

4 meters—the overlying weight compacts the snow at the base of the pack. In the dark, cold depths, a subtle alchemy occurs as delicate flakes with projecting points melt slightly under pressure and then re-freeze as larger, more spherical particles of greater density. Some of the re-freezing snow-water creates bridges between adjacent particles, further reducing the air spaces within the snowpack. Density of the snowpack progressively increases as snow accumulates, but the rate and degree of this increase vary. Sometimes layers of solid ice form within the pack through the combined effect of settling, melting, and re-freezing. Then again, extremely cold temperatures and relatively shallow snow depths can result in relatively little change in snowpack density.[4]

Snow has historically fallen during every month of the year in the Colorado Rockies. Spring typically begins with a series of "false starts" when snowstorms follow periods of warmth. Eventually, even the densest snowpack warms under the influence of increasing air temperatures and lengthening hours of sunlight. Feathery snow crystals and dense ice lenses vanish during the next few weeks as the snowpack disintegrates. Snow sublimates directly into water vapor as dry winds slip across the surface. Given the gusts that can blast across the Rockies and plains in springtime, it is surprising that any snow remains to melt into water. Yet some of the snow does melt at the surface before filtering down into the porous snow beneath or flowing across the surface crust of ice. Meanwhile, snow at depth melts and seeps downward. As melting increases, the snowpack behaves like a sponge, storing the melt water until it finally becomes saturated and water begins to percolate downward. Arriving at the base of the snowpack, some of the melt water infiltrates into the soil. Some of it accumulates to form a saturated zone that moves downslope toward a stream channel. All across the highlands the ground becomes mushy with water moving down toward the valleys.[5]

This is one of those recurrent miracles we take for granted: water filtering drop by drop into layers of sand and gravel in the soil through which it can seep or finding minute cracks in the seemingly impenetrable bedrock, forced onward by the pressure of the water behind it. Water following shallower underground paths reaches the stream channels in days to weeks, but some of the snowmelt filters down to the saturated zone below the water table, moving so slowly that it reaches the nearest stream channels months or years later. All of these millions of tiny, hidden pathways gradually fill up with water as spring continues into early summer, until the stream banks cut into mountain meadows dribble water like a leaky faucet.

Melting of the snowpack is largely invisible on the slopes while the snow is present. Early hikers may "posthole" at every step as they break through the icy surface crust and sink into the mushy snow beneath, but the only real indication of the progressive melting is the gradual rise in stream flow and the slow reemergence of snow-buried rocks and fallen logs. The most intriguing signs of all the action occurring in the snowpack appear once the melting is largely complete. Small, linear mounds of soil lie scattered across the slopes, discontinuous hieroglyphics written by rodents tunneling between their burrow entrances at the base of the snowpack. Melt water flowing downslope carries the sand and gravel dug up by the little animals, and the tunnels fill with sediment that remains briefly after the snow is gone. A few summer rains or the heavy tread of a passing elk and the perfect casts of tunnels smear into loose heaps of sediment.

Even without the mounds of pocket gophers, a mountain hill slope is not a smooth, regular surface. Snowmelt flowing across the recently thawed ground finds every little hollow and trough, concentrating into small rivulets in which water a few centimeters deep starts to erode exposed sediment grains. Occasionally, the soggy hill slopes give way abruptly in debris flows or landslides that move masses of sediment downslope. The winter streams of clear water flowing quietly patterned in green and black against the white ice give way to churning masses of milky brown color. Emily Dickinson described this transformation: "When the snows come hurrying from the hills, and the bridges often go." For most of the year, streams in the Colorado Rockies carry only a few milligrams of sediment in suspension per liter of water. During snowmelt this level can rise to more than a thousand milligrams per liter, although mostly remaining below a hundred milligrams.

The mountain tributaries of the South Platte River spread widely from north to south along the spine of the Rockies, collecting melting snow like an enormous rake. Up near the Wyoming border, the Cache la Poudre River starts in a modest lake in Rocky Mountain National Park and flows northeast before curving eastward to join the South Platte near the city of Greeley. Named by French fur trappers for a cache of gunpowder left near the channel, the Poudre was Colorado's first federally designated wild and scenic river. Only a few kilometers from Poudre Lake, the headwaters of the Big Thompson River flow southeast through Forest Canyon, one of the most rugged backcountry areas in the national park, collecting water from cirque lakes named Azure, Inkwell, Lonesome, Rainbow, and Highest Lakes before funneling into the narrow gorge of Big Thompson Canyon and joining the South Platte on the plains. North, Middle, and South St. Vrain Creeks drain the mountains south of Longs Peak. Like the Poudre, the names of these rivers reflect the history of beaver trapping. Both David Thompson and Ceran St. Vrain trapped beaver in the region during the early decades of the nineteenth century. South of the St. Vrain drainage lie Boulder Creek, Clear Creek, Tarryall Creek, and the forks of the South Platte itself. The South Fork of the

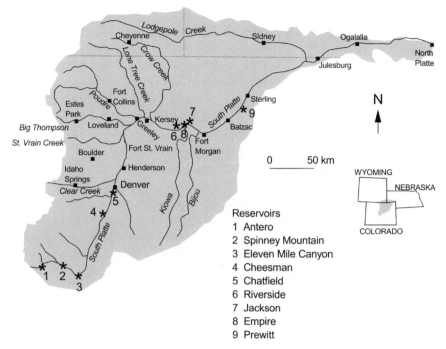

Schematic map of the South Platte River drainage basin (shaded), showing selected tributary rivers (names italicized), some of the communities and historical sites (e.g., Fort St. Vrain) mentioned in the text, and nine of the major reservoirs on or near the South Platte mainstem (many other off-channel and tributary reservoirs exist).

South Platte lies close to the northern headwaters of the Arkansas River, the next major river of the western prairie, just as the northern tributaries of the Poudre River lie close to the southern headwaters of the North Platte River. The abundance of melting snow flowing down steep slopes has carved the landscape into a dense network of streams, where only relatively narrow topographic high points separate adjacent drainages.

Spring snowmelt across the broad upper basin of the South Platte is a flush that spreads upward with time. As the nearby snow melts, stream flow at the lower elevations rises and then remains high while tributaries farther up the drainage basin swell with melting snow at the higher elevations. The result is a remarkable synchronicity in the timing of peak flow throughout the mountains. From streams near the top of the mountains at elevations of nearly 3,000 meters down to streams flowing beyond the mountain front at 1,400 meters elevation, peak flow commonly occurs between June 8 and 16 each year.

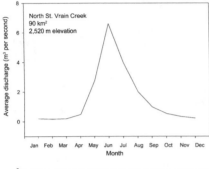

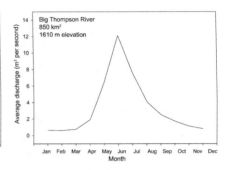

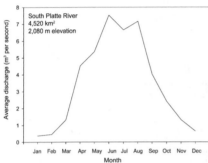

Sample hydrographs from stream sites at various elevations throughout the mountainous portion of the South Platte River basin. These curves show average monthly flow for each site. The drainage area and elevation of the river at that site are also listed. The hydrographs clearly show the strong annual peak in June and the relatively low flows during October to April.

Measurements of stream flow taken since the last decade of the nineteenth century record the consistent timing of peak flow, but changes now occurring in the mountains are altering this regular seasonal pulse. Global climate change is not simply an increase in mean air temperature. Storm tracks, extremes of temperature and precipitation, and timing of seasonal shifts also change. One of the most important alterations in regions such as the Colorado Rocky Mountains, where the gradual melting of the winter snowpack drives stream flow far beyond the mountains, is the possibility of less snowfall or faster snowpack melting. Less snowfall simply means less water, which has far from simple implications for survival in the western prairie. Faster melting can cause storage reservoirs to overflow early in the season but then be unable to store sufficient water for consumptive uses later in the summer and autumn. Global change might push the already boom-and-bust nature of seasonal fluctuations in stream flow on the western prairie to an extreme to which human and non-human communities will struggle to adjust.

Snow can also melt faster when it gets dirty. The Rocky Mountains, rearing up 4,000 meters, form a magnet to the world's winds, and the highlands catch other things besides snow. Increased dust results from changes in land use as diverse as replacing camels with four-wheel–drive vehicles in the Middle East and increasing drought and overgrazing in China. Once airborne, the dust becomes a globetrotter. Dust from the Middle East creates "blood rains" in England and settles as far away as Greenland and Caribbean coral reefs. Dust storms from China cross the Pacific Ocean and help drive air pollution levels close to federal health standards in Denver, Colorado. It is a small world after all.[6]

Ocean-crossing dust storms began to make national news during the first years of the twenty-first century. In 2006, National Public Radio reported that six dust storms hit the Colorado Rockies between December 2005 and May 2006. This resulted in more dust settling onto mountain snowpacks than scientists had recorded in at least two decades. Dust sounds vaguely benign, like something the mountain winds would just blow away. But dust settling onto an uneven snow surface acts like a dark blanket spread across the snow, increasing the rate of snowmelt much more significantly than the steadily increasing temperatures do. The combined effects of all the dust and anomalously warm temperatures during spring and summer 2006 showed up in stream flow that year. Peak flows were just over half to three-quarters of average values, even though the snowpack had been at or slightly above the thirty-year average at the end of March. The problem was that the snowpack was gone about a month early, by the end of May. Scientists predict that such changes in timing and volume of snowmelt will continue to grow more pronounced as climate warms.[7]

LIFE IN THE FAST LANE

The tributaries of the mountain tributaries—tiny, unnamed creeklets that rise from a spring in an alpine meadow or a seep at the base of a talus slope—coalesce into small lakes perched on the steep slopes near the Continental Divide. Glacier ice coalesced here in the past, and the bouldery rampart of a glacial moraine forms the downslope margin of each lake. Water overflowing from the lake cuts a channel through the moraine and leaps downslope in waterfalls and cascades. Tannic acids released by the pines stain the cold water a light, clear brown, like weakly steeped tea. Vertical drops and big rocks beat the brown water to a white froth. Any plant or animal living in these mountain creeks adapts to cold water with plenty of oxygen, fast currents, and limited sunlight where the creeks flow through forests.

Most of the animals that live in the creeks, at least on the creek bottoms, are insects. Ecologists refer to the streambed as the benthic environment from the Greek *benthos*, for depths of the sea, and the turbulent world of the creek bed creates challenges as great as those in the deep, dark sea. Where sunlight reaches the channel, algae and aquatic macrophytes can grow. In the mountain streams of the South Platte catchment, macrophytes are limited to mosses, lichens, and liverworts. Much of the photosynthesis occurs in the periphyton (from the Greek *peri* for "around" and *phyton* for "plant"), an assemblage of diatoms, green algae, blue-green algae, bacteria, and other microorganisms attached to submerged rocks and logs. This is the greenish or brownish slime a fisherman slipping on a rock may curse, but it provides a banquet for the benthic insects. Bits of fine organic detritus trapped among the living cells, like food crumbs in a shag carpet, further increase the nutritional value for insects that can digest such material. Ecologists refer to the benthic insects that feed on periphyton as scrapers or grazers. Using mouthparts structurally suited for rasping, tiny mayfly nymphs move among the creek-bed rocks as steadily as mountain goats on land. Similar to goats that scramble on muscular legs up steep, rocky slopes to reach succulent plants, the benthic grazers can move through the rushing water thanks to bodily adaptations such as flattening, streamlining, claws or hooks, and friction pads. Where the plants are too big to simply rasp off the rocks or logs, herbivore shredders mash up the green tissues into ingestible chunks.[8]

In portions of the creek where shade limits photosynthesis, plant parts dropped from the riverside forest or carried downstream on the current provide the food for aquatic insects. Detrivore shredders such as stonefly nymphs are the little street sweepers of the creek bed, converting shed plant parts into living insect tissue. Gougers help the shredders by boring into submerged logs, riddling the wood with tiny tunnels that promote decay and eventual breakage and dissolution of the wood. Collectors take care of the finest leftovers, the nearly microscopic bits carried along suspended in the water. Some filter-feeding collectors construct tiny silk nets that they drape across a crevice between rocks; others simply expose hair fringes along their bodies that trap moving particles. Net-spinning caddisfly nymphs fish from a cave, projecting their fine silk nets from a snugly fitting tube of sand grains cemented together and attached to the creek bed. It's good to have a cave to retreat into when predatory insects come around.[9]

Stoneflies, mayflies, caddisflies, dipterans, and elmid beetles together make up the benthic fauna of the mountain streams. For most, the stream is the world of their youth, from which they move to a terrestrial adult life. If insects possessed consciousness, the loss of youth would be particularly poignant: the mayflies, aptly named Ephemeroptera from the Greek "for a day," live as adults for at most a few days. Some live only an hour. Their juvenile phases last longer: aquatic insects can live in juvenile stage for more than two years. Juvenile insects are known as larvae, from the Latin for "ghost" or "mask," because they bear so little resemblance to an adult or as nymphs from the Greek for "bride," derived from the nymphs who resided in streams in classical mythology.[10]

Spring and early summer can be a lean time at the benthic insect banquet table. The snowmelt flood carries pulses of sand and fine gravel along the creek bed, scouring the periphyton. If the collectors can hang on, a lot of food is moving by in the current, but it's traveling fast. Partly because of seasonal fluctuations in water temperature and food supply, most aquatic insects living in the mountain streams take at least a year to complete the juvenile, aquatic phase of their lives. Benthic insects down on the prairie are more likely to rush through more than one generation in a year.[11]

As the little creeks join together, they form streams large enough to support fish. Much of the energy in the steepest streams is expended simply getting around the big obstacles in the creek bed. Water plunges off vertical drops and breaks into standing waves, gushing over and around boulders and logs as wide as the flow is deep. Where the water has sufficient energy to rearrange the boulders dropping in from rockfall or left by retreating glaciers, alternating drops and shallow pools form a flight of stairs in the steeper channel sections. As the creek grows larger and gentler, these steps and pools give way to pools and riffles. Rocks exposed in the creek bed become smaller, and the current is better able to rearrange them. Where a giant boulder or a logjam constricts the channel, the faster current through the constriction scours a pool into the creek bed. Backwaters upstream from the constriction and eddies along its margin trap finer sediment and organic materials, and here the fish wait for food to drift by or rest from the exertions of moving against the swift current. Benthic insects such as burrowing mayflies like eddies, too: here, they can burrow into the sand and fine gravel in search of organic detritus. The rule of thumb—or tarsus, for insects—is that the more diverse the streambed, the greater the variety of benthic insects present. Likewise, the more diverse the habitats, the greater the variety of fish present.

Beavers (*Castor canadensis*) create an important source of habitat diversity by building low dams across channels. These dams pond water and trap sediment and nutrients moving downstream. As sediment gradually fills the channel upstream from the beaver dam, floods are more likely to spill over the channel banks and submerge the adjacent low-lying valley bottom. Water filters down into the floodplain sediment, raising the water table and creating wetlands and habitat suitable for dense thickets of willows, a preferred food source for beavers. Beavers in effect keep their larders well stocked with tasty plants by maintaining the wet soils that sustain willows.

Having stated that fish diversity correlates with habitat diversity, I must admit that the mountain tributaries of the South Platte are not world record holders for fish diversity. Winter is the annual bottleneck here, with only those species that can withstand extremely cold water temperatures able to survive. Not much water is required. Fish biologists have cored down through thick winter ice to find native trout hunkered down in crevices among the boulders, surviving in only a few centimeters of water, their metabolism slowed nearly to a stop until the returning warmth of spring brings flowing water and food. Greenback cutthroat trout (*Oncorhynchus clarki stomias*) was the only fish historically abundant in the mountain streams. In addition to the physiological adaptations required to live in perennially cold water, mountain streams provide relatively few choices of neighborhood. Although they have deep pools scooped around logjams and gravel-bedded eddies above riffles, mountain streams flow through narrow valleys that lack the diversity of lowland streams, where floodwaters spread periodically into secondary channels and through floodplain wetlands.

Fishermen took it upon themselves to increase fish diversity in the mountain tributaries of the South Platte. Even as native trout grew scarce during the late nineteenth and early twentieth centuries from the combined effects of over-fishing and habitat degradation resulting from timber harvest, placer mining, and flow regulation, streams in the region became famous as a scenic fishing destination. Seeking to enhance their sport, fishermen introduced game fish that fought hard for their lives when hooked. Now, exotic brook trout (*Salvelinus fontinalis*) dominate lower reaches of the mountain tributaries, rainbow trout (*Oncorhynchus mykiss*) occupy the larger channels down to the mountain front, and brown trout (*Salmo trutta*) swim in the waters just downstream from the mountains. Native greenback cutthroats remain only in the highest-elevation tributaries, where a physical barrier such as a waterfall limits upstream migration by the introduced species.[12]

HIDDEN WATERS

The great swelling of stream flows produced by melting snow across the mountains continues hundreds of kilometers beyond the mountain front, creating higher flows all across the arid western prairie. Yet the rivers continue to flow beyond the mountain front once the snow of the high country has completely melted. This base flow fed by groundwater integrates the melting snow and falling rain of centuries that filtered deep into the subsurface and moved downslope into stream channels much more slowly. Here again the distant Rockies are like the wizard behind the curtain, invisibly controlling the dynamics of rivers on the plains. Base flow that keeps the rivers vital throughout the year comes from an aquifer—an underground storage reservoir—diffused through thick, porous layers of sand and gravel. The sand and gravel are the erosional debris of the ancestral Rockies spread in a mantle about the base of the contemporary mountains.

If a drought parches the region for years at a time, the peak flows fed by surface runoff decrease noticeably, but the base flows remain relatively constant thanks to that underground reservoir.

Pumping of subsurface water for irrigated agriculture and municipal and industrial consumption has increased so much within the past few decades, however, that underground water levels, and the base flow they feed, can drop. Groundwater levels in the mountains rise with snowmelt and seasonal infiltration, peaking between March and June. Groundwater is pumped at these high elevations mainly for individual household supplies, which does not affect water levels except during extreme droughts. Groundwater levels further downstream, on the plains, rise naturally in response to recharge from stream flow soaking into the ground. Groundwater levels on the plains also rise as irrigation water is spread across farm fields or drop as water is pumped for irrigation or municipal use. Where irrigation water infiltrates, plains groundwater tables reach their highest levels between July and September. Where subsurface water is extracted, groundwater tables have been steadily falling for decades.[13]

STREAM FLOW AND SEDIMENT

The Rocky Mountains are the great, slow-beating heart for rivers of the western prairie, pumping out snowmelt that pulses eastward across the plains each year. But this annual pulse varies in strength. An El Niño–Southern Oscillation episode strengthens the pulse; a drought weakens it. At smaller scales, a wildfire that burns the protective vegetation off the slopes and reduces the ability of the soil to absorb rainfall and snow melt dramatically increases the flow of water and sediment for a year or two in a portion of the mountains. A widespread die-off in conifers attacked by insects reduces interception of snowfall and slightly increases stream flow.

Human uses of the mountain landscape can also alter the pulse of melt water that nourishes the rivers of the western prairie. We might like to think of ourselves as doctors regulating the pulse for better health, but our effects are not usually that disciplined. Widespread timber harvest is even more effective than wildfire in reducing the stability of hill slopes and the infiltration of precipitation. This can increase stream flow, but the effect is usually offset by much greater sediment movement, producing debris flows and streams filling with sediment instead of more clear water.

Urbanization and the building of roads that accompany timber harvest can cause more persistent alterations of the pathways by which water and sediment move downstream. Snow and rain do not soak into ground covered by pavement.

Instead, the water funnels into storm sewers that rapidly dump it into streams, causing larger, quicker floods. Perhaps more important, mountain communities need dependable water supplies, and they draw from the flow of adjacent streams or dam the streams to create reservoirs. Ski resorts pull water from one stream in autumn to make snow, and the manufactured snow melts into another stream the next spring. Roads interrupt the subsurface flow paths of water moving toward stream channels. Roads also increase the movement of sediment into streams by creating unstable points on the slope that give way in landslides or by leaking sediment from erosion of unpaved roads and sand applied to paved roads to improve traction during winter. Pure mountain spring water became an advertising slogan because we think of mountains as remote and pure, but urban areas in the mountains introduce the same contaminants to mountain streams that plague urban areas in the lowlands. All of the nasty things that come out of our vehicle tailpipes and our houses and yards—heavy metals, pharmaceuticals, phthalates from plastics and endocrine disrupters from personal-care products, pesticides and other synthetic chemicals—flow with the waters coming from urban areas and roads.[14]

Each of these variations in the quantity and quality of water and sediment flowing down from mountain sources affects the rivers of the western prairie. Time-lapse photography of the past 2 million years would show the pulses of water and sediment waxing and waning as valley glaciers in the upper portions of the Rocky Mountains advanced and retreated. The contemporary landscape at the base of the mountains records each glacial change in terraces that rise like flights of steps beside the river courses. Warmer, drier intervals between glacial advances left wind-blown dunes between the rivers, although a thin veneer of grasses and cacti now covers these dunes. The largest mountain glaciers melted about 10,000 years ago, but little cirque glaciers grew and shrank back enough during the intervening time to cause periods of sediment accumulation along the rivers of the western prairie, followed by periods of erosion when the stream channels cut down through the older sediments. Fluctuating water and sediment pulses from the mountains alternately created narrow, sinuous rivers bordered by stands of deciduous trees and floodplain wetlands down on the plains or wide, shallow rivers divided among a thousand shifting sand bars and stream banks largely bare of trees.

The most recent great shift in river conditions on the western prairie occurred within the past century in response to human land uses. Changes so swift that they are clearly recorded in maps and photographs spanning only a few decades of time have left many of the native plants and animals of the plains rivers struggling to survive in the early twenty-first century.

NOTES

1. W. S. Broecker, "The Great Ocean Conveyor," *Oceanography* 4 (1991): 79–89.

2. A. O. Persson "Hadley's Principle: Understanding and Misunderstanding the Trade Winds," *History of Meteorology* 3 (2006): 17–42.

3. C. S. Ramage, "El Niño," *Scientific American* 254, no. 6 (1986): 76–83; S. E. Zebiak and M. A. Cane, "A Model El Niño–Southern Oscillation," *Monthly Weather Review* 115 (1987): 2262–78.

4. S. L. Dingman, *Physical Hydrology*, 2nd ed. (Upper Saddle River, NJ: Prentice-Hall, 2002), 166–219.

5. Ibid.

6. R. Harris, "Dust Storms Threaten Snow Packs," National Public Radio, *Morning Edition*, May 30, 2006.

7. Ibid.; T. H. Painter, J. S. Deems, J. Belnap, A. F. Hamlet, C. C. Landry, and B. Udall, "Response of Colorado River Runoff to Dust Radiative Forcing in Snow," *Proceedings of the National Academy of Sciences of the USA*, 2010, doi: 10.1073/pnas.0913139107.

8. J. V. Ward, B. C. Kondratieff, and R. E. Zuellig, *An Illustrated Guide to the Mountain Stream Insects of Colorado*, 2nd ed. (Boulder: University Press of Colorado, 2002); J. V. Ward, "Altitudinal Zonation in a Rocky Mountain Stream," *Archaeological Hydrobiology Supplement* 74, no. 2 (1986): 133–99; J. V. Ward, "A Mountain River," in *The Rivers Handbook: Hydrological and Ecological Principles*, ed. P. Calow and G. E. Petts (Oxford: Blackwell Scientific Publications, 1992), 1: 493–510.

9. Ward, Kondratieff, and Zuellig, *Illustrated Guide*; Ward, "Altitudinal Zonation"; Ward, "Mountain River."

10. Ward, Kondratieff, and Zuellig, *Illustrated Guide*; Ward, "Altitudinal Zonation"; Ward, "Mountain River."

11. Ward, Kondratieff, and Zuellig, *Illustrated Guide*; Ward, "Altitudinal Zonation"; Ward, "Mountain River."

12. E. E. Wohl, *Virtual Rivers: Lessons from the Mountain Rivers of the Colorado Front Range* (New Haven, CT: Yale University Press, 2001).

13. K. F. Dennehy, D. W. Litke, C. M. Tate, S. L. Qi, P. B. McMahon, B. W. Bruce, R. A. Kimbrough, and J. S. Heiny, "Water Quality in the South Platte River Basin, Colorado, Nebraska, and Wyoming, 1992–95," *US Geological Survey Circular* 1167 (1998); W. J. Parton, M. P. Gutmann, and D. Ojima, "Long-Term Trends in Population, Farm Income, and Crop Production in the Great Plains," *BioScience* 57, no. 9 (2007): 737–47.

14. Wohl, *Virtual Rivers*.

Onto the Plains

THROUGH THE MOUNTAIN GATEWAYS

Crossing the South Platte River in 1819, Edwin James of the Long Expedition wrote:

> The Platte at the foot of the mountains is twenty-five yards wide, having an average depth of about three feet; its water clear and cool, and its current rapid. Its descent for twenty miles below cannot be less than eight feet per mile. Its valley is narrow and serpentine, bounded by steep and elevated hills, embosoming innumerable little lawns often of a semicircular form, ornamented by the narrow margin of shrubbery along the Platte.[1]

Forty years later, Horace Greeley described a June crossing of the South Platte's tributary, the Poudre River, where it flowed from the mountain front, as "at least three feet deep for about a hundred yards, the bottom broken by the bowlders, and the current very strong."[2]

Rivers flowing eastward from the Rocky Mountains pass through a topographic boundary as abrupt as a doorway when they flow beyond the mountain front. The rivers flow through fairly narrow mountain valleys from the headwaters, but the horizons suddenly expand as the rivers pass beyond the crystalline rocks of the

DOI: 10.5876/9781607322313.c02

The Poudre River in the transition zone between the mountains and the plains, circa 1867–68. Western side of a hogback at left. The exposed cobble bar in the center of this photograph suggests that it was taken during lower stream flow rather than during the snowmelt flood. Cottonwoods and willows grow along the river, and some logs lie on the cobble bars at left. Courtesy, Denver Public Library.

mountain front. The horizons are not yet endless, however, for the rivers flow through the hogbacks before they reach the plains.

Metaphors to the contrary, the Rockies are not eternal. They have, however, been repeatedly re-created through multiple episodes of mountain building during the past 1,700 million years. A mountain range represents a tug of war between the internal forces of the planet that shift tectonic plates and fold and fault rocks upward into mountains and the external forces of weathering and erosion that fragment bedrock into sediment and carry that sediment to lower elevations. Each time internal forces lifted up the Rockies, a long period of relative stability followed the uplift. During these quiet times, weathering and erosion dismantled the mountains, carrying sediment down to the adjacent lowlands and depositing it in broad alluvial fans, wind-blown sand sheets, and river channels. The huge volumes of material shed from the mountains created vast ramps and wedges of sediment that thinned toward the east. As more sediment continued to be depos-

This view westward from the crest of a hogback shows the steep western face (foreground), the gentler eastern face (left rearground), and a sandstone unit (right) capping the hogback. The small, ephemeral gully in the valley at the center of the photograph flows south toward a larger river; the larger rivers flow east through the successive hogbacks and valleys. Rivers flowing through the transition zone alternate between narrow channels, where they cut through a hogback, and wider channels and floodplains, where they flow across the valleys between hogbacks.

ited, the earlier material was buried and lithified into sedimentary rock. Then the internal forces shifted again, and a new episode of mountain building tilted and deformed the sedimentary rocks closest to the mountain range. Weathering and erosion removed the highest portions of these rock units that had been uplifted with the mountains, leaving abruptly exposed, steeply tilted ends of rock layers closest to the mountains. Today, these hogbacks form a series of asymmetrical hills with steep western sides closest to the Rockies and more gradually sloping eastern sides. Orange-, brown-, and buff-colored sandstone, shale, and limestone exposed in the hogbacks preserve the sediments deposited from weathering of the ancient Rockies. In the dry climate of the plains, the sandstone units form small cliffs and steep slopes topped by only thin soils. Shale and limestone weather more readily, giving rise to swales between the sandstone ridges.

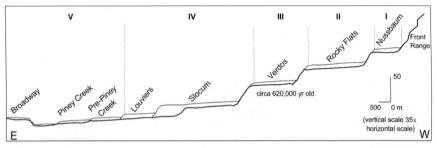

Schematic cross-sectional view of stream terraces in the Colorado Piedmont between the Front Range and the South Platte River a few kilometers north of Denver. The bold line represents the bedrock underlying relatively shallow covers of sediment on each terrace. Roman numerals indicate the five great cycles of downcutting, lateral movement, deposition, and stability. The highest surface is the oldest and the lowest surface is the youngest, although an age is known only for surface III. Each terrace is named after a local place. After Osterkamp et al. (1987, fig. 4).

This transition zone is a broadly stepped landscape punctuated by the sharp-crested hogbacks. Stream channels thread the hogbacks at water gaps where a stream was able to erode through the vertical wall of hogback cutting across its eastward path. Bench-like terraces parallel the stream channels and continue eastward for tens of kilometers. Five times during the past 2 million years, mountain glaciers drove pulses of water and sediment eastward to create these terraces. Each terrace records a time span of about 400,000 years, during which the major rivers cut downward, then began to move back and forth across the floodplain and deposit sediment before reaching a period of stability during which soils finally formed along the river bottoms.[3]

Downstream changes in river communities parallel downstream changes in topography, albeit more gradually. Although most of the biomass of headwater streams consists of benthic insects, these organisms grow more diverse and abundant from the mountains to the foothills. Insects present at high elevations remain in the streams and are joined by new species of midges, mayflies, beetles, and oligochaete worms. Cold water becomes cool water. Longnose sucker (*Catostomus catostomus*), white sucker (*C. commersoni*), and various species of minnows such as common shiner (*Luxilus cornutus*), fathead minnow (*Pimephales promelas*), and northern redbelly dace (*Phoxinus eos*) find suitable habitat along the more sinuous, cobble-bedded streams. Streamlined, flattened bodies with reduced swim bladders and large fins help longnose dace (*Rhinichthys cataractae*) do well in the fast-moving water over cobble-bedded riffles. Larger, laterally flattened or deep bodies and large swim bladders adapt green sunfish (*Lepomis cyanellus*) and orangespotted sunfish (*Lepomis humilis*) for the deeper, slow-flowing waters of sandy-bottomed pools. Most fishes of the transition zone are less than 10 centimeters long, however, and live only one or two years. Water temperature is the primary driving force behind the downstream changes in fish communities. Annual and daily water temperature ranges increase at lower elevations. Like economics in human society, temperature regime governs many of the characteristics of a fish community: the distribution of species, timing of lifecycles, feeding strategies and food webs, and behavioral responses.[4]

Fish from both cold- and warm-water communities mingle to create unique assemblages and high diversity in the transition zone. Ascending the South Platte River in summer 1842, John Charles Frémont noted that the turbid, sand-bed river became clear and the streambed changed to coarse gravel about 100 kilometers east of the mountain front. Cool-water species such as longnose sucker and long-nose dace are present as far downstream as Kersey, below the junction of the Poudre and South Platte and more than 60 river kilometers from the mountains, but warm-water species such as sand shiner (*Notropis stramineus*) and plains minnow (*Hybognathus placitus*) are also present at Kersey.[5]

LIFE IN THE STOP-AND-GO LANE

The hogbacks are the last topographic drama as the rivers flow eastward. Beyond the hogbacks, the horizon truly opens as though it could encompass the curve of the Earth. Crests of the hogbacks reach 1,980 to 1,670 meters in elevation, but beyond the transition zone elevation drops steadily to 850 meters at the junction of the North and South Platte Rivers. Rivers that have dropped approximately 1,800 meters over distances of 80 kilometers from the Continental Divide to the base of the Rockies now drop only 1,280 meters more as they flow another 900 kilometers to join the Missouri River. It was along this flat, sandy section of the river that on June 2, 1739, French explorers searching for a route from Illinois to Santa Fe, New Mexico, christened the Platte from a French word signifying "flat river."[6]

The crystalline bedrock and large boulders that so effectively resist erosion by flowing water where rivers pass through mountain valleys give way first to cobbles among the sedimentary rocks of the hogbacks and then to gravel, sand, silt, and clay farther east. Energetic floodwaters readily erode the finer sediments of the plains, and during spring snowmelt the rivers spread into floodplains and secondary channels extending hundreds of meters across.

Rivers of the mountains flow year-round thanks to the generous fall of snow and the slow release of melt water from paths deep underground. Flow also increases downstream within each mountain drainage as more tributaries contribute to the main channel. Rivers flowing eastward beyond the mountain front do not necessarily flow throughout the year or increase steadily in discharge. Tributaries heading on the plains make little contribution to the flow except during the brief, intense rain of a summer thunderstorm. They receive too little rain and snow to provide a generous overflow from subterranean reservoirs. Precipitation over the western prairie decreases eastward from 40 centimeters each year along the mountain front to less than 30 centimeters in parts of the South Platte and Arkansas River valleys before rising slightly again in northeastern Colorado. Even this relatively meager moisture does not necessarily come in a form that recharges underground supplies. Seventy percent to 80 percent of the precipitation falls from thunderstorms during April to September, and the rain bucketing down across a small area for a few minutes is as likely to flow quickly over the surface and evaporate as it is to filter down into the soil. The amount of rain also varies tremendously from year to year.

As a result of this meager and unpredictable rainfall, most tributaries that head on the plains are ephemeral and flow only briefly after rainfall. The lovely word *ephemeral* comes from the Greek *ephemeros*, for "one day," and captures the temporary and unpredictable nature of flow in such streams. Some tributaries are intermittent: going downstream, flow is present, then it's not, and then it is once more. These streams are typically fed by a groundwater spring or seep that provides a modest discharge. As long as the stream flows over thin soils or on bedrock, water remains in the channels. But if the stream crosses onto a thick layer of porous and permeable sediment, the flow can vanish into the ground, moving downstream only in the subsurface. The amount of water present in streams heading on the plains can thus be quite unpredictable in a downstream direction, depending on how water enters the stream channel—from rainfall or springs—and whether the water remains at the surface or soaks into the ground. Traveling through the Arkansas River drainage in November 1806, Zebulon Pike wrote: "Our encampment was on a creek where we found no water for several miles from the mountain, but near its base, we found springs sufficient."[7]

Discontinuous stream flow presents special challenges to aquatic insects. They can survive the dry periods by concentrating in isolated pools, although only a few species can manage this, thanks to high water temperatures in the pools and vulnerability to predation. Insects can also burrow into the streambed, which even at shallow depths can hold enough water vapor between particles of sand and gravel to sustain their tiny bodies. Several aquatic insect species go into dormant stages that can resist drying. Other species rush through their aquatic life phases and emerge as adults before the stream dries out. One species of caddisfly seals itself in its case to avoid drying out; the fishing cave of the mountain caddisfly is replaced by the moisture cave of the prairie caddisfly.[8]

Even flow in the larger prairie rivers that head in the mountains can be unpredictable, with decreases in discharge downstream as water evaporates into the dry air or seeps through the streambed and into the enormous aquifer that underlies much of the western prairie. Zebulon Pike was the first to describe this phenomenon as he traveled up the Arkansas River in November 1806: "The river was certainly as navigable here (and I think much more so,) than some hundred miles below, which I suppose arises from its flowing through a long course of sandy soil, which must absorb much of the water, and render it shoaler below than above, near the mountains."[9]

Despite the challenges of ephemeral, intermittent, or unpredictable flow, plants, insects, and fish do relatively well in the segments of prairie streams near the mountains. Abundant mosses, liverworts, and lichens create high biomass in the mountain headwaters, but biomass drops at mid-elevation sites where only algae growing attached to rocks are present. Biomass rises again on the plains as filamentous algae proliferate. Filamentous algae are the plants that resemble long green hair gently undulating in the current. Benthic insects grow more abundant on the plains, and many species not present at higher elevations appear. When biologist James Ward sampled benthic insects along the length of North St. Vrain Creek, he found 34 species in the uppermost site and 106 species at the lowermost site, on the prairie. Beetles largely absent in mountain streams make up a quarter of the species present in prairie streams, although much of the biomass comes from Diptera—true flies—and caddisflies. New species of minnows, suckers, and other types of fish adapted to warm water replace the trout of cold and cool waters at higher elevations. As many as 20 species of fish can be using a 500-meter length of stream in the transition zone, an unheard of diversity in the mountains. Besides the greater habitat diversity of the prairie streams, warm-water fish tend to be less territorial and aggressive than trout, and competition among individual fish may be less important in structuring fish communities than it is in the mountains. In other words, prairie fish make better neighbors, and many species live near one another.[10]

Life gets tougher for fish in streams farther into the plains. The seasonal snowmelt pulse, followed by a steady base flow supplied by groundwater, creates relatively stable flow, water temperature, and nutrient supply in mountain streams. Pools and riffles, wood in the channel, and pockets of sand interspersed with large boulders create diverse habitats in mountain streams. Streams on the western prairie go through boom and bust, with brief but intense rainfall runoff and then long periods of little flow. Discharge, temperature, and nutrient supply all vary more through time and space than in the mountain streams, and the sand-bed channels of the prairie create less diverse instream habitat.

Limited habitat and lack of environmental stability of rivers on the western prairie support a fish fauna that is relatively poor in species compared to wetter portions of the eastern prairie. The entire Platte River basin (South and North Platte Rivers) has an estimated 78 species of native fish. The Illinois River, in contrast, which drains one-third the area of the Platte, has 129 native species. The Platte had more species of fish during the Pleistocene ice age, but stream flows and habitats became less predictable as regional climate grew warmer and drier across the western prairie during the past 10,000 years. These prehistoric changes foreshadow the future, in which global warming is likely to further reduce the number of fish species surviving on the western prairie. Many species of fish found in the fossil record during times of cooler and wetter climate are now extinct from the region. The disparity between fish species diversity in the Platte and the Illinois is not unique to these two particular rivers. Species diversity in streams of the western prairie is much lower than in streams of the eastern prairie because western streams have simpler habitat, greater distance from the centers from which fish dispersed after the glaciers retreated, and a harsh physical environment with low dissolved oxygen in stream water, high temperatures, and wildly fluctuating flows.

Among the notable absences from western prairie streams compared to streams of the eastern prairie are sunfish. The relative lack of species in the sunfish family, which includes largemouth and smallmouth bass, likely reflects the lack of deep pools in western prairie streams. Large-bodied fishes find refuge during floods and droughts and safety from predators in deep pools of the Illinois River, where large-bodied, late-maturing fishes are more common than in the Platte River.[11]

We know more about fish in these rivers than about aquatic insects or microscopic organisms. Even the smallest native fish species can be the "charismatic megafauna" of a western prairie stream, and fish are more likely to engage the imagination and sympathy of people than are bacteria. The ability of native fish to withstand environmental change also provides an important signal of the state of river health.

All of the fish inhabiting rivers of the western prairie are survivors. When conditions deteriorate, they can move readily whenever water provides a travel corridor. They are small in size and can change where they live and what they eat, depending on what is available. They can withstand unpredictable floods as well as shallow, poor-quality water during drought. Fish ecologists distinguish three types of communities among these tough survivors. Large streams flowing over sand beds support the most distinctive fish communities (see table 2.1). These communities include several endemic species adapted to turbidity and widely fluctuating flow. Barbels bearing chemosensory and tactile sense organs allow the

Table 2.1. Characteristic fish species of large sand-bed streams

pallid sturgeon (*Scaphirhynchus albus*)	goldeye (*Hiodon alosoides*)
flathead chub (*Hybopsis gracilis*)	sicklefin chub (*Hybopsis meeki*)
sturgeon chub (*Hybopsis gelida*)	speckled chub (*Hybopsis aestivalis*)
sharpnose shiner (*Notropis oxyrhynchus*)	silverband shiner (*Notropis shumardi*)
chub shiner (*N. potteri*)	smalleye shiner (*N. buccula*)
Red River shiner (*N. bairdi*)	Arkansas River shiner (*Notropis girardi*)
western silvery minnow (*Hybognathus argyritis*)	plains minnow (*H. placitus*)
Red River pupfish (*Cyprinodon rubrofluviatilis*)	plains killifish (*Fundulus zebrinus*)
red shiner (*Cyprinella lutrensis*)	

fish to be less dependent on vision, and their eyes and the optic lobes of the brain tend to be small. Some species have hyper-developed cutaneous sense organs—a fish biologist's way of saying that the fish can sense what's around them using the skin of their face—and the portion of their brain devoted to processing incoming signals from these organs is well developed. Scales reduced in size and embedded in a thickened skin are less sensitive to abrasion when floods sweep along the sandy streambeds. A specially adapted metabolism makes native fish tolerant of high temperatures and low levels of dissolved oxygen.[12]

The reproductive adaptations of fish in large streams focus on opportunism and speed. Opportunistic species such as red shiner (*Cyprinella lutrensis*) spawn more than once during a reproductive season and can quickly divert the resources of their bodies to produce viable eggs when conditions are favorable or to retain ripe eggs when conditions are poor. Speed becomes important when eggs and larvae must compress their developmental stages into a few hours. Many species of fish around the world lay their eggs in streambed sediments or on submerged aquatic plants. The erosive, rapidly shifting sand bed of the western prairie streams would destroy delicate fish eggs and larvae during high flows, so some species of prairie fish deposit fertilized eggs directly into the water column during high flows. The eggs absorb water, quickly enlarge to two or three times their size at spawning, become semi-buoyant, and are carried downstream. As the eggs move downstream during the brief periods of high flow, they develop and hatch quickly—within twenty-four to forty-eight hours. The precocious larvae are relatively mobile and capable of swimming soon after hatching, further increasing their chances of reaching downstream habitat suitable for continued growth and survival. Stronger and more mobile adults re-populate upstream channel segments when conditions allow. These fish live on an army schedule: long periods of relative quiet punctuated by short bursts of frenetic activity—breed, grow up, and migrate, all in a few days.[13]

Dramatically fluctuating flows in western prairie rivers create challenges for fish, but they also create opportunities. Historically, the large rivers that head in the mountains had multiple flow paths constantly shifting among bars and islands. Differences in velocity and depth among these sub-channels created diverse habitats for fish. Juvenile or smaller-bodied fish could use the slower, shallower flows of secondary channels or backwater habitats associated with eddies. Ecologists now recognize that flow pulses—fluctuations in flow within the channel—can substantially enhance the abundance and diversity of river communities.[14]

A different community of fish species occurs in prairie ponds, marshes, and small streams that are spring-fed and thus have dense aquatic vegetation and relatively stable flows of clearer water (see table 2.2). Arkansas darters (*Etheostoma cragini*) that inhabit the Arkansas River basin prefer this type of stream. The little fish grow to an average 3–4 centimeters in length. They spend much of their time among thick mats of fine-leaf aquatic vegetation (*Ceratophyllum, Miriophyllum* spp.), where they can feed on invertebrate animals and hide from predators. Despite the groundwater source of these streams, the darters must be able to withstand daily fluctuations of up to 10°C in water temperature and maximum temperatures of 32°C. Most of the species in ponds and small streams occur as communities scattered across the western prairie that vary in species composition from north to south. These communities include populations of species present on the western prairie because they were suited to the cooler, wetter climates of glacial periods. Against the odds, they have hung on as their world grew warmer and drier. If the fish of the larger rivers are speedy opportunists, the fish of spring-fed systems are glacial relics.[15]

The third fish community lives in residual pools of intermittent streams. Unlike spring-fed pools, residual pools are more likely to dry completely between periods of continuous stream flow. Characteristic species are red shiner, fathead minnow (*Pimephales promelas*), black bullhead (*Ictalurus melas*), green sunfish (*Lepomis cyanellus*), johnny darters (*Etheostoma nigrum*), plains topminnow (*Fundulus sciadicus*), and plains killifish (*Fundulus zebrinus*). These fish belong to a few widespread species that, like many fish of the larger rivers, can reproduce and grow quickly and disperse to new environments during limited periods of higher stream flow. The difference is that the intermittent streams limit fish dispersal to a few hours or at most days of connected stream flow. Fish must then survive for months in completely isolated pools with warm water low in dissolved oxygen. To some extent, the race goes to those species that can move farthest upstream before the stream shrinks back to isolated pools: good colonizers gain access to

Table 2.2. Characteristic fish species of prairie ponds, marshes, and small spring-fed streams

creek chub (*Semotilus atromaculatus*)	pearl dace (*S. margarita*)
southern redbelly dace (*Phoxinus erythrogaster*)	northern redbelly dace (*Phoxinus eos*)
finescale dace (*P. neogaeus*)	lake chub (*Couesius plumbeus*)
hornyhead chub (*Nocomis biguttatus*)	common shiner (*Notropis cornutus*)
blacknose shiner (*Notropis heterolepis*)	Topeka shiner (*Notropis topeka*)
plains topminnow (*Fundulus sciadicus*)	Iowas darter (*Etheostoma exile*)
orangethroat darter (*Etheostoma spectabile*)	Arkansas darter (*Etheostoma cragini*)

upstream reaches, while other species are limited to downstream sites. Thanks to the vagaries of subsurface flow that supplies refuge pools and infiltration that drains them, downstream pools are not necessarily larger or more persistent than pools further upstream. Species that disperse widely thus increase their chances of winning the survival lottery.[16]

Winter survival of low temperatures creates a bottleneck to population growth and species diversity in mountain stream segments. Both winter and summer conditions create bottlenecks along intermittent streams on the western prairie. Shallow, disconnected pools can freeze during winter and grow too hot or too low in dissolved oxygen, or they can simply dry completely during late summer. To make life even more challenging, flash floods that result from summer thunderstorms can directly kill fish or wash them away from their refuge pools, although some research suggests that fish native to flashy streams know how to avoid displacement or death during floods. Floods, however, also scour the deep pools fish need, as well as creating infiltration that recharges the local groundwater that sustains isolated spring-fed pools. Deep, complex pools offer better refuge during floods, and fish biologists Kurt Fausch and Robert Bramblett found that species composition and relative abundances of fish in these pools are more stable through time than in shallow pools. Deep pools are also less likely to dry out during periods of low flow and drought.[17]

Along streams with both spring-fed and residual pools, successful fish manage to move between the two types of pools at different seasons and different stages of their lives. Juvenile Arkansas darters hatch earlier and grow faster in warmer downstream pools along tributaries of the Arkansas River than in upstream, spring-fed pools. Once the darters reach maturity, the fish do better if they can swim up to the spring-fed pools, where the water does not get as hot during summer and is less likely to freeze during winter. The race of life is to the swift among prairie fish: swift to reproduce, swift to grow to maturity, and swift to move when conditions deteriorate.[18]

Fish in all three of the prairie river communities tend to be small. Species in which adults grow to a maximum total length of less than 10 centimeters dominate streams of the transition zone and those that head on the plains, probably because of the small size of potential habitats in these streams. Most fish in streams of the transition zone and plains live six years or less, with an average lifespan of only one to two years. As might be expected, the larger habitats present downstream on the primary rivers support larger, longer-lived fish that are older when they first reproduce. Yet even in these slightly more stable habitats, continually varying flow and habitat limit the number of species and create large variations in the relative abundance of individuals.[19]

LIFE BESIDE THE STOP-AND-GO LANE

Grasses historically covered most of the land beyond the river corridors. Short-grass prairie dominated by grama (*Bouteloua* spp.) and buffalograss (*Buchloe dactyloides*) in the drier west gradually transitioned to mixed-grass prairie of bluestem (*Andropogon*), *Bouteloua*, and *Buchloe*. Approaching a river channel, meadow and marsh vegetation grew across low surfaces that were occasionally inundated by overbank floods and had higher groundwater tables. Diverse species of sedges (*Carex* spp.) and grasses (*Andropogon* spp., *Panicum* spp., *Agrostis* spp., and *Calamogrostis* spp.) grew in these meadows. Open- and closed-canopied woodland along the channel included plains cottonwood (*Populus deltoides*), peachleaf willow (*Salix amygdaloides*), green ash (*Fraxinus pennsylvanica*), box elder (*Acer negundo*), and American elm (*Ulmus americana*). These trees grew in isolated clumps rather than continuous ribbons of green along the rivers beyond the transition zone. Shrubby willows (*Salix* spp.) and indigo bush (*Amorpha fruiticosa*) also grew along the channel and on small river islands. After high flows receded in late summer, annual plants including sedges (*Cyperus* spp.), grasses (*Echinochloa* spp., *Eragrostis* spp.), and cockleburs (*Xanthium* spp.) grew on low sandbars.[20]

Riparian trees such as cottonwood (*Populus* spp.) and willow (*Salix* spp.) are tough. They can withstand flood and drought to some extent, but even they were challenged to survive along the broad, shallow rivers of the western prairie that flowed high during spring and early summer and then shrank back to a much narrower channel following the seasonal pulse of snowmelt. The main flow path shifted across the floodplain from year to year because the banks were easily eroded during high flows. Seedlings can only germinate and persist on bare, moist surfaces relatively safe from disturbance by flooding, erosion, or ice. The normal changes of a prairie river—local channel narrowing, migration of meanders that leaves freshly deposited sand on the inside of each bend, or deposition during the waning stages of a flood—create the surfaces on which seedlings can survive. Cottonwood seeds deposited on a moist sandbar during the waning stages of the spring flood may have only a year or two to germinate and grow before another spring flood completely erodes the sandbar as it reconfigures the channel. Riparian ecologists believe the abundance of cottonwoods can fluctuate dramatically during 50–150-year intervals because successful reproduction is primarily limited to slightly higher ground deposited during large floods. Only small stands of trees grew to maturity along this rapidly changing river, which was "a mile wide and an inch deep." The generous supply of sand, silt, and clay also kept the water turbid during high flows, giving rise to the description of rivers "too thick to drink but too thin to plow."[21]

Germination of new trees is even more episodic along the small, ephemeral prairie streams that are tributary to the South Platte River, where plains, narrowleaf (*P. angustifolia*), and lanceleaf cottonwood (*P. acuminata*) tower over peachleaf willow. Dramatic channel erosion and widening during the few hours of a large flood rips out large swathes of mature riverside forest. As the flood wanes, sediment deposition creates moist sandbars perfect for the germination of cottonwood seedlings. During the next two decades the trees gradually mature, stabilizing the banks and causing the channel to grow progressively narrower until the next large flood. Jonathan Friedman and Victor Lee documented these progressive changes following large floods in 1935 and 1965 along both Bijou and Kiowa Creeks, which drain north into the South Platte River. Neighboring Coal Creek was unaffected by the localized convective storms that caused flooding on the other creeks and, in the absence of big floods to reset the clock of the riverside forest, the cottonwoods along Coal Creek have not reproduced and are gradually being replaced by grassland.[22]

Many of the characteristics of the prairie rivers—flows of water and sediment, communities of fish and plants—are dramatically different than when people of European descent first described the western prairie. We can glean the history of the prairie rivers from two sources: geologic records that span hundreds of thousands of years, and the writings, drawings, and photographs created starting in the early nineteenth century by people coming westward from the United States into the enormous Louisiana Territory.

DEEP HISTORY

The oldest rocks underlying the western prairie indicate that for much of geologic history the region was intermittently part of a shallow sea. From 500 million to approximately 70 million years ago, the history of the region can be chanted:

the sea came in, the sea went out, the sea came in, the sea went out. When the sea came in, marine deposition created future sandstone, shale, and limestone rock units. When the sea went out, sediments deposited along beaches, estuaries, wetlands, and rivers created future terrestrial sandstone and shale units. Conditions began to change circa 70 million years ago when a period of mountain building raised an ancestral range about a third the height of the contemporary Rocky Mountains to the west. These mountains were eventually broken down into sediment that was carried to the adjacent lowlands. Renewed uplift created new mountains during the past 20 million years, and the presence of these younger mountains corresponds to the most recent episode of gradually increasing aridity.[23]

The Great Plains have been dry for as long as the Rocky Mountains have created an enormous rain shadow by wringing moisture from air moving eastward from the Pacific—approximately 60 million years. The plains are poised on the edge of drought. Only drought-tolerant plants can survive the winds that wick moisture away. Bunchgrasses and shrubs of the shortgrass prairie form small biological islands surrounded by exposed sand and silt. Blue grama (*Bouteloua gracilis*) and buffalograss (*Buchloe dactyloides*) can send their roots down nearly 2 meters in search of water but grow upward into the dessicating winds less than half a meter. Woody shrubs such as sand sage (*Artemisia filifolia*) and rabbitbrush (*Chrysothamnus nauseosus*) adapt to the dry conditions with a felt-like layer of fine growth on the leaves and stems that insulates the plant and reduces moisture loss.

While these plants grow on the surface, they help stabilize the underlying sediment. Their roots bind the soil in place and provide food for soil organisms from microscopic bacteria and protozoa to earthworms. Stems and leaves above the ground surface break up the ever-present winds, creating pockets of calm in the lee of the plant. A change to drier conditions, however, can overwhelm even these specially adapted plants. Regional droughts during the 1930s, 1950s, and 1970s pushed farmers in the western prairie to or beyond the edge of economic ruin by making it difficult to grow crops even with irrigation. But these droughts did not kill off enough native plants to allow the ever-present winds to remobilize the old dunes that lie across the landscape in low mounds. That requires an even more severe and prolonged drying of climate. (Dunes were remobilized during the 1930s and 1950s Dust Bowls, but that occurred where plowing disrupted the surface.)[24]

Thick layers of sediment underlying farm fields record fluctuations of climate over hundreds of thousands of years and clearly indicate that dry periods have been frequent and sustained. Before European settlement, freshly deposited sand and silt covered the broad floodplains of the South Platte and Arkansas Rivers as the waters of each year's spring flood receded. During periods of dry climate, strong winds blowing across the floodplains from the west-northwest winnowed out the silt and clay, carrying these finer sediments suspended in the turbulent air south and eastward across the plains until a decrease in the wind allowed the sediment to fall as loess. Back on the floodplain, the heavier sand grains also began to move in the wind, rolling and bouncing along the ground until swept into sand dunes. When the rains increased in frequency and volume, grasses and shrubs once again anchored the surface sediment against wind erosion. Soils had time to develop on the stable ground surface, and rivers left distinctively layered sediment sorted by size.

Alternating layers of loess, dune sand, soils, and river sediment beneath the surface of the western prairie allow geologists to infer the history of climatic shifts from drier to wetter conditions. Scientists with the US Geological Survey were among the first to recognize the great extent of wind-blown sediments across the Great Plains. Both Grove Karl Gilbert and Samuel F. Emmons published papers in 1896 that included descriptions of these records of past droughts, but the implications of their work were ignored until the Dust Bowl in the 1930s.[25]

Geologists now estimate that wind-blown sediment covers approximately 60 percent of Colorado east of the Rockies. About 30 percent of this area is covered by dune sand and 70 percent by loess. Soils formed during intervals of wetter climate trapped organic matter that can be dated with radiocarbon techniques. The soil ages bracket the times of loess deposition and dune activity. Some of the longest records come from Nebraska and Kansas, where loess was deposited during a period of warmer, drier climate that lasted from 500,000 to 100,000 years ago. Dune sands from eastern Colorado that can be up to 30 meters thick indicate periods of dune activity circa 9,000 to 5,500 years ago, 5,000 years ago, 3,000 to 1,500 years ago, and within the last thousand years. The clear implication of this record is that a climate dry enough to support sand dunes is not unusual in the western prairie.[26]

Times of dune activity correspond to the hot, dry periods when alpine glaciers in the Front Range retreated to higher elevations. Periods of intervening soil formation on the plains correspond to a cooler, wetter climate when the alpine glaciers advanced to lower elevations. Archaeological sites indicate that people living in the region also migrated with the fluctuating climate. People moved down to the plains during cool, wet periods and up into the foothills and lower mountains during times of warm, dry climate.[27]

So why did climate alternate among hot, dry and cool, wet? We can see the effects in sediments and fossils, but we can only infer the causes through reasoning by analogy from modern circulation patterns, such as those present during the

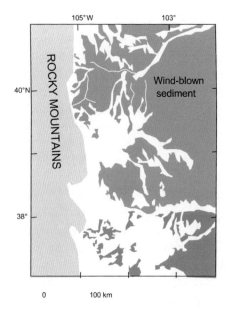

Schematic map of deposits of wind-blown sediment—sand and loess—in eastern Colorado. The white areas not covered by wind deposits have mostly been eroded by rivers; the white band in the northeastern corner indicates the course of the South Platte River. After Madole (1995, fig. 5).

1930s Dust Bowl. The El Niño–Southern Oscillation and Pacific Decadal Oscillation circulations cause temperature and precipitation to vary over a few years to decades. These are the short-term manifestations of a never-ending contest among relatively dry air coming east off the Pacific with the jet stream, cold air spilling down from the Arctic, and moist air surging northwest from the Gulf of Mexico. When the jet stream muscles everything else aside, the plains become dry and the dunes advance. When the jet stream weakens or shifts northward, moisture from the Gulf nourishes the spread of stabilizing plants that cover the loess and sand dunes and allow soils to form.[28]

The presence of ancient dunes beneath the thin veneer of vegetation becomes obvious in aerial photographs or during flights over the western prairie early or late in the day when the low-angle light reveals the subtle contours of the land. From the air, you can imagine what the region looked like under drier climates—a Sahara-like landscape with dunes spreading to the horizons and hundreds of shallow depressions between the dunes. Grasses now stabilize each mound of sand, with the dunes overall regularly spaced and shaped, as though the motion engendered by strong winds blowing from the north-northwest was suddenly frozen. Superimposed on the sinuously smooth undulations created by the rows of dunes is the oddly corrugated and pocked surface topography of each dune. North on the horizon, the Platte River forms a broad, diffuse line of dark bluish-green among the creamy-tan dunes. Little blowout dunes interrupt the harmonious lines of the larger lobes of sand. Tortuously sinuous smaller rivers wind across the interdune flats, leaving pale brown vertical banks where they cut into the edge of the dunes, and then spread into smooth patches at reservoir lakes. Continuing eastward, the empire of dunes finally begins to break up and be supplanted by a more planar landscape with dendritic drainage networks coming down from the north. The

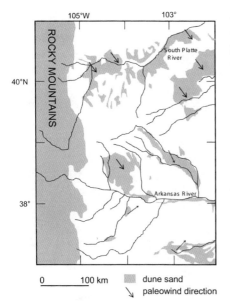

Schematic map of wind-blown sand deposits (medium gray) in eastern Colorado, showing paleowind directions (dark arrows) based on orientation of dunes. After Madole (1995, fig. 6).

last, closely packed field of transverse dunes resembles a marching army cut off by a river. Individual dunes lie more isolated and subdued beyond the Missouri River, where a reservoir creates a flat, smooth interruption of the corrugated landscape all around.

These interruptions created by reservoirs were not what the first people to reach this dry landscape saw. Whether they perceived the region as a desert depended on when they viewed the landscape with respect to the periodic droughts that affect the area, as well as on where they came from.

FIRST DESCRIPTIONS

People have lived on the western prairie for at least 12,000 years, surviving as nomadic hunter-gatherers who followed their food sources through the seasons and the greater fluctuations in climate. Clovis people, hunters of mastodon and other animals now extinct, left large projectile points at sites along the base of the mountains and farther into the plains, including the Dent site on the South Platte River. Big-game hunters gave way to hunters of smaller game and gatherers approximately 10,000 years ago. These Folsom people left smaller, beautifully fluted stone projectile points, such as those at the Lindenmeier site just north of the South Platte River. People of the Plano culture occupied the region between 10,000 and 7,500 years ago and left their tools and ornaments at places such as the Gordon Creek burial site in the transition zone along the Poudre River. The cultural tradition known as the Plains Archaic developed about 7,500 years ago as the climate of the western prairie grew warmer and drier, and it persisted until the adoption of ceramics about 2,000 years ago. Evidence of food storage pits suggests that Archaic peoples made longer stays in base camps, but they remained nomadic hunter-gatherers. Like most people, they probably spent more time along river corridors than in the uplands, but there is no evidence that they modified riverine environments. People of the Ceramic cultures adapted ceramics and replaced the atl-atl with bow-and-arrow hunting. Regional cultures of the Ceramic Period gradually diversified into the historical tribes more familiar to most people today.[29]

Apache, who were present in the basin by AD 1700, may have moved in after earlier peoples left in about 1450, perhaps in response to a prolonged drought from 1350 to 1500. The territories of the historical tribes shifted rapidly during the century preceding first European contact in Colorado, as Eurasian diseases and the domino effect of invasions from the east brought Apache, Comanche, and Ute tribes to the base of the Front Range. Arapaho and Cheyenne occupied the plains of Colorado when the first Europeans reached the area during the early nineteenth century.[30]

The first written descriptions of the western prairie date to the Lewis and Clark Expedition during the early years of the nineteenth century. This group followed the Missouri River into North Dakota and then moved west across Montana and Idaho; thus, they did not encounter the western prairie further south. The earliest descriptions of the Platte and Arkansas River valleys come from members of the Pike Expedition in 1806 and the Long Expedition in 1819–20. Edwin James wrote the scientific account of the expedition under Major Stephen H. Long. James first describes the Platte near its junction with the Missouri:

> The Platte, called by the Otoes Ne-braska (Flat river, or water,) is, as its name imports, almost uniformly broad and shoal. It is fordable at almost any place, except when swollen by freshets, which occur in the Spring season, from the melting of snow, and occasionally during the other portions of the year, from excessive rain. Its bed is composed almost exclusively of sand, forming innumerable bars, which are continually changing their position, and moving downward, till at length they are discharged into the Missouri . . .

> The range of the Platte, from extreme low to extreme high water is very inconsiderable, manifestly not exceeding six or eight feet. This is about the usual height of its banks above the surface of the sand which forms its bed. The banks are sometimes overflowed, but evidently to no great extent. The rapidity of the current, and the great width of the bed of the river, preclude the possibility of any extensive inundation of the surrounding country.[31]

Continuing upstream past the junction of the North and South Platte, Long's group crossed the South Platte, which James described as "about nine hundred yards wide, and very rapid, but so shoal that we found it unnecessary to dismount

The Platte River opposite Platte City, Nebraska, 1866. This is near what is now the city of North Platte, Nebraska, at the junction of the North and South Platte Rivers. Note the extreme width of the river, the lack of woody vegetation, and the sand in the foreground. Courtesy, Denver Public Library.

from our horses, or to unpack the mules."[32]

Descriptions of the volume of flow and the ease of crossing various channels of the Platte River drainage vary widely, depending on distance from the mountain front, time of year, and the particular year of which the traveler wrote. James described the ease in crossing the South Platte on about June 22, well downstream from the mountain front. Having crossed a railroad bridge over the South Platte much further upstream, near the junction with its tributary, the Poudre River, John Tice described the South Platte on June 12, 1871, as

> a mountain torrent one hundred and thirty yards wide, brimful, yet clear as crystal, roaring and dashing down the plain . . . No bushes encumber its edges, nor banks it has none, because the level plain sinks down with its burthen . . . Some eight miles distant, and stretching to the northwest until lost sight of in the distance, is a very straggling line of low cottonwood trees, the only sign of living vegetation.[33]

Some aspects of historical accounts, such as the dearth of riverside trees, are consistent among all writers. James notes repeatedly that the Long Expedition had difficulty finding enough wood to kindle a campfire in the evening, which they usually kept going with dried bison dung. The expedition found more trees on June 23:

> Intermixed with the narrow fringe of timber, which marks the course of the river, are very numerous trees, killed by the action of the beaver or by the effects of old age, their decorticated and bleached trunks and limbs strongly contrasting with the surrounding objects, many of them rendered doubly interesting by affording a support to the nests of the bald eagle, elevated like a beacon in the horizon of the traveller.[34]

James described immense herds of bison and other wildlife along their route, as well as a variety of plants and occasional springs. He also wrote of heat,

Wagons crossing the North Platte River at Bessemer Bend (near Casper, Wyoming) on the Oregon Trail, circa 1872–78. Scattered trees grow along the river, but the stream banks are mostly free of woody vegetation. Note the exposed sandbanks on the far side of the river, suggesting that the photograph was taken during lower stream flow, which would also have made it easier for the wagons to cross. Photograph by William Henry Jackson; courtesy, Denver Public Library.

sand, saline soils, and mirages in what he called the "inhospitable deserts of the Platte."[35]

Chroniclers of subsequent expeditions also emphasized the heat, aridity, and desert-like qualities of the landscape in the eastern Platte and Arkansas River valleys. Another military party under Lieutenant Colonel William H. Emory passed through the Arkansas valley in August 1846, and Emory wrote of wide, sandy rivers that were easily fordable and had few trees growing along the stream banks.

Within a few years, individual travelers were penning descriptions of the region, drawn to the mountain scenery or to the spectacle of the gold fields that had sprung up starting in 1859. Trails along the South Platte River formed one of the major routes to gold fields throughout Colorado. Horace Greeley wrote on June 2, 1859, that "the dearth of water is fearful" as he journeyed up the Republican River, immediately south of the Platte. Reaching the Big Sandy, a tributary of the Arkansas, Greeley wrote:

> Like the Republican, it is sometimes a running stream, sometimes a succession of
> shallow pools, sometimes a waste of deep, scorching sand. A few paltry cotton-
> woods, a few bunches of low willow, may have graced its banks or those of some

The South Platte River in Littleton, Colorado, 1903. The mature cottonwood forest was characteristic of streams near the transition zone between the mountains and the prairie. Note the wood in the channel at left, suggesting stream bank erosion. Courtesy, Denver Public Library.

dry creek running into it, in the course of twenty miles or so that we followed up its northern bank, but I do not now remember any.[36]

Sightings of flowing water and groves of riverside trees commonly increased as travelers approached the mountains. Writing on September 10, 1873, Isabella Bird described the Poudre River, a tributary of the South Platte, as having a course at the base of the mountains "marked the whole way by a fringe of small cottonwoods and aspens."

Nineteenth-century written descriptions of the Platte and Arkansas River valleys create a consistent image of an arid region dissected by water courses, the smallest of which remained dry for much of the year. Perennial rivers that headed in the mountains could spread across broad valley bottoms during the spring and early summer, but the flow remained shallow and few trees grew along the stream banks. The volume and consistency of stream flow increased with proximity to the mountain front, as did the presence of riverside groves of cottonwood and other trees. Some of these writers of European descent predicted a rich agricultural future for the region, but many dismissed the area as an inhospitable desert.[37]

A HISTORIC SNAPSHOT: THE SOUTH PLATTE RIVER BASIN CIRCA 1800

As the mountain tributaries of the South Platte crossed into the transition zone among the hogbacks and the western edge of the plains, they spread out. The rivers grew more sinuous and shifted repeatedly across their broad floodplains, leaving behind abandoned channels and backwater depressions that held shallow ponds. Boulders gave way to gravel and cold water to cool water. Cottonwood and willow trees grew along the channels. Each year's snowmelt flood removed a few of the larger, older trees and left behind moist sediments in which new seedlings could germinate. Periodic larger floods knocked down many more trees. These trees fell into the channels and created fish habitat by providing overhead cover and interrupting the current enough to allow the formation of small scour pools and overhanging banks. A rich variety of animals—insects, amphibians, reptiles, fish, birds, otter, beaver, and others—used the seasonally flooded bottomlands and perennial wetlands that spread along the rivers. In many respects, the rivers flowed through a world of ecological communities we now think of as existing elsewhere. Bison roamed from the prairie to above timberline in the mountains west of the transition zone, wolves and grizzly bears frequented the grasslands east of the transition zone, and beavers built dams and created numerous shallow ponds and wetlands along the river corridors. People lived throughout the transition zone, too, migrating seasonally between base camps along the rivers, hunting and gathering a wide variety of food.

This transition zone was a biodiversity hot spot for insects and fish. Spring-fed tributary channels originating among the hogbacks had less seasonal fluctuation in flow and supported distinctive communities of fish and insects. Entomologists estimate that more than a hundred species of aquatic insects inhabited the transition zone. The geographic ranges of warm-, cool-, and cold-water fish overlapped here. Greenback cutthroat trout (*Oncorhynchus clarki stomias*), dominant fish of the cold, clear headwater mountain streams, may have ranged as far downstream as Greeley, approximately 45 kilometers east of the mountain front. Fathead minnow (*Pimephales promelas*) and green sunfish (*Lepomis cyanellus*), plains species adapted to warm, turbid waters, ranged as far west as Fort Collins, 10 kilometers east of the mountain front. Relict populations of northern redbelly dace (*Phoxinus eos*), a cool-water minnow that was more widespread during glacial periods, still existed along the base of the mountains.

As the streams continued east, groves of riverside trees grew sparser. Discharge in the channels fluctuated more dramatically, with high flows that spread among the multiple channels contained within the outermost stream banks and low flows that shrank back to a central, shallow channel. The cool, clear water grew warmer and muddy as it flowed over sand and silt. Numerous bars and islands lay exposed among the channels during much of the year, and only a few of these were covered by shrubs or trees. Flocks of tens of thousands of migratory cranes, geese, and other birds settled briefly along the river twice each year to rest and feed during their long journeys north and south.

Tributaries originating on the plains might roar into the main channel for a few hours when a summer thunderstorm triggered a flash flood, but much of the time they remained dry, with only the debris lodged far up the stream banks indicating the streams' potential. Spring-fed tributaries flowed shallowly for a month or two each year, just enough time for the little plains fish to disperse between the pools where they spent most of the year. By midsummer these intermittent streams dried back to isolated pools of warm water, where native minnows and shiners hid under the algae when a wading bird touched down.

NOTES

1. E. James, *Account of an Expedition from Pittsburgh to the Rocky Mountains, Performed in the Years 1819 and '20*, 2 vols. (Philadelphia: Carey and Lea, 1823), 2: 3.

2. H. Greeley, *An Overland Journey from New York to San Francisco in the Summer of 1859* (Lincoln: University of Nebraska Press, 1999 [1860]).

3. C. B. Hunt, "Pleistocene and Recent Deposits in the Denver Area, Colorado," *US Geological Survey Bulletin* 996-C (1954): 91–140; R. F. Madole, "Holocene Stratigraphy of Turkey Creek, a Small Drainage Basin in the Southern Colorado Piedmont," US Geological Survey (USGS) Open-File Report 89-93 (Washington, DC: USGS, 1989); W. R. Osterkamp, M. M. Fenton, T. C. Gustavson, R. F. Hadley, V. T. Holliday, R. B. Morrison, and T. J. Toy, "Great Plains," in *Geomorphic Systems of North America*, ed. W. L. Graf (Boulder: Geological Society of America, 1987), 163–210; G. R. Scott, "Quaternary Geology and Geomorphic History of the Kassler Quadrangle, Colorado," US Geological Survey Professional Paper 421-A (Washington, DC: USGS, 1963).

4. Ward, Kondratieff, and Zuellig, *Illustrated Guide*; Ward, "Altitudinal Zonation"; Ward, "Mountain River."

5. K. D. Fausch and K. R. Bestgen, "Ecology of Fishes Indigenous to the Central and Southwestern Great Plains," in *Ecology and Conservation of Great Plains Vertebrates*, ed. F. L. Knopf and F. B. Samson (New York: Springer-Verlag, 1997), 131–66; W. J. Matthews, "Physicochemical Tolerance and Selectivity of Stream Fishes as Related to Their

Geographic Ranges and Local Distributions," in *Community and Evolutionary Ecology of North American Stream Fishes*, ed. W. J. Matthews and D. C. Heins (Norman: University of Oklahoma Press, 1987), 111–20; W. J. Matthews, "North American Prairie Streams as Systems for Ecological Study," *Journal of the North American Benthological Society* 7, no. 4 (1988): 387–409; D. L. Propst and C. A. Carlson, "The Distribution and Status of Warmwater Fishes in the Platte River Drainage, Colorado," *Southwestern Naturalist* 31, no. 2 (1986): 149–67; C. M. Tate and L. M. Martin, "Fish Communities in the Plains Region of the South Platte River, August 1993 and 1994," *US Geological Survey Fact Sheet* FS-154-95 (1995).

6. W. L. Graf, ed., *Endangered and Threatened Species of the Platte River*, Committee on Endangered and Threatened Species in the Platte River Basin, National Research Council (Washington, DC: National Academies Press, 2005).

7. Z. Pike, *The Journals of Zebulon Montgomery Pike, with Letters and Related Documents*, ed. D. Jackson (Norman: University of Oklahoma Press, 1966), 1: 350.

8. Ward, Kondratieff, and Zuellig, *Illustrated Guide*.

9. Pike, *Journals of Zebulon Montgomery Pike*, 347.

10. Ward, Kondratieff, and Zuellig, *Illustrated Guide*; Ward, "Altitudinal Zonation"; Ward, "Mountain River"; R. K. Smith and K. D. Fausch, "Thermal Tolerance and Vegetation Preference of Arkansas Darter and Johnny Darter from Colorado Plains Streams," *Transactions of the American Fisheries Society* 126, no. 4 (1997): 676–86.

11. Fausch and Bestgen, "Ecology of Fishes"; E. J. Peters and S. Schainost, "Historical Changes in Fish Distribution and Abundance in the Platte River in Nebraska," *American Fisheries Society Symposium* 45 (2005): 239–48; Matthews, "Physicochemical Tolerance and Selectivity"; F. B. Cross and R. E. Moss, "Historic Changes in Fish Communities and Aquatic Habitats in Plains Streams of Kansas," in *Community and Evolutionary Ecology of North American Stream Fishes*, ed. W. J. Matthews and D. C. Heins (Norman: University of Oklahoma Press, 1987), 155–65; Matthews, "North American Prairie Streams"; Propst and Carlson, "Distribution and Status of Warmwater Fishes."

12. Fausch and Bestgen, "Ecology of Fishes"; Matthews, "Physicochemical Tolerance and Selectivity"; Cross and Moss, "Historic Changes in Fish Communities and Aquatic Habitats"; Matthews, "North American Prairie Streams"; Propst and Carlson, "Distribution and Status of Warmwater Fishes."

13. Fausch and Bestgen, "Ecology of Fishes"; Matthews, "Physicochemical Tolerance and Selectivity"; Cross and Moss, "Historic Changes in Fish Communities and Aquatic Habitats"; Matthews, "North American Prairie Streams"; Propst and Carlson, "Distribution and Status of Warmwater Fishes."

14. C. Amoros, "Changes in Side-Arm Connectivity and Implications for River System Management," *Rivers* 2 (1991): 105–12; B. A. Payne and M. F. Lapointe, "Channel Morphology and Lateral Stability: Effects on Distribution of Spawning and Rearing

Habitat for Atlantic Salmon in a Wandering Cobble-Bed River," *Canadian Journal of Fisheries and Aquatic Sciences* 54 (1997): 2627–2736; M. Kaplinski, J. Bennett, J. Cain, J. E. Hazel, M. Manone, R. Parnell, and L. E. Stevens, "Fluvial Habitats Developed on Colorado River Sandbars in Grand Canyon," *EOS, Transactions, American Geophysical Union* 79, no. 45 (1998): F344; K. Tockner, F. Malard, and J. V. Ward, "An Extension of the Flood Pulse Concept," *Hydrological Processes* 14 (2000): 2861–83.

15. Fausch and Bestgen, "Ecology of Fishes"; Matthews, "Physicochemical Tolerance and Selectivity"; Cross and Moss, "Historic Changes in Fish Communities and Aquatic Habitats"; Matthews, "North American Prairie Streams"; Propst and Carlson, "Distribution and Status of Warmwater Fishes"; Smith and Fausch, "Thermal Tolerance and Vegetation Preference."

16. Fausch and Bestgen, "Ecology of Fishes"; Matthews, "Physicochemical Tolerance and Selectivity"; Cross and Moss, "Historic Changes in Fish Communities and Aquatic Habitats"; Matthews, "North American Prairie Streams"; Propst and Carlson, "Distribution and Status of Warmwater Fishes."

17. Fausch and Bestgen, "Ecology of Fishes"; Matthews, "Physicochemical Tolerance and Selectivity"; Matthews, "North American Prairie Streams"; K. D. Fausch and R. G. Bramblett, "Disturbance and Fish Communities in Intermittent Tributaries of a Western Great Plains River," *Copeia* 3 (1991): 659–74; S. C. Lohr and K. D. Fausch, "Multiscale Analysis of Natural Variability in Stream Fish Assemblages of a Western Great Plains Watershed," *Copeia* 4 (1997): 706–24.

18. T. R. Labbe and K. D. Fausch, "Dynamics of Intermittent Stream Habitat Regulate Persistence of a Threatened Fish at Multiple Scales," *Ecological Applications* 10, no. 6 (2000): 1774–91.

19. Fausch and Bestgen, "Ecology of Fishes"; Peters and Schainost, "Historical Changes in Fish Distribution"; Matthews, "Physicochemical Tolerance and Selectivity"; Cross and Moss, "Historic Changes in Fish Communities and Aquatic Habitats"; Matthews, "North American Prairie Streams"; Propst and Carlson, "Distribution and Status of Warmwater Fishes."

20. W. C. Johnson, "Woodland Expansion in the Platte River, Nebraska: Patterns and Causes," *Ecological Monographs* 64, no. 1 (1994): 45–84.

21. M. L. Scott, J. M. Friedman, and G. T. Auble, "Fluvial Process and the Establishment of Bottomland Trees," *Geomorphology* 14, no. 4 (1996): 327–39; J. M. Friedman, M. L. Scott, and G. T. Auble, "Management and Cottonwood Forest Dynamics along Prairie Streams," in *Ecology of Great Plains Vertebrates*, ed. F. L. Knopf and F. B. Samson, Ecological Studies 125 (New York: Springer-Verlag, 1997), 49–71.

22. J. M. Friedman and V. J. Lee, "Extreme Floods, Channel Change, and Riparian Forests along Ephemeral Streams," *Ecological Monographs* 72, no. 3 (2002): 409–25; J. M. Friedman, W. R. Osterkamp, and W. M. Lewis Jr., "The Role of Vegetation and Bed-

Level Fluctuations in the Process of Channel Narrowing," *Geomorphology* 14, no. 4 (1996): 341–51.

23. E. D. Gutentag, F. J. Heimes, N. C. Krothe, R. R. Luckey, and J. B. Weeks, "Geohydrology of the High Plains Aquifer in Parts of Colorado, Kansas, Nebraska, New Mexico, Oklahoma, South Dakota, Texas, and Wyoming," *US Geological Survey Professional Paper* 1400-B (1984).

24. T. S. Ahlbrandt, J. B. Swinehart, and D. G. Maroney, "The Dynamic Holocene Dune Fields of the Great Plains and Rocky Mountain Basins, U.S.A.," in *Eolian Sediments and Processes*, ed. M. E. Brookfield and T. S. Ahlbrandt (Amsterdam: Elsevier, 1983), 379–406; P. R. Hanson, A. F. Arbogast, W. C. Johnson, R. M. Joeckel, and A. R. Young, "Megadroughts and Late Holocene Dune Activation at the Eastern Margin of the Great Plains, North-Central Kansas, USA," *Aeolian Research* 1 (2010): 101–10; V. T. Holliday, "Middle Holocene Drought on the Southern High Plains," *Quaternary Research* 31 (1989): 74–82; J. A. Mason, J. B. Swinehart, P. R. Hanson, D. B. Loope, R. J. Goble, X. Miao, and R. L. Schmeisser, "Late Pleistocene Dune Activity in the Central Great Plains, USA," *Quaternary Science Reviews* 30 (2011): 3858–70.

25. T. S. Ahlbrandt, J. B. Swinehart, and D. G. Maroney, "The Dynamic Holocene Dune Fields of the Great Plains and Rocky Mountain Basins, U.S.A.," in *Eolian Sediments and Processes*, ed. M. E. Brookfield and T. S. Ahlbrandt (Amsterdam: Elsevier, 1983), 379–406; P. R. Hanson, A. F. Arbogast, W. C. Johnson, R. M. Joeckel, and A. R. Young, "Megadroughts and Late Holocene Dune Activation at the Eastern Margin of the Great Plains, North-Central Kansas, USA," *Aeolian Research* 1 (2010): 101–10; V. T. Holliday, "Middle Holocene Drought on the Southern High Plains," *Quaternary Research* 31 (1989): 74–82; J. A. Mason, J. B. Swinehart, P. R. Hanson, D. B. Loope, R. J. Goble, X. Miao, and R. L. Schmeisser, "Late Pleistocene Dune Activity in the Central Great Plains, USA," *Quaternary Science Reviews* 30 (2011): 3858–70.

26. Ahlbrandt, Swinehart, and Maroney, "Dynamic Holocene Dune Fields"; Z. Feng, W. C. Johnson, Y. Lu, and P. A. Ward, "Climatic Signals from Loess-Soil Sequences in the Central Great Plains, USA," *Palaeogeography, Palaeoclimatology, Palaeoecology* 110, no. 3-4 (1994): 345–58; Z. Feng, W. C. Johnson, D. R. Sprowl, and Y. Lu, "Loess Accumulation and Soil Formation in Central Kansas, United States, during the Past 400,000 Years," *Earth Surface Processes and Landforms* 19 (1994): 55–67; S. L. Forman, A.F.H. Goetz, and R. H. Yuhas, "Large-Scale Stabilized Dunes on the High Plains of Colorado: Understanding the Landscape Response to Holocene Climates with the Aid of Images from Space," *Geology* 20, no. 2 (1992): 145–48; Holliday, "Middle Holocene Drought"; R. F. Madole, "Stratigraphic Evidence of Desertification in the West-Central Great Plains within the Past 1000 Yr," *Geology* 22, no. 6 (1994): 483–86; R. F. Madole, "Spatial and Temporal Patterns of Late Quaternary Eolian Deposition, Eastern Colorado, U.S.A.," *Quaternary Science Reviews* 14, no. 2 (1995): 155–77; C. W. Martin, "Radiocarbon Ages

on Late Pleistocene Loess Stratigraphy of Nebraska and Kansas, Central Great Plains, USA," *Quaternary Science Reviews* 12 (1993): 179–88; D. R. Muhs, "Age and Paleoclimatic Significance of Holocene Sand Dunes in Northeastern Colorado," *Annals of the Association of American Geographers* 75, no. 4 (1985): 566–82; D. R. Muhs, T. W. Stafford, S. D. Cowherd, S. A. Mahan, R. Kihl, P. B. Maat, C. A. Bush, and J. Nehring, "Origin of the Late Quaternary Dune Fields of Northeastern Colorado," *Geomorphology* 17, no. 1-3 (1996): 129–49.

27. Martin, "Radiocarbon Ages"; Muhs, "Age and Paleoclimatic Significance"; Muhs et al., "Origin of the Late Quaternary Dune Fields."

28. Feng et al., "Climatic Signals from Loess-Soil Sequences"; Forman, Goetz, and Yuhas, "Large-Scale Stabilized Dunes"; Holliday, "Middle Holocene Drought"; Muhs, "Age and Paleoclimatic Significance"; Muhs et al., "Origin of the Late Quaternary Dune Fields."

29. K. Bryan and L. L. Ray, "Geologic Antiquity of the Lindenmeier Site in Colorado," *Smithsonian Miscellaneous Collections* 99, no. 2 (1941); E. S. Cassells, *The Archaeology of Colorado* (Boulder: Johnson Books, 1983); V. T. Holliday, "Geoarchaeology and Late Quaternary Geomorphology of the Middle South Platte River, Northeastern Colorado," *Geoarchaeology* 2, no. 4 (1987): 317–29; E. West, *The Contested Plains: Indians, Goldseekers, and the Rush to Colorado* (Lawrence: University Press of Kansas, 1998).

30. Cassells, *Archaeology of Colorado*; West, *Contested Plains*.

31. James, *Account of an Expedition*, 1: 459.

32. Ibid., 1: 467.

33. J. H. Tice, *Over the Plains, on the Mountains; or, Kansas, Colorado, and the Rocky Mountains; Agriculturally, Mineralogically and Aesthetically Described* (St. Louis: Industrial Age Printing, 1872), 79.

34. James, *Account of an Expedition*, 1: 469.

35. Ibid., 1: 474.

36. Greeley, *Overland Journey*, 110.

37. Tice, *Over the Plains, on the Mountains*; W. H. Emory, *Notes of a Military Reconnaissance, from Fort Leavenworth, in Missouri, to San Diego, in California, Including Part of the Arkansas, Del Norte, and Gila Rivers* (Washington, DC: Wendell and Van Benthuysen, 1848); I. L. Bird, *A Lady's Life in the Rocky Mountains* (Norman: University of Oklahoma Press, 1960 [1873]); Greeley, *Overland Journey*; James, *Account of an Expedition*; B. Taylor, *Colorado: A Summer Trip* (New York: G. P. Putnam and Son, 1867); D. Jackson and M. L. Spence, eds., *The Expeditions of John Charles Frémont*, vol. 1: *Travels from 1838 to 1844* (Urbana: University of Illinois Press, 1970).

River Metamorphosis

> Comparison of the old and new pictures of
> the same sites reveals that the 1977 channel is
> radically different from that of 70–100 years ago.
> The most striking changes apparent from the
> photographs are a decrease in channel width
> and an increase in vegetation.
>
> —*Garnett Williams, The Case of the Shrinking
> Channels—the North Platte and Platte Rivers in
> Nebraska.*

A HISTORIC SNAPSHOT: THE SOUTH
PLATTE RIVER BASIN CIRCA 1900

Some characteristics of streams in the South Platte
basin circa 1800 persisted a century later. Cities were
growing rapidly along the base of the mountains, and
irrigated farm fields spread across the plains east of the
mountains. All of these people and crops consumed
water from the rivers, and stream flow was highly regulated by dams and diversions. The effects of this regulation had not yet caused substantial changes in the appearance of the rivers, however. Rivers of the transition zone
still flowed clear and cold, although the snowmelt peaks
were declining as water was stored in reservoirs. Water
pollution mainly took the form of human and animal

DOI: 10.5876/9781607322313.c03

View of the South Platte River near Fort St. Vrain, Colorado, circa 1882–90. This site, on the South Platte upstream from its junction with St. Vrain Creek, is just east of the transition zone. Note the scattered groves of cottonwood trees and the broad, shallow channel with exposed sandbars. Photograph by William Henry Jackson; courtesy, Colorado Historical Society.

wastes, which stream flows were sufficient to dilute. Contemporary knowledge of historical plant and animal distributions comes mainly from this period, when scientists made the first systematic surveys of species present along streams of the foothills and plains. These distributions were already changing, however, in response to flow regulation and consumptive uses. Sauger (*Sander canadensis*) had been present in the South Platte near Greeley, the western extent of their range, but commercial fishing for this species ended by 1900 as sauger disappeared from that stretch of the river.

Out on the plains, stream flows fluctuated less during the year as spring snow-melt peaks were stored in reservoirs and released gradually during the growing season. These more stable flows allowed woody riparian plants to grow more densely on some of the islands and bars in the broad channels, as well as in iso-lated groves along stream banks. The water was a little cooler and clearer than it had been in 1800, and introduced fish started to encroach on the habitats used by native species. If people had been given actual snapshots of the South Platte and its tributaries in 1800 and 1900, however, they would likely have noticed few differ-ences in the streams. Differences in land use beyond the streams would be much more noticeable where people had concentrated in towns or cleared the native shortgrass prairie plants to grow irrigated crops.

SHRINKING RIVERS

The primary rivers of the western prairie look very different today than they did in 1800 or 1900. Rather than the broad, shallow channels with numerous, continually shifting sand bars that were present a century ago, the contemporary rivers flow along narrow channels between heavily wooded banks that change little from year to year. Diversion and storage of water for crop irrigation altered stream flows starting in the mid-nineteenth century and changed the bipolar flood-dry nature of stream flows to greater constancy. This made it easier for riverside trees to gain a roothold. More trees and less variable flows then interacted in complex ways that drove the metamorphosis of channel appearance.

Imagine the first farmers trying to grow wheat or corn in what some had called "the Great American Desert." There was not enough rain to support the crops, but the streams flowed brimful each spring. The first task was to bring the streams to the fields, which was easiest if the fields were next to the stream. Construction of small, relatively crude ditches used to spread water across the floodplain for crop irrigation began along the South Platte River during 1840–60. Antoine Janis diverted water from the Poudre River in 1838 or 1844. Digging by hand or using horse-drawn implements, farmers constructed larger canals to irrigate terraces higher and farther back from the streams over the next thirty years. Groups of farmers arrived from the East to establish agricultural communities, such as the Greeley Colony in 1870.

The inherent linearity of stream flow created challenges to off-stream diversions as population and water use increased. These challenges occurred first in the placer-mining areas that sprang up throughout the southern and central mountainous headwaters of the South Platte River after 1859. Miners used water to separate gold and silver mixed into valley-bottom sediments. A mining claim could effectively become worthless if another upstream miner diverted all of the stream flow to work his claim. Consequently, miners worked out their own rules of prior appropriation, commonly paraphrased as "first in time, first in right," to recognize the right of the earliest claimants to continue to access water. These rules carried through to other off-stream uses, such as agricultural irrigation, and were quickly written into law. The US Congress created the Colorado Territory in 1861. The Territorial Supreme Court's first major water law decision held that water could be diverted from a stream and that ditches could be built across public and private land to convey the water to its place of beneficial use. This was a fundamental break with the so-called Riparian Doctrine followed in other areas of the country, which stipulates that those with land next to a stream have a water right for that stream. Under prior appropriation, proximity to a stream does not create the right to use the stream's water.[1]

Nobody questioned the idea that croplands formed the destiny of the western prairie. In that first Territorial Supreme Court decision, Chief Justice Moses Hallett wrote: "In a dry and thirsty land it is necessary to divert the waters of the streams from their natural channels." The national government did its part to facilitate this destiny with the 1862 Homestead Act, which made the western prairie a part of the public domain where individuals could obtain land for a small fee. With the thought that future farmers might need help, the 1862 Morrill Act provided for the establishment of land-grant colleges that subsequently became centers for agricultural research. The federal government did not, however, develop a federal water law, preferring instead to allow the states and territories to codify their own rules and legal precedents. The result in the Colorado Territory was the Colorado Doctrine that developed starting in the 1860s. This doctrine rests on four primary components: (1) all surface and groundwater is a public resource for beneficial use by private individuals and public agencies; (2) a water right is a right to use a portion of these public resources; (3) owners of water rights can take whatever steps necessary to obtain and transfer their water to where they want to use it, including building facilities such as ditches and pipes across public and private lands; and (4) owners of water rights can use streams and aquifers for the storage and transportation of water. When Colorado became a state in 1876, Article 16 of the state constitution codified prior appropriation.[2]

Some of the effects of prior appropriation were immediate. When Bayard Taylor passed through eastern Colorado in 1866, he wrote:

> The people informed me that the farming on the St. Vrains [Creek] is fully equal to what I saw on the Boulder [Creek]—that the valleys of the Big and Little Thompson [Creeks], and even of the Cache-la-Poudre, are settled and cultivated, and will this year produce splendid crops. The line of settlement is thus not only creeping northward and southward from Denver, but, also, following the tributaries of the Platte, it advances eastward to meet the great tide approaching it. I verily believe that it will not be more than two or three years before there is a continuous belt of settlement—probably two of them—from Missouri to the Rocky Mountains.[3]

Taylor's view of the potential for growth in agricultural communities mirrored that of contemporary society but ignored limited water supplies. The earliest record of over-appropriation of water in the South Platte comes from the Poudre River in 1876, but problems with over-appropriation had spread throughout the

South Platte drainage by 1880–85. Over-appropriation seems as though it should be impossible because it literally means more water is legally allocated to users than can be physically provided. The key to this apparent paradox is the tremendous year-to-year variability in precipitation and stream flows. If water use grows by leaps and bounds during a wet year or years, everything is fine and everyone gets all their water. Problems don't arise until the first, inevitable dry year. The natural flow of the Platte River and all its tributaries was fully appropriated to human consumptive uses before 1900. Lack of understanding of the inherent variability of water supply in a dry climate, and the consequent over-allocation of water supplies, was one of the first delayed effects of prior appropriation.

Diverting water onto farm fields during the snowmelt pulse can leave the partially grown crops high and dry late in the growing season, when stream flow shrinks back to much lower volumes. During the half century 1880–1930, engineers constructed reservoirs to store snowmelt runoff for more gradual release throughout the late summer–early autumn growing season. The first relatively large reservoir in the Platte River basin was Jackson Lake on the South Platte, built in 1900 to store 58 million cubic meters (47,000 acre-feet). The federal government's 1902 Reclamation Act accelerated the construction of large structures by providing funds states could borrow for building dams and reservoirs. Jackson Lake was followed by Cheesman Lake on the South Platte in 1905 (108 million cubic meters; 87,227 acre-feet), the highest dam in the world at the time of its construction, and by Antero Reservoir on the South Platte in 1909 (141 million cubic meters; 115,000 acre-feet). The builders of these impressive structures saw their efforts in the context of Manifest Destiny. They were overcoming pessimistic nineteenth-century descriptions of the western prairie as the Great American Desert. They would harness the tremendous power of melting mountain snows and make the desert bloom. The 1909 Pathfinder Dam on the North Platte stored 1.2 billion cubic meters (1,016,500 acre-feet), making it one of the largest reservoirs in the world at that time. Each community and each territory or state saw its future as a great metropolis surrounded by productive farm fields. Storage of water, and consequent manipulation of the characteristics of stream flow, was a second delayed effect of prior appropriation.[4]

The stipulation that water must be put to beneficial use resulted in a third delayed effect of prior appropriation, as ideas about what constituted beneficial use changed through time. Initially, such use was limited to what we now call *consumptive uses*: commercial, municipal and domestic, industrial, and agricultural uses. Not until the end of the twentieth century were uses such as fish and wildlife protection, recreation, and maintaining water quality accorded legal recognition as beneficial. Until that time, prior appropriation and reserved water rights could result in a stream literally being drained dry to satisfy off-stream, consumptive uses.[5]

A fourth delayed effect of prior appropriation is sometimes paraphrased as "use it or lose it." A water right confers the right to use the resource without actually owning it. If the user does not require all of the decreed water right, the water goes to those who can use it beneficially. This situation limits or even prevents water conservation and encourages wasteful use of water to prevent the effective loss of a water right that may be difficult to reacquire later.[6]

Beginning in 1879, the Colorado General Assembly assigned to the courts the setting of water-right priority dates and amounts. This led to Colorado having more water-rights lawyers per capita than any other state except California by the twentieth century: a fifth delayed effect of prior appropriation.[7]

What began as the destiny of controlling abundant resources quickly developed into a competition as remaining available resources dwindled rapidly. Interstate rivalries grew over the limited resource of surface water for irrigation. The waters of the South Platte River were apportioned between Colorado and Nebraska by interstate compact in 1923. Although rain did not follow the plow, as some early boosters had hoped, water could be made to follow the people. Settlers on the plains of eastern Colorado saw all the snowmelt running down the sparsely inhabited western slope of the Rocky Mountains as wasted. Starting with dynamite and hand tools in the late nineteenth century and upgrading to heavy machinery for the 1953 Colorado–Big Thompson project, the people of Colorado set out to rectify Nature's errors in water distribution. The 1922 Colorado River Compact facilitated these efforts by endorsing water transfers out of the basin of origin. By the end of the twentieth century, the South Platte River had fifteen interbasin diversions sucking water out of the western streams and dumping it into tunnels beneath the Continental Divide and approximately a thousand reservoirs spread across the eastern slope to store all that transferred water. Stream flow no longer followed simple topography; it also followed money and population density. As the population of the eastern slope continued to climb steadily at the start of the twenty-first century, the aptly named Big Straw project became the latest proposal for greening (or in this case, populating) the prairie by sucking water back as it flowed down the western side of the Rockies and out of Colorado. The ability to maintain continued growth of human population and resource use in selected regions by drawing on water supplies across a much broader region is a sixth delayed effect of prior appropriation.[8]

Wheat became the dominant crop of the western prairie during and after World War I, although other crops such as sugar beets were locally important. None of these crops, however, behaved like the native bunchgrasses that return

Spillway and dam on the South Platte River in Denver, Colorado, circa 1904–15, an early example of engineering stream flow and channel shape. Courtesy, Colorado Historical Society.

nutrients to the soil. Continuous cropping depleted the reservoir of nutrients that had slowly accumulated in the upper layer of the soil. Low-yield fields were turned over to livestock pasture. The sharp hooves of grazing animals confined to pastures pulverized the soil. When drought returned to the region in the 1930s, the powdery soil blew away and eastern Colorado became part of the Dust Bowl.[9]

Limited water supplies by the 1930s helped set the stage for even larger diversions of water to the South Platte River basin from the sparsely populated headwaters of the Colorado River on the western side of the Front Range. As Dan Tyler recounts in *The Last Water Hole in the West*, his history of the Colorado–Big Thompson project, economic growth in the northern South Platte River basin was closely tied to the availability of irrigation water. Population grew by nearly 58 percent in the first decade of the twentieth century, then slowed to 28 percent and 17 percent, respectively, in the next two decades as new sources of funding for reservoirs and diversions dried up. Agricultural lands in this portion of the South Platte basin were mostly covered by row crops that required adequate and dependable irrigation throughout the growing season: the region was the leading US producer of sugar beets. Having exhausted local water sources and local funds to bring water from other areas, farmers and legislators turned to the federal government for the funds for massive water transfers.[10]

Fifty thousand tons of harvested sugar beets waiting to be processed at the Great Western Sugar Company in Fort Morgan, Colorado, 1931. Note the lines of trees along irrigation canals. Courtesy, Denver Public Library.

Farther away from the mountain front, long distances separated big rivers such as the Platte and Arkansas that flowed most of the year, and people upstream were already diverting much of the stream flow. As technology improved, settlers further east turned to water hidden beneath the ground. Groundwater irrigation in the western prairie began with the use of windmills in the late nineteenth century. If a farmer or rancher could drill down 30 meters or so, he could use the power of the ever-present wind to raise cool, clear water to the surface. This was small-scale, the type of windmill that might supply a single household or create a watering trough for cattle. Farmers dreamed of irrigated fields spreading to the horizons and looked beyond wind power to draw the water up to the surface.[11]

Conflicts over groundwater use began shortly after the pumping commenced. E. F. Hurdle constructed the first recorded irrigation wells in the South Platte basin, using steam engines to power his pumps. A neighbor sued Hurdle in 1893 for allegedly decreasing flow in a nearby river. Although the court agreed that groundwater and stream flow were probably connected in this case, it also ruled that "allegations of the wells' detrimental impacts were 'vague, conflicting, and indefinite.'" Because groundwater moves extremely slowly and along pathways hidden deep belowground, it can be very difficult to demonstrate that pumping from a single well has decreased nearby stream flows by lowering the water table that supplies the stable, year-round base flow of streams. In addition, there can be large gaps between what scientists understand and what lawyers acknowledge.

Colorado law did not legally recognize the connection between groundwater and stream flow for many decades after the 1893 case.[12]

Farmers pumped more and more groundwater during the half century between 1930 and 1980. Surface-water resources were fully appropriated and regulated. Droughts in the 1930s and 1950s drove croplands to or beyond the breaking point. Need more water? The only place to go is down. Operating under the same mind-set that made their predecessors decide to grow sugar beets in soils that supported bunchgrass and cactus, farmers had drilled nearly 2,000 irrigation wells in the South Platte valley by 1940. When the shallow aquifers were punched full of holes, new technology came along to allow farmers to access deeper layers of the subsurface and spread the water across lands previously unfeasible for irrigation. Early wells were drilled only in areas where the water table was less than 30 meters below the ground surface. After the early 1960s these wells were supplemented by turbine pumps that allowed pumping from greater depths. Development of center-pivot irrigation systems during the early 1960s brought sandy soils and rolling terrain in new areas under cultivation. When the great tide of farm expansion reached its crest, essentially all the surface and subsurface waters of the western prairie were devoted to consumptive human uses.

At present, Colorado includes more than 445,000 hectares of irrigated farmland. The Platte River basin and the underlying aquifers support approximately 810,000 irrigated hectares throughout Colorado, Nebraska, and Wyoming, with nearly 405,000 hectares in Colorado and Nebraska supplied by the South Platte River. By midsummer, the emerald green irrigated fields present a striking contrast with the native shortgrass prairie, which is already starting to fade into the shades of tan and pale gold that characterize it for most of the year.[13]

Not all of the irrigation water spread over the bottomlands adjacent to the river was used by crops. Some of the water evaporated. Some soaked into the ground. Some returned to the river. The portion that soaked into the ground raised local water tables. The earliest records of stream flow in the Platte River drainage begin in 1889, but continuous systematic records date mostly from 1930. These records show that stream flow changed in different ways throughout the Platte drainage, largely as a result of how water was used. Despite all that water being diverted from streams and stored for release later in the growing season, the average yearly peak flow along the South Platte River did not decrease during the twentieth century. The difference was made up by diversions across the Continental Divide from the headwaters of the Colorado River. Peak flows did fluctuate over periods of a few decades, however, and these fluctuations created times without large floods. Imports from the Colorado River, along with flow regulation, essentially lopped off the biggest floods and raised the smallest ones, creating

Center-pivot irrigation near Greeley, Colorado, summer 2008. This type of irrigation typically pumps groundwater from relatively deep sources and at rates sufficiently high to draw down local and regional water tables.

a smoother trend through time and keeping the *average* yearly flood about the same. Base flows increased consistently starting in the 1920s as more water came down the river for a longer period of time. Historical records suggest that by the time it neared the Colorado-Nebraska border, the South Platte in the 1800s was characterized by intermittent flows, with stretches of surface flow interrupted by stretches of dry streambed. During the 1900s the river became perennial, with continuously flowing water along its length.[14]

During the mid-nineteenth century, drier grassland species of plants occupied the higher surfaces away from the rivers. Meadow and marsh vegetation grew on floodplains. A woodland-shrubland community grew on the river islands and along the banks. All of that changed, however, as flow regulation removed the big floods and increased the base flow, altering the annual snowmelt pulse to a more steady flow. Woodlands began to expand along the North and South Platte Rivers circa 1900 and then spread downstream along the Platte River. Vegetation covered most of the former channel area along the North and South Platte Rivers by the

Railroad bridge destroyed by a 1935 flood on the South Platte River in Fort Morgan, Colorado. Note the lack of vegetation along the wide, shallow channel. Courtesy, Colorado Historical Society.

Downstream view of the South Platte River in Fort Morgan, Colorado, 2008. The channel is now much narrower, and the banks are densely vegetated.

secondary, overflow channels

main channel

Panoramic view across the banks of the South Platte in Fort Morgan, Colorado, 2008. The main channel (previous page) is out of view to the right. All of the vegetated areas in these photographs were historically part of the broad, unvegetated, braided channel.

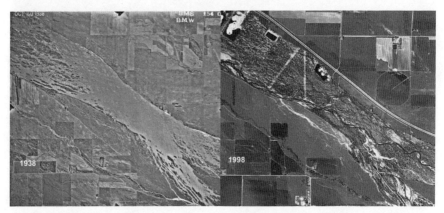

1938

1998

Matched aerial photographs of a section of the Platte River between Lexington and Overton, Nebraska. The braided channel of 1938 (left) has narrowed substantially by 1968 (right). Courtesy, Lisa Fotherby, US Bureau of Reclamation.

late 1930s, and the extent of vegetation was fairly uniform and stable throughout the Platte River system by 1986. In less than a century, the broad, open floodplains along the streams of the Platte River drainage became bands of forest connecting the eastern prairie with the mountains.[15]

Botanist Carter Johnson attributes the spread of woodlands to June flows, summer drought, and ice. Riverside trees release their seeds just in time for the June snowmelt pulse to carry the seeds downstream to new germination sites. Seedling survival, however, is a tricky business. Cottonwood and willow seeds must be deposited on moist sandbars to germinate. Sandbars cannot be eroded or deeply buried by more sediment if the seedlings are to survive. Peak flow reduced by irrigation diversions increased the chances of seedlings in this annual lottery by exposing more of the streambed during the critical window in June. Periods with a few years of lower peak flows allowed new stands of riverside trees to become

Houses and commercial buildings in Denver during a May 1864 flood on the South Platte River and Cherry Creek. Courtesy, Colorado Historical Society.

established, and these trees could then withstand subsequent higher flows better than vulnerable seedlings could.[16]

Summer droughts helped in this process of woodland spread. Droughts occur approximately every twenty years on the Great Plains, although their extent, duration, and intensity are quite variable. Droughts during the 1930s were particularly severe in the Platte River basin. These prolonged periods of low stream flow further exposed bare surfaces that could be colonized by tree seedlings.[17]

Ice may also have influenced seedling survival along the river channels. Water flowing beneath, around, and even on top of ice during winter and early spring scours away sandbars or shifts the entire channel to one side, limiting the stable ground seedlings need to survive. When a frozen river breaks up, cakes of floating ice damage seedlings or erode surfaces in which the seedlings are growing. Ice may have decreased along the Platte during the twentieth century as winter temperatures increased.[18]

Whatever the combination of factors that increased seedling survival, the end result was a dramatic spread of riverside forests. As vegetation spread along stream banks, plant roots helped hold the bank sediment in place. Stems and

Men in a boat rescuing people from a house during a 1935 flood on the South Platte River in Fort Morgan, Colorado. More trees are present along this portion of the river than in the portion shown in the photographs on page 71. Courtesy, Colorado Historical Society.

trunks slowed the movement of water flowing by, allowing sediment to settle onto the banks. The stream channels grew steadily narrower as islands and bars were stabilized with vegetation and then attached to the banks by the spreading woodland. Travelers following the major rivers of the western prairie never mentioned overbank flows during the period 1800 to 1870, but such flows began to occur after 1870 as channels grew narrower and the amount and timing of stream flows changed.[19]

Storage and diversion of water did not eliminate floods along the rivers of the western prairie. The maximum flood of record on the Platte River occurred in 1935 at all gauging stations, despite the fact that the region was in the midst of a severe drought. Some of the most catastrophic floods in the South Platte drainage occurred during June 1965, when heavy, intense rains on three different days during June 14–17 caused huge floods on Plum and Cherry Creeks south of Denver, on Kiowa and Bijou Creeks southwest of Denver, and on many small creeks north of the South Platte between Greeley and Sterling, Colorado. Up to 36 centimeters

Railroad and road bridges destroyed by the June 1965 flood on West Bijou Creek near Byers, Colorado. Courtesy, Denver Public Library.

of rain fell in a few hours during these storms, in regions that normally receive an average of 35 centimeters of precipitation throughout the year. The sheer volume of water cascading down from the sky overwhelmed the ability of even the broad valley bottoms to convey it downstream, producing a flood peak of 1,130 cubic meters per second on the South Platte River at Denver. This peak was nearly twice the highest flow recorded—618 cubic meters per second—since a gauging station was established at that site in 1889.[20]

Some of the riverside vegetation established during times of lower flows was eroded along with the stream banks during floods such as those in 1935 and 1965. This created only a temporary setback in the progressive spread of riverside forests. Sediments newly deposited by the floods provided extensive new germination sites for seedlings, and the net trend of increasing woodlands continued along the larger streams.[21]

Repeated floods have created a different scenario of forest growth and channel change along smaller streams that head on the plains and go dry for much of the year. Flow on these streams is much less altered by structures such as dams and

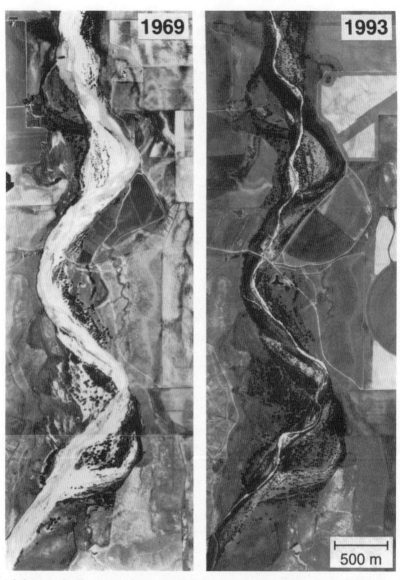

Aerial photographs illustrating changes in floodplain form and riverside vegetation between 1969 and 1993 at West Bijou Creek, a tributary of the South Platte southeast of Denver. A large flood in 1965 removed much of the woody vegetation present along the channel, leaving a wide, bare channel that appears as white or light gray in the photograph at left. The absence of large floods during succeeding decades allowed vegetation to re-grow along the channel margins and narrowly constrain the channel, as seen in the photograph at right, where the very thin white line represents the active channel. After Friedman and Lee (2002, fig. 2).

Upstream view of the Poudre River near its junction with the South Platte River in Greeley, Colorado, 2008. The extreme narrowness of the channel reflects extensive diversions of water upstream, as does the dense riverside vegetation.

diversions. Rather than growing consistently narrower during the past century, the ephemeral channels have been like a snake that distends over a meal in a few minutes and then gradually resumes its slender girth as it digests the food for days. On the ephemeral streams, extreme floods last only a matter of hours, but they widen channels, destroy existing forests, and allow germination of new seeds. Then come decades of channel narrowing as the seedlings grow to maturity.[22]

The ages of riverside trees record the flood history. Many of the cottonwood trees along Bijou and Kiowa Creeks germinated in 1935, 1965, or within a few years following each flood. Along streams that have not had a substantial flood during the past eighty years, lack of channel movement and sediment deposition has reduced new germination sites and limited the reproduction of cottonwood trees. As the cottonwood forests decline, grassland plants gradually come to dominate the stream banks and bottomlands.[23]

The magnitude of channel narrowing along the larger streams and the specifics of channel change varied throughout the western prairie. One reach along the

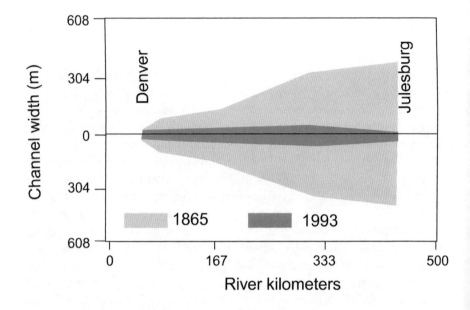

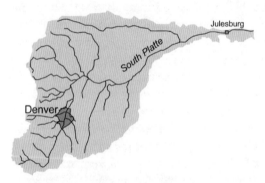

Schematic plot of channel width along the South Platte between Denver and Julesburg, Colorado. The lighter gray shading indicates conditions in 1865, and the darker gray shading indicates the much narrower channel present by 1993 as a result of changes in the flow regime. Most of the change occurred before 1938. After Dennehy et al. (1998, 8).

Arkansas River in southeastern Colorado shrank from an average channel width of 225 meters in 1926 to 30 meters in 1977. A reach along the South Platte River in northeastern Colorado decreased from 535 meters in 1867 to 109 meters in 1977. Some channels have become narrower and straight, others have grown narrower and more sinuous. The narrowest, most sinuous channels have steady stream flow, as well as silt and clay in the banks that make them more cohesive and resistant to erosion by stream flow, and they carry little sand. Whatever the specifics, during a time span just a little longer than a human life, the larger rivers of the western prairie changed from turbid, roiling channels "a mile wide and an inch deep" to narrow, limpid rivers flowing quietly between shaded green banks.[24]

FALLING WATER TABLES

Historical changes in the larger rivers of the western prairie are obvious to anyone who looks at historical photographs. Driven in part by the need to restore populations of endangered migratory birds that rely on broad floodplain wetlands along large rivers, public awareness of the extent and implications of river metamorphosis increased substantially during the last two decades of the twentieth century. Smaller rivers, however, remain the poor stepsisters of river protection. People are likely to ignore the ephemeral streams that head on the plains unless they are in flood or to assume that the streams have not changed in appearance during the past century. But the spring-fed and rain-fed streams of the western prairie have undergone changes as substantial as those of the larger rivers during the past 150 years in response to human uses of groundwater and surface lands.[25]

Small, headwater streams form a vital component of any river network. They are the starting point for the downstream journey of water, sediment, and nutrients eroding from the uplands. The ability of small streams to store and biologically process nutrients—to convert nitrogen and carbon into microbial "flesh" and then into the flesh of insects, fish, or birds—influences water quality far downstream. Small streams also provide diverse habitats and refuge sites for stream organisms. On the western prairie, the ecological functions of small streams are intimately linked to the groundwater that supplies much of their flow.

What lies beneath is particularly important for streams that head on the plains, because the porosity and permeability of the underlying rocks partly control the depth to groundwater and the presence of springs. The South Platte River and its tributaries flow across the Colorado Piedmont. Bluffs separate the piedmont, which comes from a French word for "foot of the mountains," from the High Plains to the north and east. Lava-capped mesas border the piedmont on the south. All the landscapes east of the Rockies are underlain by sedimentary rocks deposited along rivers and shallow inland seas bordering the mountains, but great chunks of this history are missing on the piedmont, where the South Platte and Arkansas Rivers and their tributaries have eroded rock units approximately 60 million to 10 million years old. Most of the piedmont sediments are now underlain by rocks approximately 100 million years old. Contemporary rivers have eroded these shale, claystone, and siltstone rock units into a low, rolling topography.[26]

View of South Pawnee Creek, a tributary of the South Platte River, in Pawnee National Grassland, Colorado. This creek dries back to disconnected pools for much of the year, but rainfall can bring floods that briefly re-connect the pools into a continuous stream. The creek makes a broad bend at the base of the low bluffs to the left in this view.

In some places further east, rocks younger than 100 million years remain present. The Ogallala Formation is the most famous of these younger rock units. Composed of lithified sand and gravel, the Ogallala retains enough tiny pore spaces to readily store and transmit subsurface water. These qualities allow the Ogallala to create an enormous groundwater aquifer that stretches from South Dakota down to Texas and from eastern Colorado across Nebraska and Kansas. Most of the agriculture of the dry western prairie relies on water held in the Ogallala. Because the Rockies are the source of the sand and gravel in the Ogallala, the unit generally thins toward the east. Otherwise, the Ogallala's geometry is sufficiently variable to create something of a lottery for farmers drilling down to pump groundwater. The top of the Ogallala might be 15 meters below the surface, or it might be 100 down. The water-bearing portion might be 50 meters thick or 100 meters thick because its sediments were deposited on an irregular surface and subsequently partly eroded. The deeper the top of the Ogallala, the more it costs to pump up the water, and the less likely the aquifer is to directly influence stream flow.[27]

Together with overlying sediments, the Ogallala forms the
principal aquifer in the Platte
River valley. The North Platte, South
Platte, and Platte Rivers connect
to this aquifer, but the plumbing is
complicated. During periods of high
stream flow, water can seep into the
aquifer from the river. During periods
of low flow, the exchange reverses and
the aquifer contributes base flow to
the river. But just as a household sink
won't drain if it is blocked, exchange
between the Ogallala and the rivers does not
occur where clay sediments or impermeable bedrock limit groundwater movement.

The Ogallala Aquifer contained more than 3,700 billion
cubic meters of water prior to intensive pumping of groundwater. Mimicking surface channels but in slow motion, water creeps southeastward
within the aquifer at about a third of a meter per day. Left alone, even the dry contemporary climate of the western prairie would continue to slowly add water to
the aquifer. Rainfall, snowmelt, and infiltration from streams recharge the aquifer
at rates that would raise the water level locally by 0.4–2.5 centimeters per year in
the absence of pumping. But of course pumping has been influencing the Ogallala for decades.[28]

Imagine someone with a straw drinking from a very thick, bathtub-size milkshake. One individual could suck at that large volume for a long time without
any perceptible effect. But little depressions would start to show up if dozens of
people put their straws into the milkshake. Each person would have to start sucking harder, too, because the thick shake would not flow quickly into the hollow
around the base of each straw. Eventually, the level of the whole milkshake would
go down.

Engineer William Code compiled thousands of well data logs from eastern
Colorado during the 1930s and 1940s, noting declines in groundwater levels. He
also detected correlations between pumping rates and flow in the South Platte
River: the water table was declining sufficiently to reduce base flow. Code was

among the first to call for legislative regulation of pumping, which was not subject to any oversight in Colorado until the state's largely ineffective 1957 Ground Water Act and the more useful 1965 Ground Water Management Act.[29]

At present, pumping continues to dominate the level of the aquifer because water is being extracted much faster than it can be naturally recharged. People pumping groundwater from the Ogallala are mining a subsurface reservoir of water that accumulated over tens of thousands of years. More than 3 million hectares of land are currently irrigated with water from the Ogallala. Approximately 150,000 pumps work night and day during the growing season to supply water to grain and cotton, as well as to the corn and sorghum that feed 40 percent of the cattle raised in the United States. Perhaps not surprisingly, an estimated half of the total water stored in the Ogallala has been removed. Not only is half the water gone, but the remaining half is deeper and much more expensive to pump to the surface.

Removal of subsurface water has other consequences besides increased pumping costs. Water might not seem like a strong material, but each water droplet in the Ogallala can exert enough force to maintain the tiny pore space it occupies and to keep the grains of sand and gravel separated from one another. Remove the water and this force vanishes, allowing the sand, gravel, and overlying sediments to compact and subside. Because the Ogallala is heterogeneous, compaction and subsidence are uneven. When they are sufficiently large, the overlying surface can lower crookedly and crack open into fissures that reach tens of meters in width and depth. The fissures can also start gully heads that erode upstream to form deeply incised channels. Sometimes landowners try to stabilize the fissures with "Detroit riprap" in the form of junked vehicles or appliances. More often the fissures are ignored. Meanwhile, less rainfall and snowmelt filters down to be stored in the compacted sediments, making it more difficult to restore the aquifer.

OASES AMONG THE BUNCHGRASS

By late summer the bunchgrasses of the shortgrass prairie stand dry and pale as baled hay. Nothing is more miraculous in this bleached landscape than the sight of clear water bubbling up from the ground in a spring. Songbirds travel long distances to drink at these springs, and herds of antelope seek out the cool water. Plants crowding the margins of the little pond surrounding the spring remain green into autumn.

Groundwater pumping for irrigated agriculture is now the great agent of drying on the western prairie, sucking down the water table that feeds the springs

Refuge pools at Pawnee National Grassland. The pool in the upper view still has water at the end of autumn. The pool in the lower view, although retaining water year-round in the past, is now dry and filled with tumbleweeds by autumn.

and the headwaters of intermittent streams. Reduced spring flow influences the entire stream network. Lower flows in the streams create less recharge from the stream back into the subsurface further downstream. Plants may not be able to send their roots sufficiently deep to reach the lowered water table. As the plants die, they transpire less water from their leaves into the atmosphere, creating a progressive drying of the air. Springs that once flowed year-round go dry as the water table drops. Wetland plant communities and local populations of insects, fish, amphibians, reptiles, birds, and mammals sustained by the water and food at each spring vanish. Downstream communities of plants and animals nourished by stream flow from the spring also vanish. Intermittent or ephemeral channels that once held water in deep pools throughout the year now dry completely along their length.

Springs and seeps provide particularly important habitat for a wide variety of life on the semiarid western prairie, yet relatively little is known about the ecology of these precious water sources. Seeps are essentially seasonal springs. Because seeps periodically dry out, they support a lower diversity of wetland plants than the more persistent springs, which can provide aquatic habitat for many animal species. Stream channels fed by springs are unusual in having more constant flow than other channels and more constant water temperature at the spring source, although ambient air temperatures affect downstream portions of the stream. Springs on the western prairie feed only very small streams separated by large expanses of dry uplands inhospitable to aquatic species. This relative isolation fosters a high percentage of species that occur only in a single stream. These endemic plants, invertebrates, amphibians, and fish can be crowded into very restricted habitat during prolonged droughts or completely extirpated if dropping water tables cause the spring to go dry for many years. Among the amphibians adapted to seeps and springs on the western prairie are tiger salamander (*Ambystoma tigrinum*), red-spotted toad (*Bufo punctatus*), chorus frog (*Pseudacris triseriata*), and plains leopard frog (*Rana blairi*).[30]

Springs in the South Platte River drainage also give rise to small, shallow marshes that form in depressions along streams or near the spring head. Impermeable rocks or soil underlie the marshes, which support herbaceous plants adapted to saturated soil. In the deepest portions grow floating-leaved plants of the genera *Lemna* and *Potamogeton* (from the Greek words for "river" and "neighbor," respectively) and submergent and floating plants of the genera *Myriophyllum*, *Ceratophyllum*, and *Elodea*. Shallower water along the margins supports emergent and floating plants that include bulrush (*Scirpus* spp.), tule (*Schoenoplectus* spp.), cattail *(Typha* spp.), rushes *(Juncus* spp.), pondweed (*Potamogeton* spp.), knotweed (*Polygonum* spp.), and waterlily (*Nuphar* spp.).[31]

Springs and seeps receive relatively little legal protection, in part because they tend to be small and easily ignored and in part because they fall between the cracks of laws governing use of surface and groundwater supplies. If a spring is to be used for potable water, it must be covered or protected from contact with the air, but the sparse human settlement and relatively few springs of the western prairie combine to make such usage rare. Many of the springs that emerge on the western prairie support only a short segment of stream flow before the water either evaporates or seeps back into the ground. Only 10 meters of surface flow are needed to maintain many spring ecosystems, yet even these small systems are disappearing as regional water tables drop.

Playas form another type of seasonal wetland scattered widely across the western prairie. When dry, these shallow ephemeral lakes are typically salt-whitened flats that appear incapable of supporting any life. And they are mostly dry, for they are not connected to springs or streams. Instead, playas form where clay-lined depressions retain runoff from rainfall for a few days or even weeks. Although widely scattered and typically small—the great majority of playas are less than 12 hectares in extent—playas of the western prairie collectively support more than a million ducks, geese, cranes, and shorebirds that stop to feed and rest in playas during their spring and fall migrations. Observers have documented at least 185 species of birds, including 30 species of shorebirds, using these ephemeral oases.[32]

An estimated 75,000 playas are spread from eastern Colorado and western Nebraska southward to western Texas and Oklahoma. In an average year, only 10 percent to 20 percent of these playas contain water, while the rest create watery mirages as they shimmer in the heat waves of summer. Yet the invertebrates and plants that spend their entire lives within playas have adapted to long periods of dryness. With the return of water comes a brief explosion of life. Leeches, midge and dragonfly larvae, and other invertebrates provide protein-rich meals for birds. Plants adapted to complete their lifecycles quickly grow and produce seeds on an accelerated schedule, creating a dense cover, varied habitats, and abundant food for birds. As the water evaporates, the birds move on, and the plants and invertebrates disappear back into roots and dormant phases to await the next flush of water and growth.[33]

Playa wetlands help to recharge the Ogallala Aquifer and create one of the most important wintering regions for ducks in the Central Flyway. Yet because less than 1 percent of the playas in the western prairie occur on public lands, their existence is vulnerable to changes in the economics and attitudes of individual landowners. Many owners are simply ignorant of the ecological importance of playas. They are bulldozed for suburban sprawl, plowed for crops, drained, or used to retain polluted wastewater from feedlots. A 2001 US Supreme Court decision that stripped isolated, ephemeral wetlands such as playas of protection by the Clean Water Act has not helped preserve playas. Beyond educating landowners about the importance of playas, one of the critical tools in preserving these features is the federal Conservation Reserve Program, which pays landowners to conserve ecologically important areas by removing them from intensive land uses. Scientists estimate that nearly 70 percent of remaining playas larger than 4 hectares are already heavily modified by drainage or water retention systems for cattle or crops, making it critical to conserve those that remain.[34]

Beneath the land-use changes that threaten playas, records kept since the 1940s and earlier indicate net declines in the water table over broad areas of the Platte River valley as a result of groundwater pumping. By 1983 the water table had dropped more than 6 meters in parts of the valley, with a projected eventual decline of 24 meters over the entire basin. There has not yet been any apparent decline in the water table of the South Platte and Ogallala Aquifers in Colorado, but the water table has declined further east and below smaller stream channels in parts of eastern Colorado. The Arikaree River basin of eastern Colorado, which is tributary to the Republican River and borders the South Platte River to the southeast, illustrates how changes in groundwater affect streams and ecological communities.

WATER IN WELLS EVERYWHERE, BUT NOT A DROP FOR THE MINNOWS

The Arikaree is a relatively small, obscure stream, draining just under 4,500 square kilometers of arid prairie in eastern Colorado. This surface area is not enough to provide reliable stream flow, and most of the Arikaree's flow is derived from the Ogallala Aquifer. Areas contributing groundwater flow to the Arikaree are mostly within 5 to 10 kilometers of the stream. Summer thunderstorms occasionally supplement the groundwater entering the stream, causing short, intense floods.[35]

About a fifth of the Arikaree's drainage basin has undergone groundwater declines of more than 8 meters as a result of intensive groundwater pumping for center-pivot irrigation systems. The Ogallala Aquifer as a whole is more like an egg crate than a bathtub, so groundwater withdrawal from individual wells can depress the water table within a localized compartment of the aquifer and severely reduce nearby stream flow. One of these compartments lies around the Arikaree, and scientists studying the stream during the summer and autumn of 2002 found that pumping from wells within 16 kilometers of the main channel can cause decreased stream flow. Sixteen kilometers is small compared to the vast extent of the entire Ogallala, but it's not unreasonable that a farmer should be surprised that his well is decreasing flow in a stream 16 kilometers away.[36]

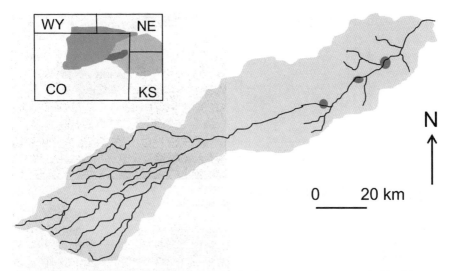

The Arikaree River basin (gray shading), showing the three stream segments studied by fish biologist Kurt Fausch and his students (dark gray circles in lower basin). The inset map shows the location of the Arikaree basin (dark gray) within the Kansas River basin in eastern Colorado, the South Platte River basin to the northwest, and the Arkansas River basin to the southwest. After Scheurer, Fausch, and Bestgen (2003, fig. 1).

These effects show up readily in a graph of stream flow and volume of pumping over time for the Lower Arikaree River. The line representing stream flow goes down just as steadily as the line representing volume of pumped groundwater goes up with the onset of center-pivot irrigation in the early 1960s. On a monthly basis, stream flow along portions of the Arikaree drops to almost nothing within a few weeks of the start of the irrigation season. Once the irrigation pumps are turned off, stream flow returns within three weeks. Combined pumping and regional drought during the first years of the twenty-first century have caused some portions of the length of the Arikaree to essentially disappear.[37]

Contemporary groundwater withdrawals do not occur in a climate of ignorance or carelessness. Sixty percent of the crops in the Arikaree basin are irrigated. Corn accounts for nearly half of these crops and sorghum, millet, and other plants for a much lower percentage. Farmers in the Arikaree basin are very conscious of water use. Most farmers use conservation practices such as no-till farming, crop rotations, and sweep rather than disk plows; and most center pivots used in the area employ low-pressure drop nozzles for greater efficiency. During the drought in 2002, however, all farmers irrigated continually rather than on their normal

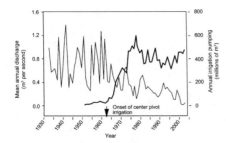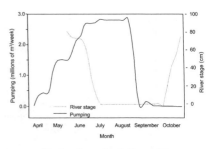

The effects of pumping groundwater for irrigating crops at the site along the Arikaree River studied by fish biologists. The graph at left shows relations between average annual stream flow (lighter line) and volume of water pumped (heavy black line) over several decades. The graph at right shows the effects during the course of a single year. After Fardal (2003).

schedule. Most farmers nonetheless were in deficit irrigation for the majority of the growing season despite the large quantity of water drawn from the aquifer.[38]

There are rules behind all of this. Just as stream flow is legally apportioned among the many consumers of water, so the state groundwater commission allows well users to pump only as much water each year as is consistent with allowing the aquifer to persist for a hundred years. Wells are permitted under the rule of a "three-mile circle." The groundwater commission uses what is known about the aquifer within a 4.8-kilometer (3-mile) radius of a proposed well to permit a flow rate from the well. The government does little, however, to monitor water usage after a well is installed.[39]

Further complications arise from the fact that the volume of water appropriated for pumping does not take into account any interactions between groundwater and surface stream flow. This means that a farmer can legally pump groundwater at a rate that dries up a nearby stream by lowering the water table beneath that stream. The widely used "safe yield" concept assumes that a long-term balance between groundwater withdrawal and recharge can be maintained if water users pump no more water than is recharged each year on average. This ignores the fact that, under natural conditions, groundwater discharges into springs and streams. Consequently, if pumping equals recharge, springs and streams may go dry because the water circuit of recharge-groundwater–stream flow is rerouted to recharge-groundwater–crop irrigation.[40]

Well appropriations were originally based on the idea of allowing the aquifer in the Arikaree basin to be depleted by 40 percent in 25 years. This was amended in 1990 to allow 40 percent depletion in 100 years, but permitted pumping rates may still be too great to maintain adequate stream flow. Given the propensity for consumptive water users to completely drain streams if left to their own devices,

March 31, 2001

May 11, 2001

May 24, 2001

June 21, 2001

Views of the same portion of the Arikaree River along which fish biologists studied fish during spring and summer 2001. The seasonal drying that appears here is typical and illustrates why pools that retain water throughout the dry season are crucial to fish survival. Courtesy, Julie Scheurer.

fish biologists proposed that a minimum flow, known as instream flow, was neces-sary to preserve aquatic communities throughout Colorado. This created a sepa-rate set of problems because water users, scientists, and environmentalists argue about exactly how much water is needed for instream flow in each river. The proposal allowed the Colorado Water Conservation Board to set instream flow levels for streams within the state, but gaps remain between policy and practice. At present, even the highest early-season flow rates on the Arikaree do not meet instream flow rights guaranteed by the water conservation board.[41]

Flow is now highly irregular along the length of the Arikaree. The main chan-nel in the upper portion of the drainage is dry most of the year. The lower 75 kilometers of stream change gradually downstream. The lower portion begins as a perennial segment with beaver dams built across a narrow, sinuous chan-nel of alternating pools and runs bordered by dense grasses, willow, and cotton-wood gallery forest. Downstream, the Arikaree becomes a seasonally intermittent stream with a wide, sandy channel bordered by grasses. This portion dries along most of its length during summer and contains few pools.[42]

Fifteen species of fish live within the Arikaree drainage. Of these, largemouth bass (*Micropterus salmoides*) is non-native, and five others—brassy minnow (*Hybog-nathus hankinsoni*), plains minnow (*H. placitus*), river shiner (*Notropis blennius*), suckermouth minnow (*Phenacobius mirabilis*), and orangethroat darter (*Etheos-toma spectabile*)—are rare species listed as threatened or endangered by the state of Colorado. Fish ecologist Kurt Fausch and some of his graduate students have studied the brassy minnow in particular.[43]

Once common in Colorado, the brassy minnow was rare by the time of a 1994 fish inventory. Like other fish of the western prairie, the brassy minnow is an amazingly resilient animal. This tiny fish, which grows to be only 10 centime-ters long, lives in harsh, fluctuating stream environments that can flood cata-strophically or dry in summer and freeze in winter. These changes in flow and temperature create drastic fluctuations in water chemistry and physical habitat as some pools fill with sand and others are scoured into the streambed by floods. In response to these conditions, the brassy minnow accelerates its reproduction and growth during higher stream flows in May and June. When high flows connect greater lengths of channel, adults disperse and mate, and the young fish grow to maturity quickly. The fish must mature quickly, while conditions in the stream are relatively good, and then race back to the safe spots where they will spend most of the year. When the water shrinks back to isolated segments of stream during the hot months of summer and the low flows of November to January, the distribution of the fish shrinks, too: adults survive in pools sufficiently deep or fed by groundwater to retain water. Ideally, these refuge pools are also connected to

A brassy minnow, which is about 7.5 centimeters long and probably in its third year of life, about the average maximum life span. Courtesy, Kurt Fausch.

channel segments with at least a trickle of flowing water, so that if a particular pool dries completely, some of the small-bodied fish might be able to struggle on to the next pool. Even in the absence of human alteration of flow along the Arikaree, survival is tricky for the brassy minnow. The persistence of the species depends on sufficient numbers of individuals being present that at least some fish will survive the unpredictable drying of the scattered refuge pools.[44]

Despite their resilience and adaptations, brassy minnows are stressed by falling groundwater levels and changing stream flows. The longer the segments of flowing stream and the deeper the pools, the greater the minnow population. Minnows spawn in flooded vegetation along floodplains during mid-April to mid-May. Larvae emerge in mid-May to mid-June. This corresponds with the start of the irrigation season, so stream segments begin to dry when the fish are at their most vulnerable stage. Consequently, fish are forced to retreat to refuges or become stranded in isolated pools. Water depth in the pools also correlates with long-term trends created by center-pivot pumping from the Ogallala.[45]

The brassy minnow, particularly the populations in the Arikaree River, are a relatively well-studied species that help us understand the conditions fish of the western prairie need to survive and how the margin of survival grows narrower as we change the distribution of surface and groundwater across the prairie. The plight of the brassy minnow in the Arikaree reflects that of dozens of other aquatic species across the western prairie.

"IT IS OBVIOUS THAT WITHOUT WATER, THERE CAN BE NO FISH."[46]

The first scientists to reach the western prairie during the early decades of the nineteenth century busily collected and described plants and animals and assessed the agricultural potential of soils and the resources to be extracted from timber or minerals. But nobody wrote anything about the fish. The first collection of western prairie fish comes from the South Platte River in 1873 during a survey under the oversight of Lieutenant George Wheeler. The Wheeler Survey—one of the four great nineteenth-century surveys of the American West undertaken by the US Army Corps of Engineers—included paleontologist Edward Drinker Cope, later famous in part for his long-running and bitter feud with the equally illustrious paleontologist Othniel Marsh. This feud, which included intense fossil-finding competition in the scientifically unexplored lands of the American West, became known as the Bone Wars. Cope was also a herpetologist, ichthyologist, and comparative anatomist who discovered, described, and named more than a thousand species of vertebrates, including hundreds of fishes. Cope established the baseline for scientific knowledge of fish species distribution across the western prairie, along with other collections such as those of Oliver Hay during the 1870s–90s. These collections came late with respect to alterations in the prairie streams already well under way for two decades, and they were limited geographically. Fishes were collected at only a dozen sites in Colorado before 1900, for example, and most of these were in the transition zone near current cities. As fish biologists Kurt Fausch and Kevin Bestgen note, native status of some western prairie species will consequently always be difficult to decipher.[47]

In spite of limited historical records, fish ecologists believe prairie fish are declining. Of thirty-seven species native to the Platte, Arkansas, and Republican River basins in eastern Colorado, six are gone (extinct) and another fourteen are going (threatened or endangered). Half of Colorado's native prairie fish species have thus either declined or been lost. Similar trends exist across the western prairie. Native red shiners (*Cyprinella lutrensis*), a species extremely tolerant of high temperatures and low oxygen levels, are now extinct in several prairie streams on the Oklahoma-Texas border, where recent severe drought killed off local populations and the presence of a reservoir prevented re-colonization. Research in Kansas indicates that fewer than half of the fish species recorded in historical collections are still present; the greatest losses have occurred in streams of western Kansas, with the most intense groundwater withdrawals and fragmentation by reservoirs.

Of forty-nine endemic fish species in the western prairie, forty-one are declining or extinct. We know much less about the life history and specific threats to many of these fish species than about those just described for the brassy minnow. Referring to North American prairie streams in a 1988 paper, William Matthews wrote that "many of the ecological features, such as hydrologic regimes, productivity, respiration, organic matter processing, and composition of the biota . . . are unknown for most streams of the interior plains." Research on the Arikaree is a spotlight shining on the darkness that is extinction. The changes documented on the Arikaree reflect those on Lone Pine Creek and Bijou Creek in the South Platte River basin and dozens of other intermittent streams of the western prairie—not least because, as Matthews also noted in the same paper, the greatest discrepancies between the streams described by nineteenth-century explorers and the streams of today seem to be in the spring-fed tributaries that were once clear, free-flowing streams and now have turbid, intermittent flows resulting mostly from rainfall.[48]

Recall the substantial groundwater declines in portions of the Arikaree River basin and the associated changes in stream flow. A minnow less than 8 centimeters in length may need 5 to 25 kilometers of river to carry out its lifecycle because the majority of those kilometers will be dry during much of the year. As water tables decline and springs and streams dry up, we push more and more prairie fish across a threshold of survival.[49]

Shrinking habitat can be isolated by dry stretches and by physical barriers fish cannot get over or around. Structures such as irrigation intakes, diversion dams, and culverts under road and railroad crossings can create barriers fish cannot swim through or jump over. For a very small fish, a vertical barrier only 5 centimeters high may be as effective a blockade to upstream movement as Glen Canyon Dam. Thousands of instream structures now effectively chop streams into isolated segments by preventing fish from migrating among suitable spawning, foraging, and refuge habitats. In her graduate thesis, fish biologist Ashley Ficke noted more than a hundred of these structures in the 1,375-square-kilometer drainage of St. Vrain Creek, one of many tributaries to the South Platte River.[50]

Death by a thousand cuts: shrinking and isolated habitats, barriers to dispersal, and then water pollution and aggressive competitors in the form of introduced species all push the western prairie fish progressively closer to that irreversible threshold of extinction. Flow regulation that reduces the snowmelt pulse and increases base flow can favor introduced fish species that prefer more stable stream flows and cooler temperatures. Fish ecologists believe introduced species are the single greatest threat to the survival of native fish. Excess nutrients and pesticides running off agricultural fields and various contaminants from roadways, municipal areas, and industries also limit fish health and survival. No perfect refuges remain. Nutrients in domestic wastewater enter streams in the transition zone from mountains to plains, and agricultural runoff carries fine sediments and fertilizers. Silt and organic muck cover these streams' cobble beds and cloud the water. Removal of wood from the streams has reduced the overhead cover and streambed scour that create good places for fish to live. Small streams further into the plains are drier than they once were, and larger streams are clearer and more consistent in their flow, favoring introduced fish.[51]

Of thirty-four fish species considered native to the Arkansas and South Platte River systems in Colorado, several are unique to aquatic ecosystems of the western prairie, including plains minnow (*Hybognathus placitus*), speckled chub (*Macrhybopsis aestivalis*), Arkansas River shiner (*Notropis girardi*), flathead chub (*Platygobio gracilis*), plains topminnow (*Fundulus sciadicus*), northern plains killifish (*Fundulus zebrinus*), and Arkansas darter (*Etheostoma cragini*). Because some of these fish typically live in fairly small habitats, an individual population can be destroyed by a very local land use. Groundwater pumping can dry up the spring-fed stream in which the population exists. A new urban neighborhood can destroy habitat for a population in a stream segment of the transition zone. An unpredictable extreme flood or drought can wipe out a population in a stream isolated by irrigation structures, and no new fish can re-populate the area. Although multiple populations of a species typically exist, as we inadvertently eliminate a population here and a population there, we are effectively concentrating all of our eggs—all of the individuals remaining in a species—into one, vulnerable basket.[52]

STRUGGLING TO SURVIVE

Journalists sometimes portray the listing of a species as threatened or endangered as a great political victory, which it too often is, but listing is only the start of protecting and recovering that plant or animal and, of course, reflects the fact that we have allowed its population to decline to perilously low levels. The next steps are to identify where the species still survives and then figure out why those locations can support the species. A fish or plant might survive along a river because of the specifics of the volume and timing of high flows, the type of sediment along the streambed or banks, the type and extent of vegetation, presence of food for the species, flow depth and velocity, and so on. Scientists must also quantify the point of no return in habitat: the minimum levels of relevant habitat characteristics necessary to ensure viability of the species. If endangered piping plovers (*Charadrius melodus*) need unvegetated sandbars along a river for nesting habitat, for example, increasing the extent of such habitat is likely to require changes in resource use by people. The people affected will want to know what constitutes a minimum area necessary to support a sustainable population of piping plovers.

Freshwater fishes and other riverine species in the western United States are among the most endangered organisms in the country. Most western rivers are over-appropriated, yet as human population in the intermountain West continues to grow, demands also increase for flow diversions from the instream flows that support these riverine species. The Poudre River, for example, has been over-appropriated since 1876, as mentioned earlier. Yet as of 2013 the Bureau of Reclamation was proposing to build another large, off-channel reservoir that would store some of the peak flow on the Poudre during the relatively few years in which high peaks occur. Under some of the proposed operating scenarios, construction of this new reservoir would keep portions of the Poudre River in the transition zone and the prairie dry during most years.[53]

More than half of all species listed under the Endangered Species Act are affected in some way by water-management projects, many of which are supported by the federal government. As a National Research Committee on endangered and threatened species of the Platte River noted, it is relatively easy to trace the connections from water-management projects to changed flow patterns and then to declines in riverine species. It is thus not surprising that people in the western United States commonly argue over how to implement the Endangered Species Act in the context of federal water projects, for the operation of these projects dramatically influences habitat and species recovery.[54]

It's not rocket science to understand that river manipulation has stressed native riverine species. It approaches rocket science to figure out how to restore the key aspects of river process and form sufficient to recover these species within the constraints imposed by human consumptive uses of land and water. This is illustrated by attempts to restore habitat for migratory birds.

Conflicts over endangered species and resource use have risen to particular prominence along the central Platte River, the 240-kilometer-long portion of the river from Lexington to Columbus, Nebraska, that starts approximately a hundred kilometers downstream from the junction of the North and South Platte Rivers. The central Platte lies just east of the 100th meridian, where the river flows from nearly arid conditions to the more humid environment typical of the eastern portion of the American prairie. The vast system of dams, diversions, canals, and groundwater pumping present along upstream tributary rivers continues downstream to the junction of the Platte with the Missouri River. The central Platte also lies within the Central Flyway, a primary north-south corridor for migratory birds. Islands, sandbars, and floodplain wetlands provide important habitat for migratory and resident birds, as well as fish and many other organisms. Among the animals that rely on the river are four federally listed species: the whooping crane (*Grus americana*), piping plover, interior least tern (*Sterna antillarum athalassos*), and pallid sturgeon (*Scaphirhynchus albus*). Concern over these species' continued viability exerts a strong influence on decisions about river management, both in the central Platte and upstream.[55]

Whooping cranes are a physically impressive bird, with a wingspan of over 2 meters. They are also the rarest crane species in the world. The decline in whoopers began decades ago in response to over-hunting and widespread habitat destruction. Estimates of whooping crane numbers during the 1860s–70s vary widely, from as many as 1,300 to 1,400 birds to as few as 500 to 700. These numbers dropped to only 15 birds in 1941. Intensive conservation efforts helped whooping cranes rebound to a 2009 population of 266 wild birds, a number that indicates the species is still perilously close to extinction. Whooping cranes were federally listed as endangered in 1967, under legislation predating the 1973 Endangered Species Act.[56]

The small wild population of whooping cranes migrates from over-wintering grounds on the Gulf Coast of Texas to breeding grounds at Wood Buffalo National Park in west-central Canada. During the two annual migration passes over the central Platte River, some of the whooping cranes stop at the river for periods ranging from a day to several weeks to feed on agricultural uplands during the day and roost along the river at night. Sightings of whooping cranes along the Platte have been documented since 1820, but open habitat the birds prefer has steadily declined.[57]

Whooping cranes once nested mostly in the northern tallgrass prairie of the upper midwestern United States and the eastern aspen parklands of Canada. Spreading out among diverse wetland habitats, the cranes followed many routes between their breeding and wintering areas. Now, like traffic on a busy multilane freeway merging into a single lane, the migrating cranes must crowd into the few remaining sites that provide suitable resting and feeding habitat, including the central Platte. The central Platte has become so important to the cranes' survival that the US Fish and Wildlife Service designated a portion of the river critical habitat for the birds.[58]

Critical whooping crane habitat along the central Platte River includes foraging areas of water that is shallower on average than water in the surrounding wetlands. Preferred foraging sites are largely devoid of vegetation greater than a meter in height and have open horizons. At these sites the cranes eat the snails, snakes, frogs, worms, and tubers of marsh plants that provide the birds with the energy to continue their long and strenuous migration. Lack of tall vegetation and open vistas allows the cranes to avoid predators while eating. If the whooping cranes are too crowded into the small remaining open areas, which are also used by the much more numerous sandhill cranes, they become more vulnerable to disease and predators.[59]

Roosting sites are another critical habitat component for cranes that stop along the central Platte. Cranes prefer to roost at sites surrounded by deeper waters that limit predation from land. The birds also choose wide, unvegetated sections of the channel with good visibility upstream and downstream, again presumably to avoid predation.[60]

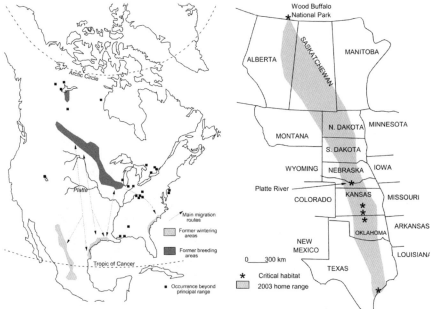

Historical distribution of whooping cranes in
North America. After Graf (2005, fig. 5-1).

2003 range of migrating whooping cranes.
After Graf (2005, fig. 5-3).

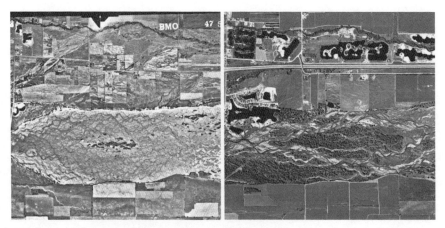

Aerial views of the Platte River near Kearney, Nebraska, in 1938 (left) and 1998 (right). Very
little vegetation (darker shading) is present within the channel in the 1938 photograph. In
contrast, much of the former channel and floodplain is covered by woody vegetation in the
1998 photograph. The wooded areas are not used by migratory cranes. Courtesy, US Bureau of
Reclamation.

Low-level aerial photograph of the Platte River in Nebraska in 2004, showing multiple shallow channels branching among densely vegetated small islands; stream banks are also densely vegetated, leaving few open places for large flocks of cranes to feed or roost. Courtesy, Will Graf.

The characteristics of preferred foraging and roosting sites whooping cranes use during their migrations are those created and maintained by the historical flow regime on the central Platte River. The most effective way to restore these habitat characteristics would be to restore the natural flow regime, but this is not particularly feasible at present given the intense human demands on water resources within the basin. In response to the crisis in whooping crane numbers and available habitat, nongovernmental organizations including the National Audubon Society and the Platte River Whooping Crane Trust began to open up the riverscape, as high flows on the Platte River once did. During the 1980s and 1990s these groups cleared wooded islands of vegetation and then periodically disked and mowed to keep vegetation short. Bulldozers lowered wooded islands to riverbed level. These actions have been effective in attracting larger flocks of roosting sandhill cranes (*Grus canadensis*), as well as whooping cranes, and the clearing is now done using public funds.[61]

The downsides of this type of habitat manipulation include reducing wooded nesting and migratory habitat for songbirds and facilitating the spread of non-native purple loosestrife (*Lythrum salicaria*). Positive aspects include improved habitat for all three federally listed bird species along the central Platte, as well as other birds that need open habitat. This habitat manipulation may also help restore lost or reduced ecological processes that may be important to proper functioning of a more natural river system.[62]

The vague phrase *ecological processes* is at the crux of river restoration. If we could go in with bulldozers and backhoes and create the ideal river channel that would then remain static, restoration would be easy. But a healthy river is anything but static. A big flood rips out mature cottonwoods, dumping the trees in the river and leaving banks of moist sand on which new cottonwoods can germinate. Fish that prefer the overhead cover and deep scour holes associated with the logs move into that portion of the stream. The new openness of the riparian forest supports different understory plants and different species of insects and songbirds. As the logs in the channel rot or float downstream, different fish move in to use the sandy channel. As the trees mature, understory plants that prefer shade and birds that like a closed canopy move into the area, while the earlier inhabitants move on to other newly disturbed sites. The entire river corridor is constantly in flux, and this flux supports a much greater abundance of species through time than would a static river. Heroclitus was right when he said "you cannot step in the same river twice." The more we understand about the wonderful complexity of interactions among river processes and plant and animal communities, the clumsier can seem our amateurish efforts to intervene through river restoration. The best we can do is to observe closely and learn as we go.

We have to learn quickly, though, when the animal at risk reaches populations as small as those of some bird species that use the central Platte River. The piping plover and the interior least tern share many habitat requirements along the central Platte. Both species are small, migratory shorebirds that breed along the broad prairie rivers, as well as elsewhere in North America. The plover, federally listed as endangered in 1985, currently has a population estimated at fewer than 500 birds along the Platte River and 6,000 birds throughout North America. Fewer than 500 interior least terns, of a total population estimated at 55,000 during the 1980s–90s, are present along the Platte River. Plover and tern populations have declined from historical levels as open, sandy nesting habitat in and along rivers has disappeared. This habitat loss reflects all the human improvements to rivers: drowning stream banks and floodplains under reservoirs, dredging and straightening channels, modifying flow, and replacing open areas with woodlands, sand and gravel mines, housing, and roadways.[63]

Piping plovers and terns typically arrive at the central Platte in spring and depart by late summer. During their stay along the river, the birds locate a mate, construct a shallow nest on sand or gravel, and lay and incubate eggs. Chicks need about twenty days after hatching before they can fly, but fledged young birds remain along the central Platte until they begin their autumn migration.[64]

Plovers and terns commonly nest near one another. Both species need bare or nearly bare islands or sandbars, favorable water levels during the nesting season, and food. Favorable water levels are those that keep land predators away—island nests have lower rates of predation than mainland nests—and that do not rise suddenly and flood the nest before the eggs are hatched or the chicks can fly. The birds obtain food in the form of invertebrates such as worms and insects or, for terns, fish from portions of open channel with pooled or slow-flowing water less than 15 centimeters deep. Plovers and terns tend to forage less than a kilometer from their nests on bars and islands. All of these requirements might seem to equal a precarious existence: after all, floods and droughts occur naturally, and these natural fluctuations would always have caused the deaths of many young birds. The key distinctions between then and now are abundance and extent. When abundant, widespread habitat supported large numbers of birds, the loss of some portions of the population in areas affected by floods or droughts could be absorbed by the species as a whole because other portions of the population bred successfully each year. With all of their eggs in one basket—or one limited area of suitable habitat—a natural flood or drought has the potential to create havoc by breaking all or most of those eggs.[65]

One basket is bad; no basket is worse. As of 2003, scientists judged that no suitable habitat for piping plovers existed along the central Platte River. Although efforts are under way to provide habitat, flow has been so low during recent years that new sandbars are not being created and existing sandbars are being colonized by vegetation. Many river reaches have also remained dry during the past few years, allowing access by land predators and limiting the birds' invertebrate food. Having created a void of habitat through past land and resource manipulation, people must now further manipulate the river corridor if they want to save plovers from the void of extinction.[66]

Pallid sturgeons, federally listed as endangered along the Platte River in 1990, are in nearly as perilous a situation along that river as whooping cranes, piping plovers, and interior least terns. Pallid sturgeons were once the great travelers of the river world. These fish were historically present in the Mississippi River from the Gulf of Mexico upstream to Iowa, along the Atchafalaya River in Louisiana, along the Missouri River from its confluence with the Mississippi upstream to Fort Benton, Montana, and along the primary tributaries of the Missouri—including 46 kilometers of the Platte upstream from its junction with the Missouri. The combined effects of damming, water diversions, flood control, channelization, and over-fishing for flesh and eggs have so greatly reduced sturgeon numbers that what was once a flowing river of migratory fish has shrunk back to a few small pools—disconnected subpopulations in Montana's Yellowstone River, the Missouri River downstream from Gavins Point Dam near Yankton, South Dakota, and the Platte River.[67]

Pallid sturgeons, which grow to more than a meter in length, probably spawn during late May to early July in the Platte River. The word *probably* reflects scientific ignorance of this species, for which sightings averaged 500 per year during the 1960s but dropped to about 7 per year during the 1980s. These rare fish prefer turbid water, making it particularly difficult for biologists to locate and study individuals or populations. Spawning seems to occur only once every two to three years for males and every three to five years for females. This is not uncommon for very large-bodied fish species, but it does make it harder for populations to rebound from a severe decline. Adults probably eat smaller fish and are most often found in sections of river with numerous islands, at the mouths of tributary streams, or at the downstream ends of islands and sandbars where currents converge. At these sites the fish find nice little spots where slower currents keep them from using too much energy but nearby faster flow brings food their way.[68]

Drawing on procedures used for other endangered species, the US Fish and Wildlife Service initially focused on the separate habitat needs of each of the four endangered species along the central Platte River. The service proposed river flows designed to meet the perceived needs of each species: a pulse flow to scour vegetation and provide more suitable sandbar habitat for terns, plovers, and cranes; higher spring and autumn flows to favor use of the river by whooping cranes during migration; higher minimum flows during summer to reduce mortality of fish eaten by terns; and so forth. One of the problems with this species-by-species approach is that it can promote micromanagement and conflicts regarding the perceived needs of individual species. In July 1997 the US Department of the Interior took a new approach when it signed the Platte River Cooperative Agreement to provide Endangered Species Act compliance for all four species simultaneously. Signatories to the agreement included water users, environmental organizations, and government agencies. The signatories created the Platte River Endangered Species Partnership as a cooperative agreement to improve and conserve habitat for the four species and to enable existing and new water uses in the basin to proceed without additional regulatory actions related to the species. In a sense, the agreement is designed to allow us to have our cake and eat it too: to restore the endangered species without further controlling existing consumptive water use or eliminating new uses. This might seem like a sleight-of-hand trick, but a critical point is that nobody seeks to restore historical abundance of habitat or non-human populations. The agreement does not attempt to restore a vanished world: rather, it attempts to restore a tiny part of that world, just enough to keep the various species present in our brave new world.[69]

Creation of the agreement and partnership is certainly a step in the right direction, but it is difficult to integrate research and management throughout a large river basin with many water users and many private and government agencies studying listed species. In 2005, for example, a National Research Council committee noted the failure to analyze or report the environmental effects of an experimental flow in 2002. These issues are not unique to the central Platte River. Large-scale river management and restoration projects currently under way on rivers as diverse as the Columbia, Colorado, Missouri, Chesapeake, and Kissimmee indicate that it is very difficult to develop the detailed scientific knowledge necessary to truly understand the complex interactions within a river ecosystem: this is the rocket science part. It is even more difficult to reach agreement among diverse stakeholders as to how to use this understanding to manage a river: this is the nearly impossible part.[70]

A useful idea to keep in mind when thinking about highly altered river systems such as the Platte River basin is the concept of a *normative river*. Instead of returning the river to pristine conditions, the primary goal of creating a normative river is to regain as much as possible of the former flow regime within the constraints imposed by flow regulation, land use and property rights, and so forth. This approach recognizes the need to perform a balancing act between restoring sufficient river function to conserve endangered species and habitat and sustaining existing human resource use. This sounds attractive, but when there is not enough water to go around, as on the western prairie, it becomes an extremely difficult and contentious balancing act. In the worst scenario, the opposing desires of different parties lead to expensive and time-consuming court cases. In the best scenario, some habitat and river function can be restored through private or governmental purchase of land and water and, if necessary, mimicking river function through actions such as mechanical removal of vegetation.[71]

Fluctuations in the population of sandhill cranes along the Platte River during the past few decades illustrate the complex interactions among human removal of riverside vegetation, stream flow and streambed topography, bird populations, and agricultural economics. From March through April, the cranes migrate from their wintering grounds in Texas and Mexico to stage in the Platte and North Platte River valleys before continuing on to breeding grounds in Canada, Alaska, and Siberia. *Stage* is the term biologists use to describe a phase in the life of the cranes when they eat as much as they can, developing fat reserves for the long flight ahead. The sight of hundreds of thousands of birds concentrating along the rivers calls to mind the great migrations of Africa or the historical migrations of bison and passenger pigeons in North America. The first effort to figure out exactly how many cranes were in the staging areas dates to 1957. With time, the technology used in these surveys changed from visual estimates to aerial infrared videography that lets scientists count the birds when they concentrate for night roosting, although visual estimates continue to be used. Biologists now estimate that 450,000 to 550,000 sandhill cranes each year use two staging areas along the 130-kilometer-long reach of the Platte River between Lexington and Grand Island, Nebraska, and a third staging area on the North Platte River near Hershey, Nebraska.[72]

Cranes roost at night in the river channel and then disperse at dawn to forage in nearby farm fields and wetlands. Although there are a great many sandhill cranes at present, they are vulnerable on at least two points: their roosting and their foraging. Suitable roosting sites are shrinking. Cranes roost in wide, shallow, unvegetated portions of the channel with water depths of 35 centimeters or less and flow velocity less than 80 centimeters per second. Most cranes are found where water is no deeper than 12 centimeters and the current moves at less than 40 centimeters per second. Bird surveys during the years 1957 to 1989 reveal that, as woody riparian vegetation encroaches on the channel and the channel narrows, cranes move to sections of the river that remain relatively wide and unvegetated, growing increasingly concentrated and vulnerable to disease and local severe storms that could kill a large percentage of the birds. The birds also accumulate less fat, presumably in part as the result of increased competition for food.

Under the US Fish and Wildlife's Partners for Wildlife Program, private landowners and environmental groups have artificially maintained wide channels and limited vegetation along approximately 30 kilometers of river during the past few decades. Heavy equipment is used to cut woody plant stems greater than 20 centimeters in diameter, and herbicides and discing with a tractor rolling a row of steel discs over the cleared area are used to limit vegetation re-growth. This can make more sediment available for river transport and downstream deposition. Studying river response at the National Audubon Society's Rowe Sanctuary near Kearney, Nebraska, Paul Kinzel and other scientists from the US Geological Survey found that decreasing stream flow and increased sediment supply caused low flows to be concentrated in small incised channels rather than spreading across broad sandbars. Higher flows are needed to create the same amount of usable habitat that would be available if the water spread shallowly across the bars, but the cranes may not use this habitat if the incised channels are near the riverbanks and easily accessible to predators.[73]

Foraging creates another point of vulnerability for sandhill cranes along the Platte. As of 1994, half of the lands around the staging areas were in cornfields, with less than 17 percent in native grassland. Cranes use both cornfields and grasslands; they probe the moist bottomland soils of the native grassland for protein-rich invertebrates that comprise 3 percent of their diet, and they eat waste corn that forms 97 percent of their diet. Cranes spend as much time searching for the 3 percent, however, as they do consuming the 97 percent, presumably because the native grassland areas are harder to find.

Corn is important, but its availability appears to be declining also. A study by Gary Krapu and colleagues published in 2004 noted that the waste corn left in fields in 1998 was less than half the amount left in 1978. Probably of more concern is the supplanting of corn by soybeans. Krapu's team did not find soybeans in the stomachs of cranes, northern pintails (*Anas acuta*), greater white-fronted geese (*Anser albifrons*), or lesser snow geese (*Chen caerulescens*) staging along the Platte, despite the fact that soybeans were widely available. Soybeans do not meet the birds' needs for a high-energy diet, and the birds must fly farther from their roosting sites to forage, thus limiting their accumulation of fat. Some of the deficit can be made up from the seeds of weeds in cropfields. Herbicides have traditionally been targeted at specific weed species so as not to kill the crop plants, which has allowed some weed species to thrive in cropfields, providing an important food source for many wildlife species. Genetically modified soybeans are poised to dominate agriculture across the United States, and these soybeans allow farmers to use glyphosphate herbicides that target all plant species except the genetically modified crop. If these trends play out as it appears they may, maintaining sufficient staging habitat for sandhill cranes and other migratory birds will require moving vegetation, re-contouring the streambed each year, and supplying some source of protein and carbohydrates: the Platte River staging area will in essence become a very large seasonal zoo. The most likely outcome, regardless of whether such intensive management is undertaken, is that bird numbers will substantially decline.[74]

Sometimes recognition of the need to balance river function and endangered species with water consumption and other resource use is forced by legislation, such as the Endangered Species Act. Sometimes this recognition is forced by human health issues. Starting in 1991, the US Geological Survey performed a nationwide assessment of surface and groundwater quality in fifty-nine river basins across the United States. The South Platte River was one of those chosen for study, and the results of the assessment helped increase public recognition of the hazards declining water quality, linked to loss of river function, posed for the health of humans and wildlife within the basin.

INVISIBLE CHANGES

Our most comprehensive picture of the health of rivers in the South Platte drainage basin comes from the US Geological Survey's National Water Quality Assessment (NAWQA) program. NAWQA scientists sampled the chemistry of surface water, groundwater, fish tissue, and streambed sediments, as well as evaluating stream ecology and habitat, at sixty different sites within the drainage during the years 1992–95. Their analyses indicate clear spatial patterns. Streams in the mountainous headwaters generally have good water quality and biological abundance and diversity, except where toxic contaminants from nineteenth-century metal mining persist. But as the streams leave the mountains and enter regions of more intensive land use in the foothills and plains, water quality and biological communities deteriorate.

"Think globally, act locally" applies to the NAWQA findings. Local land use and site characteristics have more effect on stream habitat, the integrity of aquatic communities, and water quality than do upstream or basin-wide patterns of land use. Upstream influences no longer reach as far down the South Platte as they once might have, simply because the river is so disconnected by dry segments. Each of these dry segments occurs where much or all of the stream flow is removed from the river by diversions, used for irrigating crops or municipal supplies and then returned to the river. Many of the diversions are associated with the hundred-plus municipal wastewater treatment plants within the South Platte River basin. The largest of these are the twenty-five plants along the Front Range urban corridor from Fort Collins south to Denver. These plants collectively discharge about 94 million liters of effluent per day, about 95 percent of the total daily effluent discharge in the river basin. Urban wastewater treatment is designed to remove solids and bacterial contamination. It does not remove synthetic chemicals such as insecticides or pharmaceuticals, nor does it remove nitrogen and phosphorus. An estimated 6,350 metric tons of nitrogen and 1,100 metric tons of phosphorus now enter the South Platte River basin each year from the wastewater treatment plants. Where discharge from the treatment plant supplies most or all of the stream flow, nutrient concentrations in the South Platte River can be substantially higher than elsewhere in the United States.[75]

Nitrogen and phosphorus are critical nutrients required by most living organisms, but excess levels of these elements can create problems when, for example, they stimulate algal blooms. Some species of algae excrete toxic waste products. Usually of more importance is that when the algae dies, the processes by which it decays require oxygen and thus decrease the levels of dissolved oxygen in the water. This can adversely affect other aquatic organisms. Excess nutrients also create other problems besides low dissolved oxygen.[76]

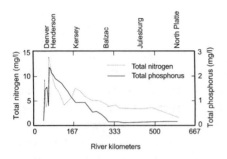

Total nitrogen and phosphorus concentrations in the South Platte River during April 1994, as sampled by NAWQA scientists. Concentrations were largest just downstream from Denver as a result of urban wastewater inputs and then generally decreased downstream. After Dennehy et al. (1998, 18).

Part of the challenge in understanding and managing nitrogen and phosphorus in streams is that so many factors influence their behavior. Consider ammonia (NH_3), for example. Nitrogen is present in various forms in natural environments, but only nitrite (NO_2^-), nitrate (NO_3^-), ammonium (NH_4^+), and orthophosphate can be directly used by living organisms. Blue-green algae and bacteria convert nitrogen to ammonia. Ammonia attaches to fine sediment, so the amount of fine sediment suspended in flowing water or accumulated on the bed partly controls ammonia concentrations. The proportion of ammonia in un-ionized form depends on water temperature and pH, as well as the concentration of ammonia present. The presence of toxic ammonia thus reflects not only nitrogen supply but also algal and bacterial activity, fine sediment, water temperature, and pH—each of which can vary over short distances or time intervals within a stream.[77]

Nitrate is usually the most abundant form of nitrogen and is typically dissolved in water and stable. High concentrations of nitrate can be harmful if consumed by warm-blooded animals because nitrate can be converted to nitrite within the gastrointestinal tract, and nitrite reacts with hemoglobin to limit oxygen transport in the blood. In extreme cases, this leads to potentially fatal conditions such as "blue-baby syndrome," in which reduced oxygen in the blood of a human infant creates a blue tinge in the baby's skin. The US Environmental Protection Agency has established drinking-water standards that specify maximum permissible nitrate levels because of these health effects. However, only a few states, none of them on the prairie, have established standards for nutrients in streams as opposed to drinking water. In addition to the obvious potential for detrimental effects to stream ecosystems, if nutrient-enriched waters are used for human consumption, carcinogenic by-products result from chemical treatment to bring the water up to drinking standards.[78]

Similar to wastewater treatment plants, return flows or infiltration of irrigation water can also produce high concentrations of nitrogen and phosphorus in surface water and groundwater within the South Platte River basin. An estimated

Sheep at a feedlot near Greeley, Colorado, 2008. Along with even larger cattle feedlots, this is one of the sources of large amounts of nitrogen to nearby streams.

36,000 metric tons of phosphorus and 180,000 metric tons of nitrogen are applied to crops in the South Platte basin each year, either as chemical fertilizers or as manure from the many feedlots present in the basin. Concentrated sources such as feedlots inevitably leak large amounts of nitrogen and phosphorus into rivers, overwhelming the capacity of riverine microbial and plant communities to process these nutrients. Water quality in agricultural portions of the South Platte basin is particularly degraded as a result of nitrates and salinity in groundwater, as well as salinity and suspended sediment in surface water.[79]

Contamination of surface waters by nutrients creates problems, but surface waters are typically able to recover relatively quickly if incoming nutrients are reduced: river flow disperses the remaining nitrogen and phosphorus and the fine sediment to which they can become attached, bacteria and algae take up some of the nutrients, and aquatic insects and fish eat the bacteria and algae. Contamination of groundwater is more problematic. Slower chemical reactions and limited biological communities in groundwater mean the excess nutrients are not as efficiently taken up by living organisms or converted into other chemical compounds, but the continuous, slow flow of groundwater gradually spreads the contaminants throughout the aquifer. High nitrate concentrations have so greatly degraded groundwater quality that wells in some cities on the eastern plains of Colorado can no longer be used to supply drinking water. Nitrate concentrations

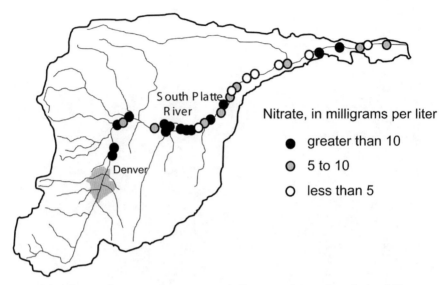

Spatial distribution of nitrate concentrations in shallow groundwater along the South Platte River as sampled by NAWQA scientists. After Dennehy et al. (1998, 17).

exceeded the US Environmental Protection Agency drinking-water standard of 10 milligrams per liter in about half of the wells sampled by NAWQA scientists. This contamination cannot be avoided by simply drilling deeper wells because the nitrates diffuse throughout the aquifer.[80]

One of the implications of the NAWQA results is that small streams are important because the plants and animals of the stream corridor effectively cleanse the water. Microbes living in streambed sediments remove nitrate from incoming agricultural return flows by incorporating nitrogen into their bodies rather than allowing it to continue downstream. Smaller streams are vital to this process because they have a higher ratio of streambed surface to water volume than do larger rivers. The efficiency of stream microbes is highest when dissolved oxygen can readily enter the streambed sediments, so streambeds covered by silt and clay retain less nitrogen than do sand-bed streams. Aquatic insects living on the streambed or within the water column also ingest nitrogen with their food. Logs and aquatic plants within the stream decrease water velocity and enhance the ability of microbes and insects to take up nitrogen. Similar processes of nitrogen storage occur in the soil of riverside areas, where the plants and soil microbes take up nitrogen and decrease nitrate concentrations in groundwater. Pumping groundwater for crop irrigation thus creates a double effect by destroying instream and riverside habitat and pushing native species to extinction and by removing the landscape-scale water filtering of excess nitrates coming off agricultural fields.[81]

Biological uptake of excess nitrogen provides an example of healthy stream corridors' self-purifying ability, but chronically high levels of nitrogen loading can overwhelm that ability. Stream segments downstream from point sources such as wastewater effluents have fewer aquatic insect species. The historical channel changes described previously also reduce the streams' ability to process nitrogen. Lower volumes of flow, lower abundance and diversity of instream and riverside species, and less diverse habitat all combine with high nitrogen loads to create a situation analogous to septic tanks overflowing during heavy rain: streams flush excess nitrogen downstream rather than processing it. Changes to each seemingly insignificant little prairie stream thus add up to a loss of essential ecosystem services that supply us with clean water.[82]

Other contaminants enter surface and groundwater from irrigated agricultural fields. Irrigated fields occupy only 8 percent of the South Platte River basin but account for 71 percent of basin water use. Corn, hay, dry beans, and other small grains are the primary crops grown using irrigation in the South Platte River basin. More than 900,000 kilograms of active pesticide ingredients are applied to these crops each year. About 90 percent of these ingredients consist of eight pesticides applied mainly to corn during spring planting and three insecticides applied as needed during the growing season, but an array of poisons linger in the water and sediment. NAWQA scientists found fifteen different pesticides in groundwater of the South Platte River basin. Some type of pesticide was detected in twenty-nine of the thirty groundwater wells sampled in the agricultural portion of the basin between Fort Lupton, Colorado, and North Platte, Nebraska. Twenty-five pesticides were present in surface water from agricultural areas. All ten sample sites between Kersey, Colorado, and North Platte had at least five pesticides present. DDT, banned in the United States since 1972, and DDT metabolites were commonly detected in tissues from fish in agricultural areas, as was the pesticide dieldrin, which was also banned during the 1970s. The DDT that is present in streambed sediments is taken up by plants and aquatic insects and then ingested by the fish that eat the plants and insects. Although the concentrations of pesticides present in the water and sediment of agricultural areas were generally low, NAWQA scientists caution that the long-term effects of exposure to mixed pesticides remain unknown.[83]

Thinking about these findings, I am reminded of a commercial for organic food on Swedish television. A man wearing a poison-gas mask and carrying a spray bottle marked poison approaches a table of diners and begins spraying their food. When they protest in horror, he shrugs and says "it's only a little." "Oh, all right, only a little," they respond. Grim humor aside, we do not know how little, if any, is safe. This is a nasty game of chance: by what percentage does "x" concentration of atrazine in the tissues of your body increase your risk of ovarian or testicular cancer? How does that percentage change when you, more realistically, have "x" concentration of atrazine, "y" concentration of metolachlor, and "z" concentration of DDT metabolites? The most frightening part of all this is that we have no idea. As cancer rates increase in industrialized societies, we gamble with our own lives and the lives of every living creature around us.

As might be expected, the least contaminated water, sediment, and fish in the NAWQA study come from forested mountain or rangeland sites within the South Platte River basin. Urban areas or sites with mixed urban and agricultural land use have the highest concentrations and greatest numbers of pesticides—diversity nobody wants to celebrate. Urban areas occupy only 3 percent of the South Platte River basin but account for 12 percent of water use (27 percent if water for power generation that largely goes to urban areas is included). In addition to excess nutrients and a wide variety of pesticides used in households and on lawns, urban areas leak volatile organic compounds to streams. These compounds are derived from substances such as gasoline and cleaning solvents. The most frequently detected volatile organic compounds in the South Platte NAWQA study were the gasoline additive MTBE and the cleaning solvent tetrachloroethene (PCE). Ever think about why snow along urban streets becomes so black within hours? Much of that filth goes with the melting snow into storm sewers and rivers.[84]

Aquatic habitat at most sites downstream from the mountainous headwaters is at least moderately degraded in the South Platte River basin, mainly because so little water is left in the streams. Urban and agricultural water withdrawals limit the dilution of contaminants entering the streams, and diversions and water storage further alter the natural flow regime and degrade stream habitat. At present, channels within the South Platte River basin resemble a vast plumbing system more than a stream network. Hundreds of structures withdraw more than 3.7 billion cubic meters (3 million acre-feet) of water each year and send the water along thousands of kilometers of ditches and pipes. Dozens of reservoirs store more than 2.5 billion cubic meters (2 million acre-feet) of water annually. Several thousand wells pump an additional 1.2 billion cubic meters (1 million acre-feet) of groundwater, and twelve trans-mountain diversions import 490 million cubic meters (400,000 acre-feet) into the South Platte basin each year from adjacent drainage systems. Stream flow in the South Platte now reflects the demands of crops and people more than snowmelt in the mountains.[85]

The cumulative effects of all these alterations in the quality and quantity of surface and groundwater, as well as habitat, show up in aquatic communities reduced

Pesticides in water

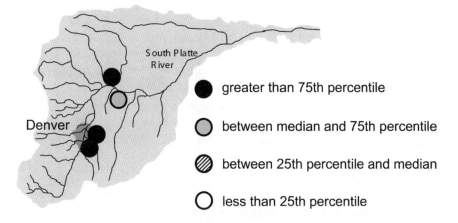

- ● greater than 75th percentile
- ◐ between median and 75th percentile
- ◕ between 25th percentile and median
- ○ less than 25th percentile

Pesticides and PCBs in bed sediment and fish tissue

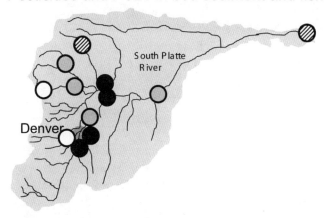

Map of South Platte River drainage basin (shaded), indicating location and results from NAWQA tests for pesticides. Circles indicate ranking of stream quality at sample site relative to all NAWQA sites sampled in the United States. Greater than 75th percentile means these sites are among the highest 25 percent of NAWQA stream sites and thus have the greatest concentrations of pesticides; less than 25th percentile means these sites are among the lowest 25 percent of NAWQA stream sites and thus have the lowest concentrations of pesticides. Bold outline of a circle indicates that one or more aquatic-life criteria were exceeded. After Dennehy et al. (1998, 22).

Irrigation ditch along the South Platte River near Fort Morgan, Colorado. During June, the time when this photograph was taken, there is more water in such canals than in the river.

in number and diversity of organisms and in aquatic organisms impaired in health. Some of the most startling findings to come to light thus far in the South Platte River basin are derived from a study of fish present in the South Platte River where the river flows through the Denver metropolitan area. The study made the front page of the *Denver Post* newspaper on October 3, 2004, when biologists found that white suckers (*Catostomus commersoni*) downstream from the Denver area's largest wastewater treatment plants had both male and female reproductive parts and that females far outnumbered males. Retired fisheries biologist John Woodling was quoted as stating, "This is the first thing I've seen as a scientist that really scared me."[86]

The effect of endocrine-disrupting chemicals had been documented elsewhere in the United States before the 2004 study on the South Platte River, but this was the first time it had been detected in Colorado. Endocrine disrupters are a group of synthetic chemicals that mimic hormones and disrupt the development of a variety of organisms, including humans. Theo Colborn and other scientists have warned since the 1990s of increasing evidence that these chemicals are destroying the ability of organisms, from invertebrates to mammals, to reproduce. Scientists, policy makers, and the public have hardly begun to consider the implications

Stream habitat degradation

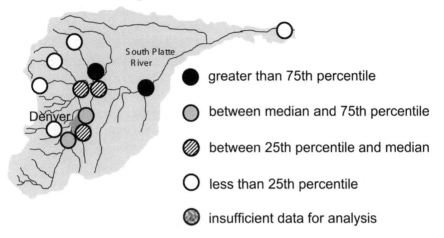

- ● greater than 75th percentile
- ◐ between median and 75th percentile
- ◨ between 25th percentile and median
- ○ less than 25th percentile
- ◉ insufficient data for analysis

Fish community degradation

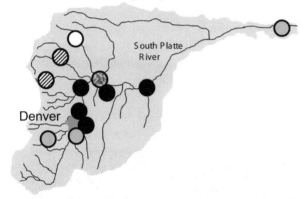

Map of South Platte River drainage basin (shaded), indicating location and results from NAWQA tests for fish community and stream habitat degradation. Circles indicate ranking of stream quality at sample site relative to all NAWQA sites sampled in the United States. Greater than 75th percentile means these sites are among the highest 25 percent of NAWQA stream sites and thus have the greatest degradation of stream habitat and fish community; less than 25th percentile means these sites are among the lowest 25 percent of NAWQA stream sites and thus have the least degradation. After Dennehy et al. (1998, 23).

of the discovery of endocrine-disrupted fish for all the prairie communities that pump their drinking water from shallow aquifers connected to the South Platte River.[87]

THE NEW ENERGY BOOM

Introduction of toxic contaminants, consumptive uses of water, and changes in land cover associated with urbanization and agriculture have all influenced the rivers of the western prairie for many decades. A more recent influence is the extraction of coal-bed methane deposits that underlie large tracts of the short-grass prairie in the Powder River Basin of eastern Wyoming and the Raton Basin of southeastern Colorado and northeastern New Mexico. Coal-bearing rock units underlying these portions of the plains generate methane (CH_4) and other gases when microbes process coal lying near the surface or when the temperature of the coal increases during deeper burial. Methane can be adsorbed onto the surface of the coal, disseminated through fractures in the coal, or dissolved in the groundwater within the coal. Miners extract the methane by pumping out the water within the coal, which allows the pressure within the coal to drop sufficiently for the gas to flow. Water pumped out of the coal beds can be relatively pure, or it can be heavily contaminated with salts formed by dissolved sodium, calcium, magnesium, sulfate, bicarbonate, and boron. This is the first problem with mining coal-bed methane.[88]

Coal-bed mining does not produce trickles of contaminated water. The three methane-bearing coal seams in the Powder River Basin can be worked by three wells per 32 hectares. Each well produces from 19 to 76 liters of water per minute. Using 45 liters per minute as an average, each well produces more than 65,000 liters of water per day. Much of this water is too saline to use for drinking or irrigating crops. If the water is simply allowed to flow down ephemeral or perennial channels, evaporation and plant uptake can concentrate the salts in the root zone to levels at which plant growth is stunted, soil crusts form and limit future infiltration of water into the soil, and the soil eventually becomes completely unsuitable for plant growth. Under lesser concentrations of salts, invasive non-native species such as salt cedar (*Tamarix* spp.), Russian olive, and leafy spurge (*Euphorbia esula*) may do better than native species that are more nutritious for grazing animals. Soil texture exerts an important control on the effects of saline water. Soils rich in silt and clay retain salt much more effectively than sandy soils, through which the salts leach downward to the groundwater.[89]

Saline water produced as a by-product of coal-bed methane extraction is currently discharged directly into streams, impounded in artificial ponds that allow the water to seep into the subsurface, applied to irrigation, or used for some other purpose such as dust control on access roads. Whatever the short-term use of the saline water, the long-term effect is soil salinization and lowered quality of surface and subsurface waters in regions where water is limited and precious.[90]

Methane was at a premium during the first decade of the twenty-first century, when coal-bed methane extraction really took off in the western prairie. Mining companies blitzed government agencies such as the Bureau of Land Management and the US Forest Service with drilling applications and made profits that kept shareholders delighted, in part because the leasing fees paid to the federal government and the states were so low. But available purification treatments for wastewater—including dilution with non-saline water, reverse osmosis, and salt precipitation using evaporation techniques—remained largely unused because they were considered too expensive or infeasible with large quantities of saline water.[91]

A second problem with mining coal-bed methane is the infrastructure necessary to extract the methane. Because a single well recovers gas from only a small part of the coal bed, hundreds to thousands of wells can be needed to mine the gas from a large region such as the Powder River Basin, which as of 2002 held an estimated 400 billion to 680 billion cubic meters of gas. Each of these wells requires access roads, drilling pads, and other infrastructure that together leave a large "footprint" on the terrain and the native vegetation, as well as changing the way rainfall and snowmelt infiltrate or run off the ground surface and carry sediment into nearby stream channels.[92]

Additional problems include unintended loss of methane to the atmosphere during mining. Methane is a highly effective greenhouse gas, as well as contributing to reduced air quality. Increasing violations of federal air standards during the first decade of the twenty-first century forced states such as Colorado to start developing more stringent regulation of emissions from coal-bed wells. Noise, mechanical operations, and traffic detract from once quiet, isolated landscapes. Drawdown of the water table in the vicinity of mining can cause loss of springs, seeps, and stream flow. The Montana Bureau of Mines and Geology estimates that coal-bed methane sites in the Powder River Basin will require between a few years and twenty years of natural recharge before groundwater levels recover. Natural gas from coal beds presently accounts for about 7 percent of total natural gas production in the United States, but the spatial extent of mining continues to grow rapidly in the western part of the country.[93]

As concerns grow about the effects of fossil-fuel consumption on atmospheric composition and global temperature, alternative energy sources appear more attractive. Among these is nuclear power, seemingly consigned to the scrap bin after the widely publicized accidents at nuclear power plants during the 1970s–80s. As nuclear power has come into wider use in countries such as China and India, the price of uranium rose from $7 per pound in 2000 to $120 per pound in 2007. The price fluctuated between $40 and $50 per pound during 2010.[94]

Colorado ranks third among the US states for its uranium reserves. Most of these are on the western slope of the Rockies, but a few are on the eastern side of the mountains in sandstone units deep beneath the soils and shallow groundwater of the plains. Uranium is currently mined near Denver, and a new mine is proposed just northeast of Fort Collins: both sites are within the South Platte River basin. Mining is conducted using "in-situ recovery" in which oxygenated water is injected 180 meters deep into the sandstone containing the uranium. After the injected water dissolves the uranium, it is pumped back to the surface, processed inside ionic exchange columns to remove the uranium, and then recycled for re-injection.[95]

Although likely to be far less disruptive and destructive than conventional mining that would strip off overlying sediment and rock to get to the uranium-bearing layer, the proposed mine near Fort Collins has generated opposition from rural landowners who fear contamination of regional aquifers by uranium and associated radioactive elements and toxic metals. These fears are justified, given a 2007 report by the Nuclear Regulatory Commission, which notes that the in-situ technique "still tends to contaminate the groundwater."[96]

Natural river systems undergo continual changes over time spans that vary from the few hours of a thunderstorm-induced flash flood to century-long fluctuations in precipitation and stream flow. Perhaps the only constant in describing river behavior is the presence of flux. Despite the continual change and resiliency that characterize the rivers of the western prairie, human-induced changes in these rivers during the twentieth century pushed many aquatic and riparian species to the brink of survival. To restore our rivers, we must understand history, but we must also think carefully about the future.

NOTES

1. G. Hobbs, "Citizen's Guide to Colorado Water Law, 2nd ed., Appendix 2.1" (Denver: Colorado Foundation for Water Education, 2003).

2. Ibid.

3. B. Taylor, *Colorado: A Summer Trip* (New York: G. P. Putnam and Son, 1867), 159.

4. Graf, *Endangered and Threatened Species*; J. Opie, *Ogallala: Water for a Dry Land*, 2nd ed. (Lincoln: University of Nebraska Press, 2000); D. Tyler, *The Last Water Hole in the West: The Colorado–Big Thompson Project and the Northern Colorado Water Conservancy District* (Niwot: University Press of Colorado, 1992).

5. Hobbs, "Citizen's Guide to Colorado Water Law."

6. Ibid.

7. Ibid.

8. Graf, *Endangered and Threatened Species*; Opie, *Ogallala*; Tyler, *Last Water Hole*.

9. Gutentag et al., "Geohydrology of the High Plains Aquifer."

10. Tyler, *Last Water Hole*.

11. Opie, *Ogallala*; N. Kryloff, "Hole in the River: A Brief History of Groundwater in the South Platte Valley," *Colorado Water: Newsletter of the Water Center of Colorado State University* 4, no. 5 (2007): 9–12.

12. Kryloff, "Hole in the River," 9

13. Ibid.; Graf, *Endangered and Threatened Species*; Opie, *Ogallala*; Tyler, *Last Water Hole*; Gutentag et al., "Geohydrology of the High Plains Aquifer"; Hobbs, "Citizen's Guide to Colorado Water Law."

14. T. R. Eschner, R. F. Hadley, and K. D. Crowley, "Hydrologic and Morphologic Changes in Channels of the Platte River Basin in Colorado, Wyoming, and Nebraska: A Historical Perspective," *US Geological Survey Professional Paper* 1277-A (1983); J. E. Kircher and M. R. Karlinger, "Effects of Water Development on Surface-Water Hydrology, Platte River Basin in Colorado, Wyoming, and Nebraska Upstream from Duncan, Nebraska," *US Geological Survey Professional Paper* 1277-B (1983).

15. Johnson, "Woodland Expansion"; C. T. Nadler and S. A. Schumm, "Metamorphosis of South Platte and Arkansas Rivers, Eastern Colorado," *Physical Geography* 2, no. 2 (1981): 95–115; G. P. Williams, "Historical Perspective of the Platte Rivers in Nebraska and Colorado," in *Lowland River and Stream Habitat in Colorado: A Symposium*, ed. W. D. Graul and S. J. Bissell (Greeley, CO: Bureau of Land Management, 1978), 11–41; G. P. Williams, "The Case of the Shrinking Channels: The North Platte and Platte Rivers in Nebraska," *US Geological Survey Circular* 781 (1978).

16. Johnson, "Woodland Expansion."

17. Ibid.

18. Ibid.

19. Eschner, Hadley, and Crowley, "Hydrologic and Morphologic Changes"; Kircher and Karlinger, "Effects of Water Development"; Nadler and Schumm, "Metamorphosis of South Platte and Arkansas Rivers"; Williams, "Historical Perspective of the Platte Rivers"; Williams, "Case of the Shrinking Channels."

20. H. F. Matthai, "Floods of June 1965 in South Platte River Basin, Colorado," *US Geological Survey Water-Supply Paper* 1850-B (1969).

21. Friedman and Lee, "Extreme Floods"; Friedman, Osterkamp, and Lewis, "Role of Vegetation"; Friedman, Scott, and Auble, "Management and Cottonwood Forest Dynamics"; Scott, Friedman, and Auble, "Fluvial Process."

22. Friedman and Lee, "Extreme Floods"; Friedman, Osterkamp, and Lewis, "Role of Vegetation"; Friedman, Scott, and Auble, "Management and Cottonwood Forest Dynamics"; Scott, Friedman, and Auble, "Fluvial Process."

23. Friedman and Lee, "Extreme Floods"; Friedman, Osterkamp, and Lewis, "Role of Vegetation"; Friedman, Scott, and Auble, "Management and Cottonwood Forest Dynamics"; Scott, Friedman, and Auble, "Fluvial Process."

24. Matthai, "Floods of June 1965"; Nadler and Schumm, "Metamorphosis of South Platte and Arkansas Rivers"; Williams, "Historical Perspective of the Platte Rivers"; Williams, "Case of the Shrinking Channels"; T. R. Eschner, "Hydraulic Geometry of the Platte River near Overton, South-Central Nebraska," *US Geological Survey Professional Paper* 1277-C (1983); L. M. Fotherby, "Valley Confinement as a Factor of Braided River Pattern for the Platte River," *Geomorphology* 103, no. 4 (2009): 562–76; M. F. Karlinger et al., "Relation of Channel-Width Maintenance to Sediment Transport and River Morphology: Platte River, South-Central Nebraska," *US Geological Survey Professional Paper* 1277-E (1983); J. E. Kircher, "Interpretation of Sediment Data for the South Platte River in Colorado and Nebraska, and the North Platte and Platte Rivers in Nebraska," *US Geological Survey Professional Paper* 1277-D (1983); W. R. Osterkamp and E. R. Hedman, "Perennial-Streamflow Characteristics Related to Channel Geometry and Sediment in Missouri River Basin," *US Geological Survey Professional Paper* 1242 (1982); S. A. Schumm, "The Shape of Alluvial Channels in Relation to Sediment Type," *US Geological Survey Professional Paper* 352-B (1960); S. A. Schumm, "Sinuosity of Alluvial Rivers on the Great Plains," *Geological Society of America Bulletin* 74 (1963):1089–1100.

25. Pike, *Journals of Zebulon Montgomery Pike*.

26. G. R. Thompson and J. Turk, *Introduction to Physical Geology* (Fort Worth, TX: Saunders College Publishing, 1998), 265–66; Eschner, Hadley, and Crowley, "Hydrologic and Morphologic Changes"; Osterkamp et al., "Great Plains."

27. Osterkamp et al., "Great Plains"; Gutentag et al., "Geohydrology of the High Plains Aquifer."

28. Kryloff, "Hole in the River."

29. Ibid.

30. B.D.J. Batt, "Prairie Ecology—Prairie Wetlands," in *Prairie Conservation: Preserving North America's Most Endangered Ecosystem*, ed. F. B. Samson and F. L. Knopf (Washington, DC: Island, 1996), 77–88; C. Hubbs, "Springs and Spring Runs as Unique Aquatic Systems," *Copeia* 4 (1995): 989–91.

31. Batt, "Prairie Ecology"; Hubbs, "Springs and Spring Runs."

32. Batt, "Prairie Ecology"; Hubbs, "Springs and Spring Runs"; T. E. Nickens, "Here Today, Gone Tomorrow," *Audubon* 108, no. 6 (2006): 42–47; Playa Lakes Joint Venture website http://www.pljv.org/.

33. Nickens, "Here Today, Gone Tomorrow."

34. Ibid.; F. S. Guthery et al., *Playa Assessment Study* (Amarillo, TX: US Water and Power Resources Service, Southwest Region, 1981); D. A. Haukos and L. M. Smith, "Past and Future Impacts of Wetland Regulations on Playa Ecology in the Southern Great Plains," *Wetlands* 23, no. 3 (2003): 577–89.

35. L. L. Fardal, "Effects of Groundwater Pumping for Irrigation to Stream Properties of the Arikaree River on the Colorado Plains," MS thesis, Colorado State University, Fort Collins, 2003.

36. M. Sophocleous, "From Safe Yield to Sustainable Development of Water Resources: The Kansas Experience," *Journal of Hydrology* [Amsterdam] 235, no. 1-2 (2000): 27–43; Gutentag et al., "Geohydrology of the High Plains Aquifer"; Fardal, "Effects of Groundwater Pumping."

37. D. Durnford, A. Squires, J. Falke, K. Fausch, R. Oad, and L. Riley, "Agricultural and Water Management Alternatives to Sustain a Vulnerable Aquatic Ecosystem on the Eastern High Plains of Colorado," *Colorado Water: The Water Center of Colorado State University* 24, no. 5 (2007): 14–19; J. A. Falke et al., "The Role of Groundwater Pumping and Drought in Shaping Ecological Futures for Stream Fishes in a Dryland River Basin of the Western Great Plains, USA," *Ecohydrology* (2010), http://onlinelibrary.wiley.com/journal/10.1002/(ISSN)1936-0592; J. A. Falke, K. R. Bestgen, and K. D. Fausch, "Streamflow Reductions and Habitat Drying Affect Growth, Survival, and Recruitment of Brassy Minnow across a Great Plains Riverscape," *Transactions of the American Fisheries Society* 139, no. 5 (2010): 1566–83, http://www.researchgate.net/journal/1548-8659_Transactions_of_the_American_Fisheries_Society; Fardal, "Effects of Groundwater Pumping."

38. Fardal, "Effects of Groundwater Pumping."

39. Ibid.; Sophocleous, "From Safe Yield to Sustainable Development."

40. Sophocleous, "From Safe Yield to Sustainable Development"; Fardal, "Effects of Groundwater Pumping."

41. Sophocleous, "From Safe Yield to Sustainable Development"; Fardal, "Effects of Groundwater Pumping."

42. J. A. Scheurer, K. D. Fausch, and K. R. Bestgen, "Multiscale Processes Regulate Brassy Minnow Persistence in a Great Plains River," *Transactions of the American Fisheries Society* 132, no. 5 (2003): 840–55; Durnford et al., "Agricultural and Water Management Alternatives"; Falke et al., "Role of Groundwater Pumping"; Falke, Bestgen, and Fausch, "Streamflow Reductions and Habitat Drying"; Fardal, "Effects of Groundwater Pumping."

43. Scheurer, Fausch, and Bestgen, "Multiscale Processes"; Durnford et al., "Agricultural and Water Management Alternatives"; Falke et al., "Role of Groundwater Pumping"; Falke, Bestgen, and Fausch, "Streamflow Reductions and Habitat Drying."

44. Scheurer, Fausch, and Bestgen, "Multiscale Processes"; Gutentag et al., "Geohydrology of the High Plains Aquifer"; Durnford et al., "Agricultural and Water Management Alternatives"; Falke et al., "Role of Groundwater Pumping"; Falke, Bestgen, and Fausch, "Streamflow Reductions and Habitat Drying"; Fardal, "Effects of Groundwater Pumping."

45. Scheurer, Fausch, and Bestgen, "Multiscale Processes"; Falke et al., "Role of Groundwater Pumping"; Falke, Bestgen, and Fausch, "Streamflow Reductions and Habitat Drying."

46. Fausch and Bestgen, "Ecology of Fishes," 157.

47. Ibid.; Cross and Moss, "Historic Changes in Fish Communities and Aquatic Habitats."

48. Scheurer, Fausch, and Bestgen, "Multiscale Processes"; Fausch and Bestgen, "Ecology of Fishes"; Peters and Schainost, "Historical Changes in Fish Distribution"; K. Fausch, "Mutual Understanding Sets the Stage; Discovery Changes the Conversation," *Colorado Water* (2006): 21–23; J. Smith, "Platte River Recovery," *Rocky Mountain News*, January 30, 2006; Matthews, "Physicochemical Tolerance and Selectivity"; Cross and Moss, "Historic Changes in Fish Communities and Aquatic Habitats"; Matthews, "North American Prairie Streams," 387 (quotation); J. A. Falke and K. B. Gido, "Spatial Effects of Reservoirs on Fish Assemblages in Great Plains Streams in Kansas, USA," *River Research and Applications* 22, no. 1 (2006): 55–68; Labbe and Fausch, "Dynamics of Intermittent Stream Habitat"; J. A. Scheurer and K. D. Fausch, "The Identification, Historical Distribution, and Habitat Requirements of Brassy Minnow in Colorado Plains Streams," *Colorado Water* 19, no. 2 (2002): 8–11; Propst and Carlson, "Distribution and Status of Warmwater Fishes"; K. B. Gido, W. K. Dodds, and M. E. Eberle, "Retrospective Analysis of Fish Community Change during a Half-Century of Landuse and Streamflow Changes," *Journal of the North American Benthological Society* 29, no. 3 (2010): 970–87; W. J. Matthews and E. Marsh-Matthews, "Extirpation of Red Shiner in Direct Tributaries of Lake Texoma (Oklahoma-Texas): A Cautionary Case History from a Fragmented River-Reservoir System," *Transactions of the American Fisheries Society* 136, no. 4 (2007): 1041–62; C. W. Hoagstrom, J. E. Brooks, and S. R. Davenport, "A Large-Scale Conservation Perspective Considering Endemic Fishes of the North American Plains," *Biological Conservation* (2010), http://www.journals.elsevier.com/biological-conservation/.

49. Fausch, "Mutual Understanding."

50. S. Gerlek, "Water Supplies of the South Platte River Basin," MS thesis, Colorado State University, Fort Collins, 1977; A. D. Ficke and C. A. Myrick, "The Swimming and Jumping Ability of Three Small Great Plains Fishes: Implications for Fishway Design," *Transactions of the American Fisheries Society* 140, no. 3 (2011): 521–31; A. D. Ficke, "Fish Barriers and Small Plains Fishes: Fishway Design Recommendations and the Impact of Existing Instream Structures," MS thesis, Colorado State University, Fort Collins, 2006.

51. Falke and Gido, "Spatial Effects of Reservoirs"; Scheurer and Fausch, "Identification, Historical Distribution, and Habitat Requirements"; Fausch and Bestgen, "Ecology of Fishes"; Peters and Schainost, "Historical Changes in Fish Distribution"; Fausch, "Mutual Understanding"; Matthews, "Physicochemical Tolerance and Selectivity"; Cross and

Moss, "Historic Changes in Fish Communities and Aquatic Habitats"; Matthews, "North American Prairie Streams"; Labbe and Fausch, "Dynamics of Intermittent Stream Habitat"; Propst and Carlson, "Distribution and Status of Warmwater Fishes."

52. Fausch and Bestgen, "Ecology of Fishes"; Peters and Schainost, "Historical Changes in Fish Distribution"; Matthews, "Physicochemical Tolerance and Selectivity"; Cross and Moss, "Historic Changes in Fish Communities and Aquatic Habitats"; Matthews, "North American Prairie Streams"; Propst and Carlson, "Distribution and Status of Warmwater Fishes."

53. Graf, *Endangered and Threatened Species*.

54. Ibid.

55. Ibid.; S. Winkler, "The Platte Pretzel," *Audubon* 91 (1989): 86–112.

56. Graf, *Endangered and Threatened Species*; Winkler, "Platte Pretzel."

57. Graf, *Endangered and Threatened Species*; Winkler, "Platte Pretzel."

58. Graf, *Endangered and Threatened Species*; Winkler, "Platte Pretzel."

59. Graf, *Endangered and Threatened Species*; Winkler, "Platte Pretzel."

60. Graf, *Endangered and Threatened Species*; Winkler, "Platte Pretzel."

61. Graf, *Endangered and Threatened Species*; Winkler, "Platte Pretzel."

62. Graf, *Endangered and Threatened Species*; Winkler, "Platte Pretzel."

63. Graf, *Endangered and Threatened Species*; Winkler, "Platte Pretzel."

64. Graf, *Endangered and Threatened Species*; Winkler, "Platte Pretzel."

65. Graf, *Endangered and Threatened Species*; Winkler, "Platte Pretzel."

66. Graf, *Endangered and Threatened Species*.

67. Ibid.

68. Ibid.

69. Ibid.; Smith, "Platte River Recovery."

70. Graf, *Endangered and Threatened Species*.

71. Ibid.

72. P. J. Kinzel et al., "Spring Census of Mid-Continent Sandhill Cranes Using Aerial Infrared Videography," *Journal of Wildlife Management* 70, no. 1 (2006): 70–77; P. J. Kinzel, J. M. Nelson, and A. K. Heckman, "Response of Sandhill Crane (*Grus canadensis*) Riverine Roosting Habitat to Changes in Stage and Sandbar Morphology," *River Research and Applications* 25, no. 2 (2009): 135–52.

73. Kinzel, Nelson, and Heckman, "Response of Sandhill Crane."

74. D. W. Sparling and G. L. Krapu, "Communal Roosting and Foraging Behavior of Staging Sandhill Cranes," *Wilson Bulletin* 106, no. 1 (1994): 62–77; G. L. Krapu, D. A. Brandt, and R. R. Cox Jr., "Less Waste Corn, More Land in Soybeans, and the Switch to Genetically Modified Crops: Trends with Important Implications for Wildlife Management," *Wildlife Society Bulletin* 32, no. 1 (2004): 127–36.

75. Dennehy et al., "Water Quality."

76. D. J. Sullivan, *Nutrients and Suspended Solids in Surface Waters of the Upper Illinois River Basin in Illinois, Indiana, and Wisconsin, 1978–97*, US Geological Survey (USGS) Water-Resources Investigations Report 99-4275 (Middleton, WI: USGS, 2000).

77. Ibid.

78. Dennehy et al., "Water Quality."

79. Ibid.

80. Ibid.

81. Ibid.; M. J. Bernot and W. K. Dodds, "Nitrogen Retention, Removal, and Saturation in Lotic Ecosystems," *Ecosystems* 8 (2005): 442–53; P. B. McMahon and J. K. Böhlke, "Denitrification and Mixing in a Stream-Aquifer System: Effects on Nitrate Loading to Surface Water," *Journal of Hydrology* 186 (1996): 105–28; G. Pinay, C. Ruffinoni, S. Wondzell, and F. Gazelle, "Change in Groundwater Nitrate Concentration in a Large River Floodplain: Denitrification, Uptake, or Mixing?" *Journal of the North American Benthological Society* 17 (1998): 179–89.

82. Dennehy et al., "Water Quality"; Bernot and Dodds, "Nitrogen Retention"; McMahon and Böhlke, "Denitrification and Mixing"; C. M. Tate and J. S. Heiny, "The Ordination of Benthic Invertebrate Communities in the South Platte River Basin in Relation to Environmental Factors," *Freshwater Biology* 33, no. 3 (1995): 439–54.

83. Dennehy et al., "Water Quality."

84. Ibid.; Parton, Gutmann, and Ojima, "Long-Term Trends in Population."

85. Dennehy et al., "Water Quality."

86. T. Stein and M. Moffeit, "Mutant Fish Prompt Concern," *Denver Post*, October 3, 2004, 1A, 18A.

87. T. Colborn and R. A. Liroff, "Toxics in the Great Lakes," *EPA Journal* 16 (1990): 5–8; T. Colborn, "The Wildlife/Human Connection: Modernizing Risk Decisions," *Environmental Health Perspectives* 102 (1994): 55–59; T. Colborn, D. Dumanoski, and J. P. Meyers, *Our Stolen Future: How We Are Threatening Our Fertility, Intelligence, and Survival: A Scientific Detective Story* (New York: Dutton, 1996); T. Colborn and K. Thayer, "Aquatic Ecosystems: Harbingers of Endocrine Disruption," *Ecological Applications* 10 (2000): 949–57; M. M. McGree et al., "Reproductive Failure of the Red Shiner (*Cyprinella lutrensis*) after Exposure to an Exogenous Estrogen," *Canadian Journal of Fisheries and Aquatic Science* 67, no. 11 (2010): 1730–43.

88. "Coal-Bed Gas Resources of the Rocky Mountain Region," *US Geological Survey Fact-Sheet* FS-110-01 (2003); V. Nuccio, "Coalbed Methane: An Untapped Energy Resource and an Environmental Concern," *US Geological Survey Fact-Sheet* FS-019-97 (1997).

89. "Coal-Bed Gas Resources"; Nuccio, "Coalbed Methane."

90. "Coal-Bed Gas Resources"; Nuccio, "Coalbed Methane."

91. "Coal-Bed Gas Resources"; Nuccio, "Coalbed Methane."

92. "Coal-Bed Gas Resources"; Nuccio, "Coalbed Methane."

93. "Coal-Bed Gas Resources"; Nuccio, "Coalbed Methane."

94. T. Hartman, "Uranium Worries," *Rocky Mountain News*, May 14, 2007, 6–7.

95. Ibid.

96. Nuclear Regulatory Commission, *Consideration of Geochemical Issues in Groundwater Restoration at Uranium In-Situ Leach Mining Facilities* (Washington, DC: US Geological Survey, 2007), NUREG/CR-6870.

FOUR

What the Future Holds

As a nation, we have viewed the river as a
pioneer trail, as a commodity, and finally as an
ecosystem.

—W. L. Graf, *Endangered and Threatened Species of
the Platte River, xxi, describing the Platte River in
central Nebraska*

A HISTORIC SNAPSHOT: THE SOUTH
PLATTE RIVER BASIN CIRCA 2000

Two and a half million people lived within the South
Platte River basin, mostly along the foothills between
Denver and Fort Collins, in 1999. The population of the
Denver area was projected to increase by an additional 1
million over the next twenty years as an estimated 36,400
hectares of farmland and ranchland were converted to
urban areas in Colorado each year. Developers and residents demonstrated a willingness to pay high prices for
water, and the value of water traded from agricultural
to urban lands in Colorado doubled from 1989 to 1991.
Much of this water came from adjacent drainage basins:
nearly a quarter of the South Platte's flow came from
the west side of the Continental Divide. At the start of
the twenty-first century, fifteen interbasin diversions

DOI: 10.5876/9781607322313.c04

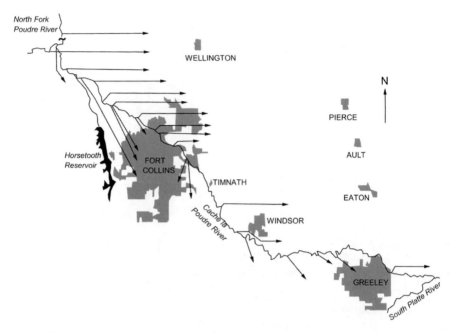

The highly fragmented course of a river in the western Great Plains. This schematic map shows the primary diversion canals (arrows) along the Cache la Poudre River between the mountain front (just east of the junction of the North Fork and main Poudre) and the city of Greeley, approximately 50 kilometers due east. Horsetooth Reservoir was built for water storage. Cities are indicated by gray shading.

brought water into the South Platte system, where 1,000 reservoirs and 500 irrigation ditches stored and distributed the water. Despite all these imports, water levels in the major bedrock aquifer underlying the Denver Basin dropped as much as 240 meters during the last twenty years of the twentieth century, and some domestic wells in the southern part of the metropolitan area went dry. Xeriscaping suburban lawns with native plants gradually grew in popularity, but each urban area still presented an anomaly of dark green trees and grass amid the olive green and tan hues of the native vegetation.[1]

The rivers of the transition zone were shrunken, simplified remnants of those present in 1800. Snowmelt flows no longer overflowed the stream banks each spring, and any floodplain wetlands present were pits from sand and gravel mining that had filled with water. Cottonwood gallery forests were slowly dying and being replaced by exotic species such as Russian olive. Most trees that fell into the streams were quickly removed by officials of the many cities crowded along

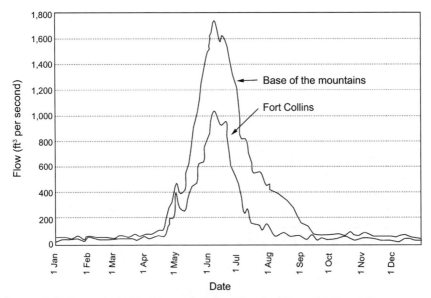

Average daily flow on the Poudre River at the base of the mountains and in Fort Collins, approximately 20 river kilometers downstream. The difference between the two values represents water diverted from the river for off-stream agricultural and municipal consumptive uses. Daily flows were averaged over the period 1976–2005.

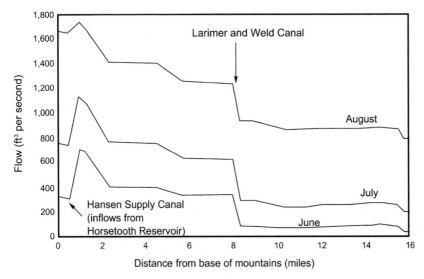

Average monthly flows during the period 1970–1994 on the Cache la Poudre River. The abrupt downstream changes in flow volume are associated with points where water is brought into or removed from the river by canals.

The Poudre River in the city of Fort Collins, winter 2009. The channel is mostly dry because of diversions. Historically, the river was sinuous in this reach, with abandoned and secondary channels and floodplain wetlands adjacent to the channel. The river channel is now relatively straight and uniform, overbank flows seldom occur, and commercial developments occupy much of the historical floodplain. Willows and cottonwoods form a dense riparian forest along the channel, but most tree trunks and large branches that fall into the river are quickly removed, limiting their ability to provide fish habitat.

the rivers at the base of the mountains. Wherever a log managed to persist, fish congregated in the vicinity. Wastewater treatment plants delivered excess nitrogen and phosphorus to the streams. These nutrients, and the diminished flows of shallow, warm water, supported long, thick strands of filamentous algae that covered the unmoving cobbles of the streambed like a green carpet. Native aquatic insects were not adapted to these conditions, and nutrient-enriched waters had lower density and diversity of insects. The rivers themselves were narrower as grasses and shrubs grew down stream banks no longer periodically ripped up and reconfigured by floods.[2]

The numerous taxa of aquatic insects present in 1800 had declined to about a dozen species that could tolerate rapid and extreme fluctuations in stream flow produced by diversions, as well as warmer and more polluted water. Cutthroat trout were nearly gone, confined to the most headwater portions of the mountain streams where a physical barrier such as a waterfall limited upstream migration of introduced brook, brown, and rainbow trout. Many of the plains fishes were reduced to dangerously low numbers of individuals isolated from one another in widely spaced populations. Stretches of dry streambed, road culverts, irrigation headgates, and erosion-control structures effectively prevented migration among these dispersed groups.

Changes in stream flow relative to historical conditions varied with distance downstream along the larger channels. At Denver, snowmelt peak flows were reduced by storage in reservoirs upstream, and portions of the South Platte went dry for much of the year except where effluent from a wastewater treatment plant created stream flow. At Kersey, about 50 kilometers east of the mountain front, peak flows and annual mean flows increased during the twentieth century as a result of water transferred from other drainage basins and base flows enhanced by return of irrigation water from flooded fields. At Julesburg, about 250 kilometers from the mountain front, flow in the river was entirely diverted at some points, but replenishment by groundwater supported flow along other segments of the river. For the most part, the broad channels had shrunk back to narrow flows of cooler, clearer water, with wide belts of riparian trees.[3]

Large populations of birds used the cottonwood forests along the Lower South Platte, but these were mostly birds not native to the region: nearly 90 percent of the eighty-two species of birds breeding along the river were not present there in 1900. Native species were in decline, as habitat generalists that thrive along forest edges replaced them. The great flocks of migratory cranes and other birds had diminished considerably from historical numbers, but the few areas of flooded bottomlands were too small to support them.[4]

Native fish were also in decline as habitats changed and water quality grew poorer. Agriculture contributed 132,000 tons of nitrogen and 14,000 tons of phosphorus to the South Platte River basin each year, with another 94,000 tons of nitrogen and 26,000 tons of phosphorus from manure in the large feedlots surrounding Greeley. National Water Quality Assessment (NAWQA) scientists found that the South Platte had the highest contamination by ammonia and nitrate and the second-highest levels of phosphorus among twenty major US rivers. Excess nutrients led to eutrophication of streams and levels of dissolved oxygen during periods of low flow that were below the standards mandated for preserving aquatic life. Native soil bacteria removed 15 percent to 30 percent of nitrate from groundwater in the South Platte basin before the water discharged back into the river, but nitrate levels in a third of the domestic wells between Denver and Julesburg exceeded standards for drinking water set by the US Environmental Protection Agency.[5]

Upstream (upper) and downstream (lower) views of the South Platte River just below its junction with the Poudre River in Greeley, Colorado, 2008. The river channel is much narrower and more densely vegetated than it was a century earlier. Black dots above the river are swallows.

View across an irrigation canal and fields irrigated using a center pivot, to the wooded belt along the South Platte River near Fort Morgan, Colorado. The slender, light gray layer at the upper right of the photograph is the grassy uplands on the other side of the river.

Changing patterns and intensity of human resource use clearly altered stream flow, water quality, river form, and riverine plant and animal communities throughout the South Platte River basin during the twentieth century. Projections of future conditions suggest that some of these trends are likely to continue and intensify. This does not by any means signify that protecting and restoring the ecological health of western prairie rivers are hopeless. Protection and restoration do require that we see clearly where we are, where we may be going, and what we can do to alter where we may be going. The preceding chapters focused on where we are and how we got here. The next three sections of this chapter outline where we may be going, and the final sections focus on what we might do to change some of the most negative scenarios of the future ecological health of the western prairie rivers.

WARMER AND DRIER

Everyone apparently wants to live in the urban corridor along the base of the Colorado Front Range. The population of the United States increased by

Closer view of the wooded belt along the South Platte River near Fort Morgan, Colorado. This belt extends across the historically active channel for about a kilometer, with several narrow channels winding through it. A part of one of these channels appears at the left in this photograph (arrow).

13 percent between 1990 and 2000. During that same period, the population of the Front Range urban corridor increased by 31 percent. The Colorado State Demographer's Office projects an additional 63 percent increase by 2030. Such rapid growth puts pressure on many natural resources, but water is the preeminent limiting factor on population growth in the region. Substantial additional water cannot be supplied by pumping subsurface aquifers: the combined effects of a dropping water table and contamination of many shallow aquifers make this source infeasible. Most surface-water supplies are already fully appropriated, so the remaining options are to further develop water transfers from adjacent basins or to convert agricultural water uses to municipal water supplies. Growing municipalities actively pursue all of these methods, but the high probability of enhanced droughts and reduced snowpack in association with changing climate looms over the future like a menacing shadow.

What might we expect in a future, warmer world? Our best knowledge always comes from what we can observe directly. Geologists use knowledge of contemporary systems to infer the past, climate modelers to predict the future. Climatologists use contemporary climatic circulation patterns and atmospheric composition to develop computer simulations of future temperature and precipitation. Hydrologists then use these climatic scenarios to predict changes in water supply. One such study of Boulder Creek, a principal tributary of the South Platte River, found that even with no change in precipitation, stream discharge in the creek decreased by 11 percent under a scenario in which the average air temperature increased by 2°C. When this temperature increase was combined with a 10 percent decrease in precipitation, stream flow decreased by 30 percent. Even using these conservative future climate scenarios, the changes in stream flow are likely to severely stress natural and human communities dependent on that flow for their water supply. Another study of the potential effects of climate change noted that many native fishes that survive in the warm waters of streams in the southern Great Plains are already near the maximum temperatures they can tolerate. It is unlikely that these species can adapt genetically with sufficient speed to survive a warming climate.[6]

The effects of climate change ripple outward like the disturbance from a rock falling into a quiet pond. Changes in air temperature and precipitation will alter not only the abundance and timing of stream flow but also such seemingly separate aspects of stream ecology as the supply of plant litter from riverside forests. The elevation of timberline in the Rocky Mountains is primarily controlled by temperature. Forest vegetation is structured in part by susceptibility to wildfire; and the occurrence of wildfire depends in part on conditions such as air temperature, precipitation, and lightning. The history of fires, combined with forest susceptibility, creates a mosaic of vegetation types and ages across the mountain landscape. Ecologists predict that climate change which alters the elevation of timberline or the type of forest present will have profound effects on the introduction of organic matter and wood to streams and thus on the biological communities in the streams.[7]

Much of the effect of warming climate on the larger rivers of the western prairie comes from changes in the snowpack and snowmelt. Rivers draining the Rocky Mountains discharge more than 70 percent of their annual water budget during two to three months of snowmelt and have instantaneous discharges 10 to 100 times the mean low flow. These streams are dominated by snowmelt in every sense: snowmelt supplies the majority of flow and regulates the shape of channels and the plants and animals that live within and along the channels. The timing of spring snowmelt shifted to earlier in the year along many western rivers during the period 1948–2000. Hydrologists project relationships between observed timing of stream flow and local temperature and precipitation to predict changes in the timing of stream flow for the period 1995–2099. Under twenty-first-century warming trends predicted by the Parallel Climate Model, the timing of peak flow on rivers in the western United States will be earlier—particularly for rivers fed by snowmelt from the Rocky Mountains, where many rivers will eventually run *thirty to forty days* earlier. As the snowpack decreases and melts earlier each spring, lower elevations in which stream flow is now dominated by snowmelt could become dominated by runoff from rainfall, which is much less predictable and more likely to occur as flash floods of short duration. It is more difficult to efficiently store and transfer rainfall-generated stream flow because of its unpredictability, which creates challenges for managing human water supplies. Aquatic and riparian organisms adapted to cold water and consistent floods in late spring–early summer may not be able to survive the changes in flow regime.[8]

Studies of changes in the flow of northern Colorado streams during the period 1948–2000 found less than five days of change in the timing of spring peak flows (other parts of the western US changed as much as thirty days during this period). If local temperature changes as little as 1°C, however, peak flow is projected to occur at least twelve days earlier. Peak flow is also predicted to occur earlier and earlier with each decade as climate warming continues, until it will be a month earlier than at present during the last decades of the twenty-first century. Changes in spring temperatures and the melting of the snowpack, rather than direct changes in precipitation, are the primary drivers of these alterations in stream flow.[9]

A more likely scenario is that precipitation will also decline, as indicated by computer models which predict that greater warming in winter at high latitudes will weaken polar air masses relative to tropical air masses. A polar mass of cold air acts like a massive mountain range to the winter jet stream's river of atmospheric moisture, forcing the jet stream to the south as it flows eastward across North America. A weaker polar air mass will create a less effective barrier, allowing the winter jet stream to move north of its historically average location. Consequently, fewer winter storms will pass over southerly regions of the Rockies such as Colorado, and rivers such as the South Platte and the Colorado that head in these mountains may decline to less than half their historical values in spring runoff.[10]

Meanwhile, down on the plains the weather will also be getting warmer and drier. Average temperatures have risen more than 1°C in the past century across the northern and central Great Plains, and annual precipitation has decreased by 10 percent. Climate models predict continued increases in temperature, particularly in the western plains and during the winter and spring. One widely accepted model predicts an increase of 4°C in Colorado and Wyoming by the end of the twenty-first century. Drying will be greatest in the rain shadow of the Rockies, with decreases of up to 25 percent in eastern Colorado. These changes in aver-age temperature and precipitation will likely be accompanied by more frequent and prolonged periods of drought that, together with diminished water supplies, will force changes in cropping and grazing or even make agriculture infeasible in some areas. The changes will also dramatically affect river ecosystems, creat-ing lower summer flows, warmer summer water temperatures, reduced summer water quality, and increased winter flows. Summer, which we're used to thinking of as the time of abundant life, may thus become the season that limits survival of plains fishes.[11]

Many fish species of the western prairie already exist near the highest water temperatures they can withstand, and they cannot migrate to cooler northern locations. One of the great challenges to survival during changing climate is the existence of migration corridors. Prairie streams in eastern Montana might sup-port brassy minnows in the future, but the fish cannot cross dry land to get there, and the rivers of the western prairie flow predominantly west to east. Prolonged drought, global climate warming, and stream flows reduced by diversions and groundwater pumping therefore have the potential to extirpate fish species native to the western prairie.[12]

FISHES CAUGHT IN THE STATUS QUO

Native prairie fishes are in trouble even in the absence of warming, drying cli-mate. Sixteen species of native fish were present in the Arikaree River basin in 1940. Seven of them may be gone from the basin: flathead chub (*Platygobio graci-lis*), plains minnow (*Hybognathus placitus*), river shiner (*Notropis blennius*), sucker-mouth minnow (*Phenacobius mirabilis*), and stonecat (*Noturus flavus*) are extirpated. Although the status of red shiner (*Cyprinella lutrensis*) and sand shiner (*Notropis stramineus*) is unknown, they have not been collected during the past ten years of fairly intensive sampling. Linger over their names for a moment. Ponder their shining bodies in the water and what caused a fish taxonomist to name one after the Latin root for *wonderful*. Then think about those still present but declining: minnows, stonerollers, chubs, suckers, bullheads, killifish, sunfish, and darters. All of these fishes once swam in segments of the Arikaree that are now permanently dry.[13]

Fish biologist Jeff Falke and his colleagues used a groundwater model to predict what might happen to stream flow in the Arikaree under three realistic scenarios of future water use: the status quo, a scenario of removing three alluvial wells but continued pumping from all wells in the regional aquifer, and removing all wells within a 4.8-kilometer (3-mile) band of the river. Removal of the three alluvial wells reflects a proposal by the Nature Conservancy to buy water rights and retire wells for conservation purposes. The 4.8-kilometer-band scenario reflects current state policy designed to curtail pumping and restore river flows for delivery of water downstream to Kansas to meet an interstate water agreement. Even under this last, most conservative scenario, only 57 percent of existing refuge pools will remain in 2045, and nearly all of them will be in an isolated fragment of river only 1.7 kilometers long. Maintaining contemporary levels of the water table and refuge pools for fishes would require reducing groundwater pumping by 75 percent, which is likely not economically or politically feasible. As Falke concluded, "Given widespread streamflow declines, ecological futures are bleak for stream fishes in the western Great Plains."[14]

TO THE LAST DROP

In response to projections of continued population growth and reduced stream flows, water managers in the South Platte River basin continue to explore means of storing every last drop of available surface water. The Northern Integrated Supply Project (NISP) provides an example of a water-supply project currently planned for the northern portion of the South Platte basin. Six small communities on the plains of Colorado and seven water districts and associations are the participants in NISP. Projections of these participants' future water needs indicate that most of them will face water shortages by 2010 without NISP, primarily because their water needs are projected to increase threefold by 2050 as regional population continues to grow. NISP is expected to provide approximately 49.3 million cubic meters (40,000 acre-feet) of water yield each year through construction of Glade Reservoir and the South Platte Water Conservation Project. The latter involves additional storage at existing reservoirs and diversions near the junction of the Poudre and South Platte Rivers. Glade Reservoir is a proposed new reservoir north of the Poudre River in the foothills just upstream from where the Poudre enters the plains. Water would be pumped from the Poudre River for storage in Glade, which is projected to have a storage capacity of 218 million cubic meters (177,000 acre-feet), and then be piped from Glade to other existing reservoirs or canals. Because flows in the Poudre are already heavily appropriated, only peak flows during wet years would be pumped into Glade.

No new dams and reservoirs have been constructed along the Colorado Front Range for more than a decade, and public opposition to Glade is substantial. There are many problems with the proposed reservoir. The site is a broad, shallow valley between hogbacks in the transition zone between the shortgrass prairie and the montane coniferous forests to the west. Agriculture and urban

Dispersed houses on former croplands near Ault, Colorado, 2008. Urban growth of this type in the vicinity of small towns is part of the justification behind increasing municipal water supplies with proposed new reservoirs such as those that form part of the Northern Integrated Supply Project.

sprawl have already heavily altered or obliterated much of the native shortgrass prairie along the base of the Front Range, and the proposed reservoir will destroy further habitat for prairie plant communities, including Bell's Twinpod (*Physaria bellii*)—a state species of concern—and animals such as prairie dogs, mule deer, and pronghorn. The broad, shallow character of the reservoir will promote loss of stored water to evaporation, exacerbated by the fact that the Poudre River will likely have insufficient peak flows to allow water pumping into the reservoir every year. During low-flow years, earlier water rights must be satisfied first, and the already shallow reservoir will shrink further as evaporation diminishes its volume. The reservoir's exposed bed will be colonized by invasive exotic species such as cheatgrass and thistle, already a serious problem in the grasslands of this area. The energy necessary to pump water to Glade and from there to other sites will become increasingly expensive and will exacerbate already worsening air-quality problems in the region associated with development of oil and natural gas. Finally, the Poudre River downstream from the diversion site will essentially stop having a spring snowmelt peak flow.[15]

Despite widespread public opposition to further flow regulation on the Poudre River, the NISP participants and the Army Corps of Engineers are pushing hard to get this project through. Whether NISP is constructed or dropped, it will set an important precedent for the future of rivers on the western prairie.

BRINGING BACK THE RIVERS

Scenarios of climate warming and consumptive use of water present a seemingly grim future for the rivers of the western prairie. But many efforts are under way to actively preserve and restore aquatic and riparian habitat along these rivers and to maintain some aspects of the natural flow regime on which river ecosystems ultimately depend.

Some of the restoration efforts focus on specific issues. The state forest services of Nebraska, Wyoming, and Colorado, for example, initiated a Riparian Forest Restoration Initiative Project for the Platte River watershed in 2007. This project is designed primarily to remove the invasive exotic riverside trees tamarisk (*Tamarix* spp.) and Russian olive (*Elaeagnus angustifolia*), which were introduced from Asia decades ago for erosion control. Exotic trees will be removed at demonstration sites, and native cottonwood and willows will be planted or maintained where they already exist. The project does not seek to restore historical conditions per se, which, of course, included only sparse riparian vegetation; rather, it focuses on ensuring that existing riparian forests are composed primarily of native plants.[16]

The volume and timing of water flow in rivers of the western prairie is the single most fundamental issue restoration efforts must address and the most difficult. River form and function reflect the supply of water and sediment to the river. Any sustainable attempt to restore form and function to provide ecosystem services such as clean water or wildlife habitat must therefore be based on restoring water and sediment fluxes. This realization has come slowly and painfully because human societies have long treated rivers as collections of disparate resources that can be partitioned rather than as integrated ecosystems that can be destroyed by resource extraction. The realization that restoring water and sediment fluxes is crucial to river restoration has also been difficult because human society as presently constituted on the western prairie is based on altering the movement of water and sediment across the landscape and into rivers. The irrigated agriculture that forms the economic basis for most communities in the western prairie absolutely depends on these alterations.

Unable to remove the dams and diversions that have fundamentally changed rivers of the western prairie during the past century, scientists seek to mitigate the negative effects of these structures using techniques such as artificial recharge of groundwater. The Tamarack Project in northeastern Colorado on the border with Nebraska provides an example. The project uses groundwater recharge to augment stream flows in the South Platte River during periods of low flow in an effort to sustain critical habitat. During times when there is no consumptive demand for water withdrawal from the river, ten pumping wells located next to the river pump the river water into recharge basins several hundred meters away. These basins are simply shallow depressions in which the water sits and infiltrates into the subsurface. Once in the ground, the water slowly returns to the river, reaching the channel during times when flow augmentation is needed. In essence, this experimental project is a sort of water banking: water is stored temporarily in the subsurface to cushion the stream flow against extreme fluctuations that could stress aquatic organisms.[17]

The Tamarack Project began in the autumn of 1996 and is considered successful in increasing water levels in warm-water sloughs and wetland complexes along the river. Other, similar projects are currently being implemented in Julesburg and elsewhere in Colorado along the South Platte River.

Other restoration attempts focus on specific segments of a river and attempt to restore the flux of water and sediment, and thereby form and function, to that segment. The most advanced version of this approach focuses on a segment of the Platte River near Kearney, Nebraska, where large concentrations of migratory birds still use the river. The states of Colorado, Nebraska, and Wyoming are partnering with the federal government to restore portions of the river near Kearney. Riverbanks and floodplain wetlands provide crucial nesting and migratory habitat to whooping cranes, piping plovers, and interior least terns; and the channel could support the pallid sturgeon. Restoration of flows and habitat for these species is complex because the necessary water and land belong to someone, but the first phase of the thirteen-year recovery plan began in 2006. The entire effort is valued at $300 million, including in-kind contributions of water and land by the states. The federal government will pay $160 million in cash, and the three states together will provide approximately $30 million and varying quantities of water and land. Much of the money will be used to purchase or lease 4,050 hectares (10,000 acres) of land from farmers along the river. Water from federal reservoirs in Wyoming and Nebraska will also be purchased to replenish river flows near Kearney during periods of the year critical for bird and fish migration and reproduction. As of 2010, however, implementation of some aspects of the recovery plan had begun to fall behind schedule, and federal funds remain subject to the annual congressional appropriations process.[18]

The Nature Conservancy's proposal to purchase and retire groundwater wells along the Arikaree River represents what is likely to be a crucial component in preserving or restoring tributaries that head on the plains. Unlike the traditional conservation approach that focuses on land acquisition, adequate protection of smaller prairie streams also requires acquisition of consumptive water rights to restore groundwater levels and stream flow.

Restoration of the shortgrass prairie landscape is at the heart of other efforts that will benefit prairie rivers. The most ambitious effort is undoubtedly the Prairie Project, in which the American Prairie Foundation is steadily acquiring private ranchlands across northeastern Montana near the 445,000-hectare Charles M. Russell National Wildlife Refuge. The Missouri River flows through this region. The foundation eventually hopes to preserve 1.2 million hectares of land in a grassland preserve that would be a third larger than Yellowstone National Park. Although some local ranchers are wary of their prospective new neighbor, the president of the foundation notes that more than 90 percent of Montana will still be in livestock production even if the foundation achieves its ambitious goal. In *Rewilding the West*, Richard Manning also proposes that we continue to use this landscape for protein production, substituting bison and elk hunting for cattle grazing as a means of sustaining local economies. As of 2010, the American Prairie Foundation had acquired approximately 49,000 hectares of land and purchased and retired grazing privileges on another 25,500 hectares in the Russell wildlife refuge.[19]

All of these efforts—removing or limiting the spread of exotic species, enhancing groundwater recharge and diverting consumptive water rights to instream flow, and restoring native prairie vegetation in adjacent uplands—are critical to maintaining and restoring the vitality of western prairie rivers. Equally important is understanding the larger context of historical alterations throughout the region and using that knowledge to identify the highest priorities and greatest opportunities for river restoration.

BEYOND THE SOUTH PLATTE RIVER

Although specifics may differ, the story of historical changes in the South Platte River largely represents the history of the Yellowstone and Missouri, the Cheyenne, Niobrara, Platte, Kansas, Arkansas, Cimarron, Canadian, and Red—the other major rivers of the western prairie. Stream flow along most rivers has been altered by dams and diversions. Channel form has been narrowed and simplified by levees, channel straightening and deepening, and the spread of riverside forests.

Water quality along many river segments has been impaired by agriculture, mining, or cities. Populations of native fish and other animals and plants have declined so far that many species are now listed as threatened or endangered.

The Kansas River is unique among major rivers of the western prairie in rising from springs fed by the Ogallala Formation and other sources across the prairie rather than originating from snowmelt in the Rocky Mountains. The principal tributaries of the Kansas River—the Republican, Solomon, Saline, and Smoky Hill Rivers—all rise from small springs and diffuse seepage. Records of fishes in these streams dating to the 1880s indicate that fish communities in the small, spring-fed streams were eliminated or reduced in complexity soon after agricultural settlement of the western prairie in the last twenty-five years of the nineteenth century. Dominant species in the large, turbid rivers persisted longer, but they too declined precipitously during the years 1950–80 as groundwater pumping lowered water tables at the western end of the drainage and nearly all of the rivers in the eastern end were impounded by dams. Several fish species that were common in the Kansas River basin as late as the 1950s were seriously threatened by the late 1980s.[20]

The severity and extent of alterations vary among the region's major rivers. The Yellowstone, the northernmost river of the western prairie within the continental United States, flows down through mountain forests and then across the grasslands almost 1,100 kilometers to its confluence with the Missouri River in North Dakota. The Yellowstone is now the longest free-flowing river remaining in the continental United States. Sparsely inhabited, with high water quality, the Yellowstone is in fairly good condition. Nebraska's Niobrara River, too, is in fairly good condition, less affected by major habitat alterations than other eastward-flowing tributaries of the Missouri River. The Arkansas River, second only to the Missouri in size among rivers of the western prairie, has more problems. From Superfund sites stemming from historical and contemporary metal mining along its headwater streams in the Colorado Rockies to numerous reservoirs and salinization in the irrigated croplands of the lower drainage basin, water quality and altered flows create challenges for the twenty native fish species in the catchment.[21]

The Missouri River, largest river of the western prairie, has been extensively altered. Much of the river was historically unconfined and braided, with unstable islands, bars, and banks; frequent overbank floods; and high turbidity and sediment transport. It was of these portions that ecologist David Galat wrote: "An unpredictable river in an unpredictable landscape best describes the historical Missouri River." Lack of predictability did not severely hamper native fish, such as the paddlefish (*Polyodon spathula*) and the pallid and shovelnose (*S. platorhynchus*) sturgeon, which adapted to large, main-channel environments along the river. Native riverside plants included cottonwoods and poplars (*Populus* spp.), willows (*Salix* spp.), American elm (*Ulmus americana*), green ash (*Fraxinus pennsylvanica*), and box elder (*Acer negundo*). The river corridor provided migration and wintering habitat for millions of waterbirds.[22]

Alteration of the approximately 1,300 kilometers of the Upper Missouri River between Fort Peck and Oahe Dams began with deforestation along the river corridor and the removal of snags in the channel during the steamboat era of the 1830s–50s. Dikes were built along the river starting in 1902, the first dam was built at Fort Peck in 1937, and levees were added starting in 1947. The dams and dikes were designed to maintain a navigation channel for the extensive barge traffic moving along the river. Today, five dams interrupt the river as it flows from its headwaters in Montana downstream across the western prairie to Nebraska. Flow regulation increases base flow during the August–December navigation season and, along with water withdrawal, decreases flood peaks. Flow regulation and channelization for water storage, navigation, and power generation are now so extensive that only 3.2 percent of relatively natural but fragmented river segments remain in the 1,720 river kilometers between Fort Peck Lake and Gavins Point Dam.[23]

Riparian ecologists have documented changes in the riverside forests as a result of flow regulation. Growth of existing trees has slowed. More important, new seedlings are not germinating to replace older trees that die. Most of the trees present along the least regulated river segments, such as the Wild and Scenic portions of the river in Montana, germinated immediately after a large flood. Where suppression of large floods by dams has largely eliminated flood deposition and meander migration, the cottonwoods are slowly disappearing and exotic species such as Russian olive are becoming more common.[24]

Even given the problems of the Arkansas and the Missouri, none of the rivers of the western prairie is so degraded or beyond repair that designation and protection of some portions of the riverine corridor are impractical. Protection requires first awareness and appreciation, then understanding and commitment.

True appreciation of the rivers of the western prairie has lagged behind that of other rivers in the United States. These rivers that historically flooded broadly across the plains and then shrank back to a narrow trickle by late summer did not offer picturesque fishing spots where a shaded bank overhangs a clear, deep pool. The tough, mostly small-bodied fishes of the western prairie did not inspire the reverence accorded to salmon, and boating was difficult or impossible on many of the shallow rivers. But appreciation for rivers such as the South Platte is at last developing. The Platte River ecosystem is one of the most diverse in the western prairie, with 58 species of fish in the central Platte and more than 300 species of vascular plants on the floodplain. Fifty species of birds nest in floodplain woodlands, with nearly half of these species neo-tropical migrants. Several hundred bird species, including large numbers of waterbirds, use the Platte's channel and woodland communities twice each year during their transcontinental migrations. All of this abundance and diversity depends on the presence of heterogeneous habitats spread across the river's channel and floodplain, adjacent wet meadows, and nearby agricultural fields. Habitat heterogeneity, in turn, depends on the movement of water and sediment down the river system.[25]

It is not only scientists who are developing a greater appreciation of the rivers of the western prairie. A study conducted during 2000 found that residents along a 75-kilometer section of the Platte were willing to pay higher water bills to enhance five ecosystem services: dilution of wastewater, natural purification of water, erosion control, habitat for fish and wildlife, and recreation. Extrapolating from a household willingness to pay an average of $250 extra each year for these services, the authors of the study noted that the more than $20 million in revenue thus generated along the entire river greatly exceeds estimated costs for the water leasing ($1.13 million) and conservation reserve program farmland easements ($12.3 million) necessary to produce the increase in ecosystem services.[26]

Although the South Platte and other rivers of the western prairie will not be restored to the broad, shallow, freely flowing rivers described by the first Europeans to visit the region in the early nineteenth century, restoration is not an all-or-nothing proposition. Scientists who work along the Missouri and Mississippi Rivers use the "string of beads" restoration concept, in which river health is protected and restored through acquisition of key floodplain habitats, such as areas near tributary confluences or remnant backwaters. These areas form beads along the river corridor that provide wildlife habitat and ecosystem services. Beads can be passively managed by removing existing structures and allowing naturally occurring floods to occur during periods of high flow. Beads can also be actively managed by pumping river water into distribution channels to flood wetland areas that remain disconnected from the main channel or artificially enhancing recharge, as at Tamarack. If we can increase the number and size of beads, such as those currently being developed at Kearney and Tamarack, then the South Platte and its tributaries may once again support sustainable populations of organisms as diverse and wonderfully adapted as brassy minnows, paddlefish, and whooping cranes, as well as provide a source of physical and spiritual sustenance for humans.

I grew up near Cleveland, Ohio, where the system of metropolitan parks encircling the urban area is known as the *emerald necklace*. Water quality in the Cuyahoga River, which caught fire three times during the twentieth century where it flows through Cleveland, has improved so much that phenomena such as large mayfly hatches—not seen in the region for decades—are occurring once more. Such examples give me hope. With care and determination, we can enrich the western prairie with many strings of river beads along the Arkansas and the Platte, the Niobrara and the Republican, the Yellowstone and the Missouri, creating vibrant necklaces of emerald, sapphire, and topaz. These rivers can once more be the family jewels of the western prairie.

NOTES

1. E. M. Strange, K. D. Fausch, and A. P. Covich, "Sustaining Ecosystem Services in Human-Dominated Watersheds: Biohydrology and Ecosystem Processes in the South Platte River Basin," *Environmental Management* 24, no. 1 (1999): 39–54; W. J. Parton, M. P. Gutmann, and W. R. Travis, "Sustainability and Historical Land-Use Change in the Great Plains: The Case of Eastern Colorado," *Great Plains Research* 13 (2003): 97–125.

2. Tate and Heiny, "Ordination of Benthic Invertebrate Communities."

3. Strange, Fausch, and Covich, "Sustaining Ecosystem Services"; Parton, Gutmann, and Travis, "Sustainability and Historical Land-Use Change."

4. F. L. Knopf, "Changing Landscapes and the Cosmopolitanism of the Eastern Colorado Avifauna," *Wildlife Society Bulletin* 14 (1986): 132–42.

5. D. K. Mueller et al., "Nutrients in Ground Water and Surface Water of the United States: An Analysis of Data through 1992," *US Geological Survey Water-Resources Investigations Report* 95-4031 (1995); Colorado Department of Health, "Ground Water Monitoring in the South Platte Valley," South Platte Monitoring Fact Sheet #10, March (Denver: Colorado Department of Health, 1995); P. B. McMahon, "Some Bacteria Are Beneficial," *US Geological Survey Fact Sheet* FS-102-95 (1995); P. B. McMahon et al., "Quantity and Quality of Ground-Water Discharge to the South Platte River, Denver to Fort Lupton, Colorado, August 1992 through July 1993," *US Geological Survey Water-Resources Investigations Report* 95-4031 (1995).

6. A. P. Covich et al., "Potential Effects of Climate Change on Aquatic Ecosystems of the Great Plains of North America," *Hydrological Processes* 11, no. 8 (1997): 993–1021; W. C. Rense, "Hydrologic Impact of Climate Change in the Colorado Front Range," *American Water Resources Association,* Spring Specialty Conference, Anchorage, 2000.

7. F. R. Hauer et al., "Assessment of Climate Change and Freshwater Ecosystems of the Rocky Mountains, USA and Canada," *Hydrological Processes* 11, no. 8 (1997): 903–24.

8. Ibid.; I. T. Stewart, D. R. Cayan, and M. D. Dettinger, "Changes in Snowmelt Runoff Timing in Western North America under a 'Business as Usual' Climate Change Scenario," *Climatic Change* 62, no. 1-3 (2004): 217–32.

9. Hauer et al., "Assessment of Climate Change"; Stewart, Cayan, and Dettinger, "Changes in Snowmelt Runoff Timing."

10. J. M. Byrne, A. Berg, and I. Townshend, "Linking Observed and General Circulation Model Upper Air Circulation Patterns to Current and Future Snow Runoff for the Rocky Mountains," *Water Resources Research* 35, no. 12 (1999): 3793–802.

11. National Assessment Synthesis Team, "Climate Change Impacts on the United States: The Potential Consequences of Climate Variability and Change; Overview: Great Plains" (Washington, DC: US Global Change Research Program, 2000); Opie, *Ogallala*; D. Ojima et al., "Potential Climate Change Impacts on Water Resources in the Great Plains," *Journal of the American Water Resources Association* 35, no. 6 (1999): 1443–54.

12. Scheurer, Fausch, and Bestgen, "Multiscale Processes"; Falke et al., "Role of Groundwater Pumping"; Falke, Bestgen, and Fausch, "Streamflow Reductions and Habitat Drying."

13. Falke et al., "Role of Groundwater Pumping."

14. Ibid., 1.

15. MWH Americas, Inc., and Anderson Consulting Engineers, Inc., "Northern Integrated Supply Project, Phase II: Alternative Evaluation," Report to Northern Colorado Water Conservancy District (2004).

16. D. Adams, M. Hughes, and G. Sundstrom, "Riparian Forest Restoration Initiative Project Proposed for the North and South Platte Rivers," *Colorado Water* 25, no. 2 (2007): 26–29.

17. Fardal, "Effects of Groundwater Pumping."

18. Smith, "Platte River Recovery."

19. M. A. Parks, "Grass Roots: A Great Plains Native Finds His Way Home," *Sierra* 95, no. 6 (2010): 50–57; http://www.americanprairie.org/; R. Manning, *Rewilding the West: Restoration in a Prairie Landscape* (Berkeley: University of California Press, 2009).

20. Cross and Moss, "Historic Changes in Fish Communities and Aquatic Habitats."

21. R. B. Zelt et al., "Environmental Setting of the Yellowstone River Basin, Montana, North Dakota, and Wyoming," US Geological Survey (USGS) Water-Investigations Report 98-4269 (Cheyenne, WY: USGS, 1999); D. A. Peterson et al., "Water Quality in the Yellowstone River Basin, Wyoming, Montana, and North Dakota, 1999–2001," US Geological Survey (USGS) Circular 1234 (Reston, VA: USGS, 2004); D. L. Galat et al., "Missouri River Basin," in *Rivers of North America*, ed. A. C. Benke and C. E. Cushing (Amsterdam: Elsevier, 2005), 426–80; W. J. Matthews, C. C. Vaughn, K. B. Gido, and E. Marsh-Matthews, "Southern Plains Rivers," in *Rivers of North America*, ed. A. C. Benke and C. E. Cushing (Amsterdam: Elsevier, 2005), 282–325.

22. Galat et al., "Missouri River Basin," 431.

23. Ibid.

24. K. D. Bovee and M. L. Scott, "Implications of Flood Pulse Restoration for *Populus* Regeneration on the Upper Missouri River," *River Research and Applications* 18, no. 3 (2002): 287–98; M. L. Scott and G. T. Auble, "Conservation and Restoration of Semiarid

Riparian Forests: A Case Study from the Upper Missouri River, Montana," in *Flood Pulsing in Wetlands: Restoring the Natural Hydrological Balance*, ed. B. A. Middleton (New York: John Wiley and Sons, 2002), 145–90; Scott, Friedman, and Auble, "Fluvial Process"; M. L. Scott, G. T. Auble, and J. M. Friedman, "Flood Dependency of Cottonwood Establishment along the Missouri River, Montana, USA," *Ecological Applications* 7, no. 2 (1997): 677–90; Johnson, "Woodland Expansion."

25. Graf, *Endangered and Threatened Species*; F. B. Samson and F. L. Knopf, eds., *Prairie Conservation: Preserving North America's Most Endangered Ecosystem* (Washington, DC: Island, 1996).

26. J. Loomis et al., "Measuring the Total Economic Value of Restoring Ecosystem Services in an Impaired River Basin: Results from a Contingent Valuation Survey," *Ecological Economics* 33, no. 1 (2000): 103–17.

II. STREAMS OF THE TALLGRASS PRAIRIE: THE ILLINOIS RIVER BASIN

Natural History of the Illinois River

We have seen nothing like this river that we
enter, as regards its fertility of soil, its prairies
and woods; its cattle, elk, deer, wildcats;
bustards, swans, ducks, parroquets, and even
beaver. There are many small lakes and rivers.
That on which we sailed is wide, deep, and still,
for 65 leagues.

—*Jacques Marquette, on reaching the Illinois River
while journeying up the Mississippi River, 1673*[1]

Illinois is known as the Prairie State, and much of its land
was once covered in tallgrass prairie. Grasses spreading
to the distant horizons, swaying in the prairie winds like
waves on the ocean, was one of the memorable sights
for people moving west from the great forests of the
eastern United States. Even otherwise prosaic writers
left eloquent descriptions of the landscape. Eliza Steele
was not a prosaic writer but rather a careful and appre-
ciative observer from whose 1841 account "A Summer
Journey in the West" subsequent writers have quoted
many passages, but she felt challenged to adequately
evoke the sweep of space on the prairie:

How shall I convey to you an idea of a prairie . . .
Imagine yourself in the center of an immense circle

DOI: 10.5876/9781607322313.c05

of velvet herbage, the sky for its boundary upon every side; the whole clothed with a radiant efflorescence of every brilliant hue. We rode thus through a perfect wilderness of sweets, sending forth perfume, and animated with myriads of glittering birds and butterflies . . . You will scarcely credit the profusion of flowers . . . We passed whole acres of blossoms all bearing one hue . . . and then again a carpet of every color intermixed, or narrow bands, as if a rainbow had fallen upon the verdant slopes.[2]

The small streams that gather to form the Illinois rise among this velvet herbage. The headwaters of the Illinois River lack the topographic drama of the mountainous headwaters of the South Platte River. Describing the headwaters of the Illinois, Father Louis Hennepin wrote in December 1679:

The river . . . rises in a plain in the midst of much boggy land, over which it is not easy to walk . . . The river Seignelay [Illinois] is navigable for canoes to within a hundred paces of its source, and it increases to such an extent in a short time, that it is almost as broad and deeper than the Marne. It takes its course through vast marshes, where it winds about so, though its current is pretty strong, that after sailing on it for a whole day, we sometimes found that we had not advanced more than two leagues in a straight line. As far as the eye could reach nothing was to be seen but marshes full of flags and alders . . . after passing these marshes . . . there are only great open plains, where nothing grows except tall grass.[3]

The drama of the Illinois headwaters lies in the spaciousness of sky stretching to distant horizons, unimpeded by trees or topography, and in the almost inconceivable abundance of wildlife. The abundance was nearly inconceivable to the first European travelers—coming from regions with relatively dense populations, intensive resource use, and centuries of hunting with firearms—and it is nearly inconceivable today as we try to imagine that lost world.

Only a few years after the governor general of New France sent Louis Joliet, Jacques Marquette, and five other Frenchmen to explore the Mississippi River in search of an inland passage to the Pacific, more Frenchmen began to travel through and describe the country they named after the Native American word *illini*. A confederacy of Peoria, Kaskaskia, Cahokia, Michigamea, and Tamoroa tribes occupied the region, and they used illini to signify a full-grown or complete and perfect man. The French corrupted the plural of this word, illiniwek, to Illinois. Father Hennepin's group, which included Rene Robert Cavelier (also known as Sieur de La Salle) and Henri de Tonti, were the first to write about the river's source. Undoubtedly, their descriptions of rich agricultural lands and abundant wildlife, timber, and water helped persuade the French to annex Illinois to Louisiana in 1711.[4]

The drainage basin of the Illinois River still impresses with its abundance in the twenty-first century. Unlike the widely spaced, compact little bunchgrasses and pale soils of the shortgrass prairie surrounding the South Platte River, the gently rolling lands surrounding the Illinois are covered in dense, vividly green vegetation supported by thick, dark soils. Water is particularly abundant. The river itself is wider and deeper than the South Platte, and many of the tributary streams carry more flow than much larger drainage basins of the western prairie. Beyond the narrow fringe of riparian forest and the high artificial levees that line the Illinois in most places lie the enormous bottomlands the river once flooded each year.

Any particular site where these floodplain wetlands are being restored seems large at first glance. Calls of yellow warblers, goldfinches, and red-winged blackbirds vibrate through the air above wet meadows. Great blue herons squawk raucously, and white egrets stalk the shallows of lakes in silent concentration. Small flocks of mallard ducks cruise the open water. Turtles sun on partly submerged logs, and a raptor soars overhead. A large black and yellow tiger swallowtail butterfly (*Papilio glaucus*) follows an undulating path above the tall, reddish-purple coneflowers (*Echinacea* spp.), pink or lavender milkweed (*Asclepias* spp.), yellow prairie dock (*Silphium terebinthinaceum*), and other blossoms that create such a diversity of color among the tall grasses. But these seemingly extensive natural areas are in fact small remnants. Along roads that descend into the river valley, crops spread to the horizons. Thousands of square kilometers once part of the riverscape now constitute the kingdom of corn and soy.

ORIGINS OF THE RIVER

What we now call the Illinois River begins at the confluence of the Des Plaines and Kankakee Rivers, 77 kilometers southwest of Chicago. The names of these rivers reflect the meeting of diverse cultures. The French named the Des Plaines for sycamore or red maple trees lining the river, which resembled the European plane tree. Kankakee is derived from a Native American word, although scholars debate its source and meaning. Exploring the river's headwaters in 1721, Pierre-François-Xavier de Charlevoix wrote:

> This morning I walked a League further in the Meadow, having almost all the
> Way my Feet in Water. Then I met with a little Pool, which communicates with
> several others of different Bigness, the largest of which is not one hundred Paces
> in Compass. These are the sources of a river called Theakiki . . . Theak signifies a
> Wolf . . . but this River is so call'd because the Mahingans, which are also called the
> Wolves, formerly took refuge here.[5]

Edwin Way Teale describes it as a corruption of the Potawatomi word *Theakiki*, signifying "slow river flowing through a wide marsh." Despite this etymology, portions of the Kankakee flow clear and shallow over a bed of sand and gravel.

The Des Plaines River extends up into Wisconsin and the Kankakee River into Indiana, but all of the Illinois River proper lies within the state of Illinois, across which it flows 450 kilometers west and then south to join the Mississippi River at Grafton, nearly 70 kilometers upstream from St. Louis. Along its way the Illinois collects the tributary waters from a dense network of streams whose spacing reflects the region's abundant precipitation and high water tables and whose names reflect Native American and European history. The Du Page and the Fox (named for the Fox Indians) drain south from the lands west of Lake Michigan. Near Hennepin, the Illinois turns south-southeast, and from here on its western tributaries are cramped by the proximity of the Upper Mississippi River: the Spoon and the La Moine enter the Illinois from the northwest but have shorter lengths than the Vermilion, Mackinaw, and Sangamon Rivers entering the Illinois from the east and southeast. The Sangamon in particular drains an area of more than 15,000 square kilometers and is a substantial river in its own right. Its name comes from a Potawatomi word signifying "where there is plenty to eat." Within the Sangamon's drainage basin lies the type locality—the classic site to which scientists refer other sites for comparison—of sediments deposited during the Sangamon interglacial, a warmer interval between the Illinoian and the later Wisconsinan advances of the immense continental ice sheet centered far to the north in Canada. The Illinois River drains a total of roughly 75,000 square kilometers of land and is commonly divided into an upper basin from the headwaters to Ottawa, Illinois (approximately 30,400 square kilometers), and a lower basin from Ottawa downstream to the junction with the Mississippi (approximately 49,900 square kilometers).[6]

The Illinois River lies within the Great Lake and Till Plains portions of the Central Lowland physiographic province, a name particularly evocative of the region's character. Everyone who writes about the Illinois River basin notes the flat, low-lying landscape, whether they glory in the abundance of its resources or lament its tedium. Across these lowlands, glaciers and glacier-driven winds dropped thick blankets of sediment, into which rivers of glacial melt water carved broad, deep valleys.

The massive continental ice sheet that repeatedly surged southward from Canada during the past 2 million years largely created the framework of the regional landscape, the details of which the Illinois River has been modifying ever since. The North American name for the second-most-recent phase of ice-sheet advance, which occurred between 200,000 and 150,000 years ago, is the Illinoian glacial. The

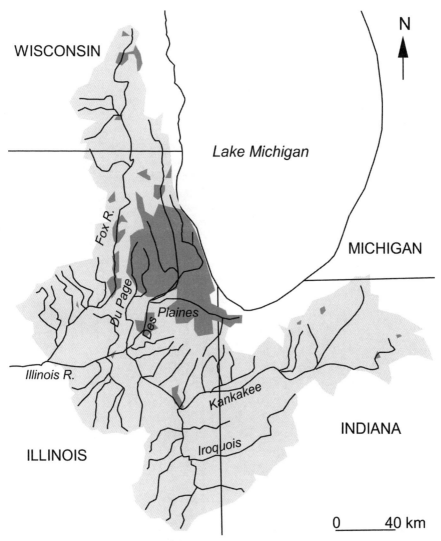

Land use and principal tributaries in the Upper Illinois River basin. River basin is outlined in lighter gray, urban areas are in darker gray. Most of the rest of the upper basin is agricultural. After Sullivan (2000, fig. 3).

Sangamon interglacial followed (circa 130,000–115,000 years ago) and then the final major advance of the Wisconsinan glacial (70,000–10,000 years ago). These ice sheets that extended across 13 million square kilometers at thicknesses of up to 3 kilometers influenced a much greater area than that actually covered by ice.

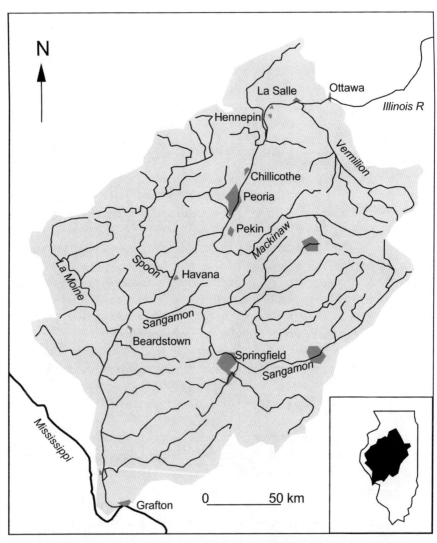

The Lower Illinois River basin (lighter gray shading), showing cities (darker gray shading) and tributary rivers mentioned in the text. The inset map at lower right shows the location of the Lower Illinois River basin within the state of Illinois. The Illinois is tributary to the Mississippi River, which flows toward the lower right in this illustration. After Warner (1998, fig. 1).

Along the margins of the glacier, melting ice released millions of tons of sediment, varying in size from huge boulders to grains of silt and sand. Some of this material remained in place as linear mounds of glacial till known as recessional

Schematic map of the location of Pleistocene-age glacial moraines in northeastern Illinois. Each of these moraines influences the sediment and water supplied to river networks in the Upper Illinois River basin.

Illinois

0   80 km

moraines. Concentric moraines outline the extent of the ice, with each moraine marking a pause in the retreat of the ice front during which a linear mound of boulders, gravel, and sand was deposited along the ice edge. On a geologic map of glacial deposits, the lobate recessional moraines that cover the upper half of the Illinois River basin resemble giant shelf fungi. Each of these moraines is 1.5 to 15 kilometers in width but rises only 15 to 30 meters above the surrounding terrain.[7]

Glacial moraines also ponded melt water when the ice sheet was retreating. The Upper Illinois River is geologically younger than the lower Illinois, which existed south of the ice sheet during the periods of glaciation. Sometime between 17,000 and 14,000 years ago, melt water ponded in the upper basin breached the Marseillaise Moraine that held the water back, creating a tremendous outburst flood known as the Kankakee Torrent. This flood that peaked at hundreds of thousands of cubic meters of water per second cut a channel south to the lower Illinois River via the Kankakee and Des Plaines Rivers. Where the Illinois River valley widens downstream from the "Big Bend" at Hennepin, Illinois, the waning stages of the Kankakee Torrent deposited thick beds of sand and gravel along the valley bottom. Quarries reveal the thickness and extent of these deposits. Gravel is now perched more than 60 meters above the contemporary river channel at Starved Rock, upstream from the Big Bend. Surging and swirling waters sculpted the thick beds of gravel into diverse shapes. Mount Joliet was a flat-topped gravel mound shaped like a cone near the Des Plaines River and the city of Joliet. The mound was so distinctive in this largely flat landscape that it became a tourist attraction as early as the 1690s. Utilitarian attitudes subsequently prevailed, however, and the mound was removed more than 130 years ago as the gravel was mined for paving and railroad ballast. What the outburst floods began, subsequent river flow continued as the Upper Illinois moved back and forth across the valley bottom over widths as great as 2 kilometers, contouring a sinuous course and leaving abandoned channel fragments to fill as backwater lakes. The river now drops only 20 centimeters per kilometer of downstream distance in this upper portion.[8]

Repeated surges of glacial ice also displaced existing river courses, muscling aside even large rivers and re-contouring the valley bottoms. The Lower Illinois River from Hennepin down to the mouth flows through a much older channel once occupied by the Upper Mississippi River. An advancing lobe of glacial ice pushed the Mississippi westward to its present location. As the glacier retreated northward, drainage across the newly uncovered landscape coalesced into the lower Illinois River. Although rivers don't always follow the path of least resistance, a large, southward-draining valley already awaited the newly forming lower Illinois, and the river moved into the obvious pathway across the landscape. Initially, the river was rather large, fed by the abundant melt water streaming from the north. As the glacier retreated further north and the supply of melt water decreased, the river valley was partly filled with sand and gravel carried downstream from the glacier on the waning flows. The diminished river nonetheless eroded a valley 45 meters to 77 meters deep and in places between 8 and 11 kilometers wide, creating an enormous trough into which the runoff from the adjacent uplands gradually found its way. It is a trough tilted imperceptibly downstream, however: gradient along this lower portion of the Illinois drops to a mere 2 centimeters of elevation per kilometer downstream.[9]

Some of the sediment released by the glaciers was also carried southward by temporary streams of melt water. As the ice front retreated, huge chunks of ice the size of an apartment building were left behind to melt more slowly under an insulating blanket of sediment. Sediment continued to accumulate around and above these isolated ice blocks, building up an outwash plain. When the ice block finally melted, the overlying sediment collapsed into the resulting cavity, leaving a depression known as a glacial kettle that might hold water permanently or seasonally. These prairie potholes and floodplain lakes create diverse habitats for fish and resident and migratory birds.

Glacial history thus created the template of extensive floodplain wetlands that could support the tremendous numbers of animals that so impressed Jacques Marquette and others. As Stephen Forbes wrote in 1928, "Illinois is essentially a river state." The glaciers and their melt waters gouged valleys far too wide and deep for the contemporary Illinois River. As the river meanders and floods across these broad bottomlands, thick soils and shallow depressions store rainfall and floodwaters, releasing them slowly back into the gently sloping river channel. Even where buried by later sedimentation, the old glacial melt water channels continue to influence the subsurface movement of water. Edwin Way Teale wrote of a farmer in the Kankakee River bottomlands whose field began to rise like a giant blister. Each year the bulge increased until it rose to almost 5 meters above the surrounding land. When scientists from Purdue University investigated the site, they realized that the field lay on the edge of a buried glacial melt water channel. Water flowing in the buried channel fed springs that caused the bulge, 70 percent of which consisted of water. Teale wrote, "The humus [organic-rich soil] it contained had swelled like a piece of dried apple soaked in water."[10]

A sheet of ice the size of Canada generates its own weather, including strong winds at the boundaries of ice and earth where differences in reflection of solar energy create dramatic temperature contrasts. When these winds blasted across sediment newly deposited by melt water streams, silt-sized sediment flew southward as loess. The loess blanketed preexisting topography, with the greatest accumulations in topographic lows such as the Mississippi and Illinois River valleys. Today, between 0.5 and 2 meters of loess lies across the landscape of the Upper Illinois River basin. This is the parent material for the extraordinarily fecund soil that once supported dense stands of tall grass and now supports the crops that feed America and the world. Loess creates rich agricultural soils, but it is also easily eroded once exposed in farm fields.[11]

Contemporary streams of the Illinois River basin have cut through the blanket of till, outwash, and loess to expose the underlying bedrock along some portions of the river valleys. This bedrock indicates that the Illinois River's portion of North America has been low-lying for a very long time.

The oldest rocks indicate a landscape with more geologic drama. Volcanic rocks record violent explosions approximately 1.5 billion years ago during the Precambrian, the oldest unit of geologic time. This episode was followed by an extended period of erosion and then two more episodes of large explosions. Intrusions of granitic magma several hundred thousand years later provided the resistant rock that was shaped into a landscape with up to 300 meters of vertical relief during a long period of erosion. Then, still in the Precambrian, the inputs of energy from Earth's interior in the form of volcanic eruptions and magma intrusions stopped, and a long period of sediment deposition began.

The Cambrian Period, which began more than 500 million years ago, is marked in Illinois by sandstone and other sedimentary rocks deposited in a broad sea that stretched across a large swathe of the continent. Shallow seas advanced and retreated repeatedly, but for the next 200 million years the area remained mostly below sea level, collecting sediment eroded from highlands to the east. Sediments eroded from the rising Appalachian Mountains were carried to what is now Illinois by river and sea currents. The St. Petersburg sandstone was deposited along the shoreline of an Ordovician (505–438 million years ago) ocean in Illinois. Thinly bedded black shales formed from organic-rich muck alternate with limestone rich in fossil organisms that lived in clear, warm, shallow tropical seas. As the sea withdrew for the last time circa 320 million years ago, gradual gentle uplift raised the landscape for the next several hundred thousand years, until slightly higher topography in northeastern Illinois caused rivers to flow to the west and south. These rivers deposited sands and silts. Intervening marshes created layers of peat that lithified into coal. A long hiatus occurs in the rock record from approximately 285 million to 144 million years ago, before sedimentary rocks of Cretaceous age (144–66 million years) appear. These rocks contain trace minerals that suggest erosion of a metamorphosed highlands as far away as the North Carolina Piedmont. Then, once more, the geologic record becomes sparse until the erosional and depositional features created by the great glaciers flowing southward from Canada.

Just as the violent history of mountain building that created the Rockies continues to dominate the landscape and rivers of the South Platte River basin today, so, too, the long geologic quiescence of the upper midwestern United States influences the contemporary landscape of the Illinois River basin. Rivers follow sinuous courses across the relatively flat topography, leaving wakes of abandoned channels and oxbow lakes. Small downstream gradients facilitate deposition of sediment and the formation of deep soils that store groundwater.

Onto this low-lying landscape falls abundant precipitation, relative to the shortgrass prairie to the west. Between 92 and 98 centimeters of precipitation falls on average each year in different portions of the region drained by the Illinois River. Approximately 70 percent of this precipitation falls as snow in the upper basin, declining to about 40 percent in the southwestern portion of the basin. Most of the precipitation falls during the spring and summer months, although at least 6 centimeters of water in some form descends from the sky during every month but January and February. What the atmosphere bestows, the plants readily take up. Unlike many plants of the western prairie, which hoard water and release only small amounts through respiration, the plants of the eastern prairie can be more prodigal in releasing water back to the atmosphere. The stomata of plants open to absorb carbon dioxide and release oxygen during respiration. Water vapor is released along with the oxygen in a process known as transpiration. In dry regions, plants adapt to limit this release, gulping more carbon dioxide during shorter intervals. Plants of the eastern prairie, in contrast, return an estimated 70 percent of the average annual precipitation to the atmosphere through transpiration. This is part of what keeps the region relatively humid: on a muggy summer day, imagine all those millions of grass blades and leafy forbs exuding water vapor into the air.[12]

The abundance of precipitation reflects in part the atmospheric conflicts generated when cool, dry air from Canada, warm, moist air from the Gulf of Mexico, and warm, dry air from the Pacific Ocean meet and mingle. These are the big three of the eastern prairie and, as in the west, their collisions create atmospheric violence: summer convective storms that pummel the landscape with hail, swift-falling rain, and tornadoes; and winter blizzards that blast snow horizontally across the landscape. Continual shifts among air masses also create large daily fluctuations in temperature and precipitation over the eastern prairie. As in the west, Pacific air dominates climate over the eastern prairie, but greater proximity to the Gulf of Mexico means collisions between moist Gulf air and dry Canadian air produce most of the precipitation that keeps the region wetter than the western prairie.[13]

Sometimes, however, the rain simply does not fall. The Illinois River basin experiences periodic and frequently severe droughts, such as those in the 1890s and the 1930s. Tree rings record wetter years of generous growth and drier years of pinched growth. The relative width of rings indicates that the five driest decades during the past 300 years were, in chronological order, 1696–1705, 1735–44, 1791–1800, 1816–25, and 1931–40. With the exception of those nine years in the mid-twentieth century, the period since settlement by Europeans has been unusually generous in terms of precipitation. In the western prairie this once would have been taken as evidence that "rain follows the plow." In the eastern prairie, it is largely taken for granted.[14]

Decadal-scale fluctuations between too much precipitation and too little in part reflect variations in sea-surface temperature in the southern Pacific Ocean. As described in chapter 1, a high-pressure system sits over the western coast of South America off Peru most years during the Southern Hemisphere summer, while a low-pressure system sits at the other side of the Pacific over northern Australia and New Guinea. At irregular intervals, this pressure distribution reverses. The low pressure that normally coincides with warm sea-surface temperatures and abundant rainfall shifts eastward to the coast of Peru, creating an El Niño circulation that brings Christmastime rainfall to western Peru. These fluctuations half a world away reverberate not only across western North America but also on the eastern American prairie. During periods of strong El Niño circulation, the high-pressure system that normally sits over the prairie and limits precipitation is replaced by a persistent low-pressure center that draws moisture in from the Gulf of Mexico. This was the pattern that gave rise to spectacular flooding across the Upper Mississippi River basin, including the Illinois River, in 1993. During the opposite, La Niña circulation pattern, drought comes to the prairie.[15]

Changes in precipitation associated with the El Niño circulation are strongest in the northern prairie. The central and southern prairie appears to be more influenced by similar fluctuations in pressure and sea-surface temperature in the North Pacific Ocean. When the northern and southern Pacific systems vary in the same direction, precipitation anomalies across the prairie can be particularly intense and widespread, as during the 1988 drought.[16]

The relatively abundant precipitation of the tallgrass prairie gives rise to abundant surface water and stream flow. On a map, tributaries of the Upper Illinois resemble arms spread wide to embrace Lake Michigan, the fingers stretched to drain every drop of water south and west away from the lake. The Kankakee River and its tributaries cover about 14,350 square kilometers south of the lake, and from these lands the Kankakee brings an average 127 cubic meters of water per second into the Illinois. The Des Plaines and its tributaries spread a network of channels hard up against the western side of the lake, draining an average 100 cubic meters per second of water from 5,860 square kilometers. The Des Plaines brings more water per kilometer of drainage basin than the Kankakee, in part because the Des Plaines also includes water diverted from Lake Michigan through a nineteenth-century canal.[17]

Discharge increases steadily downstream from the confluence of the Kankakee and the Des Plaines as lesser rivers bring their tribute to the Illinois. The Fox drains a long, narrow swathe of land that stretches up into Wisconsin. The Vermilion enters from the south, its drainage roughly parallel to the Kankakee. Originating from a marsh, this river contains one of the few whitewater river segments in Illinois where the river has cut down into the sedimentary bedrock. The Mackinaw enters well downstream from the Big Bend. Portions of this river flow clear over sand and gravel between densely forested banks and retain high water quality and significant mussel populations. The Spoon River starts near the Big Bend, then flows parallel to the Illinois before turning eastward to the larger river. Edgar Lee Masters grew up near the river and used its name in his 1916 work, *Spoon River Anthology*. The Sangamon, which like the Spoon flows mainly through agricultural lands, drains a broad swathe east of the lower Illinois. Young Abraham Lincoln traveled by canoe and flatboat along the river, and the river still includes natural areas where the connection between the channel and adjacent floodplains is preserved. Finally, the La Moine (French for "the monk") enters at the southwestern end of the Illinois drainage basin.

Between these and lesser contributors, the Illinois reaches an average of 306 cubic meters per second at Marseilles, 51 river-kilometers downstream from the Kankakee–Des Plaines junction. Discharge reaches an impressive 649 cubic meters per second at Valley City. This point, 90 river-kilometers upstream from the confluence with the Mississippi, provides the most downstream point at which to reliably measure discharge because of backwater effects from the larger Mississippi. The discharge per square kilometer of the drainage basin at Valley City is 100 times the discharge per square kilometer at the mouth of the South Platte. In

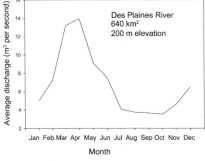

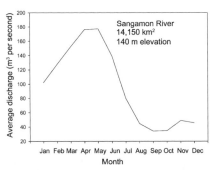

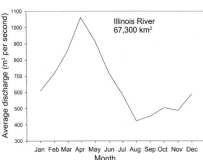

Sample hydrographs from streams at various locations throughout the Illinois River basin. These curves show average monthly flow for each site. The drainage area and elevation of the river at that site are also listed. Drainage areas listed here do not necessarily represent the total drainage area for a particular river, as not all sites are close to the mouth of each river. The hydrographs clearly show the strong annual peak between March and May.

the western prairie, water pours forth from the Rockies during the melt season but leaks drop by meager drop from the plains portion of each drainage basin. In the eastern prairie the entire drainage basin does its fair share, and the water flows more steadily from seeps and springs across the landscape throughout the year, collecting more rapidly after snow or rain.[18]

Flow in the Illinois and its many tributaries peaks between March and May, then falls to a low between August and October. Charlevoix wrote in 1721 of seeing a bison fording the mouth of the Des Plaines River under flow so shallow that the water barely reached the animal's knees. Such low water can be unpredictable, however, because floods can occur throughout much of the year. Summer thunderstorms caused flooding in parts of the Upper Illinois River basin during July 1957 and August 1987, autumn rains brought floods in September and October 1986, and rain falling on snow-covered areas caused floods in February and March 1985. The great flood of 1993, when the flooding Mississippi backed water 100 kilometers up the already flooded Illinois River, resulted from persistent rains that lasted from spring through October. These rains produced an average 127 centimeters of precipitation that year, which barely beat the previous record set in 1927, another great flood year in the Mississippi River drainage. The earlier description

October 1926 flood in Beardstown, Illinois. Beardstown lies close to the mainstem Illinois River and within the historical floodplain. Courtesy, Lincoln Library, Springfield, Illinois.

of the bison notwithstanding, the possibility that clashes between air masses can bring floods at any season, as well as the steady contributions from groundwater lying close to the surface, prevents the eastern prairie rivers from reaching the extreme lows of rivers in the western prairie: variability in discharge throughout the year on the Illinois is about two-thirds that of the South Platte River.[19]

As generous as stream flow is in the eastern prairie compared with the western prairie, recent changes in land cover have further increased the volume of water moving down stream channels. The period 1950–97 was characterized by an upward trend in annual mean stream flow at all stations where flow is measured in the Illinois River basin. The most dramatic changes have occurred in urbanized areas, where paved surfaces rapidly shed precipitation and stormwater drains quickly route this runoff into streams. Along the Des Plaines River, where 70 percent to 80 percent of the watershed is in urban or agricultural areas, median flow increased by 84 percent between 1950 and 1997. Along with flow diverted from the Chicago River, this creates a situation where contemporary flow along the Des Plaines is estimated to be much greater than it was in the mid-1800s, when only 40 percent of the watershed was developed or used for agriculture and water had not yet been diverted from other drainage basins.[20]

The Sangamon River in flood, circa 1900. This view of floodwaters spreading through the bottomland forests typifies historical conditions. Courtesy, Abraham Lincoln Presidential Library, Springfield, Illinois.

Historically, the abundance of water flowing down the channels of the Illinois River basin produced extensive flooding. As discharge increased each spring, the excess water flowed above the channel banks and across the broad valley bottoms, inundating the riverine corridor for as much as six months each year. Floodwaters create an aquatic connection between the main channel and adjacent floodplain and wetlands. During the flood season, organisms living in the river can spread out into extensive areas of shallow water where warm temperatures, abundant sunlight, and submerged vegetation create rich habitat. Flood season is a time for eating well and storing energy for breeding, growth, or migration. High levels of photosynthesis and rich decaying vegetation provide food for bottom-dwelling invertebrates and zooplankton. Many species of fish find spawning grounds and nursery habitat for young fish vulnerable to predation. Aquatic plants in backwater lakes, wetland plants in marshes, and trees in the floodplain forests time their growth and release of seeds to the flood cycle. Migrating waterfowl, shorebirds, and bald eagles find food in the rapidly growing aquatic plants, insects, and fish.[21]

River water spreading across the floodplains carries sand, silt, and clay, as well as bits of decaying plants rich in nutrients. As the floodwaters recede, vegetation

Modern view of a backwater along the Kankakee River, a principal tributary of the Illinois River. Such backwaters, now rare, were historically abundant and connected to the river during floods.

adapted to moist soil sprouts in the newly deposited sediment, creating further food sources for birds migrating south each autumn. Some of the floodplain nutrients return to the main channel in the bodies of invertebrates and fish retreating back to the channel with declining water levels. Some nutrients remain each year to gradually build the fertile bottomland soils that so delighted agriculturalists, from prehistoric Native Americans to the first settlers of European descent. Illinois scientist Stephen Forbes wrote in 1928, "Most of our streams are by nature remarkably productive because of the richness of the land from which they derive their organic content and because of their sluggish flow over a level surface by which ample time is given for the organization of their food materials into forms fit for the maintenance of animal life."[22]

Despite the abundance of water along its course, the Illinois River has a sediment problem—or, at least, European settlers have generally perceived the dynamics of sediment within the basin as constituting a problem. Historical written accounts and sedimentary deposits indicate that the river has been accumulating sediment along its valley for millennia. River currents deposit silt and sand along the river's meandering shoreline. Overbank floods start to lose velocity as they spill over the channel margins, and some of the sediment carried in suspension drops onto the riverbanks to build low natural levees. Velocity continues to drop as the floodwaters spread across the valley bottom. Fine sediments settle onto the broad, marshy floodplain and fill in the low-lying areas where remnants of abandoned channel form ponds and lakes.

Some of this excess sediment the Illinois cannot transport all the way to the Mississippi comes directly from erosion of the adjacent uplands, but most of the sediment reaches the Illinois by way of tributary streams. Tributaries draining the Till Plains are particularly rich in sediment, for even the thick vegetation cover cannot prevent intense summer thunderstorms and melting winter snows from bringing this region's loosely consolidated glacial sediment gradually down to the nearest creek. Where a tributary joins the mainstem, the sudden loss of velocity and ability to transport sediment commonly results in deposition of an alluvial fan that pushes the Illinois River across the valley from the tributary mouth. At some points along the course of the big river, these fans are so large that they constrict the river's flow and create a backwater, such as Peoria Lake.

Portions of the Illinois River basin have been modified by humans for thousands of years, as long as people have burned the forests and grasslands or cultivated land for crops. The extent and intensity of modification increased dramatically once people of European descent began to settle these lands in the early nineteenth century. Sufficient historical accounts and geologic records remain, however, to allow scientists to understand much of the function and appearance of the Illinois River prior to the nineteenth century, as well as the uplands beyond the river corridors.

"ONE WIDE SEA OF WAVING GRASS"[23]

The Illinois River basin lies near the frontier of the tallgrass prairie, where the vast mixed deciduous forests of the eastern United States give way to the grasslands of the continental interior. This is a landscape contested by trees and grass, refereed by fire and grazing. Tallgrass prairie dominated the eastern third of the American prairie prior to settlement by people of European descent, covering approximately 60 million hectares from southern Texas northward to southern Manitoba. Gradual transitions to mixed-grass prairie to the west, deciduous forest to the east, and boreal forest or aspen parklands to the north mark the boundaries of the tallgrass, where climatic extremes in the form of floods, droughts, cold winters, and late spring freezes influence the distribution of plant species.[24]

Tallgrass prairie takes its name from species including big bluestem (*Andropogon gerardi*), switchgrass (*Panicum virgatum*), Indiangrass (*Sorghastrum nutans*), and rough dropseed (*Sporobolus*). These giants among grasses reach heights of more than 2 meters aboveground and send their roots an additional 3 meters into the soil. Just as a forest is vertically layered from the emergent, tallest trees to the understory, the plants of the tallgrass prairie also create green depths. Little bluestem (*Schizachyrium scoparium*), side oats grama (*Bouteloua curtipendula*), hairy grama (*Bouteloua hirsuta*), blue grama (*Bouteloua gracilis*), western wheatgrass (*Agropyron smithii*), and buffalograss (*Buchloe dactyloides*) grow to lesser heights under the canopy of the tall grasses. The details of the species present at any spot reflect soils, moisture levels, and the history of disturbance by fire or grazing and burrowing animals: little bluestem and side oats grama prefer the drier conditions of upland prairies, prairie cordgrass (*Spartina pectinata*) and bluejoint grass (*Calamagrostis canadensis*) like the soaked soils of low points in the landscape, and big bluestem and Indiangrass prefer sites with intermediate soil moisture. Big and little bluestem can account for more than 75 percent of the vegetation in many patches of prairie, but a walk across the prairie through what might at first glance seem to be uniform grasses actually crosses something better described as a mosaic of plant assemblages. Several hundred species of grasses and forbs, interspersed with marshes and prairie potholes, create a dense carpet of vegetation.[25]

Grasses have dominated the vegetation of the uplands in the Illinois River basin for approximately 10,000 years, since the ice and the forests that grew along its margins shrank back under warmer, drier climates. Plants of the tallgrass prairie adapted to frequent disturbance. Fires that may have recurred every two to five years in some areas helped to clear back dead plant matter and facilitate the germination of new seeds by releasing nutrients bound in the plant litter. Fires were particularly important in limiting the encroachment of woody vegetation onto prairie lands. Periodically, droughts stressed the plant communities. Herbivores as large as bison, elk, and white-tailed deer and as small as rabbits and rodents acted with fire and drought to influence the diversity of plant species.[26]

Although wildfires frequently started because of lightning strikes, Native Americans also deliberately set fires to improve grazing conditions for the herbivores they hunted. During hunting, people sometimes used a ring fire in which dispersed groups set fires around a herd of bison and then used the fires to drive the animals inward or toward a passage where hunters waited. Father Hennepin wrote about Miami Indians near Kankakee, Illinois, killing as many as 120 bison in a day using this technique. Fire frequency initially increased with European settlement, then declined as settlers did what they could to suppress fires on settled lands. William Oliver wrote an especially vivid description of a nighttime prairie

Tallgrass prairie remnant preserved and under restoration at Midewin National Tallgrass Prairie in the Upper Illinois River basin.

fire in 1842: "The huge body of flame spread far and wide, leaping and plunging like the waves of the sea in a gale against a rocky coast, and emitting a continued roar like that of a heavy surf when heard from a short distance. The whole country is lighted up for miles, and the sky . . . is like a sheet of red hot metal."[27] Deliberate suppression of fires from about the 1840s onward helped woody plant species encroach on the prairie.

Despite the importance of fire, much of the prairie was wet either seasonally or permanently. Soil characteristics suggest that wetlands covered more than half of some portions of the Illinois River basin prior to European settlement. Most of the prairie was a so-called black soil prairie formed on thick, dark soils made up of decomposed vegetation mixed with mineral sediment. Between 60 and 80 percent of a prairie grass, by weight, grows belowground, and the life of the plant retreats into its rhizomes (rootstocks that spread laterally) during periods of drought or other stress. This is a landscape of cryptic life: the total biomass of all the organisms living underground in the prairie—worms, insects, mites, algae, fungi, bacteria, protozoans, and others—is likely to be greater than that of all the organisms living aboveground, despite the much greater size of the latter individuals. Many of these soil creatures help break down dead roots and other plant litter and then build this material into relatively stable organic compounds known as humus. Humus is particularly effective at storing nutrients such as potassium and nitrogen, preventing these materials from being leached deeper into the soil by infiltrating water and keeping them out of reach of living organisms. Prairie is essentially a highly efficient recycling system, churning dead plant matter back into a thick upper layer of soil on which new plants can draw for sustenance. Prairie is also conservative. More nutrients are returned to the soil each year than are taken up again by native plants, so reserves of carbon and nitrogen build up in the soil through time.[28]

Patches of tallgrass prairie occur further east, but Illinois is the real frontier of tallgrass prairie that extends to the horizons. Here the landscape and the sky open up after being crowded and hidden by the deciduous forests to the east. The prairie rivers, unlike rivers to the east that are confined by ridges and walls of rock, spread and meander freely, exuberantly overflowing their banks in season and claiming land to the distant horizons as floodplain.

Many early descriptions of this landscape stress the spaciousness of a view unimpeded by trees or steep hills and the beauty of the flowering plants growing among the grasses. Traveling across the prairie near the Illinois River in July 1840, Eliza Steele wrote: "A world of grass and flowers stretched around me, rising and falling in gentle undulations, as if an enchanter had struck the ocean swell, and it was at rest forever. Acres of wild flowers of every hue glowed around me."[29] English traveler Isabella Bird was less effusive in her 1856 account of the Illinois prairie, describing a landscape in which "the horizontal line had not a single inequality; all was hot, unsuggestive, silent, and monotonous. This was the grass prairie." But then, Bird was not a prairie connoisseur: she also left unflattering descriptions of the shortgrass prairie in the South Platte River basin. In her travels across Illinois, Bird also described grasslands "continually alternating with belts of timber and small lakes."[30]

WHERE FIRES FEAR TO TREAD

Many factors influenced the distribution of the belts of timber Bird described. Some forest patches grew on protected slopes and in ravines or in shrublands and open savanna on uplands, but many were on the floodplain, where the environment was too wet to support intense, stand-killing wildfires. These forests supported diverse fish communities, millions of migratory waterfowl and other birds, deer, elk, and abundant smaller animals. After studying 3,400 hectares at the confluence of the Illinois and Mississippi Rivers, ecologists John Nelson, Anjela Redmond, and Richard Sparks estimated that more than half of the floodplain was forested prior to European settlement, with the remainder occupied by prairie, wetlands, and lakes.[31]

Floodplain forests were generally open and contained diverse plant species. So-called flatwoods formed on level areas underlain by clay, such as portions of the Des Plaines River. The impermeable clay held standing water in spring, limiting the availability of oxygen for plant roots, then formed a hard, dry layer that further impeded the roots during summer. Swamp white oak (*Quercus bicolor*), white oak (*Q. alba*), scarlet oak (*Q. coccinea*), and American elm (*Ulmus americana*) did well in this challenging environment, creating an open, relatively sunny forest floor.[32]

Maple-basswood mesic forests, which Joel Greenberg describes as "where shadows reign," grew near the bottom of north-facing slopes with higher humidity and soil moisture and few or no fires. Sugar maple (*Acer saccharum*), basswood (*Tilia americana*), black cherry (*Prunus serotina*), red oak (*Quercus rubra*), and white oak formed the canopy in mesic forests, towering over a shrub layer of maple-leaved arrowwood (*Viburnum acerifolium*), nannyberry (*V. lentago*), and witch hazel (*Hamamelis virginiana*). These layers allowed much less sunlight to reach the forest floor, but mid-April through May, when the big trees were just leafing out and the spring warmth loosened the frozen soil, created a window of opportunity for herbaceous understory plants to flower and store sufficient energy to see them through the shady and cold periods of the year. Then the forest dominated by hues of green and brown blossomed into shades of white, pink, yellow, and blue as the successive blossoming of spring beauty (*Claytonia virginica*), great white trillium (*Trillium grandiflorum*), swamp buttercup (*Ranunculus septentrionalis*), mayapple (*Podophyllum peltatum*), and dozens of other species starred the forest floor.[33]

Maple-basswood mesic forests also grew along riverbanks with relatively well-drained soils: again, portions of the Des Plaines River provide an example. Other riverbanks supported forests composed of species tolerant of inundation by floods and the alternating erosion and deposition that accompany floodwaters. Black willow (*Salix nigra*), American elm, slippery elm (*Ulmus rubra*), sycamore (*Platanus occidentalis*), silver maple (*Acer saccharinium*), cottonwood (*Populus deltoides*), box elder (*Acer negundo*), and green ash (*Fraxinus pennsylvanica*) dominated these lowland floodplain forests.[34]

In general, hackberry (*Celtis occidentalis*), pecan (*Carya illinoensis*), elm (*Ulmus* spp.), willow (*Salix* spp.), and cottonwood were dominant tree species in the forests scattered across the prairie; but silver maple, American elm, ash (*Fraxinus* spp.), box elder, pin oak (*Quercus palustris*), bur oak (*Q. macrocarpa*), sycamore, honey locust (*Gleditsia triacanthos*), black walnut (*Juglans nigra*), and hickory (*Hicoria* spp.) were among the other tree species present. Moderately moist uplands held white oak, red oak (*Q. rubra*), basswood, sugar maple, and slippery elm; drier upland woods were dominated by black oak (*Quercus velutina*), white oak, and hickories. The numerous canopy and understory species created variegated forests. Rays of sunlight filtered down through leaves smooth-edged, lobed, toothed, and compound—sprouting in every conceivable shade of green from branches that formed a crown spreading broadly from a slender trunk or shaped like a ball, a cone, or a cumulus cloud of greenery. As in the grasslands, what might at first glance seem like an undifferentiated mass of greenery, upon closer inspection resolved into a mosaic of plant species distributed according to moisture and the history of disturbances from floods and fires.[35]

WETLANDS IN A WET LAND

Interspersed among the floodplain woodlands were patches of bluestem prairie and wetlands. The Illinois River drainage lay within what environmental historian Ann Vileisis describes as a giant mid-continent hourglass of wetlands centered on the Mississippi River. The Illinois wetlands lay in the southern portion of the upper chamber of the hourglass, where grasses and reeds grew to heights of nearly 3 meters, overtopping riders on horseback. Vileisis quotes a French traveler's 1683 description of the wetlands along the Upper Kankakee River: "As far as the eye could reach nothing was to be seen but marshes full of flags [irises] and alders." Marshes, in which vegetation emerges from standing water, formed the most extensive wetlands. Among the common marsh species were those that grow in relatively shallow water, including blue flag iris (*Iris virginica*); needle spike rush (*Eleocharis acicularis*); common reed (*Phragmites australis*), which does well in disturbed areas; pickerelweed (*Pontederia cordata*); common arrowhead (*Sagittaria latifolia*); and broad-leaved cattail (*Typha latifolia*) and narrow-leaved cattail (*T. angustifolia*). Deeper waters held white water lily (*Nymphaea tuberose*), yellow pond lily (*Nuphar advena*), bullhead lily (*Nuphar variegatum*), lotus (*Nelumbo lutea*), and other species. In 1935, Francis Ling reminisced about the Kankakee wetlands of his childhood during the last decade of the nineteenth century: "Many of the bayous and pond holes in the timber and marsh were a white carpet of waterlillies [*sic*] and the banks of the bayous and ponds were lined with marsh hollyhocks . . . In the spring the islands were one mass of flowers—spring beauties, Dutchman's breeches and violets."[36]

It is difficult to fully comprehend the extent of the largest marshes in the Illinois River basin, which are now largely gone. One of the most extensive, drained for agriculture before scientists could systematically describe it, was the Great Marsh (also known as the Grand Marsh) of the Kankakee River, which actually included both marshes and swamp forests. The Kankakee River valley lies between a glacial moraine and rolling uplands. The Kankakee was not exactly a river on a mission: water flowing in the channel actually traveled about 420 kilometers, through 2,000 meander bends, although achieving only 180 kilometers of straight-line downstream distance. At the downstream end of this tortuous portion of the river, a ledge of limestone bedrock pokes up through the valley-bottom sediment, forming a low natural dam that helps to pond water and sediment upstream. The ponded water and sediment once formed the Great Marsh, which covered somewhere between 162,000 and 405,000 hectares. Water a few tens of centimeters to more than a meter deep extended between 5 and 8 kilometers on either side of the river for much of the year. Joel Greenberg's 2002 history of the Chicago area includes a nice description from Charles Bartlett's 1907 book, *Tales of Kankakee Land:* "The river has been a mere thread of silver meandering through the sloughs, lily beds, and the [wild] rice; now trending over to the ancient bank on the right and now wandering far off to the left; here creeping around and between the members of a group of islands, and then quite losing itself in ten thousand acres of rushes and reeds."[37]

Floodplain forests of silver maple, black ash, white ash, American elm, black birch, yellow birch, bur oak, swamp white oak, and sycamore lined the river. Islands within the channel bristled with groves of beech, white oak, black oak, butternut, black walnut, sassafras, red maple, wild cherry, and pawpaw, in addition to the floodplain species. Francis Ling reminisced that "the greatest thrill of a squirrel hunt was that the whole area seemed to be alive with wild creatures . . . This area of from ten to fifteen acres seemed to be completely roofed over by the spreading tops and branches of the big beeches . . . When the squirrels were working on the beech nuts, the dropping of shells and nuts sounded like heavy rain."[38]

Forests gave way to swamp, marsh, and lakes beyond the river. These diverse watery environments supported large populations of walleye (*Stizostedion vitreum*), bullheads (*Ictalurus* spp.), buffalo fish (*Ictiobus* spp.), pickerel (*Esox americanus*), catfish (*Ictalurus* spp.), bluegill (*Lepomis macrochirus*), and crappies (*Pomoxis* spp.). Again, Francis Ling: "We never put 'if' in the fish-catching game. It was a mighty rare occasion that we didn't get all the fish we wanted." Sharing the wetlands with the fish were diverse birds, including green-winged teal, mallards, Canada geese, trumpeter swans (*Cygnus buccinators*), and wood ducks (*Aix sponsa*). Greenberg noted that the first hunters of European descent to reach the area measured birds by the acre rather than by individuals, and at times most of the floodplain lakes, such as 15,000-hectare Beaver Lake, were covered. Ling wrote:

During the migration season ducks, geese, brant and cranes were on the Kankakee area by the thousands and there were all varieties, from canvas backs to fish ducks. Canada geese . . . rested on the marsh by the thousands . . . Sandhill cranes were plentiful . . . At different places in the swamp the cranes had what we called "crane towns." Hundreds of them would meet in one locality . . . Many times I have seen as many as four or five nests in one tree. The largest town . . . was estimated to have 1,000 cranes and, believe me, there was some music when the young were in the nest! Thousands of jack snipe, sand snipe, plover and other shore birds lined the marsh shores and upland ponds.[39]

Although Ling incorrectly identifies cranes (which do not nest in trees), the abundance reflected in this description is likely accurate.

Trappers removed tens of thousands of pelts of mink, muskrats, otter, and other fur bearers from the marsh each year well into the nineteenth century. As Charles Eifrig wrote in 1918, "Such is the wonderfully rich and interesting life of the marsh. There, life is fairly piled up, flora and fauna display themselves more lavishly than in most places on dry land." For overwhelming abundance, however, it is difficult to top the numbers of passenger pigeons (*Ectopistes migratorius*), which nested in large numbers along the Kankakee River. The phrase *large numbers* barely describes a bird whose mass migrations darkened the skies and lasted for hours as flocks conservatively estimated at 2 to 3 *billion* birds passed through a region. The story of how nineteenth-century hunting frenzies and loss of habitat drove the birds to extinction has been told repeatedly.[40]

Potawatomi seasonally inhabited the Great Marsh and used it for winter hunting until forced out by federal treaties during the 1830s, when the "swampers"—Kankakee lumbermen—moved in to cut the trees, followed by farmers who eventually drained the marsh and eliminated it by 1917. The most evocative memorial to the wetlands of the region is Gene Stratton Porter's novel *A Girl of the Limberlost*, set in a large swamp south of the Great Marsh.[41]

Sedge meadows—another type of wetland formed on soils that were saturated but not submerged—took their characteristically hummocky surface from tussock sedge (*Carex stricta*), which grows in clumps a few tens of centimeters in height spaced up to a meter apart. Also growing in the sedge meadows were spike rush (*Eleocharis compressa*), river bulrush (*Scirpus fluviatilis*), and other sedge and rush species. Bogs formed in depressions that ponded melt water from abandoned ice where sphagnum moss (*Sphagnum* spp.) created and maintained acidity. Diverse plant communities of cattail marsh, tall-shrub bog, tamaracks, and low shrubs ringed the bull's-eye of each bog, and vegetative oddities such as the carnivorous round-leaved sundew (*Drosera rotundifolia*) and pitcher plant (*Sarracenia purpurea*)

Floodplain forest near Henry along the Illinois River, 2008. Note the abundant wood in the foreground that was transported by floodwaters.

consumed insects to supplement their nitrogen-deficient diet. Groundwater that moved through soils rich in calcium before returning to the surface formed fens that shared many species of grasses, sedges, and herbaceous plants with sedge meadows and wet prairie. Forested wetlands occupied swamps.[42]

Most people have an almost innate antipathy to wetlands as sources of pestilence—poisonous gases or disease-carrying mosquitoes—at worst or as "waste" land too wet for growing crops or building cities at best. Ecologists who appreciate the biological abundance and diversity of swamps, and hydrologists who appreciate their capacity to filter, cleanse, and store water, have traveled a long and arduous intellectual route in documenting the importance and usefulness of wetlands and in trying to raise public awareness of and appreciation for these lands whose very names have negative connotations: getting "bogged down" or "swamped" typically does not refer to a positive experience. The extent and diversity of wetlands in the Illinois River basin were crucial to support the biological abundance that so amazed and delighted early European visitors, but the first people of European descent systematically drained and destroyed the wetlands as fast as they could.

A COUNTRY "AS PLEASANT AS FRUITFUL"[43]

Floodplains, wetlands, and uplands supported such a wide variety of plants in part because of the many different types of soils, moisture levels, and soil and water chemistry in these environments. First the glaciers, then the rivers created diversity in the landscape. Uplands included well-drained slopes but also small glacial kettles (often termed buffalo wallows or prairie potholes) that held water at least seasonally. River bottoms included main rivers, as well as sloughs and side channels. Beyond the channels stretched floodplains where the seasonal flood pulse each spring inundated the bottomlands with water, sediment, and nutrients, then withdrew to late summer low flow. For plants that can only germinate and survive under specific conditions of soil moisture and inundation, the banks along each river channel and the floodplain beyond are as rigidly zoned as an exclusive neighborhood. Next to the channel is the natural levee, where the coarsest sediment suspended in the river water settles out as floodwaters begin to overtop the banks. Beyond this levee, which may be composed of sand and even gravel, lie the silt and clay carried farther from the main channel by overbank floods. The coarser soils of the levee drain relatively rapidly, whereas the finer soils elsewhere on the floodplain can retain water for long periods. Places where erosive floodwaters breach the levee allow rapid flow to carry coarser sediment onto the floodplain, creating small patches of sand or gravel among the silt and clay soils. When the entire river shifts sideways or cuts off a meander bend, depressions that can become floodplain lakes are left behind. These depressions slowly fill with silt and clay, but the presence of standing water throughout the year creates a different environment for plants than do the slightly drier silt and clay soils of the adjacent floodplain meadows.

The key to plant and animal diversity is diverse habitats, and the key to habitat diversity is a dynamic landscape in which fire, drought, flood, and—most of all—rivers large and small remove the existing plants and animals yet simultaneously create opportunities for new plants and animals to move in. This is the recipe for a rich landscape: (1) continental-size sheets of glacial ice that deposit sediment as they melt, release huge quantities of melt water that sculpt deep valleys, and create sufficient temperature contrasts along their margins to generate winds that carry fine sediment to the landscapes surrounding the ice sheet; (2) sufficient precipitation to nourish both continuous vegetation cover and a network of rivers; (3) a flat or gently rolling landscape on which weathering can develop soils not regularly stripped by debris flows or landslides and across which floods can spread fertilizing layers of fine sediment and organic matter; (4) cold winters that temporarily limit plant growth, allowing nutrients to gradually accumulate in the soil rather than being stored solely in the tissues of living organisms, as in the tropics; (5) an essentially north-south orientation to the river network, facilitating migration up and downstream by fish, plant, and other species as the great ice sheets waxed and waned, as well as seasonal migrations by fish, birds, and other animals under contemporary climatic conditions. Mix all five characteristics, and you have the Illinois and other river basins of the eastern prairie. The river's landscape setting critically influences the characteristics of riverine abundance and diversity, as Stephen Forbes and Robert Richardson recognized in 1919: "A river and its plankton are a flowing soil and its crop, both slipping away continuously, but both renewed constantly from an exhaustless source of supply. The fertility of the flowing water at any time is not dependent on the fertility of that which has preceded it, but on materials of fertility brought into it from the watershed."[44]

HEARTBEAT OF AN ECOSYSTEM

As on rivers around the world with extensive floodplains, the seasonal flood pulse historically set the rhythm for the entire riverine community in the Illinois drainage basin. Many species of fish, including basses and sunfishes (Family *Centrarchidae*), used the newly flooded bottomlands for spawning and nursery habitats. Because the backwater lakes along the Illinois had soft, silty bottoms that did not provide material for fish that build nests for their eggs, spawning bass and other species used the spring floods to reach inundated terrestrial plants and previously dry, compacted ground on the floodplain that provided better nesting sites. Later in the season, as declining water levels forced young fish to concentrate into remaining channels and shrinking lakes, larger fish, great blue herons (*Ardea herodias*), great egrets (*Casmerodius albus*), and other predators found well-stocked larders. Fish including bowfin (*Amia calva*) persisted in the sloughs and lakes even as levels of dissolved oxygen declined, thanks to special air bladders that allowed them to surface and gulp air directly from the atmosphere.[45]

As the floodwaters receded and the soils drained, exposed mud flats provided germination sites for moist-soil plants such as millets (*Echinochloa* spp.), nutgrass (*Cyperus strigosus*), rice cutgrass (*Leersia oryzoides*), and decurrent false aster (*Boltonia decurrens*) that could grow to maturity before the next flood. The roots of these plants helped to stabilize the newly deposited sediment and limit turbidity of the water. Seeds and tubers provided food for waterfowl during their fall and spring migrations: the valley of the Illinois River is part of the Mississippi Flyway, migratory corridor for a substantial portion of North America's shorebirds and waterfowl. Beaver (*Castor canadensis*) and muskrat (*Ondatra zibethicus*) also ate the plant tubers and rhizomes. When the floodwaters rose again the next spring, the

Floodplain wetlands at Spring Lake State Park, between Pekin and Havana along the Illinois River, 2008. The stand of forest at the rear of the view borders the main channel. This summer view includes a non-native mute swan (Cygnus olor), although other, native species of swan are present at other times of the year.

dead stems of these plants, which were mostly annual grasses and forbs, provided cover for fish spawning in the shallows and substrate for invertebrates—some of which helped recycle the dead organic matter into the river food web.[46]

The biologically rich communities of the floodplains formed along equally rich aquatic communities in the channels of the Illinois River drainage basin. Like other portions of the Mississippi River drainage, the Illinois basin is particularly endowed with mussels. Surveys conducted along the nearly 400 river kilometers downstream from the confluence of the Des Plaines and Kankakee Rivers between 1870 and 1900 found thirty-eight species of mussels, and forty-seven species are present in various portions of the drainage with diverse habitats. Some of these species have wonderfully evocative common names: creek heelsplitter (*Lasmigona compressa*), slippershell (*Alasmidonta viridis*), elktoe (*A. marginata*), snuffbox (*Epioblasma triquetra*), purple wartyback (*Cyclonaias tuberculata*), fingernail clam (*Musculium transversum*), fragile papershell (*Leptodea fragilis*), and Wabash pigtoe

(*Lasmigona complanata*). These little animals cleanse the river ecosystem, filtering organic matter from water and converting this "muck" into clam tissue that feeds fish and waterfowl.[47]

Mussels of the family Unionidae live around the world, but North America is their heartland for abundance and diversity. The 297 species of unionid mussels in North American waters not only process organic matter but also mix streambed sediments and, where they concentrate in large numbers along the streambed, provide a firm substrate for other organisms. Individual unionid mussels can live as long as a century.[48]

A mussel's life starts when it is expelled as a larva from an adult female mussel. The larva remains suspended in the stream flow for up to five days, during which time it must find a host fish to parasitize, or else the larva dies. Larvae remain attached to fish for approximately twenty-five days while the larvae develop their own organs. Once this stage is complete, larvae detach and settle to the streambed. If the habitat is suitable and the larvae survive, they become adults capable of reproducing after five years, and they usually live thirty to forty years or more. Suitable habitat for many species is water between 0.6 and 2.0 meters deep, with mean velocity in the range of 0.1–0.7 meters per second and a substrate of sand or gravel rather than clay, silt, or boulders. These conditions are most commonly present along small streams and along the margins of larger channels.[49]

Portions of the river that provide suitable habitat can be widely dispersed, and unionid mussels tend to be distributed patchily along a stream, with most individuals congregated in groups called mussel beds. Within these beds, each mussel lives partially or completely buried in the sediment. The exposed portion of the mussel's shell is likely to be encrusted with tiny plants and animals, including algae, protozoans, and larval aquatic insects such as caddisflies. One study of a mussel bed in the Upper Mississippi River found fifty-three species of invertebrates using the hard shells of mussels as a platform for their own activities. As Jonathan Swift wrote in 1733:

So, Nat'ralists observe, a Flea
Hath smaller Fleas that on him prey,
And these have smaller Fleas to bite 'em,
And so proceed ad infinitum.[50]

Sharing the stream bottom with mussels and their "smaller fleas" were numerous other species of aquatic insects. Ecologists subdivide these insects into groups based on what each species eats. The two primary sources of energy in any river system are either photosynthetic plants or organic matter in the form of leaves, twigs, and decaying wood dropped in from the adjacent riparian canopy or carried by the flow from upstream. Stream insects that eat stationary living plants are grazers. Stationary plants can be microscopic algae attached to the streambed or rooted vascular plants, such as cattails or water lilies. Insects that physically break down and then consume dead organic matter from the streambed are shredders; those that consume smaller dead organic matter are collectors. Filter feeders extend delicate net-like appendages into the flow and extract anything nourishing that is floating by, including bits of organic matter or smaller organisms such as microscopic algae floating in the water (phytoplankton) and their predators, zoo-plankton. Stream insects that eat other insects are predators.

A point of stability can be important in a rapidly changing world. Silt and sand formed the streambed through much of the Illinois River drainage network, with wood providing the only hard substrate beyond the mussel beds. Filter-feeding caddisflies (*Potamyia, Hydropsyche, Cyrnellus* spp.) preferred the relative stability of wood and mussel beds, as did some species of oligochaetes and midges. Caddisflies are like tiny fishermen setting nets, for they spin silk—a protein fiber produced by drawing a viscous liquid through a fine orifice—from which they create nets and safety lines. Although not as strong as spider silk, nets of caddisfly silk strung over crevices between rocks and logs are sufficiently durable to trap bits of plant detritus, periphyton, and microorganisms streaming by with the current. The silk is also strong enough for caddisflies to use as a safety line in current swift enough to tumble them head over abdomen: caddisflies spin a line of silk, anchor it to a rock at one end, and use it to rappel between rocks. Other species such as Nearctic alderflies (*Sialis* spp.) could be found burrowing through the mud and plant detritus near the channel shore and in the finer sediment of the main channel. Mayfly species characteristic of large rivers (*Stenonema, Stenacron, Caenis, Hexagenia* spp.) lived in the lower Illinois, reflecting the transition from narrow, shaded headwater streams to swift, deep river with enough exposed surface to support larger plants rooted in the streambed sediment. Diverse habitats throughout the Illinois River basin supported an equally diverse aquatic insect fauna.[51]

Feeding on the insects, as well as on aquatic vegetation and on each other, was a wide array of fish species. At least 74 species were present in the upper Illinois and 131 species in the lower Illinois, for a total of 140 species from 27 families in the river as a whole. The lower river's fish fauna was dominated by species of Cyprini-dae (carps, minnows), Catostomidae (suckers), Centrarchidae (bass, sunfish), and Percidae (darters, perches). Many of these fish were both abundant and large. Henri de Tonti wrote of catfish large enough to feed twenty-two men, and the fish fauna included other such large-bodied species as sturgeon and paddlefish.[52]

Some of the headwater streams began as intermittent channels where rainwa-ter running off the surface collected sufficient depth and power to begin to cut down into the soil. Black fly larvae (*Simulium* spp.) lived in the smallest trickles and, as the flow grew larger downstream, shared the little channel with mayfly nymphs. As the stream grew large enough to develop pools, caddisflies joined the black flies and mayflies, as did snails. Crayfishes such as *Procambarus gracilis* burrowed into the streambed during summer dry spells. As the pools became permanent downstream, the fauna diversified. Aquatic insects included water striders, back swimmers, and water boatmen, as well as dragonfly nymphs and beetles. Fish including horned dace (*Semotilus corporalis*) appeared, then blacknose dace (*Rhinichthys atratulus*) and southern redbelly dace (*Phoxinus erythrogaster*), followed downstream by johnny darter (*Etheostoma nigrum*), common sucker (*Catostomus commersonii*), and bluntnose minnows (*Pimephales notatus*).[53]

Other headwaters rose from springs. Although the flow was more consistent in these streams, the water commonly had insufficient dissolved oxygen to support animals, as well as levels of nitrogen and carbon dioxide too high for comfort. As water chemistry changed downstream, however, amphipods (*Gammarus* spp.), black fly larvae, beetles, dragonfly nymphs, mayflies, crayfish, and other invertebrates were able to take up residence, as on the intermittent streams. As the streams grew in size, fish such as banded darter (*Etheostoma zonale*), fantail darter (*E. flabellare*), and rainbow darter (*E. coeruleum*) appeared. Pioneering aquatic ecologist Stephen Forbes was a great fan of darters. In an 1880 article titled "The Food of Fishes" he wrote: "What the humming-birds are in our avifauna, the 'darters' are among our fresh-water fishes. Minute, agile, beautiful, delighting in the clear, swift waters of rocky streams . . . Notwithstanding their trivial size, they do not seem to be dwarfed so much as concentrated fishes—each carrying in its little body all the activity, spirit, grace, complexity of detail and perfection of finish." Forbes waxed particularly poetic about the rainbow darter, describing them as the "mountaineers among fishes. Forced from the populous and fertile valleys of the river beds and lake bottoms, they have taken refuge from their enemies in the rocky highlands where the free waters play in ceaseless torrents."[54]

Creek chub (*Semotilus atromaculatus*) also lived in small streams. The diminutive creek chub, which are typically between 10 and 30 centimeters long, take outsize measures to protect their eggs. While spawning, the fish excavate a trench and then build a ridge of gravel that can be more than a meter long and 30 centimeters wide over the trench. The eggs are interspersed among the gravel and thus protected from predators as well as smothering by finer sediment: developing fish embryos need the oxygen dissolved in flowing water, and silt and clay covering the eggs can block access to that oxygen.[55]

As flow increased downstream, alternating pools and riffles developed along the channel. In the pools lived rock bass (*Ambloplites rupestris*), smallmouth bass

(*Micropterus dolomieu*), sunfishes (*Lepomis* spp.), and yellow perch (*Perca flavescens*). Along the pool margins, beneath the roots of willows and other streamside plants exposed along the stream banks, lived several species of mussels. In the riffles, hornyhead chub (*Nocomis biguttatus*) alternately spawned and built nests of pebbles like the creek chub, creating piles of gravel that other fish such as red shiners (*Cyprinella lutrensis*), blacknose dace, and central stonerollers (*Campostoma anomalum*) also used as places to lay their eggs. The unusual combination of clear water, anchored plants, and soft streambeds of sand or mud in some headwater streams could support populations of brassy minnow; but, as in the western prairie rivers, this species has declined substantially during the past century.[56]

The brassy minnow in Illinois is the same species as that present in the Arikaree River, which actually creates challenges to conserving the fish. Brassy minnows occur across a broad geographic area, but widely dispersed populations are so different as to almost constitute different subspecies. Brassy minnows in the Illinois basin do not need to withstand the high water temperatures, low dissolved oxygen, and lack of river-long migration corridors that challenge brassy minnows in the western prairie streams. However, the existence of brassy minnows in the Illinois and other eastern prairie rivers prevents the species from being federally listed as an endangered species, thus limiting a potentially powerful legal tool for habitat protection.[57]

In the larger rivers of the Illinois drainage, gizzard shad (*Dorosoma cepedianum*), emerald shiners (*Notropis atherinoides*), and freshwater drum (*Aplodinotus grunniens*) were found in near-shore areas of the main channel. Shad are deep-bellied fish that grow to nearly 40 centimeters in length. Shad are nocturnal and prefer soft-bottomed portions of the river, where they eat anything very small: they are filter feeders that ingest bottom sediment and detritus, then use their 190 gill rakers to filter the water and sediment. Shad eat phytoplankton, zooplankton, and bits of organic matter. Sand grains that get through the filtering process help the shad digest food in their muscular gizzard. In 1888 Stephen Forbes dissected this remarkable fish and found that their diet included distillery slops. During their lifespan of up to six years, shad are mostly not nomadic. They are eaten by catfish and striped bass, but humans tend to regard them as "trash fish."[58]

Emerald shiners are well-named: streamlined, silvery-green fish that grow to only 12 centimeters in length during a life three to five years long. Moving about in schools, the little fish eat zooplankton, shifting toward the surface with their food source at dusk and then back down into deeper waters at dawn.[59]

Like shad, freshwater drum spend most of their time near the streambed, where they eat insect larvae, crayfish, bivalve mussels, and small fish. Drum are high-backed fish that can grow up to 45 centimeters in length and reach weights of nearly 25 kilograms during their thirteen-year lifespan. Their species name *grunniens* derives from the Latin for grunting. Male drum have a swim bladder able to produce sound when a special set of muscles in the body cavity vibrates against the swim bladder. Drum are also notable for their large otoliths, a bony structure in the inner ear, which resemble ivory. Native Americans used drum otoliths for jewelry and currency.[60]

Bluegill (*Lepomis macrochirus*), largemouth bass (*Micropterus salmoides*), smallmouth buffalo (*Ictiobus bubalus*), and mosquitofish (*Gambusia affinis*) used backwater habitats. Bluegills, so called because of the blue or black spot behind their gills, are the 20–40-centimeter-long gamefish beloved by juvenile anglers everywhere. These tough, widespread little fish like deep weed beds, where they feed on snails, small crayfish, insects, worms, and smaller fish. During a long spawning season that extends from spring through fall, bluegills construct nests in streambed gravel where the water is 30–60 centimeters deep, and the males then guard the nests until the eggs hatch and the fry leave.[61]

Bass is typically the fish of choice for adult anglers, a top aquatic predator and gamefish that has been introduced all over the world and caused endless trouble in other aquatic ecosystems. These olive green fish with a jagged black horizontal stripe along each flank can grow up to 40 centimeters long if male, 56 centimeters if female. They average a kilogram in weight but can grow up to 10 kilograms and put up a serious fight when hooked. In their native waters, bass typically spend the morning moving about in waters deeper than about 2.5 meters, then enjoy an afternoon siesta near a large structure, such as a big submerged log. The fish have a small home range, and their movements correspond to the movements of their prey species.[62]

Of all the species that use the backwaters, smallmouth buffalo fish are in some ways the most unique, a stalwart of the Illinois drainage that formed the bulk of early commercial fisheries. Buffalo fish are light brown in color, with a greenish tint and a hump behind the head that gave rise to their common name. Like whales, they grow large bodies from small food; these bottom feeders that eat insect larvae, zooplankton, attached algae, and organic detritus can grow to be more than a meter long and as much as 37 kilograms in weight. Buffalo fish can also feed on shellfish by grinding the shells using bony plates in their throat. Adults like abundant aquatic vegetation and a silty bottom, although they spawn over gravel patches. When the eggs hatch after one to two weeks, the benthic larvae hide beneath stones until they grow large enough to protect themselves. As with most other fish species, spawning is driven by water temperature.[63]

Similar to bass, mosquitofish have been widely introduced and caused a great deal of disruption in other aquatic ecosystems. The common name for these fish derives from their useful habit of eating the aquatic larval and pupal stages of mosquitoes, along with other small insects, zooplankton, and bits of organic material. Their fondness for mosquitoes has been the primary motivation behind their introduction to watersheds outside of their natural range in waters that drain to the Gulf of Mexico. Unfortunately, mosquitofish are aggressive and no more effective than native fish elsewhere at eating mosquitoes. They now have the dubious distinction of being nominated as one of the world's 100 worst invaders. Similar to other successful invaders, mosquitofish are adaptable (able to withstand low levels of dissolved oxygen and high temperatures), fast growing (sexually mature in six to eight weeks), and prolific (females bear multiple batches of live young each year). In the Illinois watershed, these silvery little fish grow to be only 7 centimeters long if female and 4 centimeters long if male, and they are commonly eaten by herons. Mosquitofish prefer vegetated habitats and, if they escape the herons, can live as long as three years.[64]

Historically, fish living in the Illinois River system had many habitat choices. Deep pools floored with clay alternated downstream with shallow, sandy riffles. Broad lowlands that flooded seasonally bordered the rivers, as did abandoned channel fragments that formed lakes and wetlands with water year-round. Sunwarmed waters were not far from shaded reaches beneath overhanging wooded banks that dropped logs into the channel. Channel margins held beds of reeds and aquatic plants, among which small-bodied or young fish could take refuge from predators. Food floated into eddies at meander bends, and fish could rest in the slower currents while waiting for dinner to arrive. Although the swifter current of the deep main channel required a greater expenditure of energy from fish, many species used the main channel for feeding and traveling to other habitats. Some large fish such as shovelnose sturgeon (*Scaphirhynchus platorhynchus*) were persistent residents of the main channel, whereas others such as freshwater drum spent most of their time in the main channel but sought shelter in the warmer backwaters during winter.[65]

Recent biological collections indicate that at least nine species of frogs, six species of turtles, seven species of salamanders, and two species of snakes were also present along riverine corridors in the Upper Illinois River basin. Blanding's turtles (*Emydoidea blandingi*) spent most of their time in wet habitats along the river bottoms, then moved to well-drained uplands for summer nesting. Spotted turtles (*Clemmys guttata*) along the lower Des Plaines River valley like cooler temperatures than other turtles do and spent most of the summer under the shade of dense vegetation. Snapping turtles (*Chelydra serpentina*), active predator of everything from mammals to crayfish to earthworms, prefer water deeper than about a meter and, along with spiny softshell turtles (*Apalone spinifera*), were hunted for their meat during the nineteenth and early twentieth centuries. Some of these species have declined to dangerously low population levels, such as the Illinois chorus frog (*Pseudacris streckeri*), which is listed as a state threatened species.[66]

This was the "riverscape" that struck a visitor from intensively settled Europe as being so rich. The abundance of the land glows throughout Father Hennepin's 1679 account in passages such as these:

> Many other kinds of animals are found in these vast plains of Louisiana . . . The fishery is very abundant, and the fertility of the soil is extraordinary. There are boundless prairies interspersed with forests of tall trees . . . of prodigious girth and height . . . The air there is very temperate and healthy, the country is watered by countless lakes, rivers and streams, most of which are navigable.[67]

> The river Seignelay [Illinois] on which we were sailing, is as deep and broad as the Seine at Paris, and in two or three places widens out to a quarter of a league. It is skirted by hills, whose sides are covered with fine large trees. Some of these hills are [a] half a league apart, leaving between them a marshy strip, often inundated, especially in the autumn and spring, but producing, nevertheless, very large trees. On ascending these hills, you discover prairies further than the eye can reach, studded, at intervals, with groves of tall trees . . . The current of the river is not perceptible, except in time of great rains.[68]

Historical records clearly reflect an abundance of life to match the exuberance of the floods that regularly spread across thousands of hectares of bottomlands in the Illinois River basin. The landscape and the atmosphere above it supported endless cycling. The Upper Mississippi River and its tributaries such as the Illinois flowed continually east and south, the powerful veins of the eastern prairie. Waters that emptied into the Gulf of Mexico returned as vapor traveling inland with air masses that dropped rain and snow over the prairie. Fish traveled up- and downstream and between the rivers and the adjacent floodplains, and migratory waterfowl and other birds in the millions moved between the seasonal bounties of northerly summer nesting grounds and southerly wintering areas. These great migrations had the regularity of breathing, their rhythm set by the seasons of warmth and cold and flooding and low flows.

The rhythmic ebb and flow of river waters across adjacent bottomlands is so important to the health of big floodplain rivers that ecologists have formally described the role of seasonal floods in the flood-pulse concept. First formulated by ecologist Wolfgang Junk based on his work along the Amazon River, the flood-pulse concept articulates the role of floods that inundate at least a portion of the floodplain each year. These floods provide large extents of clear, shallow water across the floodplain in which floating algae and rooted plants can photosynthe-size and provide food for a wide variety of animals. Shallowly flooded lands cre-ate fish nursery habitat and feeding areas. The shifting zone of shallow water crosses a floodplain that may be much larger than the area of permanent flowing or standing water associated with the channel. A flush of plant growth follows the shallow water during the rising limb of the flood as nutrients are deposited across the floodplain. Growth gives way to decay under the deeper, turbid water of max-imum flooding, and the receding floodwater carries back to the river nutrients released by the decay. The shifting front between terrestrial and aquatic habitats creates spatial patterns of plant species adapted to seasonally fluctuating water depth, nutrients, and sunlight. Ecologists have documented that rivers have more diverse riparian forests and greater abundances of diverse species of fish when a natural, predictable flood pulse occurs along them.[69]

Robert Richardson recognized the importance of floods and floodplain wet-lands along the Illinois early in the twentieth century, writing in 1921: "In our opin-ion and that of the most intelligent and observant fishermen, the lakes are the favorite feeding grounds of the larger and more common fishes, and this opinion is supported by the fact that . . . the heaviest fish-yields come from sections where the ratio of lake areas to river is greatest."[70]

A HISTORIC SNAPSHOT: THE ILLINOIS RIVER CIRCA 1800

By 1800, the changes in population and land use that fed on this rich landscape and that would soon accelerate were already starting. Native American popula-tions were declining, as was their use of fire in the uplands. A few people of Euro-pean descent lived in small agricultural towns. Fur trappers had removed beaver and other animals from the bottomlands, but by and large the riverscape was similar to that described by Marquette.

A large river of clear water flowed over a sandy bed, with abundant wood in the channel and diverse habitat that supported large numbers of insects, mus-sels, fish, and other aquatic organisms. The variety and abundance of river habitat increased from the headwaters downstream. Insects were particularly abundant where dense aquatic vegetation provided food and shelter from predators. The density of aquatic insects living on the streambed was greatest from autumn through spring, then declined when the winged adults emerged from the river in late spring. Fish living in shallow portions of the river ate mainly insects; fish liv-ing in deep, stable pools ate insects and other fish. Fish migrated primarily during spring and autumn as flow levels and food availability changed. Young fish lived mainly in shallow waters of the floodplain, in secondary channels or headwater streams, and along riffles. These fish grew the most during summer, many of them feeding on the abundant zookplankton.[71]

Mosaics of floodplain forest, wet meadows, ponds, and lakes covered the extensive valley bottoms. Each year's flood covered much of the bottomlands, allowing fish to move between the main channel and the floodplain, as did water, sediment, and nutrients. The variety of soils and flowing and standing water on the bottomlands supported a wide array of plants, from rooted and floating aquatic plants to open stands of trees. Aquatic turtles were common. Stinkpot turtles (*Sternothaerus odoratus*) probed streambeds for seeds, beetles, crayfish, and snails. Red-eared sliders (*Pseudemys scripta*) opportunistically ate just about anything they could catch in bottomland ponds. Common map turtles (*Graptemys geographica*) stacked atop one another to bask on well-placed logs, and smooth softshell turtles (*Trionyx muticus*) inhabited big rivers with sandy beds, where they could find insects, crayfish, and other invertebrate prey. Spring rains signaled Illinois chorus frogs (*Pseudacris streckeri illinoensis*) to emerge from their burrows and migrate to breeding pools. Northern cricket frogs (*Acris crepitans*) remained active along the margins of ponds, marshes, and streams even in very cold weather. Frogs were abundant in the lowlands: plains leopard frogs (*Rana blairi*), green frogs (*Rana clamitans*), and other frogs large and small shared the extensive shoreline habitat along rivers, lakes, marshes, and other wetlands. Small-mouthed (*Ambystoma texanum*) and blue-spotted salamanders (*Ambystoma laterale*) spent much of their time under fallen logs in the floodplain forests. Big tiger salamanders (*Ambystoma tigrinum*) emerged from their burrows at night, especially after rainy days, to feed on beetles and worms. Thousands of waterfowl and other animals used the river corridor year-round or seasonally. Most of the bottomlands were permanently or seasonally wet.[72]

Woodland songbirds—flycatchers, vireos (*Vireo* spp.), veery (*Catharus minimus*), wood thrush (*Hylocichla mustelina*), warblers, scarlet tanager (*Piranga olivacea*), rose-breasted grosbeak (*Pheuticus ludovicianus*), and others—flew up from the neo-tropics to breed and rear their young. Le Conte's sparrow (*Ammodramus leconteii*) and other sparrow species nested on the borders of marshes. Thousands of sandhill cranes (*Grus canadensis*) nested in the vicinity of Beaver Lake in the Kankakee's Great Marsh.

Land predators including gray wolf (*Canis lupus*), mountain lion (*Puma concolor*), lynx (*Lynx canadensis*), bobcat (*Lynx rufus*), fisher (*Martes pennant*), and marten (*Martes americana*) pursued prey that ranged from smoky shrew (*Sorex fumeus*) at the small end up through white-tailed jackrabbit (*Lepus townsendii*), snowshoe hare (*Lepus americanus*), pronghorn (*Antilocarpa americana*), white-tailed deer (*Odocoileus virginianus*), wapiti (*Cervus elephus*), and bison (*Bison bison*) at the large end.[73]

NOTES

1. J. Marquette, *Travels and Explorations of the Jesuit Missionaries in New France, 1610–1791,* ed. R. G. Thwaites (Cleveland: Burrows Brothers, 1898).

2. E. Steele, "A Summer Journey in the West," in *Of Prairie, Woods, and Water: Two Centuries of Chicago Nature Writing,* ed. J. Greenberg (New York: John Taylor, 1841 [1763]; Chicago: University of Chicago Press, 2008), 24.

3. L. Hennepin, *A Description of Louisiana* (New York: John G. Shea, 1880 [1683]), 140–42.

4. J. Gray, *The Illinois* (New York: Farrar and Rinehart, 1940); J. Greenberg, *A Natural History of the Chicago Region* (Chicago: University of Chicago Press, 2002).

5. J.-F.-X. Charlevoix, "Letters to the Dutchess [*sic*] of Lesdiguieres, London," in *Of Prairie, Woods, and Water: Two Centuries of Chicago Nature Writing,* ed. J. Greenberg (Chicago: University of Chicago Press, 2008 [1763]), 3–4.

6. E. W. Teale, *Journey into Summer* (New York: Dodd, Mead, 1960).

7. B. L. Rhoads and E. E. Herricks, "Naturalization of Headwater Streams in Illinois: Challenges and Possibilities," in *River Channel Restoration: Guiding Principles for Sustainable Projects,* ed. A. Brookes and F. D. Shields (Chichester: John Wiley and Sons, 1996), 331–67.

8. M. D. DeLong, "Upper Mississippi River Basin," in *Rivers of North America,* ed. A. C. Benke and C. E. Cushing (Amsterdam: Elsevier Academic Press, 2005), 326–67; J. R. Adams and E. Delisio, "Temporal and Lateral Distribution of Resuspended Sediment Following Barge Tow Passage on the Illinois River," *Long Term Resource Monitoring Program 93-R011* (Onalaska, WI: US Geological Survey Environmental Management Technical Center, 1993).

9. DeLong, "Upper Mississippi River Basin"; Adams and Delisio, "Temporal and Lateral Distribution"; Greenberg, *Natural History of the Chicago Region.*

10. S. A. Forbes, "The Biological Survey of a River System: Its Objects, Methods, and Results," *Bulletin, State of Illinois, Division of the Natural History Survey* 17, no. 7 (1928): 279; Teale, *Journey into Summer,* 74.

11. Rhoads and Herricks, "Naturalization of Headwater Streams in Illinois."

12. T. L. Arnold et al., "Environmental Setting of the Upper Illinois River Basin and Implications for Water Quality," *US Geological Survey* (USGS) *Water-Resources Investigations Report* 98-4268 (Urbana, IL: USGS, 1999); Greenberg, *Natural History of the Chicago Region*; K. L. Warner, "Water-Quality Assessment of the Lower Illinois River Basin: Environmental Setting," *US Geological Survey* (USGS) *Water-Resources Investigations Report* 97-4165 (Urbana, IL: USGS, 1998).

13. Arnold et al., "Environmental Setting of the Upper Illinois"; Greenberg, *Natural History of the Chicago Region*; Warner, "Water-Quality Assessment."

14. T. J. Blasing and D. Duvick, "Reconstruction of Precipitation History in North American Corn Belt using Tree Rings," *Nature* 307, no. 5947 (1984): 143–45.

15. C. Savage, *Prairie: A Natural History* (Vancouver: Greystone Books, 2004).

16. Ibid.

17. DeLong, "Upper Mississippi River Basin"; Greenberg, *Natural History of the Chicago Region*.

18. DeLong, "Upper Mississippi River Basin"; Greenberg, *Natural History of the Chicago Region*.

19. Arnold et al., "Environmental Setting of the Upper Illinois"; Greenberg, *Natural History of the Chicago Region*; Warner, "Water-Quality Assessment"; J. Greenberg, ed., *Of Prairie, Woods, and Water: Two Centuries of Chicago Nature Writing* (Chicago: University of Chicago Press, 2008 [1763]).

20. Arnold et al., "Environmental Setting of the Upper Illinois"; Warner, "Water-Quality Assessment."

21. DeLong, "Upper Mississippi River Basin"; Greenberg, *Natural History of the Chicago Region*; R. E. Sparks, "Need for Ecosystem Management of Large Rivers and Their Floodplains," *BioScience* 45, no. 3 (1995): 168–82.

22. Forbes, "Biological Survey of a River System," 279.

23. J. A. Clark, *Gleanings by the Way* (Philadelphia: Simon, 1842), 117.

24. Greenberg, *Natural History of the Chicago Region*; E. M. Steinauer and S. L. Collins, "Prairie Ecology: The Tallgrass Prairie," in *Prairie Conservation: Preserving North America's Most Endangered Ecosystem*, ed. F. B. Samson and F. L. Knopf (Washington, DC: Island, 1996), 39–52; M. T. Watts, *Reading the Landscape: An Adventure in Ecology* (New York: Macmillan, 1957).

25. Greenberg, *Natural History of the Chicago Region*; Steinauer and Collins, "Prairie Ecology"; Watts, *Reading the Landscape*.

26. Greenberg, *Natural History of the Chicago Region*; Steinauer and Collins, "Prairie Ecology"; Watts, *Reading the Landscape*.

27. W. Oliver, *Eight Months in Illinois; with Information to Emigrants* (Newcastle upon Tyne: William Andrew Mitchell, 1843), 27.

28. Savage, *Prairie*.

29. Steele, "Summer Journey in the West," 126.

30. I. L. Bird, *The Englishwoman in America* (London: John Murray, 1956), 139–40.

31. J. C. Nelson, A. Redmond, and R. E. Sparks, "Impacts of Settlement on Floodplain Vegetation at the Confluence of the Illinois and Mississippi Rivers," *Transactions of the Illinois State Academy of Science, Illinois State Academy of Science* 87, no. 3 (1994): 117–33.

32. Ibid.; DeLong, "Upper Mississippi River Basin"; Greenberg, *Natural History of the Chicago Region*.

33. Nelson, Redmond, and Sparks, "Impacts of Settlement"; DeLong, "Upper Mississippi River Basin"; Greenberg, *Natural History of the Chicago Region*.

34. Nelson, Redmond, and Sparks, "Impacts of Settlement"; DeLong, "Upper

Mississippi River Basin"; Greenberg, *Natural History of the Chicago Region.*

35. Nelson, Redmond, and Sparks, "Impacts of Settlement"; DeLong, "Upper Mississippi River Basin"; Greenberg, *Natural History of the Chicago Region.*

36. A. Vileisis, *Discovering the Unknown Landscape: A History of America's Wetlands* (Washington, DC: Island, 1997), 21; F. E. Ling, "The Kankakee in the Old Days," *Bulletin of the New York Zoological Society* 38, no. 6 (1935): 197–204, in Greenberg, *Of Prairie, Woods, and Water,* 84.

37. C. Bartlett, *Tales of Kankakee Land* (New York: Charles Scribner's, 1907), 1–2.

38. Ling, "The Kankakee in the Old Days," in Greenberg, *Of Prairie, Woods, and Water,* 84–85.

39. Greenberg, *Natural History of the Chicago Region;* Teale, *Journey into Summer;* Ling, "The Kankakee in the Old Days," in Greenberg, *Of Prairie, Woods, and Water,* 83 (first quote), 85 (second quote).

40. C. Eifrig, "A Day among the Waterfowl and Its Sequel," *Audubon Bulletin* (1918), in Greenberg, *Of Prairie, Woods, and Water,* 22; Bartlett, *Tales of Kankakee Land;* Greenberg, *Natural History of the Chicago Region.*

41. C. Eifrig, "A Day among the Waterfowl and Its Sequel," *Audubon Bulletin* (1918), in Greenberg, *Of Prairie, Woods, and Water,* 22; Bartlett, *Tales of Kankakee Land;* Greenberg, *Natural History of the Chicago Region.*

42. Greenberg, *Natural History of the Chicago Region.*

43. H. de Tonti, *Relation of Henri de Tonti Concerning the Explorations of LaSalle from 1678 to 1683,* trans. M. Anderson (Chicago: Caxton Club, 1898 [1680]).

44. S. A. Forbes and R. E. Richardson, "Some Recent Changes in Illinois River Biology," *Illinois Natural History Survey Bulletin* 13, no. 6 (1919): 147.

45. C. Ahn, D. C. White, and R. E. Sparks, "Moist-Soil Plants as Ecohydrologic Indicators for Recovering the Flood Pulse in the Illinois River," *Restoration Ecology* 12, no. 2 (2004): 207–13; C. Ahn et al., "Analysis of Naturalization Alternatives for the Recovery of Moist-Soil Plants in the Floodplain of the Illinois River," *Hydrobiologia* 565, no. 1 (2006): 217–28; P. T. Raibley et al., "Largemouth Bass Size Distributions under Varying Annual Hydrological Regimes in the Illinois River," *Transactions of the American Fisheries Society* 126, no. 5 (1997): 850–56.

46. Ahn, White, and Sparks, "Moist-Soil Plants"; Ahn et al., "Analysis of Naturalization Alternatives."

47. DeLong, "Upper Mississippi River Basin"; R. E. Sparks and F. S. Dillon, "Illinois River Fingernail Clam Toxicity Study," *Illinois Natural History Survey,* Aquatic Ecology-TR-93/5 (Springfield: State of Illinois, 1998).

48. Y. Morales et al., "Effects of Substrate and Hydrodynamic Conditions on the Formation of Mussel Beds in a Large River," *Journal of the North American Benthological Society* 25, no. 3 (2006): 664–76; D. C. Beckett et al., "Epizoic Invertebrate Communities on Upper

Mississippi River Unionid Bivalves," *American Midland Naturalist* 135, no. 1 (1996): 102–14.

49. Morales et al., "Effects of Substrate and Hydrodynamic Conditions"; Beckett et al., "Epizoic Invertebrate Communities."

50. Morales et al., "Effects of Substrate and Hydrodynamic Conditions"; Beckett et al., "Epizoic Invertebrate Communities"; J. Swift, *Poems II,* 2nd ed. (Oxford: H. Williams, 1958 [1733]), 651.

51. DeLong, "Upper Mississippi River Basin"; J. M. Dettmers et al., "Life in the Fast Lane: Fish and Foodweb Structures in the Main Channel of Large Rivers," *Journal of the North American Benthological Society* 20, no. 2 (2001): 255–65; J. M. Dettmers et al., "Patterns in Abundance of Fishes in Main Channels of the Upper Mississippi River System," *Canadian Journal of Fisheries and Aquatic Sciences* 58, no. 5 (2001): 933–42; I. J. Schlosser, "Fish Community Structure and Function along Two Habitat Gradients in a Headwater Stream," *Ecological Monographs* 52, no. 4 (1982): 395–414; Greenberg, *Natural History of the Chicago Region*; S. A. Forbes, "On the General and Interior Distribution of Illinois Fishes," *Bulletin of the Illinois State Laboratory of Natural History* 8, no. 36 (1909): 381–437; S. A. Forbes, "Studies of the Food of Fresh-Water Fishes," *Illinois State Laboratory of Natural History Bulletin* 2, no. 7 (1988): 433–73; S. A. Forbes, "On the Food Relations of Fresh-Water Fishes: A Summary and Discussion, *Illinois State Laboratory of Natural History Bulletin* 2, no. 8 (1988): 475–538.

52. DeLong, "Upper Mississippi River Basin"; Dettmers et al., "Life in the Fast Lane"; Dettmers et al., "Patterns in Abundance of Fishes"; Schlosser, "Fish Community Structure and Function"; Greenberg, *Natural History of the Chicago Region*; Forbes, "Studies of the Food of Fresh-Water Fishes"; Forbes, "On the Food Relations of Fresh-Water Fishes"; Forbes, "On the General and Interior Distribution"; de Tonti, *Relation of Henri de Tonti,* 109.

53. V. Shelford, *Animal Communities in Temperate North America* (Chicago: University of Chicago Press, 1913), in Greenberg, *Of Prairie, Woods, and Water,* 316–22; L. M. Page, "The Crayfishes and Shrimps (Decapoda) of Illinois," *Illinois Natural History Survey Bulletin* 33, no. 4 (1985): 335–448.

54. S. A. Forbes, "The Food of Fishes," *Illinois State Laboratory of Natural History Bulletin* 3, no. 2 (1880): 22 (quotes).

55. DeLong, "Upper Mississippi River Basin"; Dettmers et al., "Life in the Fast Lane"; Dettmers et al., "Patterns in Abundance of Fishes"; Schlosser, "Fish Community Structure and Function"; Greenberg, *Natural History of the Chicago Region*.

56. DeLong, "Upper Mississippi River Basin"; Dettmers et al., "Life in the Fast Lane"; Dettmers et al., "Patterns in Abundance of Fishes"; Schlosser, "Fish Community Structure and Function"; Greenberg, *Natural History of the Chicago Region*; Shelford, *Animal Communities*.

57. Kurt Fausch, fish biologist, Colorado State University, Fort Collins, personal

communication, September 2010.

58. DeLong, "Upper Mississippi River Basin"; Dettmers et al., "Life in the Fast Lane"; Dettmers et al., "Patterns in Abundance of Fishes"; Schlosser, "Fish Community Structure and Function"; Greenberg, *Natural History of the Chicago Region*.

59. DeLong, "Upper Mississippi River Basin"; Dettmers et al., "Life in the Fast Lane"; Dettmers et al., "Patterns in Abundance of Fishes"; Schlosser, "Fish Community Structure and Function"; Greenberg, *Natural History of the Chicago Region*.

60. DeLong, "Upper Mississippi River Basin"; Dettmers et al., "Life in the Fast Lane"; Dettmers et al., "Patterns in Abundance of Fishes"; Schlosser, "Fish Community Structure and Function"; Greenberg, *Natural History of the Chicago Region*.

61. DeLong, "Upper Mississippi River Basin"; Dettmers et al., "Life in the Fast Lane"; Dettmers et al., "Patterns in Abundance of Fishes"; Schlosser, "Fish Community Structure and Function"; Greenberg, *Natural History of the Chicago Region*.

62. DeLong, "Upper Mississippi River Basin"; Dettmers et al., "Life in the Fast Lane"; Dettmers et al., "Patterns in Abundance of Fishes"; Schlosser, "Fish Community Structure and Function"; Greenberg, *Natural History of the Chicago Region*.

63. DeLong, "Upper Mississippi River Basin"; Dettmers et al., "Life in the Fast Lane"; Dettmers et al., "Patterns in Abundance of Fishes"; Schlosser, "Fish Community Structure and Function"; Greenberg, *Natural History of the Chicago Region*; Forbes, "Studies of the Food of Fresh-Water Fishes"; Forbes, "On the Food Relations of Fresh-Water Fishes"; Forbes, "On the General and Interior Distribution."

64. DeLong, "Upper Mississippi River Basin"; Dettmers et al., "Life in the Fast Lane"; Dettmers et al., "Patterns in Abundance of Fishes"; Schlosser, "Fish Community Structure and Function"; Greenberg, *Natural History of the Chicago Region*.

65. DeLong, "Upper Mississippi River Basin"; Dettmers et al., "Life in the Fast Lane"; Dettmers et al., "Patterns in Abundance of Fishes"; Schlosser, "Fish Community Structure and Function"; Greenberg, *Natural History of the Chicago Region*.

66. DeLong, "Upper Mississippi River Basin"; Greenberg, *Natural History of the Chicago Region*.

67. Hennepin, *Description of Louisiana*, 149–51.

68. Ibid., 192–93.

69. W. J. Junk, P. B. Bayley, and R. E. Sparks, "The Flood Pulse Concept in River-Floodplain Systems," *Canadian Special Publication of Fisheries and Aquatic Sciences* 106 (1989): 110–27; J. Salo et al., "River Dynamics and the Diversity of Amazon Lowland Forest," *Nature* 322, no. 6076 (1986): 254–58; H. DéCamps et al., "Historical Influence of Man on the Riparian Dynamics of a Fluvial Landscape," *Landscape Ecology* 1 (1988): 163–73; P. B. Bayley, "The Flood-Pulse Advantage and the Restoration of River-Floodplain Systems," *Regulated Rivers: Research and Management* 6, no. 2 (1991): 75–86; P. B. Bayley, "Understanding Large River-Floodplain Ecosystems," *BioScience* 45, no. 3

(1995): 153–58.

70. R. E. Richardson, "The Small Bottom and Shore Fauna of the Middle and Lower Illinois River and Its Connecting Lakes, Chillicothe to Grafton: Its Valuation; Its Sources of Food Supply; and Its Relation to the Fishery," *Illinois Natural History Survey Bulletin* 13, no. 15 (1921): 376.

71. Schlosser, "Fish Community Structure and Function"; Forbes, "Studies of the Food of Fresh-Water Fishes"; C. A. Hart, "On the Entomology of the Illinois River and Adjacent Waters," *Bulletin of the Illinois State Laboratory of Natural History* 4, no. 6 (1895): 149–273.

72. B. W. Styles, "Faunal Exploitation and Resource Selection: Early Late Woodland Subsistence in the Lower Illinois Valley" (Evanston, IL: Northwestern University Archaeological Program, 1981); H. Garman, "Notes on Illinois Reptiles and Amphibians, Including Several Species Not before Recorded from the Northern States," *Bulletin of the Illinois State Laboratory of Natural History* 3, no. 10 (1890): 185–90; H. Garman, "A Synopsis of the Reptiles and Amphibians of Illinois," *Bulletin of the Illinois State Laboratory of Natural History* 3, no. 13 (1892): 215–390.

73. Styles, "Faunal Exploitation and Resource Selection."

Native Americans and the First European Settlers

a grassland scraped flat by a thousand years of ice,
   teeming, passive,
forgiving, unprepared, the richest soil on earth
        —*from Dan Bellm's poem "Illinois River"*[1]

The seventeenth-century river described in chapter 5 is based on what scientists have been able to glean from recent fossils and from historical records prior to European settlement. This natural river the first Europeans encountered had been influenced for millennia by indigenous peoples who burned the grasslands, hunted and fished, and grew crops in the bottomlands.

Humans reached this portion of North America at least 10,000 years ago and likely much earlier. The earliest human inhabitants appear to have lived by hunting and gathering. Archaeological sites from the Paleoindian Period (10,000–8,000 BC) feature large projectile points designed to kill the mammoths, mastodon, and other megafauna still present in North America. To date, 450 of these Paleoindian sites have been found along the stream channels of the Illinois River basin. The majority of archaeological sites—around 8,300—date from the Archaic Period (8,000–600 BC), when hunters focused on smaller game such as deer. Stone and bone tools indicate

DOI: 10.5876/9781607322313.c06

people were hunting, fishing, and gathering from a variety of food sources and living in small, dispersed bands. Archaeologists know the most about people of the Woodland Period (600 BC–AD 1050), however, for which 7,800 sites have been found, mostly concentrated along river corridors.[2]

The climate of the Illinois River basin was slightly cooler and wetter during the period of Woodland culture, but the vegetation remained similar to earlier periods of human habitation. During the Early Woodland Period, people lived in caves, rock shelters, and open-air sites along rivers. With time, the sites grew larger and were occupied for longer periods, reflecting the increase and concentration of population along rivers. Materials preserved in these sites indicate a long-distance trade network, and pottery appears during the Woodland Period. Some bison were present in the region, but they became more numerous later. Smaller game animals were important in the diet of Woodland peoples, as were fish and shellfish, but Woodland people are best known for developing domesticated crops.

FIRST FARMERS OF ILLINOIS

Some of our most detailed knowledge of prehistoric cultures comes from archaeological excavations of sites from the Late Woodland Period (AD 300–1000) in west-central Illinois between the Mississippi and Illinois River valleys. Late Woodland people grew a variety of crops and were somewhat sedentary, although they continued to hunt, fish, and gather plants. Uplands supported small, dispersed households, but the main river valleys were densely populated and supported villages of various sizes. What we know of their culture comes largely from ceramics, mortuary mounds, projectile points, and the food remains they left behind. Initially, they cultivated plants such as sunflowers (*Helianthus annuus*) and gourds (*Cucurbita* and *Lagenaria* spp.). They began to grow tobacco circa AD 1 and maize circa AD 500. Cultivated plants increased in abundance and variety with time, until people were growing the staples of prehistoric North American agriculture: tobacco, maize, beans, and squash. Woodland people gathered hickory nuts (and may have burned to encourage open oak-hickory forests), and inventing the bow and arrow circa AD 500 helped them kill deer and other mammals. Even the diversity and abundance of the Illinois River drainage had a limited carrying capacity, however, and Late Woodland communities shifted through time from larger communities to smaller, dispersed settlements in which people relied on a greater variety of food sources.[3]

People once again concentrated in large settlements during the Mississippian Period (AD 850–1450). The Mississippians were intensive farmers, mound builders, and city dwellers. Their most famous settlement, at Cahokia on the Mississippi River near St. Louis, had around 10,000 people. Construction projects such as Monks Mound, 30 meters high, 244 meters wide, and 305 meters long, attest to their organization. Approximately 2,400 Mississippian sites have been found along the Illinois River. Many of the sites have stockaded villages built around mounds. You are what you eat, and our skeletons record what we were long after we are dead. Although Mississippian farmers continued to grow beans and squash, maize-related deficiencies in the teeth and bones of people from this period indicate that maize became increasingly important in their diet.[4]

Some backwater lakes along the Illinois River began to fill with sediment during the Archaic Period as prehistoric farmers replaced natural vegetation with crops and more sediment eroded from the hill slopes. Filling accelerated during the Woodland era; and the more widespread deforestation, crops, and mound building of the Mississippian era further accelerated rates of sedimentation. It is useful to remember, however, that early French explorers consistently described clear water and white sand beds in streams of the Illinois River basin.

A cooler climate that limited the growing season may have contributed to the decline of Mississippian culture, which in AD 1500 was replaced by the Oneota culture of smaller, dispersed settlements in which people continued to mix hunting, fishing, gathering, and growing crops. It becomes a challenging detective game to understand, hundreds of years after the events of interest, what caused people to gather in larger settlements or disperse across the landscape in small groups. Whatever the causes, the archaeological record clearly indicates that prehistoric peoples in the Illinois River basin did not follow a steady trajectory of increasing population and concentration into cities but instead altered their patterns of living as their environment and available resources changed.

The Mississippian and Oneota peoples bore the brunt of the European invasion, both directly through warfare and indirectly through the diseases that preceded the Europeans westward. Archaeologists estimate a population of 10,000 people in the Illinois River valley circa AD 1080. That number had dropped to 2,000 by AD 1760 and to fewer than 300 by 1832 as Native Americans died from disease, were killed in wars, or moved westward to lands not yet claimed by Europeans. Lands occupied by individual tribes also shifted repeatedly during the eighteenth and nineteenth centuries as people displaced by Europeans along the eastern seaboard moved inland, creating a domino effect. Marquette and Joliet met Miami people when they arrived in the Upper Illinois, for example, but the Miami were forced out soon after by the Iroquois; and the Chippewa, Ottawa, and Potawatomi subsequently settled in the region.[5]

THE NINETEENTH CENTURY—PLOW, DITCH, AND DREDGE

> Here the road crossed the wet prairie, as it is called, which, in some seasons, when the lake is high, is overflown. Through this wet land we went splash, splash, nearly half the night. A rail-road is proposed here, which will render travelling more pleasant.—Eliza Steele, "Summer Journey in the West"[6]

Despite the pleasure nineteenth-century people of European descent took in the apparent biological wealth of the Illinois River lands, they immediately set out to change those lands to make them more suitable for the settled agriculture and transportation network on which their society was based. This meant clearing forests, draining wetlands, dredging and snagging rivers, and breaking up prairie sod.

Following the explorations of Joliet and Marquette, La Salle, and others, the French sent a military expedition to what is now Peoria, Illinois, in 1730. This was part of their effort to solidify trading relations with local Native American groups and to exclude the British. The French and Indian War broke out between the French and British empires in North America in 1754 and lasted for the next decade. The Native American leader Pontiac signed a peace treaty with the victorious British and led his people out of their village just above the junction of the Kankakee and Des Plaines Rivers in 1763, but European settlers did not reach the region until after the War of 1812. When the European-Americans did arrive, in 1813, they built Fort Clark. Major Stephen Long, who subsequently visited the South Platte River drainage and left his name on Longs Peak, mapped portions of the Illinois River in 1816 as part of an expedition to scout locations for additional military posts. As European settlers and soldiers moved in, many of the remaining Native Americans ceded their land to the US government and moved westward. Native Americans returned briefly for the Black Hawk War in 1832, but people of European descent were already settling the region, and Native Americans never again returned in large numbers.[7]

Europeans began to alter the Illinois River basin when fur trappers reached the region during the late eighteenth century. Trapping continued to accelerate as groups such as the American Fur Company (1816) organized the harvest of furs. Trappers removed vast numbers of beavers inhabiting the basin's extensive wetlands and small rivers. The region must have seemed an endless storehouse of wealth to the trappers: harvest the beavers, and more will be born and grow to maturity in their place. In the absence of contemporary natural history research or place-specific records of fur harvest, it is difficult to estimate the number of beavers inhabiting the Illinois River drainage basin prior to trapping. Ecologists estimate beaver populations in North America prior to European contact as between 60 million and 400 million animals. But at some point the harvest exceeded the

Painter's perception of the town of Peoria along the Illinois River, 1838. Courtesy, Bradley University.

beaver population's ability to sustain itself, and the animals largely disappeared from much of the landscape by the 1820s. An estimated 20.7 million hectares of surface area across Illinois flooded by water ponded behind beaver dams in 1600 was reduced to 207,000 hectares of beaver-created wetlands in the state by 1990.[8]

Ecologists describe beavers as both a keystone species and an ecosystem engineer. A keystone species has a disproportionate effect on the environment relative to its numbers or size. Just as removing the keystone of an arch can cause the arch to collapse, so removal of a keystone species can alter the characteristics of an entire ecosystem. An ecosystem engineer is a species that creates or modifies habitats. Beavers build low dams of wood and sediment across rivers. The dams slow the downstream passage of flood waves and help force water out of the channel and across the valley bottom, creating floodplain wetlands. Sediment and nutrients come to rest at least temporarily in the ponded water upstream from the dam, where microbes and aquatic insects can ingest the nutrients and convert them into a form that can be eaten by other animals. Aquatic plants take root in the shallows at the edge of the beaver pond, and many species of fish like the quiet, sheltered pond water. Even where beavers den in stream banks, as along the lower

Torrence Mill on the South Fork of the Sangamon River, 1895. Milldams such as this one could form barriers to fish migration. Courtesy, Abraham Lincoln Presidential Library, Springfield, Illinois.

Des Plaines and Kankakee Rivers, their ability to fell trees influences vegetation communities, and their habit of digging small canals across floodplains influences the distribution of water across river bottomlands. By enhancing the variety of riverine habitats, beavers indirectly support greater diversity of aquatic and riparian plants and animals. When the beavers are removed, their beneficial ecosystem engineering ceases, and the arch of diversity they helped support weakens or even collapses.[9]

The first trappers were followed in short order by settlers who came from Kentucky, Tennessee, Pennsylvania, and other parts of the United States, which had set up a territorial government for Illinois in 1790. The region remained part of the Northwest Territory until 1800 and the Indiana Territory during the years 1800–1809 before becoming a state in 1818. Statehood triggered a rush of settlers starting in 1819, focused mostly on the southern part of the state.[10]

European farmers initially focused on the upland prairies. Between 1817 and 1903, essentially all of the upland moist prairies in the Illinois River basin were converted to agricultural uses. The dense network of grass roots that formed the famous prairie sod was difficult to break through with plows until John Deere's 1837 invention of the self-scouring, steel-bladed plow. Until the sodbuster plow was invented, the grass roots limited settlement in the uplands, but the bottom-lands were too flood-prone for extensive early settlement. Ann Vileisis described the experiences of settlers who arrived in late summer and built on flat, rich-looking grassy areas that then flooded the following spring. Early settler Albert Herre wrote: "Every spring . . . the prairie was covered with water, so that the whole country side was a great lake. Only the sand ridges emerged here and there. Wagon traffic came to a complete stop." Receding floodwaters left wet areas suitable for malaria-bearing mosquitoes; Vileisis quotes Illinois governor John Reynolds as stating that in the early 1800s "the idea prevailed that Illinois was a graveyard."[11]

Even though flooding limited early settlement of the bottomlands, rivers pro-vided the most efficient path for transporting people and goods, and floodplain forests were logged for lumber and steamboat fuel. Railroads were just being developed, and roads were expensive and difficult to build and maintain. River networks could also be enhanced and connected with canals, as the first navi-gation canal built in the United States demonstrated in 1793 (the canal bypassed rapids on the Connecticut River). By the time they reached the Illinois River basin, Americans had decades of cultural experience and legal precedent behind them for manipulating the public resources of water and river networks for private gain perceived to benefit society. As Theodore Steinberg wrote in *Nature Incorporated*: "Over the course of the nineteenth century, the mastery of the natural world became inextricably tied to a desire for progress . . . The control of nature was beginning to harden into custom and convention."[12]

"CHICAGO PRODUCES MORE FILTH PER CAPITA THAN ANY OTHER CITY"[13]

As early as 1822, an Illinois resident named Daniel Cook championed a project to build a canal that would join the Illinois River upstream to Lake Michigan, thereby linking the river to shipping on the Great Lakes. The US Congress passed a bill authorizing the canal in 1827, and construction began in 1836. The canal, which finally opened as the Illinois and Michigan Canal in 1848, was designed to divert water from the Des Plaines and Calumet Rivers. The canal extended 160 kilometers from near Chicago to LaSalle, Illinois, at that time the head of naviga-tion above Lake Peoria. As Libby Hill notes in her history of the Chicago River, the canal faced obsolescence almost as soon as it was completed, thanks to the rapidly developing network of railroads. Within a few years, however, the city of Chicago found another use for a canal.[14]

Chicago residents had initially taken their drinking water from the Chicago River, which flows south along the western shore of Lake Michigan and into the lake at Chicago, and from shallow wells. As population and industry that included massive slaughtering yards grew along the Chicago River, its water became increasingly polluted and these sources became problematic. Repeated outbreaks of cholera and dysentery starting in 1848 led to the establishment of a city water-supply company in 1851 but failed to prevent a devastating cholera outbreak in 1854. No American city had yet built a sewer system, but Chicago engineers used lake water to dilute the sewage they sent into the Chicago River through underground pipes. Begun in 1856, this was a massive engineering project that even involved raising the elevation of all the city's streets to create sufficient slope in the sewer pipes laid under the streets. It was also a significant step forward in cleaning up the city itself: physicians and social reformers had been after the city to ensure the safe disposal of human excrement by building such pipes rather than allowing individuals to continue dumping waste in open gutters or stinking cesspools. A fundamental problem remained, however: the city sewers emptied into a river that emptied into Lake Michigan, from which the city now drew its drinking water. By the 1860s the city had moved the water intake structures further out into the lake, but this was a temporary solution.[15]

In 1865 construction began on a deeper cut that would also pull Lake Michigan water into the canal to dilute the now highly polluted Chicago River and then send the diluted water down the Des Plaines River. In other words, some wastewater would now flow southward into the Illinois River network rather than entirely into the city's drinking-water supply in Lake Michigan. Construction was finished in 1871 and, despite problems, the canal functioned as intended, presumably to the dismay of downstream residents along the Illinois River system. A man tending the navigation lock at Joliet noted that during periods of low flow, such as late September 1878, all the fish in the river were dead. Fish fled up clean tributary streams during high flow, as Edward Nelson vividly described in 1878:

> When the current of the Chicago River was first turned through the canal and the rivers, it caused the fish in them to bloat to a large size, and rising to the surface they floated down the stream in large numbers . . . When these bloated fish chanced to float into the clear water at the mouth of some tributary of the river they would revive and swim up the clear stream. Such large numbers of fish revived in this manner that all the small streams flowing into the Des Plaines and Kankakee rivers were filled with fish.[16]

Good fishing while it lasts: Nelson wrote about individual fishermen catching over 300 fish in a day, but he then described how "later in the season, as the water subsides, and the water from Chicago River predominates, the fish which came up in the spring die and are floated down the river. In July and August when the water is the worst even the mud turtles leave the river in disgust."[17]

Residents of Joliet convened public meetings to demand relief from the offensive odor issuing from the Des Plaines River. Despite the recently completed work of Louis Pasteur, people at that time commonly believed miasma—noxious odors from decaying organic matter—caused diseases such as cholera and typhoid. Meanwhile, polluted water from the Chicago River continued to enter Lake Michigan, particularly during periods of heavy rains and high flow. An additional canal, the Sanitary and Ship Canal, was built during the 1890s to completely reverse the flow of the Chicago River, sending water away from the lake and into the Des Plaines at Joliet. Completion of this second canal in 1900 created consequences described in chapter 7.[18]

VILLAINOUS RIVERS AND NATURE'S SORRY MOODS

Both rivers and canals require a minimum depth of water if they are to be used continually and efficiently for transport. In addition, features such as bends, expansions and constrictions, logjams, rapids, and secondary channels complicate river channels, making them less efficient means of conveyance than canals. But rivers can be improved. Naturally occurring wood in the channel, which has the unfortunate effect of tearing the bottom out of boats, can be removed, a process known as snagging (although perhaps it should be called de-snagging, since it involves removing the features that snag boats). Flow in the river can be kept deeper even during dry seasons by diverting water from elsewhere, dredging the channel bed in shallow sections, blocking off overbank areas to keep flow within the channel, or some combination of all three actions. All of these modifications were undertaken along the Illinois River following the first river passage by steamboat in 1829.

Throughout the Upper Mississippi River basin, including the Illinois River, steamboat traffic increased substantially after 1830, reaching its greatest volume during the period 1850–70. Mark Twain wrote in *Life on the Mississippi* of "the heyday of steamboating prosperity, [when] the river from end to end was flaked with coal-fleets and timber-rafts . . . I remember the annual processions of mighty rafts that used to glide by . . . an acre or so of white, sweet-smelling boards in each raft." Steamboats functioned best in a river cleared of snags and with a consistent minimum water depth. Twain also described the challenges of river navigation before the rivers were engineered, writing about "villainous" rivers "whose alluvial banks cave and change constantly, whose snags are always hunting up new

Steamboat on the Illinois River at Peoria. Increasing steamboat traffic resulted in snagging and dredging the river to facilitate navigation and cutting riverside forests for lumber to fuel the steam engines on the boat. Courtesy, Bradley University.

quarters, whose sand-bars are never at rest, whose channels are forever dodging and shirking, and whose obstructions must be confronted in all nights and all weathers." Steamboats also required large volumes of wood to keep the boilers generating steam, which contributed to the deforestation associated with settlement of the bottomlands that began during the second half of the nineteenth century.[19]

Local newspapers proposed that the channels of the Illinois River basin be dredged and navigation locks and dams constructed during the 1850s. Nothing large-scale was undertaken, however, at least in part because of the steadily increasing use of railroads to transport goods. Individual landowners using horse teams to draw scrapers constructed local, discontinuous ditches and levees. Not until the 1879 Illinois State Drainage and Levee Act, however, did organized levee districts using state funds quickly undertake levee construction, land drainage, and channelization that involved deepening and, in some places, straightening the rivers.[20]

Steamboat accident near Peoria, 1918; the steamboat hit a submerged tree stump. Courtesy, Bradley University.

The US Congress had ceded federal swamplands to Illinois and several other states with the 1850 Arkansas Act, also known as the Swamp Land Act, with the intent of facilitating drainage of wetlands. Drainage seldom occurred, however, as a result of both technological and economic limitations. The Illinois legislature gave counties the authority to disperse swamplands, and the counties then sold more than half of the land to non-resident speculators interested in a short-term investment or in cattle grazing. Only after other, preferable bottomlands along the rivers were already settled did farmers start to think seriously about draining the swamplands using a combination of levees to prevent overbank flooding from the rivers and ditches to drain waters off the land.[21]

Owners of the largest and most flood-prone tracts of bottomland initiated the formation of drainage districts, which enclosed areas ranging from 280 hectares to 4,800 hectares. Many of these owners were wealthy farmers, lawyers, and bankers who lived in county seats and river towns. They bought the bottomlands extremely cheaply, at prices of fifty cents to thirty dollars per acre (0.4 hectare), during the 1890s and early 1900s and quickly realized the lands' productivity. At a time when average yields ranged from twenty to forty bushels of corn per acre, the river bottomlands yielded ninety bushels or more in the first year and fifty–sixty bushels in subsequent years. Yields dropped off with time as farmers essentially mined the soil productivity banked by the rivers in centuries of overbank floods that topped the floodplains with nutrient-rich muck. The price of continued productivity was frequent flooding. One account of the period 1892–1907 along the bottomlands near the mouth of the Sangamon River documents floods in January 1897, May 1898, May 1899, April and May 1900, July and August 1902, and April 1904. These

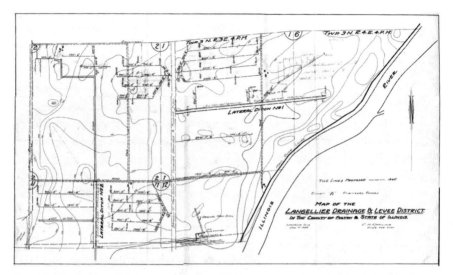

Example of a drainage district map, here for a short section of the Illinois River bottomlands near Havana, Illinois. Note the detailed mapping of topographic contours and the numerous drainage ditches. Courtesy, Havana Public Library.

floods delayed planting, ruined crops, interrupted road traffic across the bottom-lands for three weeks or longer, and inundated low-lying buildings.[22]

Much of the alteration of the Illinois River between Peoria and the confluence with the Mississippi River occurred between 1890 and 1920. During this period, bottomlands were enclosed with artificial levees to limit or prevent the type of frequent floods described for the Sangamon River. Steam-powered excavators in the form of a steam shovel on a hull were used to ditch the enclosed lands, and steam-powered pumps kept lands that had been rich in ponds and marshes dry for agriculture and settlement. The natural levees of this portion of the Illinois were 2–4 meters above low-water level and 1–3 meters above the floodplain wetlands. A flood stage of 2 meters above these levees covered the great major-ity—about 80 percent—of the floodplain. In other words, natural levees did not prevent flooding. They formed where fast-moving floodwaters lost velocity as soon as the waters began to spread across the valley bottom, with the coarsest sediments falling out of the water column beside the river. Although this process created linear mounds parallel to the river, the mounds were readily overtopped and helped slow the return of the floodwaters to the main channel as the flood receded, thus further enhancing deposition of fine sediment and nutrients on the floodplain.[23]

Levee districts set out first to heighten the natural levees so floodwaters could no longer reach the floodplains and then to drain the waters from lands enclosed within the levees to keep them dry. In the thirty-year period 1894 to 1924, approximately 75,300 hectares of floodplain were hemmed in by 500 kilometers of artificial levees. These people's energy and industry, and their effectiveness in transforming the bottomlands of the Illinois River system, are impressive. Five hundred and eighty kilometers of outlet ditches drained the lands within levee districts, and nearly forty pumping stations kept the water moving up and out. These activities changed more than half of the floodplain (64%) in this portion of the river valley from seasonal and perennial wetlands to croplands. Those who might not be fully diligent in ditching and draining could expect their neighbors' scorn. Joel Greenberg quotes a passage in Harold Kemp's 1927 University of Chicago graduate thesis. Describing a landowner who left a portion of his land unditched, Kemp wrote of "ignorance, shiftlessness, or folly" and "the story of environment winning out over the puny efforts of incompetence, while the present orderly green expanse of the once equally cursed environments along the middle roads speaks eloquently of man's ability, when rightly directed, to cope with nature, even in her sorrier moods."

Part of the moral imperative for draining wetlands came from political Progressives, who saw such drainage as a way to combat malaria. Legislation further enhanced individual efforts to dry floodplains and then to keep them dry. As Ann Vileisis wrote in *Discovering the Unknown Landscape*, her history of America's wetlands, "Lawmakers often suggested that swamps simply covered the earth and could be easily removed like a blanket from a bed. Rather than recognize that excess waters in swamps *supplied* bounteous riparian forests, vast flocks of waterfowl, and other natural riches, legislators, along with most citizens, thought that surplus water prevented lands from being even more abundant."[24]

Wetland loss accelerated with the commercial development of tile drainage. Tiles were first imported to the United States in 1835, but commercial manufacture did not take off until the 1850s. Once tiles were cheap and readily available and farmers were convinced of their efficacy, the practice of burying tiles in wet fields spread rapidly. Trenching technology progressed in parallel, from the horse-drawn machines of the 1850s to the steam-powered machines of the 1890s and gasoline-powered engines in the early 1900s. All of these innovations produced the desired results: corn yields rose by 50 percent on drained lands, and the value of those lands typically rose by 500 percent. The incidence of malaria decreased in rural areas. Vileisis quotes R.T. Brown as writing as early as 1888 that "Progressive Agriculture has removed the unsightly ponds and marshes from the farm by tile drainage, and has converted the proverbial ague seats . . . into a most salubrious climate."[25]

Other side effects also began to appear, as waterfowl populations dropped noticeably. Describing conditions prior to widespread land drainage, Albert Herre wrote: "All day long swarms of birds filled the air, and far in the night their cries sounded overhead. At the first gleam of dawn vast flights of ducks dashed to and fro and great flocks of geese sped swiftly across the sky." He then described how

> the destruction of the prairie flora and fauna began when a great machine started
> to eat its way through the prairie, leaving behind it a stream of water on which
> it floated [and] a "Big Ditch" was made. The prairie life survived to a surprising
> degree for several years more, [but] . . . the advent of tile drainage in the early 80's
> completed the transformation of the prairie into ordinary farm land and brought in
> many more people. Of course the ducks and geese stopped coming, for there was
> neither water nor food to attract them . . . The crawfish and bull frogs disappeared
> in a hurry . . . the prairie as such had disappeared, and of course its characteristic
> life with it.[26]

Tributaries entering the Illinois also had to be altered to prevent overbank flooding. Channelization transformed these typically meandering streams into straight canals cut directly toward the main channel. Smaller channels that flowed only seasonally were diverted straight into drainage ditches. Rivers efficiently perform a wide variety of ecosystem services, including providing clean water, fertile soil, and diverse habitat for numerous species of plants and animals. Nineteenth-century farmers took a much narrower view of river efficiency, though, and channelization was one of the more misguided attempts to improve river efficiency. At its most intense, channelization involves straightening and excavating the channel with machinery to create a deep, narrow trench that helps drain low-lying lands and hurries floodwaters downstream. Besides the obvious reduction of aquatic and riverside habitat, a channelized river lacks the ability to dissipate flow energy because it lacks the sources of irregularity in the channel boundaries—meander bends, instream wood, constrictions, expansions—and access to a broad flood-plain where trees and lakes further slow the downstream passage of floods. Consequently, floods roar down the neatly channelized trench, ripping away at the stream bed and banks as they go. This accelerates erosion and land loss along the channelized stream reach and creates excessive sedimentation in the downstream reach where the channelization ends.[27]

Erosion of stream bed and banks along a channelized river also increases turbidity during floods and deposition of fine sediment as floods recede. Channelized streams commonly require bank stabilization and replacement of natural riverside vegetation with riprap of rock or concrete blocks, which limits the organic matter entering streams and destroys channel-margin habitat created by rooted

Drainage canal in floodplain agricultural fields near Beardstown, 2008. This was the type of canal cut into bottomlands throughout the Illinois River basin to drain the soils sufficiently for cropland.

aquatic plants. By funneling floodwaters quickly downstream, channelization also creates boom-and-bust flows. Between floods, a channelized river has abnormally low water levels and higher water temperatures. As might be expected, many species of aquatic organisms lose both food and habitat and can no longer survive in the channelized stream.[28]

All of these activities of rearranging stream channels and floodplain topography required moving a lot of dirt, and removal of floodplain and upland forests left few plants to stabilize the displaced dirt. Land drainage became a never-ending effort. Ditches had to be cleaned as frequently as once every seven years, sometimes yielding half the volume of sediment removed initially to create the ditch. Some districts built settling basins to trap sediment. Elsewhere, sediment accumulated in ditches and small stream channels outside the levees until the channels were higher than the fields inside the levees. During floods, these ditches and channels were prone to overtopping and first breaching and then flooding the lands inside the levees. This was the start of what is still perceived as a sediment problem in the Illinois River basin.[29]

Simultaneous with the large-scale engineering of floodplains to create agricultural fields, engineering continued on the main channel to facilitate navigation. Initiation of the Illinois and Michigan Canal in 1848 had the potential to connect profitable shipping on Lake Michigan with profitable shipping on the Mississippi River, but the messy, inefficient Illinois River ruffled the smooth sailing between lake and river. A flurry of snagging, dredging, and lock and dam construction was undertaken along the length of the Illinois to facilitate boat traffic between Lake Michigan and the Mississippi River. Dredging was employed to create deeper flow over sandbars that had only 0.4–0.6 of a meter of water over them during low flow. Wing dams were built to concentrate flow in the channel center and promote scouring of the streambed and maintenance of a navigation pathway. Four dams and locks spanning the channel were built along the Illinois between 1871 and 1893, each of which created a navigation pool that maintained water depths of nearly 2 meters for distances as great as 100 kilometers upstream of the dam. These pools permanently flooded adjacent bottomlands, most of which had not been cleared and altered for croplands. The Illinois gradually became less like a river and more like a very large canal.[30]

PEARLS AND BUTTONS

Even as state and local governments were initiating organized, comprehensive alteration of the physical form of the river network, a new industry was developing that used a component of the river's biological communities. Native Americans had used the plentiful mussels of the Illinois River basin for both food and tools, as did the first European-Americans to settle in the region. Some of the mussels also developed freshwater pearls when the animal excreted a nacreous substance to coat an irritant such as a sand grain that lodged in its shell. Starting in the mid-nineteenth century, a find of a single large pearl could trigger a pearl rush because of the price for which these gems sold. By the early 1900s, a single pearl might have sold for $4,000, and the Wabash River alone yielded more than $1 million worth of pearls during a five-year period. Of course, to find a valuable pearl, you have to remove a lot of mussels from the streambed. Would-be pearl fishers were thinking about getting rich, not about preserving the mussel beds.[31]

Resourceful fishers also found other uses for freshwater mussels. William Slater shipped mussel shells collected from the Illinois River at Peoria to Europe in 1872. Among those who realized that such shells could be cut to make good buttons was the German John Boepple, who emigrated to the United States in 1887. Boepple started the mussel shell button industry in 1891 with a factory near Muscatine, Iowa. Initially, collectors gathered mussels by hand, but a device known as a crow-

Mussel fishing at Beardstown, circa 1917. Crowfoot snags hang above the boat at left. Courtesy, Abraham Lincoln Presidential Library, Springfield, Illinois.

foot was introduced by 1897. The crowfoot was a horizontal bar from which hung a series of large hooks. When this assemblage was dragged along the river bottom, the hooks lodged in the open shells of mussels, which promptly closed their shells and hung on when the hooks were lifted from the water. The crowfoot was efficient, and the number of button factories along rivers throughout the Mississippi River drainage grew rapidly, from thirteen factories in 1897 to forty-nine in 1898. Use of the crowfoot started on the Illinois River in 1907 and peaked in 1909, when 2,600 boats were harvesting mussels between the towns of Peru and Grafton, creating an average of more than five boats per kilometer of river. Although the activity gradually declined during the twentieth century as a combined result of over-harvest, pollution, and habitat alteration, mussels were still being removed from the river decades later thanks to the development in Japan of pearl culture using shell pieces during the late 1940s.[32]

Native mussels provide stable substrates for aquatic insect eggs and larvae, as well as fish eggs. Concentrations of these hard-shelled animals also create structure and habitat diversity that provide fish nursery and feeding areas. Mussels create millions of little water filters as they suck in river water and filter out particular organic matter. Organic matter that remains in the river lowers the dissolved oxygen content of the water as it decays. By removing the organic matter, the mussels thus help preserve the oxygenated water many species of fish require. Mussels convert the organic matter—their food—into their own flesh, which in turn serves as food for fish, muskrats, and raccoons.[33]

Widespread use of the crowfoot severely disrupted streambed communities. The crowfoot removed not only mature mussels but also juveniles that were too small to be of much commercial value yet were seldom returned to the river to ensure a future supply of mussels. The dragging of the assemblage of hooks and attached mussels stirred up the silt and sand of streambeds and smothered remaining mussels and bottom-dwelling insects. The crowfoot directly removed many of the little water filters and incapacitated many others. Sediment sluicing off the crop fields steadily thickened on the streambeds, and the life of the rivers shrank back to fewer species and individuals.[34]

RIVERINE GRAZERS

The over-harvest of mussels was unfortunately not unique in the annals of using river resources. As Joel Greenberg noted in a description of buffalo fish and carp in the Illinois River catchment, "The prevailing attitude towards nature during the nineteenth century was that it could be exploited without restraint." Before introduced carp dominated the commercial fishery of the Illinois River, native buffalo fish were the fish of choice or at least of bulk. Named for the humped back of adult fish, buffalo fish created a riverine analog of the famous terrestrial prairie grazers as they "plowed steadily along with their heads buried in the mud," grazing on tiny invertebrate animals. The three species of buffalo fish—smallmouth (*Ictiobus bubalus*), bigmouth (*I. cyprinella*), and black (*I. niger*)—were good-sized fish, growing half a meter or more in length. This limited their vulnerability to predators. They were also fecund: a single large female could lay up to 750,000 eggs during spring spawning. Buffalo fish did, however, have a source of vulnerability common to other large-bodied, long-lived fish: relatively late sexual maturity that limited the ability of over-fished populations to rebound. Buffalo fish can live up to eighteen years, and males reach sexual maturity at four to five years, females at six years. Despite being considered "coarse" fish less desirable for eating than other species, buffalo fish were heavily exploited, forming the bulk of commercial fishery on the river until the 1890s. Seeing no need to protect the abundant fish, farmers and fishermen caught them in shallow water during spawning season, using nets across the entrances of sloughs and floodplain wetlands and harvesting both fish and eggs. Large, weighted nets were used in deeper water.[35]

For a few decades, there was a fishing frenzy. As many as 10 million tons of buffalo fish from the Illinois River reached commercial markets in a year, and one fishing crew caught 182,000 kilograms of fish in a day. As markets became glutted, fish were dumped back into the water. Greenberg cites a description from Dr. S. P. Bartlett of the US Bureau of Fisheries, who observed dead fish covering the entire surface of the Illinois along an 80-kilometer length of river. The state of Illinois passed legislation to protect the fish by the early 1870s, but lack of enforcement rendered the laws useless. Buffalo fish, which were sufficiently resilient to be able to feed on distillery slops, gradually declined in numbers. Their populations are fairly stable today, although much reduced from historical levels.[36]

SCIENCE IN THE SEPTIC ZONE AND PISCATORIAL PARIAHS

Even as the Illinois River basin was rapidly changing under intensive resource use, scientists began to catalog and study what was present in the natural environment. In 1874 Stephen Forbes began to study fish in the river basin, and in 1877 he founded and became the first director of the Illinois Laboratory of Natural History. It is worth quoting his 1928 description of his early work: "The rivers of the country have received so little comprehensive attention from our biologists that I do not know of a single attempt anywhere in America to develop and disclose the complete biology of a river system except that which has been made by us in Illinois."[37]

The Illinois Natural History Survey has published bulletins since 1876, as well as other types of scientific reports, and many of the studies summarized in its pages provide a critical baseline for contemporary knowledge of mussels, fish, waterfowl, and other wildlife. This baseline is critical in part because it provides the only direct, systematic glimpse of earlier conditions on the river. For example, even as Forbes and David Thompson were studying native fish starting in the 1870s and the 1920s, respectively, common carp (*Cyprinus carpio*) were introduced to the Illinois River in the 1880s and spread quickly, disrupting native fish communities. The 1876 Natural History Survey bulletin listed 156 fish species in the state, including seven non-natives.[38]

In 1894 the University of Illinois established the Havana Station, the first inland biology station in the world to study river ecology, and its publications also contributed to growing documentation of the river. Forbes stated two objectives in establishing the Havana field station: "one the effect on the plant and animal life of a region produced by the periodical overflow and gradual recession of the waters of great rivers, of which the Illinois affords a notably marked example; and the other the collection of materials for a comparison of chemical and biological conditions of the water of the Illinois River at the time then present and after the opening of the sewage canal of the Sanitary District of Chicago." From the outset, the station's research mission was thus to catalog and understand the natural riverine communities and to chronicle changes in those communities resulting from human activities. Forbes recognized that productivity of the river's fishery was proportional to the area flooded each year, and in 1910 he warned: "Nothing can be more dangerous to the continued productiveness of these waters than a shutting of the river into its main channel and the drainage of the bottomland lakes for agricultural purposes."[39]

Between 1913 and 1925, the survey collected more than 1,300 bottom-dwelling organisms along nearly 400 kilometers of the Illinois River. From these organisms Robert Richardson systematically documented the changes in the river's benthic ecosystem as pollution from the sanitary canal moved steadily downstream, changing what he referred to as "clean water" zones into "sub-pollutional," "pollutional," and, at the extreme, "septic" zones. In part because of studies such as this, the Illinois has been described as the most studied river in the world.[40]

As one of the first scientists to systematically study fish of the Illinois River basin, Forbes was drawn into at least the periphery of the often virulent debate about the role of carp in the river system. Carp were first brought to the United States in 1831, as imports to the state of New York, but it was Spencer Baird, chief of the US Fish Commission as well as director of the Smithsonian Institution, who really boosted widespread introduction of the fish to American waters. Baird advocated common carp as a food fish for the farm ponds starting to appear across the landscape of the eastern and midwestern United States, and the fish commission distributed thousands of free carp. Perhaps more important, Baird waged an aggressive public relations campaign in favor of this species, which had frequently been held in low esteem since Izaak Walton's dismissal of carp in his seventeenth-century angling book. The president of the University of Wisconsin predicted that people of his state would someday thank the men who introduced "this extra fine species of fish."

This was a golden age of fish transports and stocking. Some of the biologists who pioneered scientific study of river fishes in the United States also pioneered the transfer of species across drainage divides and continents. Just as people believed they could improve the physical characteristics of rivers and adjacent landscapes, so they believed they could improve biological communities in rivers. Underlying this belief was the assumption that improvements could be controlled, but the clumsy tinkering with both the physical and biological properties of rivers created unintended consequences. As environmental historian Glenn Sandiford wrote in 2009, "The history of carp in America had already [by the late 1880s] shown that any notion of human dominion over carp—whether inspired by faith in a god or science—was illusory at best."[41]

Sandiford explores how the changing narrative and rhetoric about carp reflected different agendas during the late nineteenth and early twentieth centuries. Initially welcomed as a fast-growing and multiplying, abundant, and easily raised source of food, the carp was soon referred to as a "foreign interloper," "useless," and a "miserable scavenger." Carp are indeed fast-multiplying: an adult can lay more than 2.2 million eggs in a season. They are omnivores, able to feed on every-thing from algae and seeds to insects and crustaceans and seeking food from the water surface to the streambed. Adult carp have few effective aquatic predators, thanks to the combination of being alert and quick to move when threatened, as well as having thick scales that protect them from fish such as lampreys. Carp can withstand, and even multiply in, poor-quality water, with low oxygen levels, high turbidity, and various pollutants.[42]

By 1900 the Illinois Fish Commission was one of the few government agencies still promoting carp. Other states had quit stocking and begun eradicating carp, but the fish had escaped from numerous fish ponds and become one of the Upper Mississippi River valley's most abundant commercial fishes by the 1890s. In 1890 Forbes advocated stocking native fish in the Illinois River, although he did not dis-like carp or condemn them with the vigor of other observers.[43]

The waters of the Illinois River were perfect for carp, which prefer a shallow marsh setting with abundant aquatic vegetation. Carp spawn in waters less than 45 centimeters deep in areas recently inundated by flooding, then over-winter in deeper water. As escaped carp began to proliferate and public attitudes toward them shifted, the fish were accused of eating other fish, destroying duck habitat, tasting bad, and ruining water quality. Attitudes aside, carp were in the Illinois to stay. During electrofishing surveys along the Illinois River between 1959 and 1974, Richard Sparks and William Starrett found that carp and gizzard shad were the only species to occur abundantly in every pool of the river.[44]

As historian James Gray noted, Illinois is known as the sucker state in reference to the sucker fish, which in spring travels upstream to spawn. *Sucker democracy*, a phrase in common use during Abraham Lincoln's time, indicated that Lincoln and others from Illinois identified themselves with the state's most famous river. This did not prevent nineteenth-century Illinoisans from working hard to alter the river to suit their needs, but the bottomlands retained much of their biological abundance and diversity. It is interesting to compare an 1874 description of a por-tion of the Illinois with those penned both earlier and later:[45]

> The view from the summit of Starved Rock is very fine, and the country in the
> distance will remind the beholder of a grand landscape painting or a beautiful
> panorama. To the north and west is seen a large bottom prairie, bounded on
> each side by bluffs covered with forest trees. Through this great meadow flows
> the Illinois river, which can be seen for many miles distant, winding about in its
> serpentine course. On looking down into the river at the base of the rock, catfish

View of the Illinois River from Starved Rock, circa 1900. Courtesy, Abraham Lincoln Presidential Library, Springfield, Illinois.

and turtles can be seen sporting over the sand and rocks in the clear shallow stream; while shoals of red-horse are stemming the swift current.

The great meadow which its summit overlooks, once covered with grass and wild flowers, and sometimes blackened with herds of buffalo, is now occupied by farms in close succession. To the north, across the large bottom prairie is seen the village of Utica, with its cement mills and warehouses, and by the side of which, pass the canal and railroad. To the west, five miles below, but in plain view are the flourishing cities of LaSalle and Peru, with their church steeples glittering in the sunbeams, while steam and canal boats are seen in the river, and trains of cars passing and repassing on the different railroads. Evidence of agriculture, commerce

1888 view across the Illinois River to the city of Peoria. Courtesy, Bradley University.

and civilization are now to be seen from the summit of Starved Rock, where the scenery was once wild and lonely.[46]

The view from the summit of Starved Rock in 1874 reflected the long history of abundant bottomland forests and wetlands supporting a wealth of fish and waterfowl but also the future of an increasingly urbanized and industrialized landscape modified to support ever greater densities of people and resource extraction. The Illinois River was the vital heart of the historical landscape, its pulses of water and sediment contouring the lowlands and creating the foundation on which biological communities flourished. In the years to come the riverine heart would become progressively feebler, the flow along its network of veins and arteries constricted by dams and levees and poisoned by wastes from farms and cities.

NOTES

1. D. Bellm, "Illinois River," in *One Hand on the Wheel* (Berkeley, CA: Roundhouse, 1999), 60–62.

2. W. Green and D. J. Nolan, "Late Woodland Peoples in West-Central Illinois," in *Late Woodland Societies: Tradition and Transformation across the Midcontinent*, ed. T. E. Emerson, D. L. McElrath, and A. C. Fortier (Lincoln: University of Nebraska Press, 2000), 345–72;

D. L. Asch, "Aboriginal Specialty-Plant Cultivation in Eastern North America: Illinois Prehistory and a Post-Contact Perspective," in *Agricultural Origins and Development in the Mid-Continent*, ed. W. Green, Office of the State Archeologist Report 19 (Iowa City: University of Iowa, 1994), 25–86.

3. W. Green and D. J. Nolan, "Late Woodland Peoples in West-Central Illinois," in *Late Woodland Societies: Tradition and Transformation across the Midcontinent*, ed. T. E. Emerson, D. L. McElrath, and A. C. Fortier (Lincoln: University of Nebraska Press, 2000), 345–72; D. L. Asch, "Aboriginal Specialty-Plant Cultivation in Eastern North America: Illinois Prehistory and a Post-Contact Perspective," in *Agricultural Origins and Development in the Mid-Continent*, ed. W. Green, Office of the State Archeologist Report 19 (Iowa City: University of Iowa, 1994), 25–86.

4. J. Van Nest, "Rediscovering This Earth," in *Recreating Hopewell*, ed. D. K. Charles and J. E. Buikstra (Gainesville: University Press of Florida, 2006), 402–26.

5. L. Hill, *The Chicago River: A Natural and Unnatural History* (Chicago: Lake Claremont, 2000).

6. Steele, "Summer Journey in the West," 123.

7. Gray, *Illinois*; Greenberg, *Natural History of the Chicago Region*.

8. Gray, *Illinois*; Greenberg, *Natural History of the Chicago Region*; D. L. Hey and N. S. Phillipi, "Reinventing a Flood Control Strategy," *Wetlands Initiative* (September 1994): 4–8; M. J. Morgan, *Land of Big Rivers: French and Indian Illinois, 1699–1778* (Carbondale: Southern Illinois University Press, 2010), 102–4.

9. Gray, *Illinois*; Greenberg, *Natural History of the Chicago Region*.

10. Gray, *Illinois*; Greenberg, *Natural History of the Chicago Region*.

11. Vileisis, *Discovering the Unknown Landscape*, 63; A. W. Herre, "An Early Illinois Prairie," *American Botanist* 46 (1940): 39–44.

12. T. Steinberg, *Nature Incorporated: Industrialization and the Waters of New England* (Cambridge: Cambridge University Press, 1991), 271.

13. L. E. Cooley, *The Lakes and Gulf Waterway as Related to the Chicago Sanitary Problem* (Chicago: John W. Weston, 1890), vi, in Hill, *Chicago River*, 113.

14. Hill, *Chicago River*.

15. J. C. O'Connell, "Technology and Pollution: Chicago's Water Policy, 1833–1930," PhD diss., University of Chicago, Chicago, 1980; Greenberg, *Natural History of the Chicago Region*; Hill, *Chicago River*.

16. E. W. Nelson, "Fisheries of Chicago and Vicinity," in *Report of the Commissioner of Fish and Fisheries* (Washington, DC: Government Printing Office, 1878), 798.

17. Nelson quoted in Greenberg, *Natural History of the Chicago Region*, 180–81.

18. Ibid.; Hill, *Chicago River*; O'Connell, "Technology and Pollution."

19. R. Hoops, *A River of Grain: The Evolution of Commercial Navigation on the Upper Mississippi River*, College of Agricultural and Life Sciences Report R3584 (Madison:

University of Wisconsin, 1993); M. Twain, *Life on the Mississippi* (New York: Book-of-the-Month Club, 1992 [1883]), 18–19 (first quote), 81 (second quote).

20. J. Thompson, "Land Drainage and Conflict Resolution in the Lower Valley of the Illinois River, 1890s–1930," in *Sustainable Agriculture in the American Midwest: Lessons from the Past, Prospects for the Future*, ed. G. McIsaac and W. R. Edwards (Chicago: University of Illinois Press, 1994), 77–94; J. Thompson, *Wetlands Drainage, River Modification, and Sectoral Conflicts in the Lower Illinois Valley, 1890–1930* (Carbondale: Southern Illinois University Press, 2002).

21. Vileisis, *Discovering the Unknown Landscape.*

22. Ibid.; Thompson, "Land Drainage and Conflict Resolution"; Thompson, *Wetlands Drainage.*

23. Thompson, "Land Drainage and Conflict Resolution"; Thompson, *Wetlands Drainage*; Vileisis, *Discovering the Unknown Landscape.*

24. Thompson, "Land Drainage and Conflict Resolution"; Thompson, *Wetlands Drainage*; Greenberg, *Natural History of the Chicago Region*, 44–45; H. Kemp, "Observation of Geographic Minutiae as Exemplified by a Survey in Bloom Township, Cook County," master's thesis, University of Chicago, Chicago, 1927, 60–61; Vileisis, *Discovering the Unknown Landscape*, 76.

25. Vileisis, *Discovering the Unknown Landscape*, 127.

26. Herre, "Early Illinois Prairie," in Greenberg, *Of Prairie, Woods, and Water*, 79 (first quote), 80 (second quote).

27. R. Gillette, "Stream Channelization: Conflict between Ditchers, Conservationists," *Science* 176, no. 4037 (May 26, 1972): 890–94; Committee on Government Operations, *Stream Channelization: What Federally Financed Draglines and Bulldozers Do to Our Nation's Streams*, fifth report by the Committee on Government Operations (Washington, DC: US Government Printing Office, 1973).

28. R. Schoof, "Environmental Impact of Channel Modification," *Water Resources Bulletin* 16, no. 4 (1980): 697–701; S. S. Hahn, "Stream Channelization: Effects on Stream Fauna," in *Biota and Biological Principles of the Aquatic Environment*, ed. P. E. Greeson, Geological Survey Circular 848-A (Washington, DC: US Government Printing Office, 1982), A43–A49; D. L. Scarnecchia, "The Importance of Streamlining in Influencing Fish Community Structure in Channelized and Unchannelized Reaches of a Prairie Stream," *Regulated Rivers: Research and Management* 2, no. 2 (1988): 155–66.

29. R. L. Mattingly, E. E. Herricks, and D. M. Johnston, "Channelization and Levee Construction in Illinois: Review and Implications for Management," *Environmental Management* 17, no. 6 (1993): 781–95; Gillette, "Stream Channelization"; Committee on Government Operations, *Stream Channelization.*

30. Thompson, "Land Drainage and Conflict Resolution"; Thompson, *Wetlands Drainage.*

31. K. D. Blodgett et al., *Mussel Resources of the Illinois River System: Value to Illinois' Economy and Natural Heritage*, Long Term Resource Monitoring Program 98-R012 (Onalaska, WI: US Geological Survey Environmental Management Technical Center, 1998), 153–60.

32. Ibid.

33. Ibid.

34. Ibid.

35. Greenberg, *Natural History of the Chicago Region*, 3 (first quote); S. A. Forbes and R. E. Richardson, *The Fishes of Illinois* (Springfield: State of Illinois, 1920), 67 (second quote).

36. Greenberg, *Natural History of the Chicago Region*.

37. Forbes, "Biological Survey of a River System," 277.

38. Ibid.

39. Ibid. (first quote); S. A. Forbes, "The Investigation of a River System in the Interest of Its Fisheries," in *Biological Investigations of the Illinois River*, vol. 2 (Urbana: Illinois State Laboratory of Natural History, 1910), 12 (second quote).

40. R. E. Richardson, "The Bottom Fauna of the Middle Illinois River, 1913–1925," *Bulletin, State of Illinois, Division of the Natural History Survey* 17, no. 12 (1928): 387–475.

41. Greenberg, *Natural History of the Chicago Region*; G. Sandiford, "Transforming an Exotic Species: Nineteenth-Century Narratives about Introduction of Carp in America," PhD dissertation, University of Illinois at Urbana-Champaign, 2009, 256.

42. Sandiford, "Transforming an Exotic Species."

43. Ibid.

44. Ibid.; R. E. Sparks and W. C. Starrett, "An Electrofishing Survey of the Illinois River, 1959–1974," *Illinois Natural History Survey Bulletin* 31, no. 8 (1975): 317–80.

45. Gray, *Illinois*.

46. N. Matson, *French and Indians of Illinois River* (Carbondale: Southern Illinois University Press, 1874), 21–23.

SEVEN

Twentieth-Century River Metamorphosis

A HISTORIC SNAPSHOT: THE ILLINOIS RIVER CIRCA 1900

In describing the Illinois River circa 1900 during high water, Dr. Charles Kofoid of the Illinois Natural History Survey wrote of traveling by boat across the flooded bottomlands:

> A flock of startled waterfowl leave their feeding grounds as we pass into the wide expanse of Flag Lake. We push our way through patches of lily-pads and beds of lotus, past the submerged domes of muskrat houses built of last year's rushes, and thread our way, through devious channels, among the fresh green flags and rushes just emerging . . . The water is clear and brownish save where our movements stir the treacherous and mobile bottom. We now enter . . . the partially wooded country and cross the submerged ridge to the sandy eastern shore of Thompson's Lake . . . The "breaks" of the startled fish show that we have invaded favorite feeding grounds. The waters are evidently moving towards the river, and they bear the rich plankton of Thompson's Lake . . . Schools of young fry can be seen feeding upon the plankton in the warm and quiet waters . . . Turning

DOI: 10.5876/9781607322313.c07

Mouth of the Illinois River circa 1900. Courtesy, Abraham Lincoln Presidential Library, Springfield, Illinois.

back towards the river we pass through the heavy timber where the still brown water, cool and clear, overlies the decaying leaves and vegetation of last season's growth, now coated with the flood deposits of winter.[1]

This description of a seemingly idyllic landscape is offset by Kofoid's mention in his account of huge masses of cattle-yard refuse, agricultural erosion creating "a turbid yellow flood pouring out from the Spoon River," and sewage.[2]

What happens when a clear stream with a sand bed—of the sort described in some of the earliest written accounts of the Illinois River catchment—goes to turbid water flowing over a silty bed? Almost everything changes. Phytoplankton—microscopic algae floating in the water—decrease in abundance, and the zooplankton and other minute creatures that feed on the phytoplankton change in abundance and diversity. Fish eggs deposited on the streambed, which rely on water flowing through the porous bed to deliver oxygen to the developing embryos, are more likely to smother. The species present in the bottom-dwelling community of plants, insects, and other invertebrates change. The abundance and diversity of fish that feed on these smaller creatures also change. Exchanges of water among the stream, the shallow subsurface water, and the groundwater decrease; this alters the nutrients, dissolved oxygen, and water temperature in the river. The forms and amounts of nitrogen present in the stream change, further altering the biota. The effects of the "turbid yellow flood" extend far beyond the obvious changes in the river's appearance.

View of the Sangamon River circa 1900. Most riverside forests have been removed, and crop fields at the right in this view extend to the edge of the channel. Courtesy, Abraham Lincoln Presidential Library, Springfield, Illinois.

The human population of Illinois had just begun its dramatic growth. The population of slightly over 800,000 in 1850 had increased to more than 8 million by 1950. Approximately 1 million people joined that population every decade from 1890 to 1930, and this period was one of extensive conversion of landscapes to human use. Farmers had cleared about half of the floodplain along the Illinois River between Peoria and Beardstown by 1904 and closer to 70 percent of the floodplain between Beardstown and the mouth of the Illinois. Cleared land was already parceled out between levees and drained by ditches and pumps.

Between these swathes of cleared land remained stands of timber and brush, as well as undrained floodplain wetlands, shallow lakes, and ponds. Although most of the headwater streams were channelized between the 1880s and early 1900s, a few un-channelized headwater streams still meandered across gently sloping wet prairies. In 1920 Stephen Forbes and Robert Richardson described the headwaters of the Kankakee River as having

> an almost imperceptible flow, and in many places wild rice, rushes, lily-pads, and aquatic grasses so choke the channel as to cause the flooding of the marshes during summer freshets . . . The small tributaries are usually lost in the marsh before reaching the main stream. On the immediate border of the river there is a strip ranging in width from one fourth to one and one half miles which is heavily timbered. The only other timber is found on so-called islands whose surfaces rise 10 to 20 feet above the general level of the marsh. The open marsh is covered with a rank growth of wild grasses, bulrushes, sedges, reeds, wild rice, and other semiaquatic vegetation . . . The valley of the Kankakee . . . resembled an immense

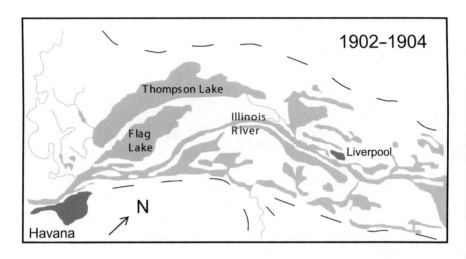

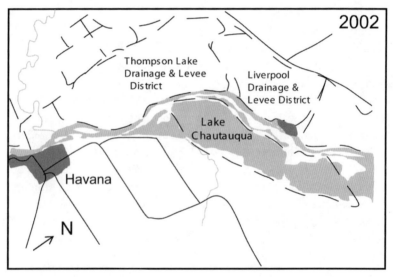

Channel and floodplain changes along 20 kilometers of the valley bottom along the Illinois River near Havana, Illinois, between 1902–4 and 2002. Gray areas are rivers or lakes. Long dashed lines indicate bluffs along the valley margins; short dashed lines are levees. Downstream is to the left. After Thompson (2002, maps 7.1 and 7.2).

sponge, slowly absorbing the water during the wet season and as slowly giving it forth during the dry, so that the flow throughout the year was quite regular and uniform in amount.[3]

Backwater along the Illinois River circa 1900. The extent and duration of flooding in such backwaters strongly influence the productivity of the river ecosystem. Courtesy, Abraham Lincoln Presidential Library, Springfield, Illinois.

The uppermost portions of the drainage network, where runoff could not cut a channel through the dense cover of tallgrass, were loosely connected wet-prairie sloughs. Marshy wetland grasses covered the sloughs and swales, which slowly and continuously leaked their stored water to create perennial flow in all but the driest years. The tallgrass prairie covering much of the watershed burned periodically, and only scattered trees were present along the smaller streams. Riparian forests grew beside medium-size and larger rivers that could provide sufficient moisture to protect the trees from prairie fires. Trees from the riverside forests fell into the channels, creating overhead cover and local scour holes that provided good fish habitat. Alternating pools and riffles formed in the sand beds of these meandering channels, which flooded across the valley bottom each year. Remaining portions of natural floodplain were sufficient to continue to support abundant and diverse aquatic communities.[4]

The statistics on commercial fish catches tell some of the story about the condition of the Illinois River circa 1900. In 1908, a stretch of the river approximately 330 kilometers in length produced 10 percent of the total catch of freshwater fish in the United States. Although more than half of these fish were pollution-tolerant carp introduced to the river basin during the 1880s, this catch was greater than that of any other river in North America that year except rivers such as the Columbia, with huge runs of salmon returning from the ocean to spawn. More than 2,000 commercial fishermen worked the Illinois River, catching 11 million kilograms each year, which averaged out to 200 kilograms per hectare (178 pounds per acre) of permanent water. How to put 11 million kilograms of fish into perspective? The size of individual fish varies and the average size varies among the three species of buffalo fish, but using 25 kilograms as an average weight, the annual catch on the Illinois River during the heyday of catching buffalo fish works out to about 440,000 fish. That's a fine kettle of fish.[5]

THE UNSANITARY CANAL

Like many cities of the time, nineteenth-century Chicago dumped raw sewage into nearby water bodies, relying on dilution and downstream dispersal to remove the waste. The problem with Chicago was that it had too many people to get away with this: dilution was an insufficient solution to pollution. Because Chicagoans consumed more water in terms of total volume and per capita average than any other American city, water filtration was considered too expensive. Instead of developing methods to treat the waste, Chicago and its engineers reconfigured drainage for the region. The Sanitary and Ship Canal, completed in 1900, was the largest public works excavation undertaken up to that time. Newly designed steam shovels moved millions of tons of earth and rock to create a canal 47 kilometers long and up to 90 meters wide. Completion of the canal demonstrated the feasibility of connecting the Pacific and Atlantic Oceans by way of a canal across the Isthmus of Panama a few years later.

Downstream cities along the Illinois River did not object when the canal diverted sewage into the Illinois and all the way downstream to the Mississippi River starting in 1900 because they did not obtain drinking water from the river, and the extra flow could enhance navigation. Only St. Louis, which took its drinking water from the Mississippi a few kilometers below the confluence of the Illinois and Mississippi Rivers, expressed concern about the possibility of typhoid and cholera. Facing the threat of a legal injunction from St. Louis that would have limited the use of their $33,000,000 canal, Chicagoans rushed to clear the last plug of earth and ice between the Chicago River and the canal. Libby Hill quotes an article from the *Chicago Tribune* describing the final dramatic swing of the dredge arm on January 2, 1900, that opened a 7-meter drop between the river and the canal: " 'It is open! It is open!' went up from scores of throats . . . 'It is the Niagara of Chicago.' "[6]

The newly opened canal was subsequently lengthened during 1903–7 to replace the Illinois and Michigan Canal. The state of Illinois pointed out that limited amounts of sewage entering by way of the existing Illinois and Michigan Canal already polluted the upper reaches of the Illinois River and conducted studies to evaluate the effect of the proposed new canal. Although these studies documented poor water quality above La Salle as a result of Chicago's urban and industrial sewage, as well as immediately downstream from Peoria and Pekin as a result of biological wastes where distillery and feedlot operators heaped stable refuse along riverbanks, the state concluded that the cities of Illinois must use the river for sewage disposal and supported the proposed Sanitary and Ship Canal. The state also speculated that, under conditions in which about half of the water reaching Peoria during dry years was a combination of water from Lake Michigan and sewage from Chicago, the proposed diversion might improve water quality by increasing dilution.

The Sanitary District of Chicago released a report maintaining that water-quality problems in St. Louis resulted from the slaughterhouses and distilleries at Peoria and Pekin. Explaining that running streams, adequately diluted, purify themselves from sewage pollution, the report went on to state that "all talk of Chicago sewage injuriously affecting the drinking water at St. Louis is thus completely and effectually disposed of by the work of these investigators." The Illinois Fish Commission went on record stating that the increased sewage would provide fish food and increase fish populations, although the commission did express concern about the effects of industrial wastes on fish populations. Although the idea of increased urban and industrial waste providing fish food might seem laughable, studies of the stomach contents of diverse fish species supported this contention. Stephen Forbes found that many fish ingested distillery slopes, and he wrote about channel catfish (*Ictalurus punctatus*) he dissected in 1888: "A dead rat, pieces of ham, and other animal débris [from slaughterhouses] attest the easy-going appetite of this thrifty species."[7]

The Sanitary District of Chicago opened the Sanitary and Ship Canal in January 1900 and immediately started diverting 1 million cubic meters (274 million gallons) of sewage into the Illinois River each day. Of the total 84 cubic meters per second of flow diverted from Lake Michigan, 34 were used for water supply and 50 for dilution of contaminants. Water-quality studies conducted during the next few years found that the upper stretches of the river and the water below Peoria remained very polluted. Meanwhile, the Army Corps of Engineers and the governments of Canada and several Great Lake states complained that too much water was being diverted from Lake Michigan, lowering the water level throughout all the lakes by 15 centimeters and interfering with navigation. There was no immediate impact on commercial fisheries, however, and the US Supreme Court concluded that Chicago's sewage was unlikely to cause outbreaks of disease in St. Louis, thereby allowing continued operation of the canal.[8]

Turning water into the newly completed Sanitary and Ship Canal, January 2, 1900. Courtesy, Abraham Lincoln Presidential Library, Springfield, Illinois.

Rather than decimating the commercial fisheries, operation of the canal actually seemed to improve them: catches rose steadily each year until 1908. Supporters of the canal claimed that higher water levels produced more overbank flooding and breeding areas and that microorganisms feasting on the decomposing sewage provided abundant fish food. The presence of introduced carp was likely equally important. Carp not only tolerated turbid and polluted water but also propagated so rapidly that they became the most abundant species caught, moving up from 10 percent of the catch in 1894 to more than 65 percent in 1908. Substantial increases in the number of fishermen working the river between 1900 and 1910 further inflated catches.[9]

The year 1908 was the last good one for commercial fisheries on the Illinois River. After that, two primary factors combined to suppress fish populations. First, continued conversion of floodplain forest and wetlands to croplands removed nearly half the spawning areas along the river corridor. Second, the continuing sewage input from Chicago finally overwhelmed the river's ability to biologically cleanse itself. The decomposition processes of organic matter, including sewage, remove dissolved oxygen from the surrounding water. If a river is overloaded with decomposing material, oxygen levels eventually drop too low to support some forms of aquatic life. Studies during the first three decades of the twentieth century documented a steady downstream progression of low levels of dissolved oxygen, accumulation of sewage along the streambed, and associated destruction of bottom-dwelling microorganisms, insects, and invertebrates. Robert Richardson documented changes from snail-dominated bottom fauna in clean waters to various species of midge larvae and leeches in sub-pollutional waters, midge larvae and *Tubifex* worms in pollutional zones, and the sewage-dwelling bacteria *Sphaerotilus natans* in the septic zone. Stands of aquatic plants that previously covered up to half of the bed of floodplain lakes had disappeared by 1920. Fish in these oxygen-starved waters, lacking food and habitat, also started to disappear. Populations of catfish and buffalo fish declined in the lower river and largely vanished from the upper river. By 1918, biologist Victor Shelford was writing: "Our fish resources have been depleted through neglect, carelessness, and the pollution of waters."[10]

In 1928, David Thompson linked deformities in carp to pollution. Fish showing these deformities became known as knothead carp for the knobs that developed along the sides of their heads behind each eye. These fish grew only about half as large as normal carp, had difficulty breathing, and, upon dissection, were found to have bones with different shape and thickness than normal carp. Thompson attributed the knothead growths to a piscine form of Rickets disease, which results from a lack of vitamin D in the diet. *Potamogeton* and other rooted aquatic plants mostly disappeared from Peoria Lake and other parts of the Illinois River heavily affected by sewage between 1915 and 1920, and non-chlorophyll-bearing plankton lacking in vitamins replaced those with chlorophyll. The changing food supply resulted in vitamin deficiencies in carp.[11]

A particularly vivid description of conditions along the river during this period was penned in 1913 by Stephen Forbes and Robert Richardson of the Illinois State Laboratory of Natural History: "The water here was grayish, sloppy, and everywhere clouded with tufts of Sphaerotilus and Carchesium. The odor was continuously foul, with a distinct privy smell in the hottest weather. Bubbles of gas were continually breaking at the surface from a soft bar of sludge . . . On the warmest days putrescent masses of soft, grayish black, mucky matter . . . were floating on the surface."[12]

It was not until 1918, however, that scientists proposed that sewage was negatively affecting biological communities of the Illinois River. Biologists with the Illinois Natural History Survey noted that higher flows in the river reduced summer water temperatures, thereby slowing decomposition of the sewage and allowing it to spread further downstream before being decomposed. The survey also documented the biological effects of the sewage advancing down the river like a slowly moving flood wave. Changes in bottom-dwelling organisms approached Peoria by

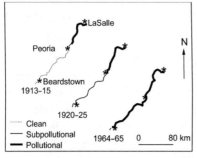

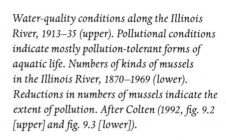

Water-quality conditions along the Illinois River, 1913–35 (upper). Pollutional conditions indicate mostly pollution-tolerant forms of aquatic life. Numbers of kinds of mussels in the Illinois River, 1870–1969 (lower). Reductions in numbers of mussels indicate the extent of pollution. After Colten (1992, fig. 9.2 [upper] and fig. 9.3 [lower]).

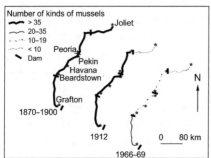

1915, moved through the waters of Lake Peoria by 1925, and reached Beardstown by 1964. Changes in the biological community occurred as species tolerant of pollution replaced species present before. Many of these tolerant species provided relatively poor food for commercially harvested fish and waterfowl, which also declined in number and variety. Mussels were particularly badly affected, dropping from more than thirty-five species to fewer than ten as the front of pollution advanced.[13]

The effects of the unsanitary canal on the Illinois River were not as straightforward, however, as a simple downstream progression. The extra flow diverted into the river raised water levels and increased the extent of floodplain inundation, which initially benefited fish and other organisms until the increased pollution created critically low levels of dissolved oxygen. As water levels rose, some riverside trees died off, causing a loss of mature pin oak (*Quercus palustris*) and pecan (*Carya illinoensis*) trees that provided food for mallard ducks (*Anas platyrhynchos*) and wood ducks (*Aix sponsa*). The dead trees provided nest sites for cavity-nesting birds such as tree swallows (*Iridoprocne bicolor*) and prothonotary warblers (*Protonotaria citrea*), which increased in numbers until the 1940s, when the last of the dead trees fell over and bird populations declined markedly.[14]

These responses to increased pollution and flow played out over decades, but scientists in the first decades of the twentieth century struggled to understand the immediate and longer-term effects of the changes in the river's flow. Victor Shelford wrote angrily in 1918:

> There has been too much bald scientific and business sophistry in the matter [of fish and river pollution]. Ichthyologists, biologists, engineers, sanitarians, industrial chemists, and business men, without consultation, cooperation, or critical analysis, have proceeded on the basis of their imperfect and fragmentary knowledge to draw inferences as to the effect of this or that on fishes. The inferences of some scientists are not especially more in keeping with an equitable decision relative to a policy favorable to the public interest than was the exclamation of a manufacturer when confronted with a law intended to stop his factory from polluting streams: "What! stop a great industry because of a few fish!" . . . We have all sinned alike until it becomes imperative that we take stock of our knowledge, now that we are under the pressure of numerous problems demanding immediate solution.[15]

Shelford went on to discuss nine fundamental questions that needed to be addressed in assessing the effects of pollution on the river ecosystem: Is the animal used in testing the toxicity of a polluting substance one of representative sensitiveness? What is the most sensitive stage in the life history of the test animal and of any useful animals associated with it? When is the pollution most concentrated? What is the toxicity of untreated polluting effluents, of each residual of processes of partial recovery, or of treatment by additions to the effluent? Do animals turn back from the polluting substance and thus escape destruction, or do they swim into it and die? Do polluting substances cover the bottom and make conditions unsuitable for eggs? If the supply of useful animals is depleted, will recovery be rapid or slow? Can correct decisions be reached without investigation of individual cases that arise? What is the real value of the waste when the amount of the damage it causes is added to its commercial value? The number and breadth of these questions give some insight into how difficult it is to unravel the complexities of ecosystem response to pollutants. Scientists continue to struggle today to answer these questions precisely in relation to new suites of pollutants in surface and groundwaters.[16]

The year 1921 may have been a nadir in terms of sheer volume of sewage entering the Illinois River. Urban population in the river basin increased from 2.7 million people in 1920 to 3.6 million in 1922, with most of this increase occurring in Chicago. The Sanitary District of Chicago began treating drinking water with chlorine in 1912 and started operating sewage treatment plants on the Des Plaines and Little Calumet Rivers in 1922. This helped reduce sewage loading to the Illinois,

View across the Illinois River of a portion of Peoria, Illinois, in 1900, showing manufacturing. Courtesy, Bradley University.

although these plants treated mostly domestic waste and waste from meat-packing plants, leaving the organic and inorganic effluent from a wide variety of other manufacturers untreated. These untreated manufacturing wastes contributed more than 40 percent of the total waste load by the late 1920s. By that time only pollution-tolerant organisms could survive in the upper Illinois, which looked and smelled polluted as far downstream as La Salle. Commercial fisheries declined to 2.3 million kilograms in 1931.[17]

Oxygen levels in the Illinois began to improve, as most of the larger cities along the river built sewage treatment plants during the late 1920s and early 1930s, but treatment of industrial wastes lagged behind. A 1937 survey found that industries were discharging wastes equivalent to the sewage produced by 2 million people into the river. Conditions improved only gradually: over 90 percent of factory effluent received some treatment by 1950, but substances such as phenols, acids, and oils remained a major source of contamination. Fingernail clams (Sphaeriidae) disappeared from the river during the 1950s, perhaps because of high ammonia levels; populations of canvasback ducks (*Aythya valisineria*), diving ducks that ate the clams, then rapidly declined. Even the carp declined, and fish catches fell to 0.9 million kilograms by 1960, after which commercial fishing largely ceased. Industrial wastes entering the river in 1963 still equaled the sewage produced by 900,000 people.[18]

Water-quality conditions along the Illinois River did not really improve substantially until passage of federal water pollution controls acts, including the 1977 Clean Water Act. During the 1970s, the Sanitary District of Chicago launched the $3.8 billion Tunnel and Reservoir Plan, also known as the Deep Tunnel Project. The project collects sewer overflows during major rainfalls into several huge tunnels and reservoirs until the water is processed in district facilities. About $4 billion in federal and local funds spent on waste treatment in the Illinois drainage basin between 1965 and 1975 produced improvements during the next decade. In the Chicago River, pollution-tolerant sludge worms and midge larvae were about the only organisms able to survive on the streambed until the early 1980s. As the sanitary district began adding oxygen to the water and stopped adding chlorine, diversity increased as snails, fingernail clams, leeches, and other invertebrates returned. During the period 1981–85, Lake Michigan diversions averaged 97 cubic meters per second, with 47 used for water supply and 50 for dilution. Water-quality indicators such as temperature, dissolved oxygen, and turbidity were generally better during the years 1985–89 than they had been during 1979–84. Some organisms less tolerant of pollution began to return, including a species of sauger (*Stizostedion canadense*) that now supports a nationally ranked annual fishing tournament. Fish species present in the sanitary canal increased from three in the period 1974–77 to twenty-two in 1988–91.[19]

The ages of freshwater mussels collected during the decade 1990–99 suggest that mussels began to re-colonize parts of the upper Illinois during the early 1980s. Scientists found five or more species in recently formed mussel beds at four sites along the upper river. They also collected individuals of six species that had been extinct along the entire main channel. Populations in tributary streams presumably supplied the pioneers to re-colonize the main channel, but biologists have also documented backwater lakes in which the interactions among the physical properties of the lake, waterfowl, fish, and diverse mussel fauna have preserved native mussel diversity and limited the encroachment of exotic species of mussels. Native unionid mussels are among the most endangered groups of animals in the world, and scientists documenting re-colonization in the upper Illinois carefully noted that, although the present community does not approximate the community in existence prior to 1900, time and continued improvements in river condition may allow the mussels to return.[20]

VANISHING UNIONID MUSSELS

Commercial harvest of mussels along the Illinois River continued even as increasing municipal and industrial pollution was limiting the river's ability to support diverse and abundant aquatic life. Commercial harvest returned during the second half of the twentieth century because the pearl culture in Japan relied on shell pieces. Mussel fishers for the Japanese industry focused on the Illinois River mussel stocks after those in the Tennessee River system had been severely depleted. William Starrett undertook a survey of pearly mussels (Unionacea) throughout the Illinois River system in connection with the resurgence of commercial mussel harvest. Whereas forty-nine species of mussels were found throughout the river system during the period 1870–1900, Starrett found only twenty-four species during 1966–69, five of which were represented by a single individual. Nonetheless, 500,000 kilograms of mussels were harvested from the river as late as 1991. The harvest was closed in 1994, in part as a result of continued declines in mussel abundance and diversity and in part because of the threat to populations of native mussels posed by the introduced zebra mussel (*Dreissena polymorpha*).[21]

Native to freshwater lakes of southeastern Russia, zebra mussels first entered the Great Lakes system at Lake St. Clair in 1988 through ballast water emptied from ships. Zebra mussels spread from Lake Michigan through the canal and into the Illinois River by way of their tiny larvae, which drift downstream with the current until the larvae are large enough and find suitable habitat on which to settle. First found in the Illinois River during 1991 about 100 kilometers downstream from Peoria, zebra mussels increased dramatically during the next two years. The large flood throughout the Upper Mississippi River basin in 1993 probably helped disperse the mussels and produced a population explosion on the lower Illinois River, with densities as high as 60,000 mussels per square meter of streambed. Although these extreme numbers declined during the next two years, zebra mussels are on the Illinois to stay. Their microscopic larvae were found drifting in the river's waters at densities of greater than 100 larvae per liter during 1994 and 1995, resulting in more than 60 million larvae passing a site on the river each second.[22]

Like a boxer reeling from repeated hard punches, North American mussels are going down from the combined effects of commercial harvest, habitat disruption and loss, water pollution, and introduced species: our native mussels are one of the most endangered groups of organisms in the world. Of 297 taxa in North America, a third are endangered, more than 14 percent are threatened, and another 24 percent are of special concern. In other words, at least 71 percent of the mussel species are either gone or in trouble. The 24 mussel species Starrett found during the 1960s have held steady until today, although their abundance is only about one-fifth what it was in the 1960s.[23]

One of the limitations to recovery of mussel populations along the Illinois is likely the presence of contaminants not removed during wastewater treatment. A 1998 study noted that portions of the river where fingernail clams and other bottom-dwelling organisms died out during the years 1955–58 have not been re-colonized by these organisms, despite the presence of populations in tributary streams and isolated portions of the main river. The scientists conducting the study found that fingernail clams, which obtain their food by filtering organic matter from the water and streambed sediments, could not effectively filter feed where sodium cyanide was present. Sodium cyanide enters surface waters as a by-product of mining or manufacturing processes involving metals.[24]

The effect of a single highly toxic chemical compound on mussels indicates the complex interrelations between water quality and biological communities along the river. Dispersal and concentrations of pollutants are strongly influenced by the movements of water and sediment along the river, which in turn are largely controlled by the complex river engineering begun during the nineteenth century and accelerated during the twentieth century. It is useful to review twentieth-century engineering modifications to the river corridor before returning to water quality during the twentieth century.

BINDING THE ILLINOIS: LOCKS AND DAMS

During the twentieth century, the Illinois River was drawn into the steadily accelerating process of engineering channels in the Upper Mississippi River basin to improve navigation for commercial barges. The US Congress autho-rized the Army Corps of Engineers in 1907 to establish a navigation channel 1.8 meters (6 feet) deep along the Upper Mississippi River. During the period 1930–40, this channel was deepened to 2.7 meters (9 feet). Creation of the naviga-tion channel—a central portion of the river along which a minimum depth of water was guaranteed throughout the year—relied on the combined effects of dredging, wing and spur dikes, and locks and dams. Despite the American tradi-tion of celebrating individualism and uniqueness, engineers redesigned rivers to increase conformity. Dredging removed the sediment flowing steadily into the rivers from the cleared and cropped uplands, ensuring uniform channel dimen-sions. Wing and spur dikes aided the dredging efforts by directing the current toward the central channel in a manner that encouraged scouring of sediment from the streambed. Dams, which included locks to facilitate passage of barges upstream and downstream, backed up sufficient water to maintain some mini-mum depth in shallow portions of the river, helping to ensure uniform flow depth.[25]

Aerial view of locks downstream from Peoria under construction during the 1930s. Courtesy, Bradley University.

Navigation dams added to the Illinois River during the 1930s were specifically designed to guarantee the 2.7-meter-deep navigation channel that was becoming standard throughout the Upper Mississippi. The series of locks and dams creating the Illinois Deep Waterway was completed by 1933, and barge traffic immediately increased. As river historian James Gray wrote in 1940, "Today, a lively procession of boats moves up and down the Illinois. They carry machinery and manufactured goods out of Chicago; corn from the rich agricultural districts of Illinois; coal from the rich bituminous district." Larger boats worked the lower Illinois, taking cargo to St. Louis, and smaller boats moved along the upper stretches of the Illinois near Marseilles.[26]

As indicated in Gray's description, most of this navigation was aimed at moving bulk commodities such as grain, but the necessity to move troops quickly and efficiently during World War II also influenced river engineering. A passage Gray wrote in 1940 reflects the contemporary attitude toward rivers: "The waterways might still be useful. Army engineers set resolutely about the task of making

A 2008 view of the lock and dam complex along the Illinois River at Starved Rock (upper) and the lake-like backwater created upstream from the dam (lower). The monotony of the lower view reflects the physical uniformity created by backwaters above lock and dam complexes.

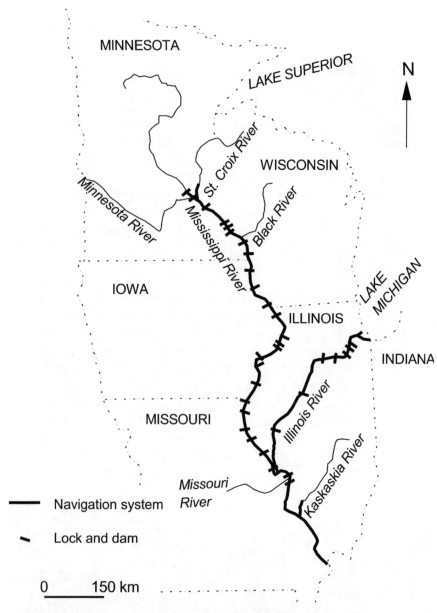

Map of the extent of the navigation system and the location of locks and dams on the Upper Mississippi River and the Illinois River. After Bhowmik and Adams (1989, fig. 1).

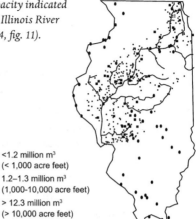

Locations of dams in Illinois, with mean storage capacity indicated by dot size. Only larger dams are shown outside the Illinois River basin. After Critical Trends Assessment Project (1994, fig. 11).

·   <1.2 million m³
(< 1,000 acre feet)
▪   1.2–1.3 million m³
(1,000-10,000 acre feet)
●   > 12.3 million m³
(> 10,000 acre feet)

America's system of streams navigable. To the passive unruliness of nature they opposed new mechanized forces. Rocks that stood in the way of future traffic were blasted out; the caprices of the Illinois's 'mighty crooked water' were sternly corrected."[27]

As barge traffic grew steadily during the period 1940–80, new lock and dam complexes were built along the Illinois and the Mississippi. At present, seven locks and dams regulate water depth along the Illinois River, which continues to serve as a primary commercial transport corridor between the Great Lakes and the Mississippi River. Operation of these lock and dam complexes is intimately connected to a variety of changes that occurred along the Illinois River during the twentieth century, starting with the transport and storage of sediment.

TO DRAIN OR NOT TO DRAIN?

Contrasting trends affected the extent of wetlands in the Illinois River basin during the twentieth century. Illinois lost nearly 30 percent of its wetlands during the period 1906–22 as drainage technology improved, as described in chapter 6. Franklin D. Roosevelt's New Deal agencies such as the Civilian Conservation Corps re-drained previously drained lands in Illinois and adjacent states. But the period around World War II also saw the formation of Ducks Unlimited, which began to restore wetlands. The US Fish and Wildlife Service undertook the first national survey to document the distribution, quality, and extent of wetlands; its 1956 publication highlighted the massive loss of wetlands and the consequent decline in waterfowl numbers, as well as introducing the word *wetlands* to common use. In 1958 the US Congress responded with a Wetlands Easement Program funded by duck stamp money that helped private landowners preserve wetlands. In contrast, the US Department of Agriculture's (USDA's) Soil Conservation Service continued to promote wetland drainage until the early 1960s, and massive postwar suburban sprawl resulted in large losses of wetlands. Wetlands received some legal protection under Section 404 of the 1972 Clean Water Act. Conflicting attitudes toward what Ann Vileisis has described as "a landscape on the periphery" and "the most controversial landscape in America" continued throughout the twentieth century, and by the 1980s Illinois and neighboring states had lost more than 80 percent of their wetlands.[28]

Steadily dropping populations of water birds accompanied the loss of wetlands, as described by Albert Herre in chapter 6. The birds also faced other challenges, such as lead poisoning from spent bird shot ingested by the birds while feeding. Frank Bellrose first called the public's attention to lead poisoning in a pioneering study along the Illinois River and its backwaters. When Bellrose published the definitive study "Lead Poisoning as a Mortality Factor in Waterfowl Populations" in 1959, he estimated that 2–3 percent of the entire North American waterfowl population died from lead poisoning each year. Little or no controversy arose from this study, but Bellrose kept working on the issue. He eventually realized that as much as 40 percent of the waterfowl population ingested lead shot during a single season of exposure. Sometimes a bird ingested a large amount of shot, was acutely poisoned, and died quickly. More commonly, the bird ate one or two pellets and died slowly, losing 30–50 percent of its normal weight over several weeks. When a few birds weakened or died, predators and scavengers ate their bodies and no one noticed. Occasional massive die-offs attracted more attention. Each autumn, thousands of hunters blasted away at the birds, and lead shot littered the beds of lakes and rivers from the northern breeding grounds to the southern wintering grounds. Species that fed most actively on the bottom ingested the most shot. Mallards (*Anas platyrhynchos*) were particularly susceptible, as were black ducks (*Anas rubripes*), mottled ducks (*Anas fulvigula*), pintails (*Anas acuta*), canvasbacks (*Aythya valisineria*), redheads (*Aythya americana*), and ring-necked (*Aythya collaris*) ducks.

Controversy erupted twenty years after Bellrose's initial study, when the US Fish and Wildlife Service proposed in 1974 to require the use of steel shot for hunting waterfowl in selected areas. Steel shot is less dense than lead, and a blast of steel shot does not scatter as widely or as far. As Bellrose wrote in a 1986 review of the issue, "The lower density of steel shot can be compensated for by increasing shot size and velocity, thus delivering similar levels of energy to the target [bird]. No significant differences in crippling rates [result]." Despite the cries of outrage from hunters, the ban on lead shot improved the chances of a duck being able to survive among the diminished wetlands of the Illinois and other rivers.[29]

BRINGING THE FARMLANDS TO THE RIVER VALLEYS: SEDIMENTATION IN THE ILLINOIS RIVER BASIN

The contemporary Illinois River flows along an outsize valley with dimensions formed by an earlier iteration of the Mississippi River and glacial outburst floods, such as the Kankakee Torrent. This contributed in part to the Illinois River's historical sinuosity and its continuing low gradient. The energy of a river to transport sediment can be calculated as stream power, the product of discharge and downstream gradient. Other things being equal, a river of low gradient has less power to carry the sediment supplied to it from adjacent hill slopes and tributary streams. The earliest historical descriptions of the Illinois River emphasize the clarity of the water and the "clean sand" along much of the river bottom. The river and its backwaters now tend to remain turbid as a result of silt and clay that remain suspended in the water. Two changes during the past century have reduced the Illinois's ability to carry sediment: an increase in sediment supplied to the river and the loss of gradient and velocity in sections of the river impounded behind dams.

Agriculture is the primary source of increased sediment to the Illinois River. Intense row cropping became common practice during and following World War II, as increasingly larger farm machinery, good prices for crops, and abundant synthetic fertilizers made it easier for farmers to attain high yields. Row cropland increased about 67 percent in the Illinois River basin between 1945 and 1986, reflecting an important change in the agricultural landscape and the economy. Family farms with crops surrounded by patches of woodland and native vegetation, some planted as part of conservation practices instituted after the 1930s Dust Bowl, gave way to the Green Revolution and the objective of feeding the world using giant farm machinery, intensive application of fertilizers and pesticides, and an industrial approach to maximizing food production. Buffer strips of native vegetation around farm fields and along stream courses were ripped out to make way for industrial-scale row cropping.

Buffer strips are like the mussel beds of the agricultural landscape, in that they act as filters. Hard rains running off the bare soil of farm fields carry along sediment and dissolved chemicals. A strip of woodland and shrubs slows down the water, allowing it to soak into the ground. Sediment is deposited in the buffer strip but typically not in sufficient depths to smother the vegetation, which continues to grow and stabilize the newly added sand, silt, and clay. Nitrogen and phosphorus

Settlers and cleared croplands along the Illinois River, 1904. Note the erosion of unvegetated stream banks at the center of the photograph. Courtesy, Abraham Lincoln Presidential Library, Springfield, Illinois.

from the fertilizer runoff are taken up by the native plants or processed by soil microbes, and even the toxic pesticides are at least partially stored in place rather than leaking into the nearest river. Removal of these buffers, along with cropping on lands formerly left uncleared, increased the erosion rate of soils across the Illinois River basin and decreased the filtering of agricultural runoff. Nani Bhowmik and Mike Demissie found in 1989 that 62 percent of sediment entering the main river comes from upland areas, most of which are used to grow crops. Illinois farmers are smoothing out the undulations in their already flat state. An estimated 5 to 23 centimeters of topsoil has eroded from Illinois uplands since settlement by Europeans. Soil erosion from croplands across Illinois is presently estimated at 143 million metric tons each year, and much of this goes into the lowest points on the landscape: rivers and wetlands. Unfolding events continue to support the apocryphal assertion of a Native American who watched European farmers busting the sod: "Grass no good upside down." Tallgrass prairie historically covered 8.9 million hectares in the state of Illinois. By the end of the twentieth century the prairie had been reduced to 930 hectares, a decline of 99.9 percent.[30]

The widespread channelization discussed previously further contributed to increased sediment in the main river. When a channel is straightened and deepened, its downstream gradient and velocity increase, providing more energy to

Cornfields behind the levee along the Illinois River at Beardstown, 2008.

erode the channel bed and banks and to keep the sediment mobilized by this erosion moving downstream. Richard Phipps, Gary Johnson, and Paul Terrio of the US Geological Survey used tree roots and tree rings to document changes in the tributary Kankakee River, where channelization shortened the mainstem from 420 kilometers to 140 kilometers in length and doubled the gradient from 8 to 16 centimeters per kilometer. Prior to channelization, the upstream portion of the Kankakee meandered back and forth across a valley bottom 5–8 kilometers wide in the Grand Marsh. Channelization of the river through the marsh began in 1860, and by 1918 the entire upper river was channelized and the Grand Marsh was converted to croplands. This resulted in an increased sediment load within the channelized reach and increased sediment deposition downstream, although the rush of sediment downstream was not immediate. Lateral tree roots initially grow just beneath the surface. By measuring the depth of these now deeply buried roots and using tree rings to determine when the burial occurred, Phipps and his colleagues found in 1995 that sedimentation rates had increased most dramatically after 1950, presumably as a result of more intensive agriculture and soil erosion in the drainage basin, combined with soil compaction and increased stream flow during large floods that occurred between 1950 and the 1995 study.

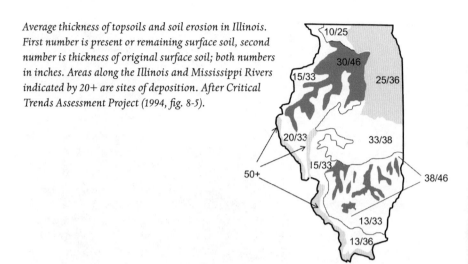

Average thickness of topsoils and soil erosion in Illinois. First number is present or remaining surface soil, second number is thickness of original surface soil; both numbers in inches. Areas along the Illinois and Mississippi Rivers indicated by 20+ are sites of deposition. After Critical Trends Assessment Project (1994, fig. 8-5).

The study by Phipps and his colleagues explored the results of channelization along one stretch of one tributary to the Illinois River. The great majority of tributary streams in some portions of the Illinois River basin were channelized, and all are surrounded by agricultural lands: the cumulative effects of these activities add up to a tremendous volume of sediment coming into the river corridor. The "sternly corrected" rivers appear to be reminding us sternly of basic physics: steeper channelized rivers with smoother banks equals more energy to erode and transport sediment, which translates to more sediment deposited in the quieter waters of bottomlands and large sinuous rivers.[31]

The combined effects of increased sediment eroding from uplands and moving through channelized and leveed rivers hit the backwater lakes particularly hard. Diversion of Lake Michigan water at Chicago starting in 1900 further increased the flow and increased the water level in the remaining backwater lakes still connected to the channel. If flowing water is carrying sediment, some of that sediment will settle out wherever the flow slows down. Consequently, some of the sediment moving down the main river with higher flows was diverted into the backwater lakes, which began to fill with sediment at a faster rate than previously. As Frank Bellrose and his coauthors wrote in 1979: "Soil erosion, the high velocities of tributaries, and the sluggish flow of the main channel—together have brought about an environmental disaster: backwater lakes of the Illinois River are filling at a rapid rate leading to their early extinction." Construction of the lock and dam complexes essentially created more sections of very low flow velocity along which sediment could accumulate on the bed of the main channel. Locks and dams have created more than fifty backwater lakes in which sediment has steadily accumulated over the past six decades.

As of 1993, Nani Bhowmik estimated that the total sediment input to the main Illinois River valley was 25 million metric tons per year. This equates to 361 tons of sediment per square kilometer of the drainage basin each year. Typical values of sediment yield from relatively flat landscapes with good vegetation cover are closer to 1 ton per square kilometer per year. Even where easily eroded loess soils such as those in Illinois are present, typical values are closer to 100–200 tons per square kilometer. The lands of the Illinois River thus yield abnormally large amounts of sediment. Of the 25 million tons entering the river, 6.3 million metric tons per year continue through the Illinois to the Mississippi River, and the rest are deposited somewhere in the Illinois River valley. This valley is accumulating sediment at an average rate of 2–5 centimeters per year, with much higher rates in many of the backwater areas.[32]

Peoria Lake is one of the best-studied backwaters. This largest and deepest bottomland lake along the Illinois River is a natural lake created where sediment deposition at tributary mouths constricted the river flow. The gradient of the Illinois along this portion of its valley is so low that the river drops only 3 centimeters per kilometer traveled. Today, the lake receives the majority of its sediment from the main channel, with an additional 40 percent coming from several smaller tributary channels. Although water does flow through Peoria Lake, the lake's average depth has declined steadily from 2.4 meters in 1903 to 1.5 meters in 1965, 1.2 meters in 1976, and 0.8 meters in 1985. Put another way, the lake has lost 68 percent of its 1903 volume as approximately 113.5 million cubic meters (92,000 acre-feet) of sediment have accumulated along the lake bottom. These numbers reflect the fact that the Illinois River carries a lot of sediment. About 90–95 percent of this sediment is carried suspended in the river flow, and most of it is silt and clay. Average annual sediment load on the Illinois River at Henry during the period 1983–86 was 78 parts sediment per million parts water. This might not sound like much, but it quickly adds up to 2,930 metric tons of sediment per day. Nani Bhowmik predicted in 1993 that within ten to fifteen years the lake would have lost most of its capacity outside of the navigation channel. This prediction has not fully come true because the lake is now being actively dredged.[33]

At least some of this sediment that might otherwise settle from the river is continually stirred up by the passage of barges. Bhowmik noted in 1993 that the average commercial barge tow along the Illinois is nine barges (three wide by three long), creating an aggregate craft 32 meters wide and 180 meters long that requires a draft varying from 0.6 to 2.7 meters. The passage of each barge stirs up the bottom sediments and increases the concentration of sediment suspended

*View of Peoria Lake, 1917.
Courtesy, Abraham Lincoln
Presidential Library,
Springfield, Illinois.*

in the water column by up to five times (from 103 milligrams per liter to 500 milligrams per liter). Although this effect lasts only ten to fifteen minutes after a barge tow passes, Bhowmik noted that ten barges passed his monitoring sites during four days. This level of activity is likely sufficient to stress bottom-dwelling organisms such as mussels, insects, and plants by increasing turbidity and thus reducing the penetration of sunlight, as well as potentially smothering the bottom dwellers. Barges and other motorized boats also generate waves that enhance erosion of stream banks and contribute more sediment to the river, as well as uprooting aquatic plants that can stabilize bed and bank sediment. The effects of barge- and wind-generated turbidity tend to last much longer in backwater lakes, where seven to twelve days may be required before silt and clay settle from suspension in the water column. Moderate to strong winds recur more frequently than seven days in Illinois, helping to keep the sediment continually in suspension. Barges generate turbidity trails up to 1.6 kilometers long, some of which enter backwaters adjacent to the river. For the river ecosystem, Mark Twain's "lively procession of boats" is more like the fatally dangerous stream of cars on a busy street a squirrel tries to cross.[34]

Peoria Lake is unique only in its size. Of 300 backwater lakes present along the lower Illinois River in 1903, only 53 remain today. Many of the remaining lakes have lost from 30 percent to 100 percent of their capacity to sediment deposition. These rates of sediment accumulation are gradually changing the backwaters to

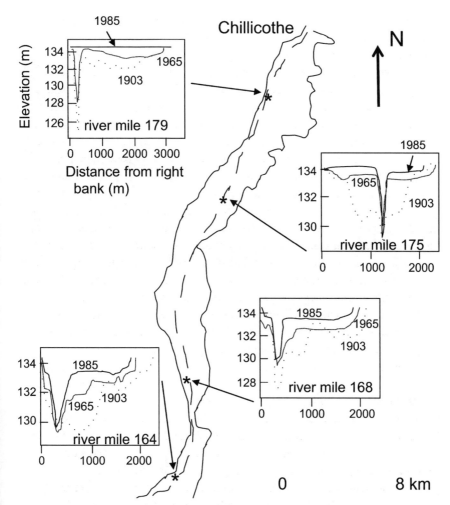

Map of Peoria Lake (shorelines indicated by solid lines, central channel indicated by dashed line), with inset cross-sections showing changes in lake volume from 1903 to 1985. After Bhowmik and Demissie (1989, fig. 2).

marshes. Clear water with aquatic plants growing on the lake bed transforms to excessively turbid, biologically barren areas and eventually to marsh habitat and terrestrial floodplains. In 1965, William Starrett and Arnold Fritz described how Quiver Lake, downstream from Peoria Lake near Havana, had changed: "Today Quiver Lake is devoid of aquatic plants. The formerly deep basin of the lake has been filled in with 4- to 8-foot deposits of silt."[35]

A tow five barges in width on the Illinois River at Havana, 2008.

Largemouth bass (*Micropterus salmoides*) provide an example of how these changes in backwaters affect individual species. Bass winter in backwaters; as sedimentation continues to fill these areas, fluctuating river levels and turbidity more severely limit depths and water quality for over-wintering fish. Other species appear to have crossed a threshold as habitat disappeared. Populations of game fish and ducks declined drastically from 1958 to 1964 along a 320-kilometer reach of the Illinois. The Illinois River valley was one of the most important autumn waterfowl staging areas in the United States before the 1950s. Biologist Frank Bellrose recorded 3.6 million mallard ducks during one week of the fall migration in 1944. Within a few years, the population of birds such as diving ducks had largely disappeared, and it has not yet recovered. The amazingly rapid loss of diving ducks provides a cautionary tale: although a river ecosystem can absorb a great deal of change, it can be pushed beyond the point of rapid or easy recovery.[36]

Biologists attribute declines in the numbers of diving ducks and other species to a feedback loop started by increased sedimentation. Sedimentation, along with waves and turbidity generated by barges, limits the ability of submerged aquatic plants to survive. This directly affects dabbling ducks such as pintail (*Anas acuta*), green-winged teal (*A. carolinensis*), and wigeon (*A. americana*), which correlate with the abundance of wetland plants. Reductions in aquatic plants also indirectly affect diving ducks that feed on fingernail clams. Removal of aquatic plants makes the streambed and banks more susceptible to erosion and helps smother the clams on which the ducks feed. The net result is to remove habitat and food for aquatic insects, fish, waterfowl, and mammals such as muskrats. Species composition shifts as fish populations previously dominated by sight predators such as northern pike (*Esox lucius*) and nest builders such as bowfin (*Amia calva*) become dominated by species that can locate their food by scent and scatter their eggs on lake beds of silt, such as carp. More important, rooted aquatic plants take up ammonia; in their absence, ammonia can build up to toxic levels in bottom sediments, limiting aquatic insects and possibly fish.[37]

Various attempts are under way to limit the adverse effects of sedimentation in backwater lakes. Soil and water conservation districts have intensified their efforts to reduce upland erosion. In 1989 the six districts around Peoria Lake were selected for a demonstration project that combines traditional soil conservation practices, such as contour plowing and shelterbelts around croplands, with removal of land from agricultural production through the Conservation Reserve Program. These changes are designed both to control the flow of sediment into the lake and to stabilize the streams transporting upland sediment. Combined with dredging the lake sediments, upland conservation practices have helped slow the rate of sedimentation in the lake.[38]

Aquatic vegetation including arrowhead (*Sagittaria latifolia*), sago pondweed (*Potamogeton pectinatus*), and wild celery (*Vallisneria americana*) has also been manually planted in backwater lakes. Floating breakwaters have been installed to limit the constant recycling of un-stabilized sediments between the lake bed and the water column in backwater lakes. By reducing wave energy, the breakwaters reduce disturbance of the lake bed and the substrate in which plants are growing. Where such techniques have been applied, the new vegetation beds have higher densities and more species of fish, birds, and muskrats than adjacent areas. Vegetation beds were so successful in attracting animals that netting was eventually placed around the plants to limit grazing pressure.[39]

Some observers have proposed a laborious process of returning sediment to the uplands from which it eroded. In addition to the expense and investment of energy required for such a human-mediated recycling of sediment, use of sediment along the river corridor can be problematic if the sediment is contaminated with heavy metals or synthetic chemicals. Having used reclaimed lake sediment to grow vegetables, biologist Stephen Ebbs and his colleagues demonstrated that although some of the vegetables grew exceptionally well in the lake sediment, they had elevated concentrations of zinc and molybdenum. Although the projected dietary intake of copper, molybdenum, and zinc from these plants was significantly higher than that from plants grown in a reference soil, these levels remain below levels believed to cause health hazards and are therefore considered safe to eat. Sediment containing residues of pesticides or other synthetic chemicals would more likely pose a hazard to humans consuming food grown in this material.[40]

The Army Corps of Engineers is also dredging sediment and creating stabilized sediment mounds in the Illinois River to make artificial islands. Construction of artificial islands has only been undertaken within the past few years, and it is too soon to determine how stable these islands will be, but they have the potential to enhance habitat complexity in the river by creating side channels and to improve navigation by keeping the main channel narrower and deeper. One observer facetiously likened these mounds to those built at Cahokia and elsewhere by prehistoric cultures. The reference to Cahokia is a reminder that people have been reconfiguring topography for a very long time. Geologists recently proposed that the past 300 years be designated as a new geological time period, the Anthropocene, in recognition of the enormous volume of sediment moved by humans, which now exceeds that moved by rivers or glaciers. We have in a geomorphic sense become the Illinois and other rivers, trying to control or mimic all historical river functions as we attempt to mitigate the results of past landscape engineering.[41]

One of the unique aspects of the Illinois River is that, as one of the most studied rivers in the world, the multitude of changes that occurred during the twentieth century are well documented. In 1966 Harlow Mills, William Starrett, and Frank Bellrose summarized the state of the river at that time and its changes during the preceding decades in *Man's Effect on the Fish and Wildlife of the Illinois River*. It is worth quoting at length from their concluding section before exploring in further detail the pollutants impacting the river, as their summary was written just before scientists began to realize the effects of the synthetic chemicals that have been manufactured and dispersed into the environment in ever greater quantities since World War II.

> It is difficult to believe that so much has happened to the Illinois River since [Charles] Kofoid published his comprehensive work in 1903. Starting with the diversion of Lake Michigan waters into the river in 1900, the ecology of this stream has been changed drastically several times. This diversion added to the fish habitat in the lower stretches and removed it completely in the upper river. Drainage enterprises removed half of the floodplain that the river once used and eliminated fish and waterfowl habitat. Navigation dams created new water areas while

destroying important waterfowl marshes. Domestic pollution has fluctuated up and down as new sewage treatment plants have been activated and then found to be inadequate as the rising tide of human population in the basin caught up with them. Chemicals have been released into the waters from developing industries on the river's banks and in the watershed. Although these actions have caused conditions to fluctuate widely, the net result has been an ever-diminishing biological resource as the aquatic habitat and its inhabitants have been degraded by the activities of man . . . We trust that the deleterious trends now apparent in the Illinois River can be changed . . . There must be desire . . . to translate present knowledge into action.[42]

POLLUTANTS IN THE ILLINOIS RIVER BASIN

If written words were like a movie, this section of the book might come with a warning, a sort of "PG" or "R" rating to alert the reader that what follows may be disturbing. The key point to keep in mind is that, unfortunately, the Illinois River is not unique in the United States or the world with respect to pollutants. This is our world—*our only world*—and it is vital that we recognize what is happening. We can change conditions to better protect and restore river environments, as demonstrated repeatedly by advances such as the Clean Water Act, but first we must be aware that there is a problem.

Sediment has been repeatedly identified as the most widespread source of pollution in many surface waters of the United States. All of the topographic rearrangement begun by nineteenth-century farmers and accelerated during the twentieth century shows up in sediment pollution. Soil erosion contributes 30.8 million metric tons of sediment to the streams of the Upper Illinois River basin each year. This equates to 1,013 tons of sediment per square kilometer each year, which is similar to the quantity of sediment coming from some of the world's steepest and most rapidly eroding mountainous areas. Concentrations of suspended solids range from less than 10 milligrams per liter to more than 50 milligrams per liter, with observed maximum concentrations of greater than 1,500 milligrams per liter. These maximum concentrations are unusually high for a river that does not drain mountainous terrain or a landscape recently disrupted by wildfire or a volcanic eruption. Concentrations are usually highest in summer, when agricultural activity disturbs the surface and rainfall runs off the ground, carrying sediment into stream channels. Once in the rivers, higher flows can keep the sediment moving downstream and erode the stream banks and bed. Because of the tremendous amount of sediment that enters streams in the Upper Illinois River basin each year, erosion remains the primary non-point source of contaminants.[43]

The LaMoine River, a tributary of the Illinois River, flowing turbid with suspended sediment, August 2008.

In addition to sediment, the heavy metals and synthetic chemicals that may limit recycling of backwater sediments along the Illinois River also limit human water consumption and the health of aquatic communities throughout much of the river basin. As in the case of the South Platte River basin, the US Geological Survey's National Water Quality Assessment (NAWQA) program, conducted in the 1990s, provides a baseline for understanding the sources and levels of contamination of surface and groundwaters, stream sediments, and tissues of living organisms in the Illinois River basin.

The Upper and Lower Illinois River basins form two of the fifty-nine regions of the United States assessed for the NAWQA program. As noted by Kelly Warner and Arthur Schmidt, the authors of an overview of the NAWQA findings, the Illinois River is the primary channel for transport and disposal of much of the state's human, animal, industrial, and agricultural wastes. Maintaining high standards of water quality is a challenge for a drainage that starts with a major metropolitan area like Chicago—and its unsanitary canal—in its headwaters and continues through additional metropolitan, industrial, and agricultural regions.

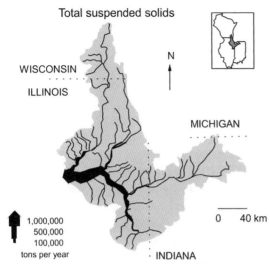

Total suspended solids

WISCONSIN
ILLINOIS

N

MICHIGAN

1,000,000
500,000
100,000
tons per year

0   40 km

INDIANA

Estimated annual load of total suspended solids in streams of the Upper Illinois River basin, 1978–97. The relative widths of the stream lines represent progressive downstream increases in sediment load. After Sullivan (2000, fig. 18).

As of 1990, agricultural land made up 75 percent of the Upper Illinois River basin, urban areas constituted 17 percent, and only 5 percent was in forest. Percentages of land in agriculture and forest have been declining since the 1970s. Effects of differing land uses show up clearly in the patterns of different contaminants in the Illinois River basin.[44]

Synthetic chemicals create a major source of contamination for surface and groundwaters in the upper Illinois River basin. The ability of microbes, plants, and river ecosystems to store, absorb, or break down these chemicals is limited. The NAWQA program measured several types of synthetic chemicals, including pesticides and volatile organic compounds. Chemical and physical properties of volatile organic compounds, such as the solvent tetrachloroethylene or the gasoline-related compound toluene, allow them to move freely between water and air phases. This means they can flow with tap water, vaporize while one is taking a hot shower or washing clothes, and be breathed in by the nearest humans. Production and use of these compounds increased greatly during the second half of the twentieth century. By 2000, about 60,000 known synthetic chemicals were used in manufacturing. Because almost no research has been devoted to how these chemicals combine with one another or with soil, air, and water, we remain ignorant of the by-products and degradation products that result when the original chemicals are released into the environment.[45]

In addition to the synthetic chemicals, more than 10,000 pesticides with over 250 active ingredients were in use during the late twentieth century. These chemicals stream into rivers from point sources such as municipal and industrial wastewaters and accidental spills. They trickle and seep in with storm runoff and groundwater discharge. Atmospheric deposition sprinkles them across rivers and floodplains. Individual chemicals can be dissolved in water or can attach to fine sediment or organic matter. Many of these chemicals, particularly those with low solubility in water, accumulate in the tissues of living organisms through time and can be passed on to other organisms. Many of the chemicals are toxic, carcinogenic, teratogenic, and mutagenic: precise technical terms for something that causes death, cancer, developmental changes or abnormalities (think of birds with crossed bills or frogs with legs coming out of their heads), or chromosomal changes, respectively. Scientists know relatively little about the hazards these chemicals create for living organisms, however, because there are so many chemicals, many of which have not been in existence long enough for investigators to document long-term health hazards. This ignorance is reflected by the fact that drinking-water or other water-quality standards have been set for almost none of these chemicals.[46]

Pesticides entering stream waters in the Upper Illinois River basin come from both agricultural and municipal sources. Herbicides are applied to more than 95 percent of the corn and soybean fields in Illinois and insecticides to about 40 percent. Although the total amount of active ingredients applied has decreased by about a quarter since 1982, herbicide application in agricultural areas of the upper Illinois basin is among the highest in the nation. Compounds such as atrazine, alachlor, and metolachlor constitute the bulk of these applications. Alachlor is a carcinogen that affects the liver. Metolachlor is a potential carcinogen that bioaccumulates in fish. Atrazine and alachlor are banned in the European Union, but herbicide atrazine is the most heavily used agricultural pesticide in the United States. It is important to recognize, however, that agricultural applications average 1.35 kilograms per hectare, whereas up to 11 kilograms per hectare are applied on suburban lawns. An estimated 1.7 million kilograms are applied each year in suburban Chicago, and another 54,500 kilograms of unused pesticides go into Chicago landfills each year. Seventy-five percent to 90 percent of Chicago households use pesticides including atrazine, 2,4-D, diuron, malathion, and diazinon against weeds and insects.[47]

Atrazine is toxic to humans. It adversely affects the function of the heart, lungs, liver, kidney, and brain, as well as causing developmental effects such as birth defects, structural anomalies, and adverse hormone changes. Atrazine creates these effects even when present in vanishingly small amounts. Communities with occasional or annual mean atrazine concentrations greater than three parts atrazine per billion parts water are considered high-risk by the US Environmental Protection Agency (EPA). During the period 1993 to 1998 there were fifty-three such watersheds nationwide, including the Illinois River. Perhaps most striking is

Crop duster spraying pesticides onto a cornfield along the Illinois River, August 2008.

the fact that the risks from atrazine can be reduced without a large reduction in total economic surplus by decreasing the rate of atrazine application and either charging consumers more for pesticide-free crops or replacing herbicides with mechanical weed removal. Under either scenario, the improvements in drinking-water quality and human health indicate that net benefits are likely to be higher than the cost of reduction. Documenting these effects, Aklilu Tesfamichael and his colleagues call into question the basic economics of contemporary agricultural practices.[48]

Chemicals do not stay where we put them. Imagine the world as composed primarily of fluxes rather than as the static landscape we may be more used to visualizing. Fluxes of air, soil, water, and organisms—and the chemicals traveling with them—continually redistribute the matter and energy on which all life depends. Now these fluxes also redistribute highly toxic materials that kill and deform. As the poet Dan Bellm wrote in his poem "Illinois River,"

> herbicide sprayed from a tank under the air-conditioned tractor and accumulating
> in the black soil, turning up years later in the drinking water at the bottom of the
> page in a newspaper report.[49]

NAWQA samples detected seventeen different pesticides at least once in both urban and agricultural areas in the Illinois River basin. These were not necessarily the same seventeen pesticides at different sites. Alachlor was detected primarily at agricultural sites and malathion at urban sites, for example, whereas atrazine was everywhere. The highest concentration at urban sites came from 2,4-D, which is highly toxic to fish and persists for up to three months in aquatic environments. The EPA has established drinking-water standards for only four of the pesticides tested for in the Upper Illinois (alachlor, atrazine, 2,4-D, and simazine). Each of these standards was exceeded for some sites in the basin. Of these compounds, atrazine and simazine are used extensively in city parks for weed control (atrazine) and algae control (simazine). Atrazine and simazine can persist in soil for six to twenty-four months, so they can continue to enter streams long after they are applied to a site. As might be expected, large spikes in pesticide levels in stream waters occur during May, when applications to urban and agricultural lands start each year. Each rainstorm that follows during the growing season can bring a new load of contaminants into streams. Atrazine in the agricultural Kankakee and Iroquois River basins, for example, exceeded EPA maximum contaminant levels for drinking water during runoff periods throughout the spring and summer.[50]

Volatile organic compounds (VOCs) are so-named not because they are created through natural, biological reactions but because they include carbon molecules in their structure. VOCs include compounds used as solvents, degreasers, lubricants, and fumigants and compounds used in dry-cleaning, production of plastics, pharmaceuticals, pesticides, textiles, and fluorocarbons. Semi-VOCs include polycyclic aromatic hydrocarbons produced during municipal incineration and coal combustion and phenols used in the manufacture of oil additives, drugs, resins, and plasticizers. Most point-source discharges of these compounds in the Upper Illinois River basin occur in the lower Des Plaines River basin within the metropolitan Chicago area. Sites where NAWQA samples included multiple VOCs were mostly within 3 kilometers of a point source, and concentrations along the Des Plaines River and in the Chicago area sometimes exceeded EPA maximum contaminant levels for individual compounds. Chloroform was the most common compound, followed by tetrachloroethylene, 1,1,1-trichloroethane, and others, with much of the detection occurring at sites downstream from wastewater treatment plants. Wastewater—an increasingly tragic word in a world with limited clean water—is primarily treated for particulate matter and biological contaminants. The water is physically screened, then aerated to allow dissolved gases to escape. Sludge and scum are removed, and chlorine is added to kill bacteria. Everything else dissolved in the water goes back into the nearest stream or the ocean.[51]

Pesticides and volatile organic compounds can reflect contemporary contaminant sources. Concentrations in surface waters increase rapidly as contaminated storm runoff enters a river but may then decrease as the contaminant is dispersed downstream, settles into bottom sediment, or is chemically altered under the influence of microbes present in the river. Groundwater moves more slowly, and contaminants must travel deeper into the ground with infiltrating water before they reach it. Biologically influenced chemical reactions occur more slowly than in streams, if at all. Groundwater thus provides a more conservative record that can reflect contemporary or past contaminant sources. Once in groundwater, however, contaminants can be harder to remove and can continue to slowly poison wells and seep into rivers. NAWQA samples from more than forty wells in shallow (less than 53 meters depth) groundwater in recently urbanized areas near Chicago found VOCs such as the gasoline additive methyl tert-butyl ether and chloroform in 74 percent of the wells, pesticides in 74 percent of the wells, and nitrate concentrations greater than 2 milligrams per liter in 30 percent of the wells. Although drinking water is not drawn from these particular wells, their contents reflect the shallow groundwater that is most commonly used for drinking water and that can recharge streams. Generations of readers have been impressed by the abilities of the fictional detective Sherlock Holmes to infer an individual's living habits from observations such as the wear in his shoes or clothing. Contemporary scientific sleuths can likewise infer our collective living habits from the contaminants dispersed in sediment, surface water, and groundwater.[52]

Synthetic chemicals can also persist in stream sediments and the tissues of living organisms for decades or longer, so their presence reflects sources of contaminants that may no longer be present. The use and manufacture of polychlorinated biphenyls (PCBs) have been banned in the United States since 1979 because of the severe health hazards they pose to humans and other organisms, yet NAWQA sampling during the 1990s found that, except for the notoriously contaminated Hudson River, the Upper Illinois basin had the highest concentrations of PCBs in stream sediments in the United States (8,850 micrograms per kilogram). Concentrations of DDT and chlordane, pesticides banned for agricultural use in the United States in 1972 and 1983, respectively, are also very high in the Upper Illinois compared to the rest of the United States. Concentrations of these contaminants are highest in urban areas such as near the Skokie River, which may reflect the use of DDT to control Dutch elm disease in urban areas. NAWQA samples of fish tissue also sometimes contained high concentrations of DDE (a breakdown product of DDT), dieldrin (another pesticide now banned), and chlordane.

NAWQA scientists carefully looked for patterns in contaminant occurrence. Analyzing whole fish, fillets, and fat from thirty-five fish species, scientists found that a significant part of the variation in contaminant concentration among samples reflected either the position of the fish species in the food web or the percentage of body-fat content in the species or individual. Bigger, predatory fish ingested the toxins accumulated in the bodies of their prey, and fish with greater body fat stored more toxins in their fat cells. The tendency of a variety of contaminants to concentrate in fat cells of most living organisms provides another reason to be concerned by the increase in obesity in the United States. Despite these patterns related to fish characteristics, concentrations of chlordane, DDT, and PCBs in fish were generally higher in urban areas, and concentrations of dieldrin were higher away from urban areas. Of these contaminants, only PCBs reached concentrations that exceeded US Food and Drug Administration advisory levels for human consumption, and all the samples that exceeded these levels were from the Illinois and Des Plaines Rivers in and downstream from Chicago.[53]

Contaminants residing in the tissues of fish limit not only human consumption of those fish but also the ability of the fish to survive. NAWQA scientists found that the structure of fish communities, in terms of number and type of species, correlates strongly with water-quality conditions. Streams in agricultural regions, despite excess sediment and nutrients, tend to have relatively diverse fish communities that include species such as shorthead redhorse (*Moxostoma macrolepidotum*), rosyface shiner (*Notropis rubellus*), blacknose dace (*Rhinichthys atratulus*), and northern hog sucker (*Hypentelium nigricans*), which are intolerant of pollution and habitat degradation. Streams in more heavily urbanized areas have fish communities dominated by fewer, more tolerant species such as goldfish (*Carassius auratus*), carp-goldfish hybrids, and green sunfish (*Lepomis cyanellus*).[54]

Other studies of aquatic communities in the Upper Illinois River basin illustrate these trends. Indices of biotic integrity, which include measures of fish, stream insects, and stream habitat, range from poor to excellent in streams draining rural areas. Streams with more than 10 percent of urban land in their drainage basin consistently have fair or poor scores on such indices. Faith Fitzpatrick, Mitchell Harris, and other scientists conducting these studies attributed low urban scores to elevated concentrations of trace elements, including arsenic, cadmium, chromium, copper, lead, and mercury—all of which are highly toxic and accessible to living organisms—in the sediment of urban streams. Differences in scores among the agricultural streams in part reflect physical stream characteristics. Streams with relatively steep slopes and rocky beds, for example, tended to have higher scores than streams with relatively low slopes and sandy or silty beds, in part because the latter streams were more likely to have been channelized.[55]

Water-quality studies in the Lower Illinois River basin paint a similar picture. Primary water-quality issues include sedimentation, toxic chemicals in sediments,

Aerial view of the city of Peoria, 1974. Courtesy, Bradley University.

high concentrations of nutrients and agricultural chemicals, and low levels of dissolved oxygen. During the 1988 summer low-flow period, dissolved oxygen concentrations in the Lower Illinois River decreased to two parts oxygen per million parts water: the EPA criterion for supporting aquatic life is five parts per million. When they describe clear, flowing water sparkling in the sunlight, writers like to use evocative phrases such as *living waters*. When contaminants suck up sufficient oxygen to make the fish and other organisms suffocate, we have to write about dead waters.[56]

Many of the varieties of contaminants present in water and sediment along the Lower Illinois River also show up in the tissues of organisms within the river corridor. A study by Anna Tryfonas and colleagues of red-eared slider turtles (*Trachemys scripta elegans*) found high concentrations of metals in the sediment of backwater lakes relative to the concentrations in water, soil, and plant tissues. Sliders were chosen for study because they are long-lived and widely distributed, and they constitute a large proportion of the total biomass found in backwater lakes along the Illinois. Sliders living in backwater lakes contained detectable levels of five metals in their eggs and nine metals in their eggshells. Scientists conducting the study were particularly concerned by the levels of tin, which enters the river from boat antifouling compounds, and nickel. In addition to creating health hazards for the turtles, these metals can be passed on to the foxes, crows, raccoons, skunks, and other animals that eat turtle eggs.[57]

Another study by a team led by Tryfonas focused on lead concentrations in the tissues of mallards and wood ducks using waterfowl management areas along the Illinois River. These ducks can ingest lead shotgun pellets or acquire metals through contaminated sediments or through transfer up the food chain from other organisms. Because ducks can accumulate lead in their organs, the animals are used as indicators of environmental contaminants. Concerns about lead pellets resulted in a ban on the use of lead shot for waterfowl hunting in the United States in 1991. The effects of this ban show up in the 1997–98 study, in which lead concentrations in the livers of ducks were lower than previously reported and were within background levels. Results such as these provide one example of why there is reason to hope and to act to reduce environmental contaminants.[58]

TOO MUCH OF A GOOD THING

Nutrients are one of the primary groups of water contaminants assessed for the NAWQA program. As mentioned in the discussion of the South Platte River basin, excess nutrients can decrease levels of dissolved oxygen present in stream water, occur in forms toxic to fish, and create health hazards for humans. Nitrogen enters streams from agricultural fertilizers (195,000 metric tons per year in the upper Illinois River basin) and urban wastewater treatment plants (23,600 metric tons per year). To put these volumes in perspective, the average annual flux of total nitrogen to the Gulf of Mexico from the Mississippi River during the period 1981–2005 was 1.47 million metric tons. This means the Illinois River basin, which comprises 1 percent of the land area in the Mississippi River drainage, contributes 13 percent of the nitrogen coming down the Mississippi. Concentrations of nitrogen in the Lower Illinois River were under 3.0 milligrams per liter circa 1900; between 1980 and 1998 they averaged 5.5 milligrams per liter. Most of this increase resulted from agriculture. The largest changes in nitrogen export for the Mississippi River basin as a whole occurred between the 1950s and the 1980s, when fertilizer inputs increased from less than 1 million metric tons to more than 6 million metric tons per year. At sites within the upper Illinois River where intensive row cropping is present, such as Aux Sable Creek and the Mazon River, concentrations of nitrate nearly reach dangerous concentrations of 10 milligrams per liter—the maximum for drinking-water standards in the

United States. Concentrations above this level create a risk of health effects, such as blue-baby syndrome.[59]

Phosphates are the most common form of phosphorus in natural waters. Orthophosphate, which typically constitutes the majority of dissolved phosphates, can be readily assimilated by plants and can promote eutrophication, or excessive plant growth and consequent lack of dissolved oxygen as the plants decay. Concentrations of phosphate in the upper Illinois basin mainly reflect the locations of wastewater treatment plants, which pass on household fabric and dishwasher detergents and industrial phosphates used to prevent iron oxide or calcium carbonate crystallization in water. Daniel Sullivan, in his NAWQA summary report, describes phosphate concentrations in the urbanized Upper Illinois and Des Plaines River basins as "remarkably high."[60]

NAWQA scientists assessing concentrations of nutrients in the upper Illinois River during the period 1978–97 estimated that 54 percent of nutrients originate from non-point sources, including agricultural lands, urban areas, groundwater, atmospheric deposition, and plants. The remaining 46 percent come from point sources, primarily wastewater treatment plants. This is reflected in geographic patterns of nutrient distribution. Levels of all nutrients except nitrates were generally highest in streams draining urban areas of the Des Plaines River basin, where municipal and industrial waste discharges are widespread. It's easy to point a metaphorical finger at nineteenth-century Chicago sluicing its sewage downstream in a canal, but our modern wastewater treatment clearly leaves plenty to be desired.[61]

Levels of nitrates in the Upper Illinois River basin were greatest in streams draining agricultural areas, where abundant fertilizers are applied to farm fields. Plants help to reduce nitrate levels. Crops absorb and use some of the nutrients in which they are regularly drenched, as reflected in seasonal patterns of nutrient concentrations. These concentrations drop during the spring and summer growing season, reach the lowest levels in late summer to early autumn, and then zoom back up to the highest levels when plants go dormant during winter. Plants can only do so much, however, when much of the basin is covered by pavement or regularly fertilized crops, and dilution is ineffective when nitrate concentrations increase downstream as each city or farm district adds its load to the river. Levels of nitrate, phosphorus, and orthophosphate at the most downstream site measured in the Upper Illinois River basin were among the highest measured by NAWQA in the entire Mississippi River basin. The Des Plaines River basin had higher levels of most nutrients than the adjacent Fox and Kankakee basins because of land-use patterns and the presence of Chicago's canal, into which three large Chicago wastewater treatment plants discharge. Loads of nitrate

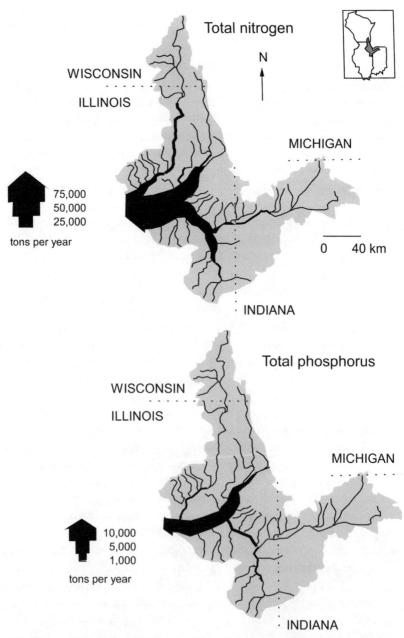

Estimated annual load of total nitrogen (upper) and total phosphorus (lower) in streams of the Upper Illinois River basin, 1978–97. After Sullivan (2000, fig. 16 [nitrogen] and fig. 17 [phosphorus]).

and sediment, however, were greater from the agricultural Fox and Kankakee basins.[62]

NAWQA scientists estimated that the total nitrogen export from the Upper Illinois River basin during the period 1978–97 was 83,300 metric tons per year. The phosphorus export was 4,900 metric tons per year. These represent enormous amounts: the nutrient yields from the Upper Illinois are among the highest in the Mississippi River basin. Exports from the Upper Illinois could be much higher, however: only about 30 percent of the estimated total nitrogen input to the basin (272,000 metric tons per year) and 6 percent of the total phosphorus input (85,300 metric tons per year) actually leave the basin. The remainder are processed and stored by crops and within the network of streams. Despite the loss of riparian corridors and buffer strips, streams still effectively create a huge filtering system that helps protect downstream areas such as the lower Mississippi and the Gulf of Mexico from the harmful effects of even greater nutrient loading.[63]

Excess nutrients resulting from major urban areas, including Chicago, and from agricultural lands thus constitute one of the major water-quality issues in the Upper Illinois River basin. This makes it vital to understand the complicated dynamics of nitrogen and phosphorus, the primary nutrients in river water. The nitrogen cycle starts with nitrogen gas, N_2, in the atmosphere. Before this gas can be used by terrestrial organisms, it must be fixed, or combined with hydrogen, oxygen, or carbon. About 60 percent of the fixed nitrogen that reaches land in forms such as nitrate (NO_3^-) and ammonium (NH_4^+) comes courtesy of biological fixation as a result of the respiratory activities of bacteria. Another 24 percent of fixed nitrogen reaches land through precipitation or so-called dry deposition—settling of wind-blown dust—carrying previously fixed nitrogen. The remaining 16 percent of nitrogen reaches the land from the application of industrially fixed nitrogen in fertilizer.[64]

Rivers are important conduits for nitrogen, transporting various forms from the land to the oceans. Rivers are not simple pathways for nitrogen, however; they also filter nitrogen as organisms all along the river corridor remove and transform dissolved nitrogen into plant and animal tissue. Because of these transformations, rivers carry to the oceans only about 18–20 percent of the total nitrogen loss from the land.[65]

The amount of nitrogen entering a river reflects the sources of the nitrogen and the pathways nitrogen follows across the landscape en route to the river. Land use exerts a strong influence on nitrogen inputs to rivers. Factors such as soil thickness and the steepness of adjacent hill slopes, which influence whether water and nitrogen move quickly into rivers or move sufficiently slowly to allow soil microbes and plants to take up some of the nitrogen, also control the amount of nitrogen entering a river. Much of the biological activity that removes nitrogen before it reaches rivers occurs in the soils beneath riverside vegetation.[66]

Not all rivers are created equal when it comes to nitrogen processing. Small headwater streams are disproportionately important because rates of dissolved nitrogen uptake from the water column are especially high in shallow streams where algae and microbes coat the streambed sand, rocks, and logs with periphyton communities. When stream plants and animals are particularly active during spring and summer, headwater streams typically send downstream less than half of the nitrogen they receive from the surrounding watershed. Any individual headwater stream might not seem very important by itself, but together these small streams can account for most of the total river kilometers within a watershed.[67]

The details of rivers large and small influence nitrogen dynamics. Nitrogen uptake can be significantly higher where water ponds upstream from a logjam or a beaver dam. Silt, clay, and fine bits of organic matter settle from the water and are stored on the streambed, where microbes and aquatic insects feed on the nutrients. The composition of the streambed also influences the exchange of surface and subsurface waters. Clay and silt tend to impede this exchange, whereas more porous and permeable sand and gravel enhance it. Flows between the surface and subsurface influence nitrogen levels because removal of nitrogen from waters passing through stream sediments is an important component of nitrogen uptake.[68]

Ecologists coin evocative phrases for the inequalities of nitrogen processing, writing about biogeochemical hot spots in patches of river with disproportionately high reaction rates relative to surrounding areas and hot moments that occur during short periods of time with much higher reaction rates than longer intervening time periods. Riverine hot spots form beneath riverside vegetation or patches of streambed where ground and surface waters converge. Riverine hot moments occur when floodwaters flush nutrients accumulated in secondary channels or overbank areas. Nitrogen is thus taken up and biologically processed most effectively where diverse channel and floodplain conditions and flow variability maintain hot spots and hot moments. Although the amount of nitrogen exported from rivers can vary substantially within a relatively small region, this export can be accurately predicted using features that reflect the existence of hot spots, such as the proportion of the catchment covered by wetlands.[69]

Understanding nitrogen dynamics is particularly important now that human activities have markedly increased nitrogen inputs to rivers such as the Illinois and decreased the ability of river ecosystems to process nitrogen by removing floodplain wetlands and forests, changing the grain sizes present on the streambed and the plants and animals living in the streams. The net results of these

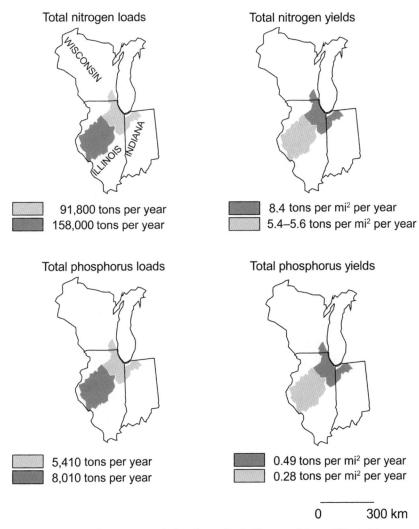

Total nitrogen loads

91,800 tons per year
158,000 tons per year

Total nitrogen yields

8.4 tons per mi² per year
5.4–5.6 tons per mi² per year

Total phosphorus loads

5,410 tons per year
8,010 tons per year

Total phosphorus yields

0.49 tons per mi² per year
0.28 tons per mi² per year

0   300 km

Total loads and yields for nitrogen and phosphorus for the Upper and Lower Illinois River basins. After Sullivan (2000, figs. 19 and 20).

changes are much higher nitrogen loads in rivers and eutrophication in many of the coastal areas into which the rivers empty. The Mississippi River basin and the increasing eutrophication and resulting dead zone in the Gulf of Mexico are a much-publicized example of these effects. Much of the increased nitrogen in the Illinois, the Mississippi, and other rivers comes from inorganic fertilizer use, but

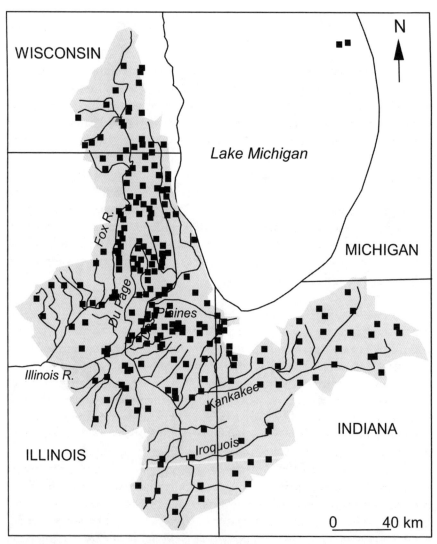

Location of municipal wastewater treatment plant point-source discharge sites (dots) in the Upper Illinois River basin (shaded). After Sullivan et al. (1998, fig. 5).

emissions from fossil-fuel combustion also contributed substantially to the doubling of nitrogen inputs to the United States from human activity during the years 1961 to 1997.[70]

Important changes in nutrient discharge within the Upper Illinois River basin occurred during the 1978–97 period assessed for NAWQA. Surface runoff within the city of Chicago has been diverted since 1985 into a series of underground tunnels called the Tunnel and Reservoir Plan (TARP). These tunnels capture and store storm runoff until it can be treated and discharged as effluent. TARP is designed to eliminate the discharge of raw sewage during storms, which had occurred when heavy rains overwhelmed septic systems. As a result of these and other changes, ammonia (NH_3, not to be confused with ammonium, NH_4^+) decreased at most sites during the period 1978–97, whereas nitrate increased. Much of this change occurred in urban areas, where wastewater treatment plants convert ammonia to nitrate. Ammonia is toxic to fish and other aquatic organisms even in very low concentrations, so converting it to nitrate is an improvement.[71]

As we alter the amount of silt and clay entering streams and being deposited on streambeds, the temperature and exposure to sunlight of the stream water, the dissolved oxygen levels and communities of microbes and algae, and the chemicals dissolved in the water, we inadvertently engage in a modern form of alchemy, transmuting not base metals into gold but nitrogen, carbon, and other elements into diverse forms—some of which are toxic to living organisms, while others are not. Although it can be difficult to follow the complicated fate of nitrogen molecules, the existence of consistent national sampling and analysis programs such as those of the US Geological Survey are crucial. Because the US Environmental Protection Agency has been unable to set national standards for many aspects of surface-water impairment, such standards are left to individual states. The result is that many streams abruptly become impaired or unimpaired as they cross state boundaries, even in the absence of any actual change in stream conditions: impairment, like beauty, is in the eyes of the beholder.

STRAIGHTER AND DEEPER: CHANNELIZATION

As mentioned earlier, channelization contributed to the sediment problems in the Illinois River basin during the twentieth century. To channelize a river is to treat it like a machine by seeking to maximize efficiency and the single function of conveying water downstream. But a river is not a machine performing a single, simple function. Channelization was so ubiquitous throughout the basin by the end of the twentieth century that it is appropriate to explore its implications more thoroughly.

Throughout the United States as a whole, more than 550,000 kilometers of streams were directly modified through processes such as channelization and the building of levees. Eighty percent of the channelization occurred in just fifteen states, one of which was Illinois; and the majority of the levees were built in California, Florida, and Illinois. A few of the sub-basins within the Illinois River basin provide examples. Forty-eight percent of the 1,490 kilometers of streams in the Des Plaines River basin were channelized. Thirty-four percent of the 1,276 kilometers of the Fox River were channelized, as was 28 percent of the length of the Sangamon and 43 percent of the Kankakee. In general, 35 percent to 50 percent of the streams were channelized in more than half of the major drainage basins in the state of Illinois. These changes affected small streams most heavily. First-order streams are those so small that they have no tributaries; these are the true headwaters. Every first-order stream was channelized in the Des Plaines, Kankakee, and Sangamon River basins. River networks formed on relatively homogeneous, gently sloping landscapes such as those in Illinois resemble the branching pattern of a tree when viewed on a map. For this reason, they are called dendritic networks. A channelized network is more like a crude drawing with stick figures in which shorter, straighter lines replace the gently sinuous branches of the dendritic network.[72]

Little streams play a big role in river networks. In addition to the disproportionately large amount of nitrogen removed from the water and transformed into plant and animal tissues, riffles along headwater streams provide abundant spawning habitat for many species of fish, and pools provide rearing habitat for juveniles that may move downstream to larger rivers as they become adults. Habitat provided by small streams differs from that in large streams, so small streams help increase the diversity of plant and animal species present in a river network. Because headwater streams constitute as much as two-thirds of the total length of a river network, they make substantial contributions to the network's total production of aquatic insects. Many of these headwater aquatic insects are carried downstream to serve as food for animals living in larger river segments, or they emerge as winged adults to provide food for land animals.[73]

Although ecologists have emphasized the importance of headwater streams for three decades, our unfortunate history of ignoring and mistreating these streams continues in court cases, such as the US Supreme Court's 2001 decision that isolated waters do not deserve the protection accorded to other waters under the Clean Water Act. *Isolated* in this context is defined based on a navigable surface-water connection to other bodies of water. Small streams were thus left without water-quality standards, oil-spill prevention and cleanup, pollution discharge permits, and discharge of dredged or fill materials—all of which are covered in individual sections of the Clean Water Act. A 2006 Supreme Court judgment that lacked a majority vote only increased confusion as to how headwater, intermittent, and ephemeral streams are to be treated. In a 5–4 vote, the court ruled that there are limits to the federal government's ability to regulate wetlands but failed to agree on those limits, leaving it to lower courts to make decisions on a case-by-case basis.[74]

The extent of channelized streams in the Illinois River drainage reflects broader changes in the landscape. Eighty-five percent to 90 percent of the vast wetlands that covered Illinois prior to European settlement were drained for agriculture. Over 80 percent of the land in the state is now farmed, and the prairie has been largely eradicated for agriculture. By the end of the twentieth century, croplands extended to the margins of streams throughout the headwaters, and the scattered woody vegetation present along headwater streams was removed as part of routine drainage management.[75]

As noted earlier, channelization often increases stream erosion and exacerbates downstream sedimentation because the increase in channel gradient creates greater flow energy within the channel. This was not always the case, however, along channelized headwater streams in the Illinois River basin. Channelization extended the entire stream network in areas where poorly defined wet-prairie sloughs had formed continuous surface flow during rainstorms or snowmelt and then shrunk back to discontinuous marshes during drier times. These newly channelized streams continued to have extremely low downstream gradients, however, dropping as little as 1 meter or even 1 decimeter per kilometer traveled (0.001–0.0001 meters/meter). At these gradients, stream power remained low even after channelization, limiting the channel's ability to erode its bed and banks. Bed erosion was also limited by the fact that the wide, deep, trapezoidal channels cut by the ditchers often intersected compacted glacial sediments or cohesive clay deposited on the bed of an ancient lake.

Bruce Rhoads and other scientists investigating the response to early-twentieth-century channelization along the Spoon River found that, instead of incising, the river began to erode its banks slightly. Sediment produced through this erosion was deposited in bars along the sides or in the middle of the channel. Eventually, these bars became stable, developing thick grasses and soils on top. The river wound back and forth between the bars, which effectively created a meandering low-flow channel within the straight channelized ditch. Habitat diversity associated with the low-flow channel supported a more diverse fish community than was present in channelized streams that lacked bars. Thus the river gradually regained some of its lost ground.[76]

Fish communities responded to channelization in different ways. Fish species diversity and abundance increased in some channelized headwater streams because the ditching processes extended channel networks into previously unchanneled portions of the landscape, thereby creating new habitat and longitudinal connectivity for fish. Comparison of channelized and natural portions of other streams indicates that although the same species of game fish are present in both reaches, fish diversity and density are greater in the natural reaches, whereas

Partridge Creek, a small tributary stream in the Illinois River basin. The upper photograph shows the upstream, un-channelized portion of the creek. The lower photograph shows the channelized portion of the creek, which is developing slight bends and bars.

fish biomass is greater in the channelized reach. Greater biomass results mainly from the presence of large carp, which can make up three-quarters of the total fish biomass in channelized streams. Carp are tolerant of the greater turbidity and contamination that may be present in channelized streams that lack a riverside buffer zone of native vegetation capable of trapping some sediment and contaminants. Fish in natural portions of the streams were found predominantly in eddies or near wood in the channel. Both eddies and wood are likely to be absent in channelized streams, especially if the streams undergo periodic maintenance.[77]

Other comparisons, such as those by Kelly Frothingham, Bruce Rhoads, and Edwin Herricks along the Embarras River just to the east of the Illinois River basin, demonstrate greater biomass in un-channelized reaches because of the greater availability of deep pools that provide habitat for mature fish. Fishery biologists use the Index of Biotic Integrity (IBI) to evaluate the quality of a fish community based on the total number of species present, type of species, distribution of fish flesh among various levels of the food web, and overall fish abundance and condition. Rhoads also found that un-channelized river reaches and channelized reaches in which habitat structure had redeveloped over time since the original channelization had greater IBI scores than channelized reaches that remained straight and uniform.[78]

Farmers maintain the ability of channelized streams to convey water rapidly downstream by removing sediment, wood, and other organic material that accumulates in the channel. Although a clause requiring drainage commissioners to formally consider environmental quality in stream maintenance plans was added to state regulatory statutes governing land drainage in the early 1970s, Rhoads and Herricks noted in 1996 that the clause was rarely heeded or enforced. The authority of drainage districts to conduct channelization and maintenance was curtailed by a ruling on the Clean Water Act Regulatory Program (Section 404) issued by the US Army Corps of Engineers and the Environmental Protection Agency in 1993. Interpretation and enforcement of the ruling varied substantially among district offices of the Army Corps of Engineers even before a federal court overturned the ruling in 1998. The Clinton presidential administration issued a revised ruling in 2001, but maintenance of channelized streams has largely proceeded unimpeded. As Rhoads and others noted in a 1999 review on the topic, the condition of channelized streams in the Illinois River basin will not change substantially until the public and individual landowners support rehabilitation of these streams. This is the vital lesson for anyone who cares about rivers and environmental health: nothing will change or improve until we know and care enough.[79]

Artificially created sinuosity along a ditch draining agricultural lands in the Illinois River basin. The intent behind this slightly curvaceous channel form is presumably to create something more natural in appearance, to dissipate some of the energy of high flows by increasing the hydraulic roughness of the channel boundaries, and to provide some habitat diversity within the channel.

EXOTIC SPECIES

Human introduction of exotic species—those that did not evolve in the Illinois River basin or migrate into the basin without human assistance—also affected much of the basin during the second half of the twentieth century. Exotic species introduced both deliberately and accidentally compete with native species and alter aquatic and riparian habitat and food webs. As noted in the discussion of native mussels, exotic zebra mussels reached the Illinois River circa 1991. Scientists are still evaluating their effects on native mussel populations in the Illinois system, but zebra mussels are believed to threaten native mussels in other parts of the Mississippi River network. Other exotic species that reached the Illinois fairly recently include *Daphnia lumholtzi*, a species of zooplankton first detected in the Illinois River near Havana in June 1995.[80]

What does an exotic Daphnia matter? As is commonly the case in rivers, what we do not see or think much about turns out to be vital. Originally from tropical and subtropical lakes in eastern Africa, eastern Australia, and India, the exotic Daphnia, commonly known as water flea, may have entered American waters with imported Nile perch. The water flea is adapted to warmer temperatures than are native zooplankton, so it competes with the natives for food resources in late summer when water flea populations rise. This competition may in turn limit the food for fishes that depend on zooplankton during late summer but cannot handle the water flea's spines. When magnified, it becomes apparent that the tiny water flea bristles with a long spine at its head and another at its tail. Not all exotic species turn out to be as disruptive, but we do not know ahead of time which ones will upset the aquatic applecart.[81]

Other exotic species in the Illinois River basin have received much more attention than the exotic Daphnia. Among the most notorious are the so-called Asian carp, four species introduced relatively recently. Bighead carp (*Hypophthalmichthys nobilis*) and silver carp (*H. molitrix*) were introduced in 1973, black carp (*Mylopharyngodon piceus*) in 1993, and grass carp (*Ctenopharyngodon idella*) in 1990. Bighead carp are filter-feeders imported to clean fish farms, but, as seems to happen commonly, they escaped from the impoundments. Silver carp are filter-feeders specializing in plankton that feed constantly: their voracious appetite depletes food supplies for native fishes. Black carp feed on snails and mussels.[82]

Imported from Malaysia to the United States in 1963 as a means of controlling aquatic vegetation, grass carp were called white amur because of widespread negative attitudes toward carp. Individual grass carp escaped from aquaculture ponds and spread into the channels of the Mississippi River basin. Grass carp can tolerate a wide range of environmental conditions and are capable of extensive movement once released into river systems. They spawn and incubate in side channels, where they eat the aquatic plants. The roots of aquatic plants help anchor bottom sediments. Their stems and leaves dampen waves generated by barges and wind. Together, roots and upper portions of the plant reduce re-suspension of fine sediment and turbidity of the water. Aquatic plants also provide habitat and food for native species of fish and aquatic insects. When aquatic plants declined in side channels and backwaters of the Illinois River during the late 1950s, these formerly clear, biologically productive waters became more turbid and supported less life. Plants struggling to survive in turbid waters where sediment accumulated and reduced habitat area were further stressed by the appearance of voracious grass carp, which, like many exotic species, rapidly increase in population in their new environment. The carp also compete with native herbivores, including migratory waterfowl such as canvasback ducks (*Aythya valisineria*) and muskrats (*Ondatra zibethicus*).[83]

As with common carp in the late nineteenth century, the four recently imported carp species were initially greeted with enthusiasm. Enthusiasm mostly turned to disgust, though, as evidenced by the title of a 2006 article in *Maclean's*, "Barbarians at the Gate." Today, people refer to "bottom feeders" in various contexts with disdain, the phrase having originated in reference to fish species such as carp. In more crude, judgmental language, carp are also dismissed as "trash fish." Yet as recently as 2005, the Illinois Department of Natural Resources awarded pins and certificates to anglers who released large common and other carp back into the water alive rather than killing the fish. A new wrinkle on the shifting attitudes toward these and other exotic fishes involves charges of xenophobia, racism, and nativism by the ecologically ignorant against those who oppose introduced species. As Glenn Sandiford noted about the original piscatorial pariah, the common carp, positive and negative attitudes toward Asian carp reflect an "argument among people about the place of a rather nondescript fish in their different and often competing visions of aquatic nature."[84]

Although probably not capable of completely altering the aquatic ecosystem or driving other aquatic species to the brink of extinction by itself, the grass carp and other exotic species create one more source of stress for native species driven to dangerously low population levels by the combined effects of habitat alteration, river pollution, and competition from exotics. Historical records indicate that at least sixty-two fish species were once present in the Illinois portion of the upper Des Plaines River, for example. By 1967 only twenty-eight species were found. Although this number increased to forty species in 1976, a 1989 survey found that common carp made up 90 percent of the total mass of fish found in this portion of the river. The most at-risk native species are those officially listed as threatened and endangered—the so-called t and e species.[85]

DISAPPEARING NATIVE SPECIES

A species is already in serious trouble by the time it reaches official threatened or endangered listing at the state or federal level. Once the species is listed, scientists and managers are challenged to understand what population levels and distribution are necessary for the species to sustain sufficient genetic variability, as well as what ecological conditions the species needs to survive and how those conditions can be preserved or restored. Protecting a species is rarely a simple matter. Most species of plant or animal require a wide range of environmental conditions. Many species also require periodic changes, such as the occurrence of an annual flood that reconfigures channels and inundates valley bottoms.

Reduction or, along some reaches that are leveed and drained, loss of the annual flood pulse has substantially changed channels throughout the Illinois River basin. Diversion of water from Lake Michigan, construction of navigation locks and dams, draining of floodplain wetlands that are then separated from the main channel by levees, and reduction of multiple channels to a single stabilized channel have all reduced the yearly flood and its effects on the riverine landscape. The effects of this reduction show up in declining diversity and abundance of aquatic fish and insects, as well as the disappearance of riverside plants adapted to the yearly flood.

The decurrent false aster (*Boltonia decurrens*) is one of the most thoroughly studied of these plants because it is a species endemic to the Illinois River that is now threatened with extinction. The false aster, which requires open areas to become established, used to colonize large portions of the floodplain, including wet prairies, shallow marshes, and the open shores of creeks and lakes after the annual spring floodwaters receded. Because the false aster is tolerant of oxygen-limited soils and of being underwater for long periods, it was once abundant and grew in continuous stands along the entire valley of the Lower Illinois River. As the construction of dams interrupted the dispersal of false aster seeds floating downstream and the construction of levees reduced the suitable habitat available to the plant, the false aster was only able to survive by exploiting areas disturbed by human activity. By the end of the twentieth century, the false aster was restricted to isolated populations separated by the three navigation dams along the Lower Illinois and was listed as threatened by the state and federal governments. The 1993 flood, the flood of record on the Upper Mississippi River system, illustrated what was needed to restore populations of the false aster. Ecologists Marian Smith and Paige Mettler studied the effects of the flood and wrote that populations of the false aster "that had been near extirpation exploded in size." At one site that had 50 false asters in 1992, for example, scientists counted more than 20,000 individual plants in 1994. Perhaps by itself, the decurrent false aster is not so important. It may not be a keystone species or an ecosystem engineer, but the false aster may be like a canary in a coal mine: its inability to survive in the altered Illinois River basin reflects the state of the entire ecosystem and the potential future fate of many other species.[86]

Existing land use in the Illinois River basin creates economic and political conditions that make it unlikely that the natural flood regime will be restored throughout the river system. The Army Corps of Engineers is experimenting with summer drawdown of navigation pools, however, as a means of expanding suitable false aster habitat without affecting navigation on the river. More than half the length of the Illinois is restricted by federal levees, but the corps can mimic floods by pumping water out of backwater areas or using gates or culverts to let water in behind the levees in a manner that facilitates false aster establishment and growth. Restoring false aster populations will help not only an endangered species but the

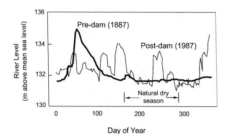

Schematic illustration of changes in the annual flow regime along the Illinois River as a result of navigation dams. The pre-dam hydrograph (bold line) was characterized by a spring flood and summer low flow. The post-dam hydrograph (lighter line) has a less predictable pattern of high and low discharge throughout the year. After Smith and Mettler (2002, fig. 4-10).

entire river ecosystem by restoring wet-marsh and slough vegetation that creates natural filter strips and thereby slows runoff and stores sediment.[87]

Many species of aquatic animals are also struggling to survive in the altered channels of the Illinois River basin. This chapter provides an overview of the multitude of twentieth-century changes. Agricultural clearing, ditching, and draining eliminated prairie grasses, caused water tables to drop, and created upland erosion that changed small, clear-flowing perennial streams into turbid, intermittent creeks with silty beds. Dams and levees reduced the annual flood and limited movement of aquatic animals among the main channel, side channels, and the floodplain. Most headwater springs and marshes are gone. Most small to medium streams are channelized. Levees line the larger streams. Aquatic habitats have become more homogeneous. Riverside and instream vegetation is much reduced. Dams and other structures create numerous barriers to fish migration. Urban and industrial wastewaters and agricultural runoff contaminate streams. Exotic species compete with natives. Storm runoff moves more quickly into and through streams, and summer flows are lower. Backwater lakes fill with sediment and are murky, as waves and passing barges keep silt and clay suspended in the water column. As Charles Rabeni wrote in 1996, "By any biological or physical measure, the aquatic resources of the prairie are highly altered in comparison to their original condition." As might be expected under these circumstances, there are many threatened and endangered species in the Illinois River system.[88]

Scientists can document the effects of all these changes on fish communities in part because fish distribution in the Illinois River has been studied for more than a century. Of a total of 140 fish species, 5 percent were increasing at the end of the twentieth century, 5 percent were introduced, and 23 percent were stable, but 6 percent (8 species) were gone and 61 percent were declining. In other words, two-thirds of the fish species in the Illinois were decreasing in abundance or had been eliminated from parts of their historical range.[89]

As with other stories of loss along the river, there is reason for hope. Fish communities have responded to improvements made during the past few decades. Sci-

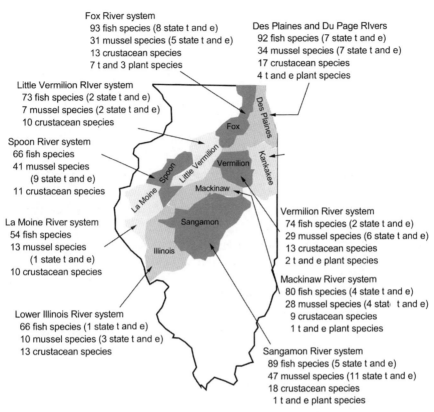

Fox River system
93 fish species (8 state t and e)
31 mussel species (5 state t and e)
13 crustacean species
7 t and 3 plant species

Des Plaines and Du Page RIvers
92 fish species (7 state t and e)
34 mussel species (7 state t and e)
17 crustacean species
4 t and e plant species

Little Vermilion RIver system
73 fish species (2 state t and e)
7 mussel species (2 state t and e)
10 crustacean species

Spoon River system
66 fish species
41 mussel species
(9 state t and e)
11 crustacean species

La Moine River system
54 fish species
13 mussel species
(1 state t and e)
10 crustacean species

Lower Illinois River system
66 fish species (1 state t and e)
10 mussel species (3 state t and e)
13 crustacean species

Vermilion River system
74 fish species (2 state t and e)
29 mussel species (6 state t and e)
13 crustacean species
2 t and e plant species

Mackinaw River system
80 fish species (4 state t and e)
28 mussel species (4 stati t and e)
9 crustacean species
1 t and e plant species

Sangamon River system
89 fish species (5 state t and e)
47 mussel species (11 state t and e)
18 crustacean species
1 t and e plant species

Sub-basins within the Illinois River drainage basin, with a listing of numbers of fish, mussel, and crustacean species known to have occurred in those sub-basins in the past, along with the numbers of state threatened and endangered (t and e) species. In some cases these t and e species are no longer present in the basin. Data from Page et al. (1991).

entists examining data on fish populations from 1957 to 2000 found that the fish present in the Upper Illinois River after 1983 differed from those present between 1957 and 1983. Species richness increased after 1983 as at least small numbers of individuals of thirty-eight species re-colonized the upper river. Among the species returning to the upper river were black crappie (*Pomoxis nigromaculatus*), orang-espotted sunfish (*Lepomis humilis*), smallmouth bass (*Micropterus dolomieui*), bull-head minnows (*Pimphales vigilax*), and sand shiners (*Notropis stramineus*), all of which are less tolerant of pollution and poor water quality. These changes reflect improved water quality, although fish response lagged behind water-quality improvements made in the mid- to late 1970s by nearly a decade. Improvements in water quality also correlate with decreasing abundance of tolerant species, such as common carp and goldfish. At the time of Roy Heidinger's 1989 study of fish in the heavily polluted upper Des Plaines River, for example, carp made up 90 percent of the fish biomass. The Lower Illinois River, which was never as impacted by the Chicago canal as the upper river was, may have served as a source area for less tolerant species of fish re-colonizing the upper river.

Recovery of fish communities may be limited, however, by pollutants persisting in streambed sediments. A 1994 report by the Illinois Department of Energy and Natural Resources noted that bottom-dwelling fishes in the Upper Illinois River had poor body condition and a high incidence of external abnormalities, signs that toxic contaminants are moving up the food web from streambed sediment to aquatic insects and then fish. All the king's horses and all the king's men . . . we can restore river habitat and even some function, but some forms of contamination persist for a very long time.[90]

This does not mean we give up: it means we try harder and proceed carefully. Further improvement and restoration of the biological integrity of streams in the Illinois River basin require new strategies that reflect the many interacting parts of the river ecosystems. Because changes in one component can cascade through a river ecosystem, people trying to restore rivers must think carefully about the potential implications of any particular management action. If flow increases because of urbanization, for example, that creates more physical energy in the stream, which can result in erosion of the streambed and banks. Changes in water depth and velocity, as well as configuration and stability of the streambed, alter the habitat in which organisms feed, rest, spawn, or grow to maturity. Increased turbidity limits the presence of aquatic plants, as does the unstable streambed. Fewer or different aquatic plants alter the energy source for the river community, producing changes in the number and type of aquatic animals. Contaminants from the urban area also limit the survival of aquatic organisms. The volume of water and its distribution through time not only influence habitat and water quality but also provide cues for organisms that time their lifecycles—such as fish spawning on floodplains—by fluctuations in stream flow. Individual animals and species also interact through competition, predation, disease, and parasitism; all of these interactions are indirectly affected by changes in physical and chemical characteristics of the stream that alter the number and type of individual organisms present. Eventually, the increased stream flow resulting from urbanization can limit the abundance of individuals and the diversity of species present along a river.[91]

One solution? Start reclaiming some of the urbanizing land. Instead of water flowing from paved surfaces into storm drains that efficiently speed the water into streams, allowing the water to flow across even tiny wetlands enhances infil-

tration and gradual water movement into streams through underground pathways, as well as helping to trap some of the contaminants coming off urban lands.
Allowing even a narrow margin of native riverside vegetation to return to creeks
and streams both small and larger further filters some of these contaminants and
improves stream health in urban areas.[92]

By the end of the twentieth century, river restoration had become a multi-
billion-dollar industry across the United States as people realized what was being lost
when river ecosystems responded to the multitude of changes in water, sediment,
and contaminants entering rivers; engineering of river form; and exotic species.[93]

NOTES

1. C. Kofoid, "The Plankton of the Illinois River, 1894–1899, with Introductory Notes
upon the Hydrography of the Illinois River and Its Basin," *Bulletin of the Illinois State
Laboratory of Natural History* 6, no. 2 (1903): xlii–xliii.

2. Ibid.

3. Forbes and Richardson, *Fishes of Illinois*, xxxvii.

4. Thompson, *Wetlands Drainage*; C. F. Rabeni, "Prairie Legacies—Fish and Aquatic
Resources," in *Prairie Conservation: Preserving North America's Most Endangered Ecosystem*,
ed. F. B. Samson and F. L. Knopf (Washington, DC: Island, 1996), 112; Critical Trends
Assessment Project, *Summary Report: The Changing Illinois Environment; Critical Trends*
(Springfield: Illinois Department of Energy and Natural Resources, 1994).

5. R. Sparks, "The Illinois River-Floodplain System," in *Restoration of Aquatic
Ecosystems: Science, Technology, and Public Policy*, Committee on Restoration of Aquatic
Ecosystems: Science, Technology, and Public Policy, Water Science and Technology
Board, National Research Council (Washington, DC: National Academy Press, 1992),
412–32.

6. C. E. Colten, "Illinois River Pollution Control, 1900–1970," in *The American
Environment: Interpretations of Past Geographies*, ed. L. M. Dilsaver and C. E. Colten
(Lanham, MD: Rowman and Littlefield, 1992), 193–214; S. A. Changnon and J. M.
Changnon, "History of the Chicago Diversion and Future Implications," *Journal of Great
Lakes Research* 22, no. 1 (1996): 100–118; Hill, *Chicago River*, 131–32; S. A. Forbes, "Studies of
the Food of Fresh-Water Fishes," *Illinois State Laboratory of Natural History Bulletin* 2, no. 7
(1988): 433–73.

7. Colten, "Illinois River Pollution Control," 194 (first quote); Changnon and
Changnon, "History of the Chicago Diversion"; Hill, *Chicago River*; Forbes, "Studies of
the Food," 457 (second quote).

8. Colten, "Illinois River Pollution Control"; O'Connell, "Technology and Pollution."

9. Colten, "Illinois River Pollution Control."

10. Ibid.; Sparks, "Illinois River-Floodplain System"; Richardson, "Bottom Fauna of the Middle Illinois River"; V. E. Shelford, "Ways and Means of Measuring the Dangers of Pollution to Fisheries," *Illinois State Natural History Survey Bulletin* 13, no. 2 (1918): 25.

11. D. H. Thompson, "The 'Knothead' Carp of the Illinois River," *Bulletin, State of Illinois, Division of the Natural History Survey* 17, no. 8 (1928): 285–320.

12. S. A. Forbes and R. E. Richardson, "Studies on the Biology of the Upper Illinois River," *Bulletin of the Illinois State Laboratory of Natural History* 9 (1913): 507.

13. Colten, "Illinois River Pollution Control."

14. Sparks and Starrett, "Electrofishing Survey"; F. C. Bellrose, F. L. Paveglio, and D. W. Steffeck, "Waterfowl Populations and the Changing Environment of the Illinois River Valley," *Illinois Natural History Survey Bulletin* 32, no. 1 (1979): 1–53.

15. Shelford, "Ways and Means," 26.

16. Ibid.

17. Colten, "Illinois River Pollution Control"; O'Connell, "Technology and Pollution."

18. Colten, "Illinois River Pollution Control."

19. Sparks, "Illinois River-Floodplain System"; Greenberg, *Natural History of the Chicago Region.*

20. B. E. Sietman et al., "Post-Extirpation Recovery of the Freshwater Mussel (Bivalvia: Unionidae) Fauna in the Upper Illinois River," *Journal of Freshwater Ecology* 16, no. 2 (2001): 281–82; J. K. Tucker and E. R. Atwood, "Contiguous Backwater Lakes as Possible Refugia for Unionid Mussels in Areas of Heavy Zebra Mussel (Dreissena polymorpha) Colonization," *Journal of Freshwater Ecology* 10, no. 1 (1995): 43–47; Forbes and Richardson, "Studies on the Biology."

21. Blodgett et al., *Mussel Resources*; K. L. Warner and A. R. Schmidt, *National Water Quality Assessment Program: The Lower Illinois River Basin*, NAWQA Fact Sheet 94-018 (Washington, DC: US Geological Survey, 1994); J. A. Stoeckel et al., "Larval Dynamics of a Riverine Metapopulation: Implications for Zebra Mussel Recruitment, Dispersal, and Control in a Large-River System," *Journal of the North American Benthological Society* 16, no. 3 (1997): 586–601; W. C. Starrett, "A Survey of the Mussels (Unionacea) of the Illinois River: A Polluted Stream," *Illinois Natural History Survey Bulletin* 30, no. 5 (1971): 267–403.

22. Blodgett et al., *Mussel Resources*; Warner and Schmidt, *National Water Quality Assessment Program*; Stoeckel et al., "Larval Dynamics."

23. Blodgett et al., *Mussel Resources.*

24. Sparks and Dillon, "Illinois River Fingernail Clam."

25. Gray, *Illinois*; Hoops, *River of Grain.*

26. Gray, *Illinois*, 264; Hoops, *River of Grain.*

27. Gray, *Illinois*, 264.

28. S. P. Shaw and C. G. Fredline, "Wetlands of the United States—Their Extent and Their Value to Waterfowl and Other Wildlife" (Washington, DC: US Department of the

Interior, 1956); Vileisis, *Discovering the Unknown Landscape*, 2 (first quote) and 5 (second quote).

29. F. C. Bellrose, "Lead Poisoning as a Mortality Factor in Waterfowl Populations," *Illinois Natural History Bulletin* 27 (1959): 235–88; G. C. Sanderson and F. C. Bellrose, *A Review of the Problem of Lead Poisoning in Waterfowl*, Illinois Natural History Survey, Special Publication 4 (Champaign: Illinois Natural History Survey, 1986).

30. N. G. Bhowmik and M. Demissie, "Sedimentation in the Illinois River Valley and Backwater Lakes," *Journal of Hydrology* 105, no. 1-2 (1989): 187–95; Sparks, "Illinois River-Floodplain System"; Steinauer and Collins, "Prairie Ecology"; Critical Trends Assessment Project, *Water Resources*, vol. 2: *The Changing Illinois Environment: Critical Trends* (Springfield: Illinois Department of Energy and Natural Resources, 1994); S. A. Changnon and M. Demissie, "Detection of Changes in Streamflow and Floods Resulting from Climate Fluctuations and Land Use-Drainage Changes," *Climatic Change* 32, no. 4 (1996): 411–21; K. P. Singh and G. S. Ramamurthy, "Gradual Climate Change and Resulting Hydrologic Response," in *Conference on Climate and Water*, vol. 1 (Helsinki: International Association of Hydrological Science, 1989), 476–85.

31. N. G. Bhowmik, *Physical Impacts of Human Alterations within River Basins: The Case of the Kankakee, Mississippi, and Illinois Rivers*, Long Term Resource Monitoring Program 93-R004 (Onalaska, WI: US Geological Survey Environmental Management Technical Center, 1993); R. L. Phipps, G. P. Johnson, and P. J. Terrio, *Dendrogeomorphic Estimate of Changes in Sedimentation Rate along the Kankakee River near Momence, Illinois*, US Geological Survey (USGS) Water-Resources Investigations Report 94-4190 (Washington, DC: USGS, 1995); A. Brookes, *Channelized Rivers: Perspectives for Environmental Management* (Chichester: John Wiley and Sons, 1988).

32. Bellrose, Paveglio, and Steffeck, "Waterfowl Populations," 29; Bhowmik and Demissie, "Sedimentation in the Illinois River Valley"; Bhowmik, *Physical Impacts of Human Alterations*; N. G. Bhowmik, *Sediment Sources Analysis for Peoria Lake along the Illinois River*, Long Term Resource Monitoring Program 94-R006 (Onalaska, WI: US Geological Survey Environmental Management Technical Center, 1994); D. E. Walling and B. W. Webb, "Erosion and Sediment Yield: A Global Overview," in *Erosion and Sediment Yield: Global and Regional Perspectives*, International Association of Hydrological Science (IAHS) Publication 236 (Wallingford, UK: IAHS, 1996), 3–19.

33. Bhowmik and Demissie, "Sedimentation in the Illinois River Valley"; Bhowmik, *Physical Impacts of Human Alterations*; Walling and Webb, "Erosion and Sediment Yield"; Bhowmik, *Sediment Sources Analysis*.

34. Adams and Delisio, "Temporal and Lateral Distribution"; N. G. Bhowmik and R. J. Schicht, *Bank Erosion of the Illinois River*, Illinois Institute of Natural Resources Report of Investigation 92 (Urbana: Illinois Institute of Natural Resources, 1980); Sparks, "Illinois River-Floodplain System."

35. Bhowmik and Demissie, "Sedimentation in the Illinois River Valley"; Bhowmik, *Physical Impacts of Human Alterations*; Bhowmik, *Sediment Sources Analysis*; Warner and Schmidt, *National Water Quality Assessment Program*; N. G. Bhowmik and J. R. Adams, "Successional Changes in Habitat Caused by Sedimentation in Navigation Pools," *Hydrobiologia* 176-77 (1989): 17–27; W. C. Starrett and A. W. Fritz, "A Biological Investigation of the Fishes of Lake Chautauqua, Illinois," *Illinois Natural History Survey Bulletin* 29, no. 1 (1965): 88.

36. R. E. Sparks et al., "Disturbance and Recovery of Large Floodplain Rivers," *Environmental Management* 14, no. 5 (1990): 699–709; Sparks, "Illinois River-Floodplain System"; R. E. Sparks, "Environmental Inventory and Assessment of Navigation Pools 24, 25, and 26, Upper Mississippi and Lower Illinois River: An Electrofishing Survey of the Illinois River," University of Illinois at Urbana-Champaign Water Resources Center Special Report 5, UILU-WRC-77-0005 (Urbana-Champaign: Water Resources Center, University of Illinois, 1977); Bellrose, Paveglio, and Steffeck, "Waterfowl Populations"; P. T. Raibley, K. S. Irons, T. M. O'Hara, K. D. Blodgett, and R. E. Sparks, "Winter Habitats Used by Largemouth Bass in the Illinois River, a Large River-Floodplain Ecosystem," *North American Journal of Fisheries Management* 17 (1997): 401–12.

37. Sparks et al., "Disturbance and Recovery"; Sparks, "Environmental Inventory and Assessment"; Bellrose, Paveglio, and Steffeck, "Waterfowl Populations."

38. R. W. Nichols, "Controlling Soil Erosion in the Illinois River Basin," Second Conference on the Management of the Illinois River System: The 1990s and Beyond, University of Illinois Water Resources Center Special Report 18 (Urbana-Champaign: Water Resources Center, University of Illinois, 1989).

39. Sparks et al., "Disturbance and Recovery"; Sparks, "Illinois River-Floodplain System."

40. S. Ebbs, J. Talbott, and R. Sankaran, "Cultivation of Garden Vegetables in Peoria Pool Sediments from the Illinois River: A Case Study in Trace Element Accumulation and Dietary Exposures," *Environmental International* 32, no. 6 (August 2006): 766–74; M. L. Machesky et al., "Sediment Quality and Quantity Issues Related to the Restoration of Backwater Lakes along the Illinois River Waterway," *Aquatic Ecosystem Health and Management* 8, no. 1 (2005): 33–40; R. G. Darmody and J. C. Marlin, "Sediments and Sediment-Derived Soils in Illinois: Pedological and Agronomic Assessment," *Environmental Monitoring and Assessment* 77, no. 2 (July 2002): 209–27.

41. R. LeB. Hooke, "On the History of Humans as Geomorphic Agents," *Geology* 28, no. 9 (2000): 843–46.

42. H. B. Mills, W. C. Starrett, and F. C. Bellrose, *Man's Effect on the Fish and Wildlife of the Illinois River*, Illinois Natural History Survey Biological Notes 57 (Urbana: Illinois Natural History Survey, 1966), 22–23.

43. Sullivan, *Nutrients and Suspended Solids*; Walling and Webb, "Erosion and Sediment Yield."

44. Warner and Schmidt, *National Water Quality Assessment Program*; Sullivan, *Nutrients and Suspended Solids*.

45. D. J. Sullivan et al., *Surface-Water-Quality Assessment of the Upper Illinois River Basin in Illinois, Indiana, and Wisconsin: Pesticides and Other Synthetic Organic Compounds in Water, Sediment, and Biota, 1975–90*, US Geological Survey (USGS) Water-Resources Investigations Report 96-4135 (Urbana, IL: USGS, 1998).

46. Ibid.

47. Warner and Schmidt, *National Water Quality Assessment Program*; A. A. Tesfamichael, A. J. Caplan, and J. J. Kaluarachchi, "Risk-Cost-Benefit Analysis of Atrazine in Drinking Water from Agricultural Activities and Policy Implications," *Water Resources Research* 41, W05015 (2005): 13 pp; R. Eisler, *Atrazine Hazards to Fish, Wildlife, and Invertebrates: A Synoptic Review*, US Fish and Wildlife Service Biological Report 85 (1.18) (Washington, DC: US Fish and Wildlife Service, 1989).

48. Warner and Schmidt, *National Water Quality Assessment Program*; R. Eisler, *Atrazine Hazards to Fish, Wildlife, and Invertebrates: A Synoptic Review*, US Fish and Wildlife Service Biological Report 85 (1.18) (Washington, DC: US Fish and Wildlife Service, 1989); A. A. Tesfamichael, A. J. Caplan, and J. J. Kaluarachchi, "Risk-Cost-Benefit Analysis of Atrazine in Drinking Water from Agricultural Activities and Policy Implications," *Water Resources Research* 41, W05015 (2005): 13 pp.

49. Bellm, "Illinois River," 60.

50. Sullivan et al., *Surface-Water-Quality Assessment*.

51. Ibid.

52. W. S. Morrow, *Anthropogenic Constituents in Shallow Ground Water in the Upper Illinois River Basin*, US Geological Survey (USGS) Water-Resources Investigations Report 02-4293 (Urbana, IL: USGS, 2003).

53. Sullivan et al., *Surface-Water-Quality Assessment*.

54. P. M. Ruhl, *Surface-Water-Quality Assessment of the Upper Illinois River Basin in Illinois, Indiana, and Wisconsin: Analysis of Relations between Fish-Community Structure and Environmental Conditions in the Fox, Des Plaines, and Du Page River Basins in Illinois, 1982–84*, US Geological Survey (USGS) Water-Resources Investigations Report 94-4094 (Urbana, IL: USGS, 1995).

55. F. A. Fitzpatrick et al., "Urbanization Influences on Aquatic Communities in Northeastern Illinois Streams," *Journal of the American Water Resources Association* 40, no. 2 (2004): 461–75; F. A. Fitzpatrick et al., "Effects of Urbanization on the Geomorphology, Habitat, Hydrology, and Fish Index of Biotic Integrity of Streams in the Chicago Area, Illinois and Wisconsin," *American Fisheries Society Symposium* 47 (2005): 87–115; M. A. Harris et al., *Physical, Chemical, and Biological Responses to Urbanization in the Fox and Des Plaines River Basins of Northeastern Illinois and Southeastern Wisconsin*, US Geological Survey (USGS) Scientific Investigations Report 2005-5218 (Urbana, IL: USGS, 2005).

56. Warner and Schmidt, *National Water Quality Assessment Program*; K. L. Warner, *Analysis of Nutrients, Selected Inorganic Constituents, and Trace Elements in Water from Illinois Community-Supply Wells, 1984–91*, US Geological Survey (USGS) Water-Resources Investigations Report 99-4152 (Urbana, IL: USGS, 2000); W. S. Morrow, *Volatile Organic Compounds in Ground Water of the Lower Illinois River Basin*, US Geological Survey (USGS) Water-Resources Investigations Report 99-4229 (Urbana, IL: USGS, 1999).

57. A. E. Tryfonas et al., "Metal Accumulation in Eggs of the Red-Eared Slider (*Trachemys scripta elegans*) in the Lower Illinois River," *Chemosphere* 63, no. 1 (March 2006): 39–48.

58. J. M. Levengood, "Cadmium and Lead in Tissues of Mallards (*Anas platyrhynchos*) and Wood Ducks (*Aix sponsa*) using the Illinois River (USA)," *Environmental Pollution* 122, no. 2 (2003): 177–81.

59. Sullivan, *Nutrients and Suspended Solids*; B. T. Aulenbach et al., *Streamflow and Nutrient Fluxes of the Mississippi-Atchafalaya River Basin and Subbasins for the Period of Record through 2005*, US Geological Survey (USGS) Open-File Report 2007-1080 (Washington, DC: USGS, 2007); Committee on Environment and Natural Resources, *Integrated Assessment of Hypoxia in the Northern Gulf of Mexico* (Washington, DC: National Science and Technology Council, 2000).

60. Sullivan, *Nutrients and Suspended Solids*, 26.

61. Ibid.; Aulenbach et al., *Streamflow and Nutrient Fluxes*; Committee on Environment and Natural Resources, *Integrated Assessment of Hypoxia*.

62. Sullivan, *Nutrients and Suspended Solids*; Aulenbach et al., *Streamflow and Nutrient Fluxes*; Committee on Environment and Natural Resources, *Integrated Assessment of Hypoxia*.

63. Sullivan, *Nutrients and Suspended Solids*; Aulenbach et al., *Streamflow and Nutrient Fluxes*; Committee on Environment and Natural Resources, *Integrated Assessment of Hypoxia*.

64. E. K. Berner and R. A. Berner, *The Global Water Cycle: Geochemistry and Environment* (Englewood Cliffs, NJ: Prentice-Hall, 1987); R. O. Hall and J. L. Tank, "Ecosystem Metabolism Controls Nitrogen Uptake in Streams in Grand Teton National Park, Wyoming," *Limnology Oceanography* 48 (2003): 1120–28; B. J. Peterson et al., "Control of Nitrogen Export from Watersheds by Headwater Streams," *Science* 292, no. 5514 (April 6, 2001): 86–90; A. J. Ranalli and D. L. Macalady, "The Importance of the Riparian Zone and In-Stream Processes in Nitrate Attenuation in Undisturbed and Agricultural Watersheds: A Review of the Scientific Literature," *Journal of Hydrology* 389, no. 3-4 (2010): 406–15; S. P. Seitzinger, R. V. Styles, E. W. Boyer, R. B. Alexander, G. Billen, R. W. Howarth, B. Mayer, and N. Van Breemen, "Nitrogen Retention in Rivers: Model Development and Application to Watersheds in the Northeastern U.S.A.," *Biogeochemistry* 57-58 (2002): 199–237; N. Van Breemen et al., "Where Did All the Nitrogen Go? Fate of Nitrogen Inputs to Large Watersheds in the Northeastern U.S.A.," *Biogeochemistry* 57, no. 1 (2002): 267–93.

65. Peterson et al., "Control of Nitrogen Export"; Van Breemen et al., "Where Did All the Nitrogen Go?"

66. R. M. Fanelli and L. K. Lautz, "Patterns of Water, Heat, and Solute Flux through Streambeds around Small Dams," *Ground Water* 46 (2008): 671–87; C. Gu, G. M. Hornberger, J. S. Herman, and A. L. Mills, "Effect of Freshets on the Flux of Groundwater Nitrate through Streambed Sediments," *Water Resources Research* 44 (2008): W05415; C. Gu, G. M. Hornberger, J. S. Herman, and A. L. Mills, "Influence of Stream-Groundwater Interactions in the Streambed Sediments on NO_3^- Flux to a Low-Relief Coastal Stream," *Water Resources Research* 44 (2008): W11432; R. J. Naiman and J. M. Melillo, "Nitrogen Budget of a Subarctic Stream Altered by Beaver (*Castor canadensis*)," *Oecologia* 62 (1984): 150–55; R. J. Naiman, J. M. Melillo, and J. E. Hobbie, "Ecosystem Alteration of Boreal Forest Streams by Beaver (*Castor canadensis*)," *Ecology* 67 (1986): 1254–69; B. J. Nihlgard, W. T. Swank, and M. J. Mitchell, "Biological Processes and Catchment Studies," in *Biogeochemistry of Small Catchments: A Tool for Environmental Research*, ed. B. Moldan and J. Cerny (Chichester: John Wiley and Sons, 1994), 133–61; E. H. Stanley and A. J. Boulton, "Hyporheic Processes during Flooding and Drying in a Sonoran Desert Stream, I: Hydrologic and Chemical Dynamics," *Archives for Hydrobiology* 134 (1995): 1–26; G. Wang, H. Ma, J. Qian, and J. Chang, "Impact of Land Use Changes on Soil Carbon, Nitrogen and Phosphorus and Water Pollution in an Arid Region of Northwest China," *Soil Use and Management* 20 (2004): 32–39; M. Thouvenot-Korppoo, G. Billen, and J. Garnier, "Modelling Benthic Denitrification Processes over a Whole Drainage Network," *Journal of Hydrology* 379 (2009): 239–50; T. M. Scanlon, S. M. Ingram, and A. L. Riscassi, "Terrestrial and In-Stream Influences on the Spatial Variability of Nitrate in a Forested Headwater Catchment," *Journal of Geophysical Research* 115 (2010): G02022; L. E. Band et al., "Forest Ecosystem Processes at the Watershed Scale: Hydrological and Ecological Controls of Nitrogen Export," *Hydrological Processes* 15, no. 10 (2001): 2013–28.

67. Peterson et al., "Control of Nitrogen Export"; Ranalli and Macalady, "Importance of the Riparian Zone."

68. Fanelli and Lautz, "Patterns of Water"; Gu et al., "Effect of Freshets"; Gu et al., "Influence of Stream-Groundwater Interactions"; Naiman and Melillo, "Nitrogen Budget"; Naiman, Melillo, and Hobbie, "Ecosystem Alteration."

69. H. M. McGinness, M. C. Thoms, and M. R. Southwell, "Connectivity and Fragmentation of Flood Plain-River Exchanges in a Semiarid, Anabranching River System," in *The Structure, Function and Management Implications of Fluvial Sedimentary Systems*, ed. F. J. Dyer, M. C. Thoms, and J. M. Olley, International Association of Hydrological Science (IAHS) Publication 276 (Wallingford, UK: IAHS, 2002), 19–26; M. E. McClain et al., "Biogeochemical Hot Spots and Hot Moments at the Interface of Terrestrial and Aquatic Ecosystems," *Ecosystems* 6, no. 4 (2003): 301–12; R. Lowrance et al., "Riparian Forests as Nutrient Filters in Agricultural Watersheds," *BioScience* 34, no. 6

(1984): 374–77; J. W. Harvey and C. C. Fuller, "Effect of Enhanced Manganese Oxidation in the Hyporheic Zone on Basin-Scale Geochemical Mass Balance," *Water Resources Research* 34 (1998): 623–36; I. F. Creed and F. D. Beall, "Distributed Topographic Indicators for Predicting Nitrogen Export from Headwater Catchments," *Water Resources Research* 45 (2009): W10407.

70. E. W. Boyer, C. L. Goodale, N. A. Jaworski, and R. W. Howarth, "Anthropogenic Nitrogen Sources and Relationships to Riverine Nitrogen Export in the Northeastern U.S.A.," *Biogeochemistry* 57-58 (2002): 137–69; E. W. Boyer et al., "Riverine Nitrogen Export from the Continents to the Coasts," *Global Biogeochemical Cycles* 20, no. 1 (2006): GB1S91; J. N. Galloway et al., "Nitrogen Cycles: Past, Present, and Future," *Biogeochemistry* 70, no. 2 (2004): 153–226; R. W. Howarth et al., "Nitrogen Use in the United States from 1961–2000 and Potential Future Trends," *Ambio* 31, no. 2 (March 2002): 88–96; Seitzinger et al., "Nitrogen Retention in Rivers."

71. Sullivan, *Nutrients and Suspended Solids*; Aulenbach et al., *Streamflow and Nutrient Fluxes*; Committee on Environment and Natural Resources, *Integrated Assessment of Hypoxia*.

72. Mattingly, Herricks, and Johnston, "Channelization and Levee Construction."

73. J. L. Meyer et al., "The Contribution of Headwater Streams to Biodiversity in River Networks," *Journal of the American Water Resources Association* 43, no. 1 (2007): 86–103; M. C. Freeman, C. M. Pringle, and C. R. Jackson, "Hydrologic Connectivity and the Contribution of Stream Headwaters to Ecological Integrity at Regional Scales," *Journal of the American Water Resources Association* 43, no. 1 (2007): 5–14; T. Gomi, R. C. Sidle, and J. S. Richardson, "Understanding Processes and Downstream Linkages of Headwater Systems," *BioScience* 52, no. 10 (2002): 905–16; R. L. Beschta and W. S. Platts, "Morphological Features of Small Streams: Significance and Function," *Water Resources Bulletin* 22, no. 3 (1986): 369–79.

74. T.-L. Nadeau and M. C. Rains, "Hydrologic Connectivity of Headwaters to Downstream Waters: Introduction to the Featured Collection," *Journal of the American Water Resources Association* 43, no. 1 (2007): 1–4.

75. Rhoads and Herricks, "Naturalization of Headwater Streams in Illinois"; K. M. Frothingham, B. L. Rhoads, and E. E. Herricks, "A Multiscale Conceptual Framework for Integrated Ecogeomorphological Research to Support Stream Naturalization in the Agricultural Midwest," *Environmental Management* 29, no. 1 (January 2002): 16–33; Nelson, Redmond, and Sparks, "Impacts of Settlement."

76. Rhoads and Herricks, "Naturalization of Headwater Streams in Illinois"; Frothingham, Rhoads, and Herricks, "Multiscale Conceptual Framework"; K. Landwehr and B. L. Rhoads, "Depositional Response of a Headwater Stream to Channelization, East Central Illinois, USA," *River Research and Applications* 19, no. 1 (2003): 77–100.

77. Frothingham, Rhoads, and Herricks, "Multiscale Conceptual Framework"; C. E. Petersen, "Water Quality of the West Branch of the DuPage River and Kline Creek,

Illinois, as Evaluated Using the Arthropod Fauna and Chemical Measurements," *Great Lakes Entomologist* 24, no. 3 (1991): 127–31; R .J. Wade et al., "Integrating Science and Technology to Support Stream Naturalization near Chicago, Illinois," *Journal of the American Water Resources Association* 38, no. 4 (2002): 931–44.

78. K. M. Frothingham, B. L. Rhoads, and E. E. Herricks, "Stream Geomorphology and Fish Community Structure in Channelized and Meandering Reaches of an Agricultural Stream," in *Geomorphic Processes and Riverine Habitat*, ed. J. M. Dorava et al. (Washington, DC: American Geophysical Union Press, 2001), 105–17; B. L. Rhoads, J. S. Schwartz, and S. Porter, "Stream Geomorphology, Bank Vegetation, and Three-Dimensional Habitat Hydraulics for Fish in Midwestern Agricultural Streams," *Water Resources Research* 39, no. 8 (2003): ESG 2-1–2-13.

79. Rhoads and Herricks, "Naturalization of Headwater Streams in Illinois"; B. L. Rhoads et al., "Interaction between Scientists and Nonscientists in Community-Based Watershed Management: Emergence of the Concept of Stream Naturalization," *Environmental Management* 24, no. 3 (October 1999): 297–308.

80. J. A. Stoeckel et al., "Establishment of *Daphnia lumholtzi* (an Exotic Zooplankter) in the Illinois River," *Journal of Freshwater Ecology* 11, no. 3 (1996): 377–79.

81. Ibid.

82. P. T. Raibley, D. Blodgett, and R. E. Sparks, "Evidence of Grass Carp (*Ctenopharyngodon idella*) Reproduction in the Illinois and Upper Mississippi Rivers," *Journal of Freshwater Ecology* 10, no. 1 (1995): 65–74.

83. Ibid.; R. C. Heidinger, "Fishes in the Illinois Portion of the Upper Des Plaines River," *Transactions of the Illinois Academy of Science* 82, no. 1 (1989): 85–96.

84. Raibley, Blodgett, and Sparks, "Evidence of Grass Carp"; Sandiford, "Transforming an Exotic Species," 299.

85. Raibley, Blodgett, and Sparks, "Evidence of Grass Carp"; Heidinger, "Fishes in the Illinois Portion."

86. M. Smith and P. Mettler, "The Role of the Flood Pulse in Maintaining *Boltonia decurrens*, a Fugitive Plant Species of the Illinois River Floodplain: A Case History of a Threatened Species," in *Flood Pulsing in Wetlands: Restoring the Natural Hydrological Balance*, ed. B. A. Middleton (New York: John Wiley and Sons, 2002), 117.

87. Ibid.

88. T. M. Koel, "Spatial Variation in Fish Species Richness of the Upper Mississippi River System," *Transactions of the American Fisheries Society* 133, no. 4 (2004): 984–1003; Rabeni, "Prairie Legacies," 112.

89. Rabeni, "Prairie Legacies"; J. R. Karr, L. A. Toth, and D. R. Dudley, "Fish Communities of Midwestern Rivers: A History of Degradation," *BioScience* 35, no. 2 (1985): 90–95.

90. M. A. Pegg and M. A. McClelland, "Spatial and Temporal Patterns in Fish Communities along the Illinois River," *Ecology of Freshwater Fish* 13, no. 2 (2004): 125–35;

M. E. Retzer, "Changes in the Diversity of Native Fishes in Seven Basins in Illinois, USA," *American Midland Naturalist* 153, no. 1 (2005): 121–34; Heidinger, "Fishes in the Illinois Portion"; Illinois Environmental Protection Agency (IEPA), *Illinois Water Quality Report, 1994–1995*, vol. 1: *Illinois' Assessment of Water Resource Conditions*, IEPA/BOW96/06a (Springfield: IEPA, 1996); Critical Trends Assessment Project, *Ecological Resources*, vol. 3: *The Changing Illinois Environment: Critical Trends* (Springfield: Illinois Department of Energy and Natural Resources, 1994).

91. Karr, Toth, and Dudley, "Fish Communities."

92. E. S. Bernhardt, E. B. Sudduth, M. A. Palmer, J. D. Allan, J. L. Meyer, G. Alexander, J. Follastad-Shah, B. Hassett, R. Jenkinson, R. Lave, J. Rumps, and L. Pagano, "Restoring Rivers One Reach at a Time: Results from a Survey of U.S. River Restoration Practitioners," *Restoration Ecology* 15, no. 3 (2007): 482–93; E. S. Bernhardt et al., "Synthesizing U.S. River Restoration Efforts," *Science* 308, no. 5722 (April 29, 2005): 636–37.

93. Bernhardt et al., "Restoring Rivers One Reach at a Time"; Bernhardt et al., "Synthesizing U.S. River Restoration Efforts."

EIGHT

What the Future Holds

A HISTORIC SNAPSHOT: THE
ILLINOIS RIVER CIRCA 2000

Several state governmental agencies set out to inventory the condition of streams in Illinois toward the end of the twentieth century. Scientists developed a Biological Stream Characterization to categorize streams based mostly on the diversity, abundance, and condition of aquatic insects and fish. Streams of category "A" exhibit conditions comparable to those at the time of European settlement. "B" streams are in good condition and support game fishes, but species diversity is below expectations. "C" streams are in fair condition, with reduced fish diversity and game fishes limited to bullheads, sunfishes, and carp. "D" streams are in poor condition, with substantially reduced diversity and a community dominated by species tolerant of pollution and degraded habitat. "E" streams are in such poor condition that they support only a few individuals of the most tolerant species of insects and fish. Although only 4 percent of the stream kilometers in Illinois were in category A when the assessment was completed in 1992, 54 percent were rated as in good condition, with less than 1 percent in category E. These numbers, which reflect the most recent comprehensive

DOI: 10.5876/9781607322313.c08

A - Unique

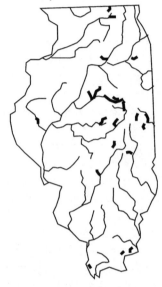

B - Highly valued

C - Moderate

D/E - Limited or restricted

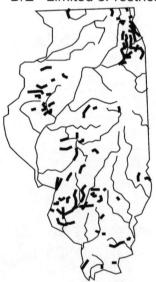

Biological characterization of Illinois streams, showing stream segments in each of the primary categories highlighted as darker lines. Segments that appear to be disconnected from the drainage network are along streams too small to be included in these maps. After Critical Trends Assessment Project (1994, fig. 6).

inventory for the state, represent an improvement over a similar survey in 1972, which had 35 percent of the streams in good condition and 11 percent in poor condition.[1]

If Charles Kofoid, Stephen Forbes, and Robert Richardson could visit the Illinois River basin today, they might find it difficult to recognize the river. Floating masses of putrid sewage that marred their excursions along channels and backwaters are gone, but so are most of the side channels and backwaters. The main river is narrowly constrained by high levees or, where cities lie next to the river, concrete-covered banks. People live mostly in towns or small cities. Bridges across the river at regular intervals provide access to the channel, which is lined by narrow bands of forest in most places. Tows attached to multiple barges move upstream and downstream on the brown water. The landscape adjacent to the river remains largely agricultural, as it was in 1900, but the fields are larger. Rows of corn and soybeans stretch to the small stands of trees forming the horizons on all sides. Large silos for storing grain rise at intervals above the crops. Ends of crop rows along the roads are labeled with signs listing the type of fertilizer or genetic engineering used on the plants. Crop dusters buzz the fields from above, and huge machines spread thousands of tons of fertilizers and pesticides across the surface. The rich topsoil that is one of the region's greatest natural assets has been compromised by more than a century of erosion. Soil eroding from the fields goes into drainage ditches, tributary streams, and eventually the main river, where it fills the pools created by backwaters from navigation dams. Clear water flowing over streambeds of white sand has been replaced by murky water and silty bottoms. Stream banks everywhere are bands of slippery mud. Aquatic insects such as stoneflies have mostly declined in diversity during the past century, with species tolerant of pollution and able to utilize a wide variety of habitats replacing those sensitive to pollution that specialize in particular types of habitat. Fewer types of fish and fewer individual fish swim in the river, and fewer mussels filter the turbid water.[2]

There remain places, however, that time travelers from 1900 would recognize. State parks, national wildlife refuges, and privately owned preserves protect and restore patches of riverine bottomlands all along the course of the main river and its tributaries. At these refuges it takes little imagination to understand how rich the river corridor once was in wild plants and animals. In summer, blossoms of white, yellow, lavender, orange, red, and blue rise waist-high among thick stands of grasses. Grassy banks slope down toward a shallow lake dotted with little islands of sedges and reeds. Dark silhouettes formed by small stands of trees across the lake merge gradually into the pale blue sky at the horizon. Great blue herons have staked out territories at regular intervals along the shoreline. Ducks move slowly

View from the summit of Starved Rock, 2008. A lock and dam complex now crosses the river, creating a large backwater upstream.

across the water. The rhythmic percussion of a pileated woodpecker rings out from trees farther back from the lake, above the continual sounds of frogs and insects. Waters flooding across these bottomlands are manipulated with pumps and gates to mimic the natural cycle, and sediment and contaminants move with the waters, but some of the river corridor's natural function and form remains.

CLIMATE CHANGE

Flow increased along most streams throughout the Illinois River basin during the last quarter of the twentieth century, particularly in its northern third. Changing land use, especially urbanization, contributes to this increase, but the higher flows also reflect an increase of greater than 10 percent in annual precipitation. Are these increases likely to persist during the next few decades?[3]

Unlike the arid western prairie, where there is great fear of intensified droughts as a result of future climate change, relatively few studies have focused on the specific impacts to the Illinois River basin under differing scenarios of climate change.

Contrasting views along different sections of the Illinois and Michigan Canal, 2008.

Field of soybeans and storage silo in former floodplain of the Illinois River, 2008. Prior to agricultural usage of this land, it would have been floodplain and valley-bottom wetlands.

Studies that encompass the entire American prairie project an average 2°–4°C increase in winter temperatures and a 2°–3°C increase in summer by 2030, accompanied by a less productive growing season because of decreased precipitation. Precipitation changes may be more severe in the central and western prairie, but it remains unclear how global changes in climate will affect the Illinois River basin over the next few decades. If precipitation declines sufficiently to impact crop yields in the eastern prairie, changes in application of fertilizer, pesticides, and irrigation water will likely have the most important impact on the Illinois River and its tributaries, given the extensive portion of the drainage basin devoted to crops.[4]

REVERSING THE RIVER

In a story carried by the Associated Press in 2010, Chicago mayor Richard Daley proposed that local water resource managers and the US Army Corps of Engineers study the feasibility of reversing flow in the Chicago River back to its original direction, into Lake Michigan. Some environmentalists and Great Lakes advocates have lobbied Chicago for years to reverse the river's flow as a means of restoring a significant influx of freshwater to the lake and reducing water pathways for invasive species such as Asian carp to move between the Mississippi River network and the Great Lakes. Dick Durbin, a US senator from Illinois, has also requested that the US Congress commission a study to examine (1) re-engineering regional waterways in a manner that continues to allow boat passage but blocks the migration of invasive species and (2) restoring the Chicago River to its original direction. The Chicago River will continue to flow into the Illinois River basin for the foreseeable future, but perhaps eventually the unsanitary canal will become only a historical site.[5]

In the meantime, the Army Corps of Engineers is employing various tactics to limit the migration of exotic species. Of particular concern at present are so-called Asian carp, a blanket term for common carp, goldfish (*Carassius auratus*), Crucian carp (*C. carassius*), grass carp, black carp, bighead carp, and silver carp. All of these big fish, which grow to an average of 18 kilograms in weight, are hearty eaters: some of them eat 40 percent to 60 percent of their body weight each day in algae and other microscopic organisms, stripping the base of the food web on which other fish also rely. Because these fish are established in the Illinois River drainage basin, the concern is that they will migrate upstream through the canal to Lake Michigan and then spread through the Great Lakes ecosystem. The corps has constructed dispersal barriers in the Sanitary and Ship Canal that emit electrical fields designed to repel fish. The first electric barrier, completed in 2002, cost $2.2 million. A second barrier was completed in 2005. Worried that determined fish will bypass these barriers by way of the Des Plaines River or other pathways during floods, in 2010 the corps also built a 22-kilometer-long fence of concrete barriers and wire mesh that passes water but not fish. These are praiseworthy efforts, but time will tell how well they actually succeed. The tricky part with respect to invasive exotic species is that if even a few individuals get through to a new environment, they can be the fertile pioneers that establish a whole new population.[6]

RESTORATION OF PRAIRIE

Rivers are intimately connected to the uplands adjacent to valley bottoms. Hill slope processes and tributary streams bring water, sediment, nutrients, and contaminants into the mainstem river and floodplains, and numerous animal species move between uplands and bottomlands. It is within this context that recent efforts to restore native tallgrass prairies in Illinois can play an important role in the future of the Illinois River and its tributaries.

Efforts to restore native plants and historical landscape processes such as fire to tallgrass prairies date to Aldo Leopold's work in Wisconsin during the 1930s. Lessons learned in these early efforts have been applied to recent prairie restoration projects in Illinois, most of which feature intensive hand cultivation of native plants grown from seeds in a greenhouse, along with control of non-native species. An area of 314 hectares is being returned to native grassland using these techniques at the Fermilab in Bativia, Illinois, and similar efforts are planned for 7,760 hectares at the Midewin National Tallgrass Prairie in Wilmington, Illinois. Midewin, formerly an army ammunition plant, is named from a Potawatomi word for healing.[7]

This restoration does not occur quickly. Because they are expensive and labor-intensive, most restorations are planted with a one-time seeding that includes relatively few species in the seeding mixes. Fragmentation, invasion by exotic species, and altered fire regimes remain challenges for many years. Experts on prairie restoration point out that although some new restorations are successful at re-creating the plant community, most do not effectively re-create the communities of soil invertebrates, insects, and small mammals, let alone large mammals, once present on the tallgrass prairies. Yet these restoration efforts are vital work, not only because of the hope they provide for rehabilitating heavily eroding uplands but also because of their ability to heighten the profile of tallgrass prairies—to increase contemporary residents' awareness of, and interest in, the possibilities of their landscape.[8]

NATURALIZATION OF CHANNELS

Preceding chapters have chronicled the massive historical changes along streams of the Illinois River basin. For more than a century, people have dramatically altered the streams through snagging, dredging, over-harvesting of mussels and other organisms, channelization, building levees and draining floodplain wetlands, clearing native vegetation from the uplands and increasing sediment entering streams, and introducing sewage, excess nutrients, synthetic chemicals, and other pollutants into the water. Yet despite these alterations of the physical and chemical processes and biological communities of the river corridors, a report published by the National Research Council in 1992 identified portions of the Illinois River as one of the three remaining large floodplain river systems in the United States that retain enough natural characteristics to allow for restoration. Other rivers explicitly identified were portions of the Atchafalaya and Upper Mississippi Rivers.[9]

A few years prior to the 1992 report, a 1987 workshop attended by approximately 200 people ranging from private citizens to members of environmental organizations, university faculty, and government agencies met in Peoria to define management problems along the Illinois River, as well as potential solutions. A comprehensive solution requires managing each of the drainage basin's major components: uplands, tributary channels, and mainstem rivers and floodplains. Upland management focuses on reducing erosion from agricultural lands using techniques such as conservation tillage and grassed waterways. Management of tributary streams can include planting riverside trees to stabilize banks and provide organic matter inputs to streams and limiting maintenance clearing of channelized streams. Management of larger rivers and floodplains can include retiring lands from agricultural production and restoring a more natural pattern of flooding by allowing floodwaters to access bottomlands, actively replanting native bottomland species, and removing barriers that disconnect side channels and backwaters from the main channel. These diverse components of restoration can create a cascading effect analogous to the downstream flow of water and sediment if upland restoration reduces sediment and contaminants entering lowlands, tributary stream restoration further buffers channels from incoming sediment and contaminants and enhances riverside habitat, and mainstem restoration opens up extensive former habitats and the river-floodplain fluxes that maintain those habitats.[10]

One of the more widespread restoration strategies planned in the Illinois River basin is the Illinois Rivers 2020 program, launched in 1999. Projected to last twenty years and to cost more than $1 billion, this voluntary, incentive-based program is a cooperative partnership among the Illinois River Coordinating Council, the state's department of natural resources, the US Army Corps of Engineers, and other government agencies. A sort of liposuction for lakes, the program includes dredging sediment from locations other than the navigation channels along the Illinois River basin—primarily lakes and backwaters—and using the sediment for habitat development.

Program proponents note that the 24,000 hectares of Illinois River backwaters lost more than 70 percent of their capacity during the twentieth century, in some cases going from depths of 1.8–2.4 meters early in the century to depths of only half a meter as a result of sediment filling. A 12-kilometer stretch known as Babbs Slough, just upstream of Peoria Lake, once held water up to 2 meters deep separated from the main channel by a string of islands and was famous for waterfowl hunting. Now the islands have coalesced to a long, narrow peninsula, the slough is only 20 centimeters deep, and waterfowl habitat is minimal. The plan is to dredge sediment in an effort to convert shallow, marginal backwaters into habitat of higher quality, with characteristics such as the 3-meter depth necessary for over-wintering fish. Some of the dredged sediment will be added to floodplains to restore elevations and soil moisture that existed prior to 1900. Other sediment will be used to build new islands in the river and to enlarge existing islands. Long, narrow islands will increase plant and bird habitat in particular and help reduce bank erosion by absorbing waves generated by barges. There is not likely to be a shortage of sediment, and additional uses such as restoration of former surface-mine areas and highway projects have also been proposed. Getting the sediment out in a useful form does require some innovations. Traditional hydraulic dredging techniques add a substantial amount of water to the sediment and pump the mixture out through pipes, producing a slurry that must be dried before use. New mechanical dredging techniques developed for this program do not add moisture, allowing the sediment to be dried more quickly and facilitating sediment transport by barges rather than trucks. Mechanical dredges also use a so-called clamshell bucket that minimizes turbidity by holding the sediment tightly as it is lifted from the river bottom.[11]

At the most fundamental level, successful restoration will focus on the management actions that remain possible under the constraints imposed by existing urban and agricultural land uses in the river's drainage basin. The Illinois River basin will not be restored to its condition in 1700, 1800, or even 1900. A return to some biologically rich past baseline condition is not necessary, however, to restore river function and biological communities to self-sustaining levels. What is necessary is to identify the critical physical and chemical processes that create and maintain habitat diversity, water quality, and biological abundance and diversity and then to restore these processes where possible at selected sites along the river corridor. This "string of beads" approach to restoration focuses on critical parcels spaced along the river corridor—beads—that can be restored to provide ecological connectivity within the river system. Restoring the beads requires an understanding of how water, sediment, and dissolved chemicals move down tributaries to the main channel; how physical and chemical constituents and organisms move between the main channel and floodplains; and how organisms migrate up and down the main river corridor. To paraphrase E. M. Forster, it is a matter of "only connect": intellectually connect the dots of understanding how the different components of the river basin connect, and restore or protect the physical and ecological mechanisms that create connectivity.

In the Illinois River basin, much of the connection must occur through the mechanism of floods. As Marian Smith and Paige Mettler wrote in their 2002 paper about restoring the decurrent false aster to floodplains along the Illinois River, "The United States has never viewed flooding from a systemwide perspective." Instead, our country has a history of taking a locally focused approach in which individual landowners, drainage districts, and even state and federal government agencies treat segments of channel or parcels of floodplain lands in isolation, modifying them without sufficient thought to the effects these modifications have on the entire river corridor. The results of this history are twofold. First, successive modifications have left relatively little of the river corridor in a naturally functioning state in which a complex channel network with deeps and shallows, side channels and backwaters, and wood, sand, and silt along the streambed provide diverse habitats for plants and animals and seasonal floods nourish wetlands and aquatic and riparian species. Second, there has been little recognition of the beneficial effects of flooding in providing a mechanism for sediment, nutrients, and organisms to move between channels and floodplains. By thinking about the Illinois River *basin* rather than just individual, artificially isolated sections of rivers and bottomlands, scientists and managers can effectively restore the Illinois River ecosystem one "bead" at a time. Flows of water, sediment, nutrients, and organisms will then string the beads together to create an effect greater than the individual parts.[12]

Examples of existing restoration beads along the river come from activities undertaken within the past few years by the Nature Conservancy, an international environmental stewardship organization. Nature Conservancy projects at Emiquon and Spunky Bottoms illustrate how people who care about watershed health are restoring some of the historical functions of the Illinois River.

In 2002 the Nature Conservancy acquired approximately 2,800 hectares at Emiquon, which is along the Illinois River about 70 kilometers southwest of Peoria. Emiquon was once a backwater lake connected to the Illinois River during high water. The lake was drained and leveed during the 1920s and farmed for eighty years. The intent of the new preserve is to restore a biologically diverse complex of backwater wetlands that supports native plants and animals. Conservancy stewards work jointly with scientists from the Illinois State Water Survey and the University of Illinois to develop computer models that can be used to evaluate the effects of different management scenarios on river processes, habitat, and biological communities. By reintroducing overbank flows that create different water depths and time spans of inundation, for example, the Nature Conservancy hopes to reestablish prairie grasses and forbs, as well as bottomland hardwood forests. Moist-soil plants including millets (*Echinochloa* spp.) and the endangered decurrent false aster are a particular focus of this work. These plants require regular spring flooding that eliminates flood-intolerant competitor species and creates open moist areas in which seeds of the millets and aster can germinate. Mud flats must be exposed from about July 10 to October 1 so the moist-soil plants can grow to maturity without being overtopped by water. The plants then produce seeds that can be eaten by waterfowl. Scientists studying the interactions among plants and floods at Emiquon find that the areal extent of the floodplain inundated and the depth of water exert particularly important influences on these floodplain ecosystems.[13]

Restoration of floodplain wetlands is in its early stages at Emiquon. In 1896, Stephen Forbes described the area:

> The forest itself, beginning at water's edge with a billowy belt of pale green willows, is an untamed tract of primitive wilderness. Elms and pecans and sycamores tower overhead. The shallow lakes and swamps are glorious in their season with the American lotus and the white water lily. Waterfowl abound, and fish lie in the shallows, basking in the summer sun. The microscopic life in a cubic meter of water is at certain times far in excess of the amount recorded for any other situation in the world.[14]

This contrasts with Jeanne Handy's description of a visit to the Emiquon project site in 2004:

> Rather than this bountiful diversity in what had formerly been two shallow floodplain lakes . . . I see instead acres and acres of dirt, interrupted only briefly by farm remnants . . . With the harvest already complete, the ground appears so barren, so used. Try as I might, I am unable to envision the scene that greeted Forbes. Others, however, can and have.[15]

This ability to see the possibilities of the future drives restoration.

At Spunky Bottoms, about 80 kilometers south of Emiquon, the Nature Conservancy acquired another 800 hectares in 2002 that were historically drained and used for agriculture. The conservancy began restoring floodplain wetlands by limiting the amount of water pumped out of the low-lying areas and working with the Army Corps of Engineers to restore connections with the main channel that will allow fish such as gar and paddlefish access to the floodplain. The conservancy has planted more than 7,500 bottomland hardwood trees, as well as hundreds of pounds of seed for prairie grasses in the upland areas. Other wetland species have emerged from soil seed banks that survived decades of farming. As the native vegetation and a more natural flow regime return, waterfowl and other animals using the site are rising in numbers and diversity. More than 16,000 waterfowl migrate through the preserve in spring, which also has one of the largest populations of northern cricket frogs (*Acris crepitans*) in Illinois. River otters (*Lutra canadensis*), American bitterns (*Botaurus lentiginosus*), and least bitterns (*Ixobrychus exilis*)—all rarely seen in the surrounding areas—now seek fish in the river.

Another example of active restoration along the mainstem of the Illinois River comes from a project undertaken by the Wetlands Initiative, a nonprofit organi-

Floodplain wetlands at Emiquon, August 2008. The apparent monotony of this view masks a wealth of biochemical processes and ecological communities.

zation that is reestablishing more natural conditions on 1,050 hectares of former corn and soybean fields north of Peoria at Hennepin and Hopper Lakes. Restoration began in 2001 when managers turned off the drainage district's pumps, which had been keeping bottomland areas dry. Existing levees and other drainage structures were left alone so scientists could withdraw water from the river, manipulate water levels across the bottomlands, and measure the resulting patterns of water quality and habitat. Eventually, the project site will include about 500 hectares of lake, 180 hectares of seasonally flooded prairie and shoreline marsh, nearly 300 hectares of prairie, 30 hectares of wetlands, and 60 hectares of forest. All of this will cost an estimated $15 million. Balanced against the cost of losses in cropland production are the benefits of restored wetlands in terms of commercial and recreational fishing, hunting, and other forms of recreation; better habitat for plants and animals; and improved water quality. An assessment of these costs and benefits concluded that restoration is economically efficient and will positively impact the regional economy, with a total net benefit of nearly $2 million for the entire project.[16]

In general, projects seeking to restore bottomland function along the Illinois River can keep existing levees and manage water levels on the sites independent

Restored floodplain wetlands at Spunky Bottoms, 2008.

of water levels in the river to produce desired wetland plants to attract and feed migrating waterfowl. Private duck-hunting clubs and government wildlife management agencies commonly use this strategy, which mimics the natural flood regime by flooding bottomlands from late autumn through late spring and then exposing them during the summer low-flow season by means of pumping water into and out of impoundments or emptying impoundments of water through gates. This strategy, however, does not allow access of fish to bottomland sites that provide essential spawning and feeding grounds for species such as basses and sunfishes. It also limits dispersal of floating plant seeds and exchange of nutrients between the channel and adjacent floodplain. Breaching the levees or installing gates within them can restore both a more natural flooding regime and connectivity with the river to bottomlands, and this management strategy is likely to be increasingly adopted as more sections of bottomland are restored along the Illinois River. The Nature Conservancy, for example, plans to use gates in the levees to restore historical floods and river-floodplain connectivity at Emiquon.[17]

At the same time projects such as Emiquon, Spunky Bottoms, and Hennepin and Hopper Lakes focus on restoration along the Illinois River, other projects

Restored floodplain lakes and wetlands at Hennepin, 2008.

focus on restoration along tributaries to the main river. Scientists engaged in this work refer to it as *stream naturalization*. They have chosen this term because restoration of streams in the intensively farmed lands of much of the Illinois River basin is unlikely. Restoration implies a return to some level of stream form and function present historically. As Bruce Rhoads and others have pointed out, because transformation of the landscape occurred prior to the collection of detailed environmental information in many parts of the Illinois River basin, scientists have limited knowledge of the condition of smaller streams prior to European settlement. Environmental conditions such as land cover, erosion, and nutrient availability have been so thoroughly altered throughout entire watersheds of smaller streams that it is unlikely that pre-settlement stream conditions would be sustainable even if scientists could determine those conditions. The agricultural communities that occupy much of the Illinois River basin landscape wish to maintain high levels of agricultural productivity on privately owned lands, so it is not feasible to change conditions throughout the watershed beyond a certain level. In other words, it might be possible to change some agricultural practices, such as levels of fertilizers and pesticides applied to farm fields, but it is unlikely that agricultural lands will be substantially reduced unless they are replaced by urban land use, which creates its own challenges for river restoration. Under these conditions, scientists have focused on naturalization that "defines a viable management goal for water-sheds situated in landscapes characterized by intensive human modification of the biophysical environment." In other words, what can be done to improve stream form and function in the midst of thousands of hectares of farm fields?[18]

It turns out that many things can be done. For channelized streams routinely maintained by clearing and dredging, managers can allow the stream to develop a low-flow meandering channel within the larger trapezoidal channel created by channelization. Left to their own devices, many channelized streams in Illinois start to recover their historical sinuosity by developing an inset partially meander-ing channel within the larger straight channel. This occurs as sediment moving down the stream starts to form bars along the sides of the channels. These bars are offset in a downstream direction: a bar forms along the left bank, forcing the current toward the right and eroding a slight bend, then another bar forms down-stream along the right bank, forming another slight bend, and so on down the stream. Because the channelized stream is far wider and deeper than necessary to convey water downstream, the formation of a slightly sinuous inset channel does not reduce the downstream movement of water channelization was designed to ensure. As the bars along the inset channel become stabilized by grasses and sedges, the low-flow channel develops alternating downstream deeps and shal-lows that increase habitat diversity for aquatic plants and animals. This is exactly what has happened along the Spoon River, a tributary of the Vermilion River in east-central Illinois that was channelized along its entire length during the early twentieth century.[19]

Even such subtle changes in channel form produce results in biological com-munities. Scientific study tends to focus on fish diversity, which is fundamentally limited by the availability of physical habitat. Gradual natural modification of channelized streams during the past thirty years has contributed to increasing use of slightly more diverse habitats by greater numbers of fish species. Fish in headwater streams of Champaign County in east-central Illinois, for example, are more diverse and abundant than they were from the late nineteenth century to the mid-twentieth century. By the 1990s, improved water quality in the Illinois River and some of its tributaries allowed breeding populations of native fish to return, although exotics such as carp persist.[20]

Beaver can also help restore channels. If beaver are reintroduced to a watershed or allowed to re-colonize the area on their own, many of the benefits associated with their dam building can be returned to the river corridor. By 2006, the Illinois Department of Natural Resources estimated that "unexploited" (i.e., untrapped

A portion of the channelized Spoon River near Emiquon, August 2008. The channel here remains relatively uniform and the water is very turbid, with suspended sediment from agricultural runoff.

or otherwise hunted) beaver populations in the Mississippi River bottomlands of southern Illinois had reached more than three colonies per square kilometer, with an average of five or six beaver per colony.

Allowing channels to naturally restore some habitat diversity may require active limitation of channel maintenance. A study of Poplar Creek near Elgin, Illinois, conducted in 2000 found that public outreach to community organizations undertaking channel "cleaning" was critical to channel naturalization. A segment of Poplar Creek 350 meters long was artificially straightened in the early 1900s. Local volunteer groups had been undertaking controlled burns and removal of wood in the stream once or twice a year for several years in the belief that wood in the stream contributed to flooding and decreased habitat quality. By explaining that wood actually improves fish habitat and is unlikely to increase flooding within a channelized stream, scientists were able to facilitate the natural processes of wood recruitment to the stream, thus increasing habitat diversity and fish abundance and diversity.[21]

The example of Poplar Creek highlights the critical importance of involving local communities in channel naturalization. When human residents learn more about the processes by which streams maintain physical form and physical and biological function, they can not only limit activities that impair form and function but can also become stewards of the natural landscape who work to restore river health. Work by the Nature Conservancy along the Mackinaw River in central Illinois, for example, demonstrates that focused outreach efforts can persuade farmers to use suggested conservation-oriented agricultural practices. Agriculture uses more than 75 percent of the Mackinaw's 300,000 hectares. Despite declines in habitat and water quality, however, the stream network still provides habitat for 66 fish species, 31 mussels, 264 birds, and several at-risk species of plants and animals. Scientists working in the Mackinaw watershed now monitor the effectiveness of constructed wetlands in improving water quality and evaluate how large wetlands need to be to reduce nutrients from agricultural runoff. A 100-hectare experimental farm is used to demonstrate river-friendly farming.[22]

In addition to restoring the annual flood and connectivity of the channel-floodplain system, improvements in water quality are necessary to restore biological communities throughout the Illinois River basin and to protect human health. More effective wastewater treatment facilities are an important part of this process. Individual communities sometimes balk at the costs necessary to update or replace aging infrastructure, but strategies tailored to specific situations and that combine artificial wastewater treatment with natural purification processes can substantially reduce these costs. An example of using natural processes is nitrogen farming, as advocated by the Wetlands Initiative.[23]

Nitrogen farming targets the excess nitrogen flushed down the Illinois and Mississippi Rivers from agricultural fields. So much nitrogen now reaches the Gulf of Mexico that it fuels enormous algal blooms. These blooms reduce dissolved oxygen levels to the point that so-called dead zones as large as 18,000 square kilometers in area form each year in the Gulf. The Illinois River basin contributes a disproportionate share of this nitrogen. A team of scientists led by William Mitsch and funded by the National Oceanic and Atmospheric Administration (NOAA) promoted the idea that restored wetlands can be used to reduce this nitrogen flow. As a result of microbial reactions occurring in wetlands, these areas can dispel nitrate to the atmosphere as nitrogen gas: scientists have found that bacteria can remove 80 percent of the nitrate load entering a wetland. The NOAA group estimated that 9.7 million hectares of restored wetlands and riverside vegetation zones are needed to control nitrogen flow to the Gulf, which would cost an estimated $40 billion. Within the Illinois River basin, 162,000 hectares of restored wetlands could reduce the river's nitrate load to levels measured in 1900, representing

Soybean fields behind the levee (grassy band topped by trees at right) along the middle Illinois River. These crop fields, which were once floodplain wetlands and forests, now contribute large amounts of nitrogen to the Illinois and Mississippi Rivers and the Gulf of Mexico.

14 percent of the reduction needed to improve conditions in the Gulf of Mexico. These 162,000 hectares constitute less than 2 percent of the total watershed area of the Illinois River and approximately a third of the river's historically flooded bottomlands.[24]

Given the intensive agriculture in much of the Illinois River basin, these requirements for wetland extent and costs still sound daunting. Wetlands to be restored, however, can be located and financed through nitrogen farming in which bottomlands are flooded with nutrient-rich water for a period as short as six to eight days, sufficient time for nitrate to be converted and dispersed. Farmers who possess sufficient water and suitable soils can thus harvest nitrate and earn credits measured by the tons of nitrogen they remove from the river. These credits could be sold to industries, municipalities, and other farmers who produce excess nitrate. Such a market-based system is facilitated by Environmental Protection Agency criteria currently being developed for allowable total maximum daily loads of nitrogen specified by watershed or stream reach. The system will be most flexible if nutrient standards differ among stream reaches, so that nutrient-rich water can be transported from conventional farms or cities downstream to nitrogen farms: in other words, water quality with respect to nitrates would be sacrificed along some stream segments or farm ditches to improve water quality throughout the Illinois River basin as a whole. Acquiring and restoring bottomland nitrogen farms in the Illinois River basin are estimated to cost $770 million, or $55 million per year. This is less than the estimated $110 million per year to reduce nitrate loads in streams through conventional biological or chemical treatment using concrete tanks, pumps, and chemical and electrical energy; in addition, conventional treatment does not create habitat for wetland plants and animals.[25]

It is difficult to overstate the importance of wetlands in the Illinois River basin. About 10 percent (371,400 hectares) of natural wetlands remained in the state of Illinois by the 1980s; only about 2,400 hectares of these wetlands were undisturbed by sedimentation or pollution and of high quality. Yet these small fragments provide a life raft for plants and animals overwhelmed in a sea of humanity. Forty-two percent of the native plant species in Illinois are wetland plants. As many as 266 species of birds use wetlands during some stage of their lifecycle, and at least 39 of the 59 mammal species in the state use wetland habitats, as do 37 of the 41 species of amphibians and 47 of the 60 species of reptiles. High-quality, relatively undisturbed wetlands are concentrated along the Fox, Des Plaines, and Kankakee Rivers and the middle Illinois River valley, and these sites are a high priority for protection: although we can restore some function to altered wetlands, it is much more effective to prevent their degradation in the first place.[26]

Also a high priority for protection are the stream segments identified by the 1992 study as biologically significant either because they have an A rating in the Biological Stream Characterization or because they support populations of federal or state threatened, endangered, or "watch list" species of plants or animals. Scientists with the Illinois Department of Natural Resources identified 132 of these stream segments throughout Illinois.[27]

BEYOND THE ILLINOIS RIVER

As in the case of the South Platte and rivers of the western prairie, the details of river form and function and of historical alteration vary among the rivers of the eastern prairie, but the basic outline is similar between the Illinois and other rivers. Many of these rivers begin in forested uplands before flowing onto what was once the tallgrass prairie; a few flow entirely across prairie lands. Historically, the rivers spread across broad bottomlands to create a mosaic of meadows, marshes, and lakes around the sinuous channels. Removal of native vegetation and introduc-

Locations of high-quality wetland communities identified by the Illinois Natural Areas Inventory, indicated by star symbols. These represent relatively undisturbed sites. After Critical Trends Assessment Project (1994, fig. 27).

tion of row crops on the uplands dramatically increased sediment yields to the rivers, leading to increased turbidity and sedimentation. Draining of bottomlands for crops and cities and confining the rivers between levees disconnected channels and floodplains and caused massive habitat loss for many aquatic and riparian plants and animals. Agricultural and urban contaminants and introduced species magnify the effects of habitat loss and have led many aquatic species to be listed as threatened or endangered.

The extent and severity of environmental change vary among the rivers of the eastern prairie. Rivers such as the Upper Mississippi, the largest river in the region, retain much of their natural function and continue to provide relatively extensive habitat. Despite the presence of eleven dams in the headwaters and twenty-six locks and dams on the mainstem, the Upper Mississippi still has a fairly natural hydrograph and more than 80 percent of the connectivity between the mainstem and adjacent floodplains. The Upper Mississippi drainage supports 145 fish species, of which 7 are endangered, as are 3 species of mussel. Similarly, the Wapsipinicon River in Iowa still retains mature stands of riparian forest and floodplain meadows and wetlands, although almost 90 percent of the basin is agricultural. Draining a long, narrow swathe of eastern Iowa down to its junction with the Mississippi near Clinton, Iowa, the Wapsipinicon basin supports 74 fish species, only one of which is endangered.[28]

The Rock and Des Moines Rivers, in contrast, are highly altered and polluted. The Rock River heads in southern Wisconsin and flows southeast through Illinois before entering the Upper Mississippi at Moline, Illinois. The lands it drains are used for agriculture and urban communities, and only 2 percent of the basin remains in wetlands. Agricultural and municipal pollutants compromise the rivers throughout the catchment, which move sluggishly among 19 hydroelectric dams on the mainstem and 272 dams throughout the basin. The Des Moines River of Minnesota and Iowa is the largest river draining the central tallgrass prairie, but it has many problems. Two major dams and 58 small to medium dams regulate flow throughout the drainage. Agricultural and urban lands throughout the basin leak large quantities of nitrates, pesticides, and sediment. Habitat loss caused by impoundments along the river has caused declining numbers of aquatic vertebrates, especially turtles; and of the 84 fish species, 3 are endangered.[29]

It is worth repeating that even for the most altered rivers, such as the Rock and the Des Moines, a string of beads formed by parcels of land covered with native vegetation and managed to restore or imitate natural cycles of water and sediment movement would improve water quality and other ecosystem services and help save the species of plants and animals that are struggling to survive. Even a casual visitor to an eastern prairie river can find a place enlivened by numerous species of birds and abundant butterflies, where it is possible to fall asleep to a chorus of frogs and walk through floodplain forests and along shallow lakes and wetlands. These remnants of a once vast natural landscape provide a strong nucleus from which to build in preserving and restoring the river corridors of the eastern prairie.

NOTES

1. Critical Trends Assessment Project, "Ecological Resources"; Illinois Environmental Protection Agency, "Illinois Water Quality Report."

2. D. W. Webb, "The Winter Stoneflies of Illinois (Insecta: Plecoptera): 100 Years of Change," *Illinois Natural History Survey Bulletin* 36, no. 5 (2002): 195–274.

3. Critical Trends Assessment Project, "Water Resources."

4. Covich et al., "Potential Effects of Climate Change."

5. www.mywebtimes.com.

6. Sandiford, "Transforming an Exotic Species."

7. Greenberg, *Natural History of the Chicago Region*, 470.

8. S. Packard and C. F. Mutel, eds., *The Tallgrass Restoration Handbook: For Prairies, Savannas, and Woodlands* (Washington, DC: Island, 1997); S. Shirley, *Restoring the Tallgrass Prairie: An Illustrated Manual for Iowa and the Upper Midwest* (Iowa City: University of Iowa Press, 1994); J. R. Thompson, *Prairies, Forests, and Wetlands: The Restoration of Natural Landscape Communities in Iowa* (Iowa City: University of Iowa Press, 1992).

9. National Research Council, *Restoration of Aquatic Ecosystems: Science, Technology, and Public Policy* (Washington, DC: National Academy Press, 1992).

10. Sparks, "Illinois River-Floodplain System."

11. B. Iverson, "Silt: A Problem Turned Solution?" *Outdoor Illinois* 8 (2000): 5–7; J. C. Marlin and R. G. Darmody, "Returning the Soil to the Land: The Mud to Parks Project," *Illinois Steward* 14 (2005): 11–18.

12. Smith and Mettler, "Role of the Flood Pulse," 136; T. M. Koel and R. E. Sparks, "Historical Patterns of River Stage and Fish Communities as Criteria for Operations of Dams on the Illinois River," *River Research and Applications* 18, no. 1 (2002): 3–19.

13. Ahn, White, and Sparks, "Moist-Soil Plants."

14. Quoted in J. T. Handy, "The Reawakening," *Illinois Times* [Springfield], November 25, 2004.

15. Ibid.

16. T. Prato and D. Hey, "Economic Analysis of Wetland Restoration along the Illinois River," *Journal of the American Water Resources Association* 42, no. 1 (2006): 125–31.

17. Ahn et al., "Analysis of Naturalization Alternatives."

18. B. L. Rhoads et al., "Interaction between Scientists and Nonscientists in Community-Based Watershed Management: Emergence of the Concept of Stream Naturalization," *Environmental Management* 24, no. 3 (October 1999): 304.

19. Landwehr and Rhoads, "Depositional Response."

20. Rhoads and Herricks, "Naturalization of Headwater Streams in Illinois"; Sandiford, "Transforming an Exotic Species"; Raibley, Blodgett, and Sparks, "Evidence of Grass Carp."

21. Wade et al., "Integrating Science and Technology"; Rhoads et al., "Interaction between Scientists and Nonscientists."

22. Wade et al., "Integrating Science and Technology"; Rhoads et al., "Interaction between Scientists and Nonscientists."

23. R. B. Helm, G. Hewitt, and D. R. Good, "Improving the Illinois," *Water Environment and Technology* 6, no. 6 (1994): 44–46; D. L. Hey, "Nitrogen Farming: Harvesting a Different Crop," *Restoration Ecology* 10, no. 1 (2002): 1–10.

24. Hey, "Nitrogen Farming"; R. Kadlec and R. Knight, *Treatment Wetlands* (Chelsea, MI: CRC-Lewis, 1996); D. L. Hey, K. R. Barrett, and C. Biegen, "The Hydrology of Four Experimental Constructed Marshes," *Ecological Engineering* 3 (1994): 319–43; W. J. Mitsch et al., "Reducing Nutrient Loads, Especially Nitrate-Nitrogen, to the Surface Water, Ground Water, and the Gulf of Mexico." *Topic 5 Report, NOAA* (Silver Spring, MD: National Oceanic and Atmospheric Administration, 1999); R. H. Meade, "Contaminants in the Mississippi River 1987–92," *US Geological Survey Circular* 1133 (1995).

25. Hey, "Nitrogen Farming."

26. Critical Trends Assessment Project, "Ecological Resources"; Illinois Environmental Protection Agency, "Illinois Water Quality Report."

27. Critical Trends Assessment Project, "Ecological Resources"; Illinois Environmental Protection Agency, "Illinois Water Quality Report."

28. DeLong, "Upper Mississippi River Basin."

29. Ibid.

Epilogue

RIVERS IN THE ANTHROPOCENE

Intervals of geologic time are named to record either some particular place where rocks of that age were first described, as in the Jurassic Period, named for rocks first described in the mountainous Jura region between France and Switzerland, or to indicate their relative position in the timescale, as in the Holocene, named from the Greek *holos* for "whole" and *kainos* for "new or recent": the Holocene was, until very recently, the youngest interval of geologic time. At the very end of the twentieth century, geologists began to publish papers estimating that humans have now cumulatively moved more sediment than glaciers, rivers, and other natural erosive processes combined. Initially, this was simply a fascinating observation for many scientists. Then more papers in a similar vein began to appear. Mining decades of systematic records of water, sediment, and chemical fluxes along rivers, scientists realized that people are not only moving sediment around locally but are also significantly altering global fluxes to the ocean. Humans have collectively increased soil erosion and the global sediment transport of rivers by an estimated 2.3 billion metric tons per year (out of a total 12.6 billion metric tons), for example, yet they have reduced the flux of sediment reaching the ocean by 1.4 billion metric tons per year as a result of trapping sediment in reservoirs. Simultaneously, diverse evidence continues to accumulate that humans are significantly altering atmospheric chemistry and global climate. In recognition of these so-called anthropogenic effects (from Greek *anthropos* for "human being" and *genic* for "caused by"), a new interval of geologic time to be known as the Anthropocene will soon be designated.[1]

The exact dates of this interval are under debate. An argument can be made for the start of intensive agriculture. Replacement of native vegetation by crops clearly appears in river sediments around the world, whether it occurred 3,000 years ago in the Middle East or 200 years ago in the United States. The volume of sediment entering rivers increased as a result of agriculture, and excess sediment was stored along valley bottoms. An argument can also be made for the start of the Industrial Revolution as the initiation of the rapid population growth and intense resource use that now characterize the Anthropocene. Regardless of the exact starting date, humans today so strongly influence landscapes and fluxes of matter and energy around the world that formal designation of a new era seems appropriate.

With a human population of 7 billion and growing, Earth's surface, including rivers, will not return within the foreseeable future to any baseline conditions that might have existed prior to intensive human resource use. Complete restoration of "natural" river form and function is thus unlikely in densely used areas such as the US prairies. On the other hand, we clearly cannot continue with the progressive loss of ecosystem services such as clean water without paying an unimaginably high price. So what can we do? Methods proposed to protect and restore some river services include miniaturization of river ecosystems—a sort of downsizing to create a smaller but still functional version of a river corridor, given the continuing demands for consumptive water uses. Water banking involves an entity such as a federal agency purchasing water from willing sellers and keeping that water from going to consumptive uses, such as irrigated agriculture. A related approach is stream mitigation banking, in which developers offset construction impacts by purchasing credits generated by for-profit companies that restore damaged streams on a speculative basis, as approved by federal regulatory agencies. And strings of river beads reflect the understanding that preserving some portions of an ecologically healthy river corridor can be quite effective, even if the river's entire length cannot be restored. Each of these approaches relies on being able to identify thresholds of river response and function on which minimum levels of protection and restoration can be based. A key point here is that river function and the provision of ecosystem services are not typically linear. You cannot count on sustaining a very small population of a certain fish species, for example, with a very small amount of water because some minimum flow volume is likely necessary to create sufficient habitat and ability for the fish to disperse and maintain genetically healthy populations: below that minimum flow volume, there will likely be no fish at all.[2]

The science underlying knowledge of river response to different strategies of protection is fundamental, but public awareness and willingness to support rivers—at personal, communal, and political levels—are equally critical. My hope is that each of us will think of rivers not as gutters down which our wastes can be flushed or as drainage canals that simply convey water where we wish but rather as ecosystems. Because many people in the industrialized world have become aware of tropical rainforests as diverse, vibrant, and imperiled ecosystems, public support for certified, sustainably harvested wood has caused even the largest retailers to change the way they buy wood products. Surely we can develop an equal appreciation for the rivers in our own backyards and begin to regulate our actions to reflect this appreciation. This can start by being aware of rapid changes in energy production that are just starting to affect the American prairies.

ENERGY OF THE FUTURE

Our nation's choices can affect rivers in unexpected ways. This book has traced the history of how land and water use in drainages of two diverse portions of the American prairie have altered the water and sediment entering rivers and thus the form and function of river ecosystems. As we continue into the twenty-first century, increasing evidence of climate changes triggered by greenhouses gases, and rising prices for petroleum fuels and associated national economic problems, are facilitating diversification of the sources from which we obtain energy. In the western prairie, this has already affected rivers through accelerated drilling of oil and natural gas, but increased production of ethanol may also have a large effect on rivers. In 2007 the group Environmental Defense examined the potential implications of expanded ethanol production on the Ogallala Aquifer. As of 2007, five ethanol plants were producing 270,600 cubic meters of ethanol each year from lands underlain by the aquifer. Once the nine additional plants under construction become operational, they can produce up to 2.4 million cubic meters per year. This would require an additional water withdrawal of 223–454 million cubic meters of water each year from the most depleted parts of the aquifer. The aquifer cannot sustain this level of withdrawal.[3]

In addition to subsurface water levels and, by association, springs and stream flow, increasing ethanol production will affect land cover. A 2007 report by the US Government Accountability Office estimated that more than 2.2 million hectares of grasslands were converted into crop production from 1982 to 2003, a continuing trend largely spurred by crop prices rising as a result of ethanol demand. Loss of grasslands and wetlands across the prairie would be much higher were it not for the US Department of Agriculture's (USDA) Conservation Reserve Program. This program has paid to retire almost 15 million hectares of environmentally sensitive cropland, but by 2007 the USDA had halted new enrollment of lands and anticipated actually returning nearly 2 million hectares to crop production over the next few years. This change would substantially impact the eastern as well as the western prairie, for many of the retired croplands are in river-bottom wetlands in the eastern prairie.[4]

In the western prairie, more corn production for ethanol means further consumptive demands on limited water supplies. In both the eastern and western prairie, more corn production means loss of natural land cover and increased sediment, nitrogen, phosphorus, and pesticides entering rivers. This alternative fuel comes with tremendous hidden costs.

A BETTER FUTURE FOR RIVERS AND PEOPLE

Much remains to be done to protect and restore river ecosystems throughout the South Platte and Illinois River basins and all the other prairie rivers represented by these two case studies. People of European descent crossed these wide rivers physically, encountering them during early explorations of the prairie and its resources and then moving beyond them on horseback or on boats, overcoming hazards of grounding, snagging, and drowning. Then we crossed the rivers metaphorically, opposing with our dredges, dams, drains, and levees the tendency of the rivers to flood widely, to break up into multiple channels, and to meander slowly across wide bottomlands. In the course of these alterations we gained a great deal: reliable supplies of water for crop irrigation and municipal use, access to rich bottomland soils for agriculture, extensive waterways for moving large quantities of material on barges, and sluices that conveniently carried away a large variety of wastes. We also lost a great deal, which now seems like unimaginable environmental wealth: waters a human could safely drink without treating or purifying it; millions of hectares of bottomland forests, wetlands, and river habitat; and millions and millions of fish and birds, as well as the organisms that supported them and preyed upon them. We narrowed and simplified the rivers of the American prairie, and it remains an open question whether we lost more than we gained.

Every river system of the American prairie has experienced widespread and intensive changes during the past two centuries as a result of human uses of land

and other resources. As a result, the form and function of these rivers have been altered so substantially that the rivers can be said to have metamorphosed. These metamorphoses impose severe stresses on native species of aquatic and riparian plants and animals, many of which have declined in abundance or even disappeared. Changed river conditions have also in many cases compromised the rivers' ability to provide ecological services to humans, including clean water, fertile bottomland soils, and recreation. River systems can be restored to some of their historical function, however, without significantly disrupting the human societies that now occupy these basins. We have the technical knowledge necessary for restoration and protection, and we have the financial resources: what we need is the collective will to dedicate the time, energy, and money necessary to restore and protect the rivers of the American prairie.

Acquiring beads of land along the strings of rivers in these basins is a critical first step, as is managing the lands to restore some of the natural processes that create diverse habitat and connect channels and floodplains. To paraphrase a popular movie about baseball, "build it and they will come" can also apply to river and wetland plants and animals. These organisms will utilize suitable habitat if they can reach it—if their migration pathways are not blocked and the distance between patches of habitat is not too great to travel—and if the organisms have not vanished into extinction.

Simultaneous with the acquisition and management of riverine lands must be changes in the use of resources—particularly water—and the disposal of wastes throughout the drainage basin. Protecting "beads" will be of limited value if no water is available to flow down the river between them or to inundate the floodplains within the beads. Similarly, plants and animals will not be able to survive within the beads if the water and sediment are poisoned by synthetic chemicals, heavy metals, or excess nutrients. Changing the patterns of resource use and waste disposal throughout a river basin is more difficult than acquiring isolated plots of land along the river. Many fairly recent examples, however, illustrate that these changes are possible. Soil erosion from agricultural lands declined as a result of land-conservation practices implemented after the 1930s Dust Bowl (although unfortunately many of these practices have subsequently been abandoned, leading once again to higher rates of soil erosion). Phosphate levels in streams across the United States went down substantially after individual states started banning phosphate detergents in the 1970s. Concentrations of metals in streams within the Illinois River basin decreased during the last two decades of the twentieth century in response to improved pollution control measures. Sewage entering the rivers declined in response to expanded and better wastewater treatment facilities throughout the basin. These recent improvements demonstrate what can be accomplished if society makes land and water conservation a priority. We can continue to build on these past improvements to restore and protect the ecosystems that are most vital to our own survival—our country's rivers.

The prairie is our continent's heartland, of which the Mississippi River and its tributaries are the great heart. The pulse of these rivers nourishes the adjacent bottomlands and the extensive biological—including human—communities that depend on the bottomlands' water, nutrients, and habitats; but the influence of this pulse reaches far beyond the bottomlands. Biological productivity in the Gulf of Mexico rises or falls as flows from the Mississippi River network enrich or poison the waters of the Gulf. We must continue to cross the wide rivers of the prairie and the frontiers they represent, but now the frontiers to be crossed are those of knowledge and responsibility as we restore and protect our irreplaceable natural heritage.

NOTES

1. Hooke, "On the History of Humans"; J.P.M. Syvitski, C. J. Vörösmarty, A. J. Kettner, and P. Green, "Impact of Humans on the Flux of Terrestrial Sediment to the Global Coastal Ocean," *Science* 308 (2005): 376–80; J. Zalasiewicz, M. Williams, A. Smith, and 18 more, "Are We Now Living in the Anthropocene?" *GSA Today* 18, no. 2 (2008): 4–8.

2. S. M. Burke, R. M. Adams, and W. W. Wallender, "Water Banks and Environmental Water Demands: Case of the Klamath Project," *Water Resources Research* 40 (2004): W09S02; R. Lave, M. M. Robertson, and M. W. Doyle, "Why You Should Pay Attention to Stream Mitigation Banking," *Ecological Restoration* 26, no. 4 (2008): 287–89.

3. "High Stakes in Farm Bill," *Rocky Mountain News*, September 30, 2007, E-5.

4. Government Accounting Office (GAO), *Agricultural Conservation: Farm Program Payments Are an Important Factor in Landowners' Decisions to Convert Grassland to Cropland* (Washington, DC: GAO, 2007).

English-Metric Unit Conversions

Length	
1 inch	2.54 centimeters
0.6 mile	1 kilometer
3.29 feet	1 meter

Area	
2.47 acres	1 hectare

Weight	
2.2 pounds	1 kilogram
2,205 pounds	1 metric ton

Volume	
35.6 cubic feet	1 cubic meter
1 acre-foot	1,233 cubic meters

Concentration	
0.035 ounces	1,000 milligrams
1 gallon	3.78 liters
0.1323 ounces/gallon	1,000 milligrams/liter

Selected Bibliography

WESTERN PRAIRIE AND MOUNTAINS: BOOKS

Bird, I. L. *A Lady's Life in the Rocky Mountains*. Norman: University of Oklahoma Press, 1960 [1873].

Botkin, D. B. *Beyond the Stony Mountains: Nature in the American West from Lewis and Clark to Today*. Oxford: Oxford University Press, 2004.

Brookfield, M. E., and T. S. Ahlbrandt, eds. *Eolian Sediments and Processes*. Amsterdam: Elsevier, 1983.

Calow, P., and G. E. Petts, eds. *The Rivers Handbook: Hydrological and Ecological Principles*. Oxford: Blackwell Scientific Publications, 1992.

Cassells, E. S. *The Archaeology of Colorado*. Boulder: Johnson Books, 1983.

Dingman, S. L. *Physical Hydrology*, 2nd ed. Upper Saddle River, NJ: Prentice-Hall, 2002.

Emory, W. H. *Notes of a Military Reconnaissance, from Fort Leavenworth, in Missouri, to San Diego, in California, Including Part of the Arkansas, Del Norte, and Gila Rivers*. Washington, DC: Wendell and Van Benthuysen, 1848.

Graf, W. L., ed. *Endangered and Threatened Species of the Platte River*. Committee on Endangered and Threatened Species in the Platte River Basin, National Research Council. Washington, DC: National Academies Press, 2005.

Greeley, H. *An Overland Journey from New York to San Francisco in the Summer of 1859*. Lincoln: University of Nebraska Press, 1999 [1860].

Guthery, F. S., F. C. Bryant, B. Kramer, A. Stoecker, and M. Dvorack. *Playa Assessment Study*. Amarillo, TX: US Water and Power Resources Service, Southwest Region, 1981.

Jackson, D., and M. L. Spence, eds. *The Expeditions of John Charles Frémont*, vol. 1: *Travels from 1838 to 1844*. Urbana: University of Illinois Press, 1970.

James, E. *Account of an Expedition from Pittsburgh to the Rocky Mountains, Performed in the Years 1819 and '20*. 2 vols. Philadelphia: Carey and Lea, 1823. http://dx.doi.org/10.5962/bhl.title.61840.

Manning, R. *Rewilding the West: Restoration in a Prairie Landscape*. Berkeley: University of California Press, 2009.

Opie, J. *Ogallala: Water for a Dry Land*, 2nd ed. Lincoln: University of Nebraska Press, 2000.

Pike, Z. *The Journals of Zebulon Montgomery Pike, with Letters and Related Documents*, vol. 1. Ed. D. Jackson. Norman: University of Oklahoma Press, 1966.

Samson, F. B., and F. L. Knopf, eds. *Prairie Conservation: Preserving North America's Most Endangered Ecosystem*. Washington, DC: Island, 1996.

Taylor, B. *Colorado: A Summer Trip*. New York: G. P. Putnam and Son, 1867.

Tice, J. H. *Over the Plains, on the Mountains; or, Kansas, Colorado, and the Rocky Mountains; Agriculturally, Mineralogically and Aesthetically Described*. St. Louis: Industrial Age Printing, 1872.

Tyler, D. *The Last Water Hole in the West: The Colorado–Big Thompson Project and the Northern Colorado Water Conservancy District*. Niwot: University Press of Colorado, 1992.

Ward, J. V., B. C. Kondratieff, and R. E. Zuellig. *An Illustrated Guide to the Mountain Stream Insects of Colorado*, 2nd ed. Boulder: University Press of Colorado, 2002.

West, E. *The Contested Plains: Indians, Goldseekers, and the Rush to Colorado*. Lawrence: University Press of Kansas, 1998.

Wohl, E. E. *Virtual Rivers: Lessons from the Mountain Rivers of the Colorado Front Range*. New Haven, CT: Yale University Press, 2001.

WESTERN PRAIRIE AND MOUNTAINS: ARTICLES, BOOK CHAPTERS, GOVERNMENT PUBLICATIONS

Batt, B.D.J. "Prairie Ecology—Prairie Wetlands." In *Prairie Conservation: Preserving North America's Most Endangered Ecosystem*, ed. F. B. Samson and F. L. Knopf, 77–88. Washington, DC: Island, 1996.

Bovee, K. D., and M. L. Scott. "Implications of Flood Pulse Restoration for *Populus* Regeneration on the Upper Missouri River." *River Research and Applications* 18, no. 3 (2002): 287–98. http://dx.doi.org/10.1002/rra.672.

Bryan, K., and L. L. Ray. "Geologic Antiquity of the Lindenmeier Site in Colorado." *Smithsonian Miscellaneous Collections* 99, no. 2 (1941): 1–95.

Byrne, J. M., A. Berg, and I. Townshend. "Linking Observed and General Circulation Model Upper Air Circulation Patterns to Current and Future Snow Runoff for the Rocky Mountains." *Water Resources Research* 35, no. 12 (1999): 3793–802. http://dx.doi.org/10.1029/1999WR900149.

"Coal-Bed Gas Resources of the Rocky Mountain Region." *US Geological Survey* (USGS) *Fact-Sheet* FS-110-01. Washington, DC: USGS, 2003.

Colorado Department of Health. "Ground Water Monitoring in the South Platte Valley." *South Platte Monitoring Fact Sheet #10*, March. Denver: Colorado Department of Health, 1995.

Covich, A. P., S. C. Fritz, P. J. Lamb, R. D. Marzolf, W. J. Matthews, K. A. Poiani, E. E. Prepas, M. B. Richman, and T. C. Winter. "Potential Effects of Climate Change on Aquatic Ecosystems of the Great Plains of North America." *Hydrological Processes* 11, no. 8 (1997): 993–1021. http://dx.doi.org/10.1002/(SICI)1099-1085(19970630)11:8<993::AID-HYP515>3.0.CO;2-N.

Cross, F. B., and R. E. Moss. "Historic Changes in Fish Communities and Aquatic Habitats in Plains Streams of Kansas." In *Community and Evolutionary Ecology of North American Stream Fishes*, ed. W. J. Matthews and D. C. Heins, 155–65. Norman: University of Oklahoma Press, 1987.

Dennehy, K. F., D. W. Litke, C. M. Tate, S. L. Qi, P. B. McMahon, B. W. Bruce, R. A. Kimbrough, and J. S. Heiny. "Hydraulic Geometry of the Platte River near Overton, South-Central Nebraska." *US Geological Survey Professional Paper* 1277-C (1983).

Dennehy, K. F., D. W. Kitke, C. M. Tate, S. L. Qi, P. B. McMahon, B. W. Bruce, R. A. Kimbrough, and J. S. Heiny. "Water Quality in the South Platte River Basin, Colorado, Nebraska, and Wyoming, 1992–95." *US Geological Survey Circular* 1167 (1998).

Eschner, T. R. "Hydrologic and Morphologic Changes in Channels of the Platte River Basin in Colorado, Wyoming, and Nebraska: A Historical Perspective." *US Geological Survey Professional Paper* 1277-A (1983).

Eschner, T. R. "Hydraulic Geometry of the Platte River near Overton, South-Central Nebraska." *US Geological Survey Professional Paper* 1277-C (1983).

Eschner, T. R., R. F. Hadley, and K. D. Crowley. "Hydrologic and Morphologic Changes in Channels of the Platte River Basin in Colorado, Wyoming, and Nebraska: A Historical Perspective." *US Geological Survey Professional Paper* 1277-A (1983).

Falke, J. A., K. R. Bestgen, and K. D. Fausch. "Streamflow Reductions and Habitat Drying Affect Growth, Survival, and Recruitment of Brassy Minnow across a Great Plains Riverscape." *Transactions of the American Fisheries Society* 139, no. 5 (2010): 1566–83. http://dx.doi.org/10.1577/T09-143.1. http://www.researchgate.net/journal/1548-8659_Transactions_of_the_American_Fisheries_Society.

Falke, J. A., K. D. Fausch, R. Magelky, A. Aldred, D. S. Durnford, L. K. Riley, and R. Oad. "The Role of Groundwater Pumping and Drought in Shaping Ecological Futures for Stream Fishes in a Dryland River Basin of the Western Great Plains, USA." *Ecohydrology* (2010). http://onlinelibrary.wiley.com/journal/10.1002/(ISSN)1936-0592.

Falke, J. A., and K. B. Gido. "Spatial Effects of Reservoirs on Fish Assemblages in Great Plains Streams in Kansas, USA." *River Research and Applications* 22, no. 1 (2006): 55–68. http://dx.doi.org/10.1002/rra.889.

Fardal, L. L. "Effects of Groundwater Pumping for Irrigation to Stream Properties of the Arikaree River on the Colorado Plains." MS thesis, Colorado State University, Fort Collins, 2003.Fausch, K. D., and K. R. Bestgen. "Ecology of Fishes Indigenous to the Central and Southwestern Great Plains." In *Ecology and Conservation of Great Plains Vertebrates*, ed. F. L. Knopf and F. B. Samson, 131–66. New York: Springer-Verlag, 1997.

Fausch, K. D., and R. G. Bramblett. "Disturbance and Fish Communities in Intermittent Tributaries of a Western Great Plains River." *Copeia* 3 (1991): 659–74. http://dx.doi.org/10.2307/1446392.

Feng, Z., W. C. Johnson, Y. Lu, and P. A. Ward. "Climatic Signals from Loess-Soil Sequences in the Central Great Plains, USA." *Palaeogeography, Palaeoclimatology, Palaeoecology* 110, no. 3-4 (1994): 345–58. http://dx.doi.org/10.1016/0031-0182(94)90091-4.

Ficke, A. D., and C. A. Myrick. "The Swimming and Jumping Ability of Three Small Great Plains Fishes: Implications for Fishway Design." *Transactions of the American Fisheries Society* 140, no. 6 (2011): 521–31.

Forman, S. L., A.F.H. Goetz, and R. H. Yuhas. "Large-Scale Stabilized Dunes on the High Plains of Colorado: Understanding the Landscape Response to Holocene Climates with the Aid of Images from Space." *Geology* 20, no. 2 (1992): 145–48. http://dx.doi.org/10.1130/0091-7613(1992)020<0145:LSSDOT>2.3.CO;2.

Fotherby, L. M. "Valley Confinement as a Factor of Braided River Pattern for the Platte River." *Geomorphology* 103, no. 4 (2009): 562–76. http://dx.doi.org/10.1016/j.geomorph.2008.08.001.

Friedman, J. M., and V. J. Lee. "Extreme Floods, Channel Change, and Riparian Forests along Ephemeral Streams." *Ecological Monographs* 72, no. 3 (2002): 409–25. http://dx.doi.org/10.1890/0012-9615(2002)072[0409:EFCCAR]2.0.CO;2.

Friedman, J. M., W. R. Osterkamp, and W. M. Lewis Jr. "The Role of Vegetation and Bed-Level Fluctuations in the Process of Channel Narrowing." *Geomorphology* 14, no. 4 (1996): 341–51. http://dx.doi.org/10.1016/0169-555X(95)00047-9.

Friedman, J. M., M. L. Scott, and G. T. Auble. "Management and Cottonwood Forest Dynamics along Prairie Streams." In *Ecology of Great Plains Vertebrates*, ed. F. L. Knopf and F. B. Samson, 49–71. Ecological Studies 125. New York: Springer-Verlag, 1997.

Galat, D. L., C. R. Berry, E. J. Peters, and R. G. White. "Missouri River Basin." In *Rivers of North America*, ed. A. C. Benke and C. E. Cushing, 426–80. Amsterdam: Elsevier, 2005. http://dx.doi.org/10.1016/B978-012088253-3/50013-4.

Gido, K. B., W. K. Dodds, and M. E. Eberle. "Retrospective Analysis of Fish Community Change during a Half-Century of Landuse and Streamflow Changes." *Journal of the North American Benthological Society* 29, no. 3 (2010): 970–87. http://dx.doi.org/10.1899/09-116.1.

Gutentag, E. D., F. J. Heimes, N. C. Krothe, R. R. Luckey, and J. B. Weeks. "Geohydrology of the High Plains Aquifer in Parts of Colorado, Kansas, Nebraska, New Mexico, Oklahoma, South Dakota, Texas, and Wyoming." *US Geological Survey Professional Paper* 1400-B (1984).

Hauer, F. R., J. S. Baron, D. H. Campbell, K. D. Fausch, S. W. Hostetler, G. H. Leavesley, P. R. Leavitt, D. M. McKnight, and J. A. Stanford. "Assessment of Climate Change and Freshwater Ecosystems of the Rocky Mountains, USA and Canada." *Hydrological Processes* 11, no. 8 (1997): 903–24. http://dx.doi.org/10.1002/(SICI)1099-1085(19970630)11:8<903::AID-HYP511>3.0.CO;2-7.

Haukos, D. A., and L. M. Smith. "Past and Future Impacts of Wetland Regulations on Playa Ecology in the Southern Great Plains." *Wetlands* 23, no. 3 (2003): 577–89. http://dx.doi.org/10.1672/0277-5212(2003)023[0577:PAFIOW]2.0.CO;2.

Hoagstrom, C. W., J. E. Brooks, and S. R. Davenport. "A Large-Scale Conservation Perspective Considering Endemic Fishes of the North American Plains." *Biological Conservation* (2010). http://www.journals.elsevier.com/biological-conservation/.

Hobbs, G. "Citizen's Guide to Colorado Water Law, 2nd ed., Appendix 2.1." Denver: Colorado Foundation for Water Education, 2003.

Holliday, V. T. "Geoarchaeology and Late Quaternary Geomorphology of the Middle South Platte River, Northeastern Colorado." *Geoarchaeology* 2, no. 4 (1987): 317–29. http://dx.doi.org/10.1002/gea.3340020404.

Hubbs, C. "Springs and Spring Runs as Unique Aquatic Systems." *Copeia* 4 (1995): 989–91. http://dx.doi.org/10.2307/1447053.

Johnson, W. C. "Woodland Expansion in the Platte River, Nebraska: Patterns and Causes." *Ecological Monographs* 64, no. 1 (1994): 45–84. http://dx.doi.org/10.2307/2937055.

Karlinger, M. F., T. R. Eschner, R. F. Hadley, and J. E. Kircher. "Relation of Channel-Width Maintenance to Sediment Transport and River Morphology: Platte River, South-Central Nebraska." *US Geological Survey Professional Paper* 1277-E (1983).

Kinzel, P. J., J. M. Nelson, and A. K. Heckman. "Response of Sandhill Crane (*Grus canadensis*) Riverine Roosting Habitat to Changes in Stage and Sandbar Morphology." *River Research and Applications* 25, no. 2 (2009): 135–52. http://dx.doi.org/10.1002/rra.1103.

Kinzel, P. J., J. M. Nelson, R. S. Parker, and L. R. Davis. "Spring Census of Mid-Continent Sandhill Cranes Using Aerial Infrared Videography." *Journal of Wildlife Management* 70, no. 1 (2006): 70–77. http://dx.doi.org/10.2193/0022-541X(2006)70[70:SCOMSC]2.0.CO;2.

Kircher, J. E. "Interpretation of Sediment Data for the South Platte River in Colorado and Nebraska, and the North Platte and Platte Rivers in Nebraska." *US Geological Survey Professional Paper* 1277-D (1983).

Kircher, J. E., and M. R. Karlinger. "Effects of Water Development on Surface-Water Hydrology, Platte River Basin in Colorado, Wyoming, and Nebraska Upstream from Duncan, Nebraska." *US Geological Survey Professional Paper* 1277-B (1983).

Knopf, F. L. "Changing Landscapes and the Cosmopolitanism of the Eastern Colorado Avifauna." *Wildlife Society Bulletin* 14 (1986): 132–42.

Krapu, G. L., D. A. Brandt, and R. R. Cox Jr. "Less Waste Corn, More Land in Soybeans, and the Switch to Genetically Modified Crops: Trends with Important Implications for Wildlife Management." *Wildlife Society Bulletin* 32, no. 1 (2004): 127–36. http://dx.doi.org/10.2193/0091-7648(2004)32[127:LWCMLI]2.0.CO;2.

Kryloff, N. "Hole in the River: A Brief History of Groundwater in the South Platte Valley." *Colorado Water: Newsletter of the Water Center of Colorado State University* 4, no. 5 (2007): 9–12.

Labbe, T. R., and K. D. Fausch. "Dynamics of Intermittent Stream Habitat Regulate Persistence of a Threatened Fish at Multiple Scales." *Ecological Applications* 10, no. 6 (2000): 1774–91. http://dx.doi.org/10.1890/1051-0761(2000)010[1774:DOISHR]2.0.CO;2.

Lohr, S. C., and K. D. Fausch. "Multiscale Analysis of Natural Variability in Stream Fish Assemblages of a Western Great Plains Watershed." *Copeia* 4 (1997): 706–24. http://dx.doi.org/10.2307/1447289.

Loomis, J., P. Kent, L. Strange, K. Fausch, and A. Covich. "Measuring the Total Economic Value of Restoring Ecosystem Services in an Impaired River Basin: Results from a

Contingent Valuation Survey." *Ecological Economics* 33, no. 1 (2000): 103–17. http://
dx.doi.org/10.1016/S0921-8009(99)00131-7.

Madole, R. F. "Stratigraphic Evidence of Desertification in the West-Central Great Plains
within the Past 1000 Yr." *Geology* 22, no. 6 (1994): 483–86. http://dx.doi.org/10.1130
/0091-7613(1994)022<0483:SEODIT>2.3.CO;2.

Madole, R. F. "Spatial and Temporal Patterns of Late Quaternary Eolian Deposition,
Eastern Colorado, U.S.A." *Quaternary Science Reviews* 14, no. 2 (1995): 155–77. http://
dx.doi.org/10.1016/0277-3791(95)00005-A.

Matthai, H. F. "Floods of June 1965 in South Platte River Basin, Colorado." *US Geological
Survey Water-Supply Paper* 1850-B (1969).

Matthews, W. J. "North American Prairie Streams as Systems for Ecological Study."
Journal of the North American Benthological Society 7, no. 4 (1988): 387–409. http://dx.doi
.org/10.2307/1467298.

Matthews, W. J. "Physicochemical Tolerance and Selectivity of Stream Fishes as Related
to Their Geographic Ranges and Local Distributions." In *Community and Evolutionary
Ecology of North American Stream Fishes*, ed. W. J. Matthews and D. C. Heins, 111–20.
Norman: University of Oklahoma Press, 1987.

Matthews, W. J., and E. Marsh-Matthews. "Extirpation of Red Shiner in Direct
Tributaries of Lake Texoma (Oklahoma-Texas): A Cautionary Case History from a
Fragmented River-Reservoir System." *Transactions of the American Fisheries Society* 136,
no. 4 (2007): 1041–62. http://dx.doi.org/10.1577/T06-059.1.

Matthews, W. J., C. C. Vaughn, K. B. Gido, and E. Marsh-Matthews. "Southern Plains
Rivers." In *Rivers of North America*, ed. A. C. Benke and C. E. Cushing, 282–325.
Amsterdam: Elsevier, 2005. http://dx.doi.org/10.1016/B978-012088253-3/50010-9.

McGree, M. M., D. L. Winkelman, N.K.M. Vieira, and A. M. Vajda. "Reproductive Failure
of the Red Shiner (*Cyprinella lutrensis*) after Exposure to an Exogenous Estrogen."
Canadian Journal of Fisheries and Aquatic Sciences 67, no. 11 (2010): 1730–43. http://dx.doi
.org/10.1139/F10-092.

McMahon, P. B. "Some Bacteria Are Beneficial!" *US Geological Survey Fact Sheet* FS-102-95
(1995).

McMahon, P. B., K. J. Lull, K. F. Dennehy, and J. A. Collins. "Quantity and Quality of
Ground-Water Discharge to the South Platte River, Denver to Fort Lupton, Colorado,
August 1992 through July 1993." *US Geological Survey Water-Resources Investigations
Report* 95-4031 (1995).

Mueller, D. K., P. A. Hamilton, D. R. Helsel, K. J. Hitt, and B. C. Ruddy. "Nutrients in
Ground Water and Surface Water of the United States: An Analysis of Data through
1992." *US Geological Survey Water-Resources Investigations Report* 95-4031 (1995).

Muhs, D. R. "Age and Paleoclimatic Significance of Holocene Sand Dunes in
Northeastern Colorado." *Annals of the Association of American Geographers* 75, no. 4
(1985): 566–82. http://dx.doi.org/10.1111/j.1467-8306.1985.tb00094.x.

Muhs, D. R., T. W. Stafford, S. D. Cowherd, S. A. Mahan, R. Kihl, P. B. Maat, C. A.
Bush, and J. Nehring. "Origin of the Late Quaternary Dune Fields of Northeastern
Colorado." *Geomorphology* 17, no. 1-3 (1996): 129–49. http://dx.doi.org/10.1016
/0169-555X(95)00100-J.

Nadler, C. T., and S. A. Schumm. "Metamorphosis of South Platte and Arkansas Rivers, Eastern Colorado." *Physical Geography* 2, no. 2 (1981): 95–115.

National Assessment Synthesis Team. "Climate Change Impacts on the United States: The Potential Consequences of Climate Variability and Change; Overview: Great Plains." Washington, DC: US Global Change Research Program, 2000.

Nickens, T. E. "Here Today, Gone Tomorrow." *Audubon* 108, no. 6 (2006): 42–47.

Nuccio, V. "Coalbed Methane: An Untapped Energy Resource and an Environmental Concern." *US Geological Survey Fact-Sheet* FS-019-97 (1997).

Ojima, D., L. Garcia, E. Elgaali, K. Miller, T.G.F. Kittel, and J. Lackett. "Potential Climate Change Impacts on Water Resources in the Great Plains." *Journal of the American Water Resources Association* 35, no. 6 (1999): 1443–54. http://dx.doi.org/10.1111/j.1752-1688.1999.tb04228.x.Osterkamp, W. R., M. M. Fenton, T. C. Gustavson, R. F. Hadley, V. T. Holliday, R. B. Morrison, and T. J. Toy. "Great Plains." In *Geomorphic Systems of North America*, ed. W. L. Graf, 163–210. Boulder: Geological Society of America, 1987.

Osterkamp, W. R., and E. R. Hedman. "Perennial-Streamflow Characteristics Related to Channel Geometry and Sediment in Missouri River Basin." *US Geological Survey Professional Paper* 1242 (1982).

Parks, M. A. "Grass Roots: A Great Plains Native Finds His Way Home." *Sierra* 95, no. 6 (2010): 50–57.

Parton, W. J., M. P. Gutmann, and D. Ojima. "Long-Term Trends in Population, Farm Income, and Crop Production in the Great Plains." *BioScience* 57, no. 9 (2007): 737–47. http://dx.doi.org/10.1641/B570906.

Parton, W. J., M. P. Gutmann, and W. R. Travis. "Sustainability and Historical Land-Use Change in the Great Plains: The Case of Eastern Colorado." *Great Plains Research* 13 (2003): 97–125.

Peters, E. J., and S. Schainost. "Historical Changes in Fish Distribution and Abundance in the Platte River in Nebraska." *American Fisheries Society Symposium* 45 (2005): 239–48.

Peterson, D. A., K. A. Miller, T. T. Bartos, M. L. Clark, S. D. Porter, and T. L. Quinn. "Water Quality in the Yellowstone River Basin, Wyoming, Montana, and North Dakota, 1999–2001." *US Geological Survey* (USGS) *Circular* 1234. Reston, VA: USGS, 2004.

Propst, D. L., and C. A. Carlson. "The Distribution and Status of Warmwater Fishes in the Platte River Drainage, Colorado." *Southwestern Naturalist* 31, no. 2 (1986): 149–67. http://dx.doi.org/10.2307/3670555.

Ramage, C. S. "El Niño." *Scientific American* 254, no. 6 (1986): 76–83.

Rense, W. C. "Hydrologic Impact of Climate Change in the Colorado Front Range." *American Water Resources Association.* Spring Specialty Conference, Anchorage, 2000.

Scheurer, J. A., K. D. Fausch, and K. R. Bestgen. "Multiscale Processes Regulate Brassy Minnow Persistence in a Great Plains River." *Transactions of the American Fisheries Society* 132, no. 5 (2003): 840–55. http://dx.doi.org/10.1577/T02-037.

Scott, M. L., and G. T. Auble. "Conservation and Restoration of Semiarid Riparian Forests: A Case Study from the Upper Missouri River, Montana." In *Flood Pulsing in Wetlands: Restoring the Natural Hydrological Balance*, ed. B. A. Middleton, 145–90. New York: John Wiley and Sons, 2002.

Scott, M., G. T. Auble, and J. M. Friedman. "Flood Dependency of Cottonwood Establishment along the Missouri River, Montana, USA." *Ecological Applications* 7, no. 2 (1997): 677–90. http://dx.doi.org/10.1890/1051-0761(1997)007[0677:FDOCEA]2.0.CO;2.

Scott, M. L., J. M. Friedman, and G. T. Auble. "Fluvial Process and the Establishment of Bottomland Trees." *Geomorphology* 14, no. 4 (1996): 327–39. http://dx.doi.org/10.1016/0169-555X(95)00046-8.

Smith, R. K., and K. D. Fausch. "Thermal Tolerance and Vegetation Preference of Arkansas Darter and Johnny Darter from Colorado Plains Streams." *Transactions of the American Fisheries Society* 126, no. 4 (1997): 676–86. http://dx.doi.org/10.1577/1548-8659(1997)126<0676:TTAVPO>2.3.CO;2.

Sophocleous, M.. "From Safe Yield to Sustainable Development of Water Resources: The Kansas Experience." *Journal of Hydrology [Amsterdam]* 235, no. 1–2 (2000): 27–43. http://dx.doi.org/10.1016/S0022-1694(00)00263-8.

Sparling, D. W., and G. L. Krapu. "Communal Roosting and Foraging Behavior of Staging Sandhill Cranes." *Wilson Bulletin* 106, no. 1 (1994): 62–77.

Stewart, I. T., D. R. Cayan, and M. D. Dettinger. "Changes in Snowmelt Runoff Timing in Western North America under a 'Business as Usual' Climate Change Scenario." *Climatic Change* 62, no. 1–3 (2004): 217–32. http://dx.doi.org/10.1023/B:CLIM.0000013702.22656.e8.

Strange, E. M., K. D. Fausch, and A. P. Covich. "Sustaining Ecosystem Services in Human-Dominated Watersheds: Biohydrology and Ecosystem Processes in the South Platte River Basin." *Environmental Management* 24, no. 1 (1999): 39–54. http://dx.doi.org/10.1007/s002679900213. Medline:10341061.

Tate, C. M., and J. S. Heiny. "The Ordination of Benthic Invertebrate Communities in the South Platte River Basin in Relation to Environmental Factors." *Freshwater Biology* 33, no. 3 (1995): 439–54. http://dx.doi.org/10.1111/j.1365-2427.1995.tb00405.x.

Tate, C. M., and L. M. Martin. "Fish Communities in the Plains Region of the South Platte River, August 1993 and 1994." *US Geological Survey Fact Sheet* FS-154-95 (1995).

Williams, G. P. "The Case of the Shrinking Channels: The North Platte and Platte Rivers in Nebraska." *US Geological Survey Circular* 781 (1978): 636–37. http://dx.doi.org

Williams, G. P. "Historical Perspective of the Platte Rivers in Nebraska and Colorado." In *Lowland River and Stream Habitat in Colorado: A Symposium*, ed. W. D. Graul and S. J. Bissell, 11–41. Greeley, CO: Bureau of Land Management, 1978.

Winkler, S. "The Platte Pretzel." *Audubon* 91 (1989): 86–112.

Zelt, R. B., G. Boughton, K. A. Miller, J. P. Mason, and L. M. Gianakos. "Environmental Setting of the Yellowstone River Basin, Montana, North Dakota, and Wyoming." *US Geological Survey (USGS) Water-Investigations Report* 98-4269. Cheyenne, WY: USGS, 1999.

EASTERN PRAIRIE: BOOKS

Bird, I. L. *The Englishwoman in America.* London: John Murray, 1856.

Brookes, A. *Channelized Rivers: Perspectives for Environmental Management.* Chichester: John Wiley and Sons, 1988.

Clark, J. A. *Gleanings by the Way*. Philadelphia: Simon, 1842.

Forbes, S. A., and R. E. Richardson. *The Fishes of Illinois*. Springfield: State of Illinois, 1920.

Gray, J. *The Illinois*. New York: Farrar and Rinehart, 1940.

Greenberg, J. *A Natural History of the Chicago Region*. Chicago: University of Chicago Press, 2002.

Hennepin, L. *A Description of Louisiana*. New York: John G. Shea, 1880 [1683].

Hill, L. *The Chicago River: A Natural and Unnatural History*. Chicago: Lake Claremont, 2000.

Marquette, J. *Travels and Explorations of the Jesuit Missionaries in New France, 1610–1791*. Ed. R. G. Thwaites. Cleveland: Burrows Brothers, 1898.

Matson, N. *French and Indians of Illinois River*. Carbondale: Southern Illinois University Press, 1874.

Morgan, M. J. *Land of Big Rivers: French and Indian Illinois, 1699–1778*. Carbondale: Southern Illinois University Press, 2010.

Oliver, W. *Eight Months in Illinois; with Information to Emigrants*. Newcastle upon Tyne: William Andrew Mitchell, 1843.

Packard, S., and C. F. Mutel, eds. *The Tallgrass Restoration Handbook: For Prairies, Savannas, and Woodlands*. Washington, DC: Island, 1997.

Shirley, S. *Restoring the Tallgrass Prairie: An Illustrated Manual for Iowa and the Upper Midwest*. Iowa City: University of Iowa Press, 1994.

Steinberg, T. *Nature Incorporated: Industrialization and the Waters of New England*. Cambridge: Cambridge University Press, 1991.

Teale, E. W. *Journey into Summer*. New York: Dodd, Mead, 1960.

Thompson, J. R. *Prairies, Forests, and Wetlands: The Restoration of Natural Landscape Communities in Iowa*. Iowa City: University of Iowa Press, 1992.

Thompson, J. R. *Wetlands Drainage, River Modification, and Sectoral Conflicts in the Lower Illinois Valley, 1890–1930*. Carbondale: Southern Illinois University Press, 2002.

Twain, M. *Life on the Mississippi*. New York: Book-of-the-Month Club, 1992 [1883].

EASTERN PRAIRIE: ARTICLES, BOOK CHAPTERS, GOVERNMENT PUBLICATIONS, DISSERTATIONS

Adams, J. R., and E. Delisio. "Temporal and Lateral Distribution of Resuspended Sediment Following Barge Tow Passage on the Illinois River." *Long Term Resource Monitoring Program 93-R011*. Onalaska, WI: US Geological Survey Environmental Management Technical Center, 1993.

Ahn, C., D. M. Johnston, R. E. Sparks, and D. C. White. "Analysis of Naturalization Alternatives for the Recovery of Moist-Soil Plants in the Floodplain of the Illinois River." *Hydrobiologia* 565, no. 1 (2006): 217–28. http://dx.doi.org/10.1007/s10750-005-1915-5.

Ahn, C., D. C. White, and R. E. Sparks. "Moist-Soil Plants as Ecohydrologic Indicators for Recovering the Flood Pulse in the Illinois River." *Restoration Ecology* 12, no. 2 (2004): 207–13. http://dx.doi.org/10.1111/j.1061-2971.2004.00361.x.

Arnold, T. L., D. J. Sullivan, M. A. Harris, F. A. Fitzpatrick, B. C. Scudder, P. M. Ruhl, D. W. Hanchar, and J. S. Stewart. "Environmental Setting of the Upper Illinois River

Basin and Implications for Water Quality." *US Geological Survey (USGS) Water-Resources Investigations Report* 98-4268. Urbana, IL: USGS, 1999.

Asch, D. L. "Aboriginal Specialty-Plant Cultivation in Eastern North America: Illinois Prehistory and a Post-Contact Perspective." In *Agricultural Origins and Development in the Mid-Continent*, ed. W. Green, 25–86. Office of the State Archeologist Report 19. Iowa City: University of Iowa, 1994.

Aulenbach, B. T., H. T. Buxton, W. A. Battaglin, and R. H. Coupe. "Streamflow and Nutrient Fluxes of the Mississippi-Atchafalaya River Basin and Subbasins for the Period of Record through 2005." *US Geological Survey (USGS) Open-File Report* 2007-1080. Washington, DC: USGS, 2007.

Band, L. E., C. L. Tague, P. Groffman, and K. Belt. "Forest Ecosystem Processes at the Watershed Scale: Hydrological and Ecological Controls of Nitrogen Export." *Hydrological Processes* 15, no. 10 (2001): 2013–28. http://dx.doi.org/10.1002/hyp.253.

Bayley, P. B. "The Flood-Pulse Advantage and the Restoration of River-Floodplain Systems." *Regulated Rivers: Research and Management* 6, no. 2 (1991): 75–86. http://dx.doi.org/10.1002/rrr.3450060203.

Bayley, P. B. "Understanding Large River-Floodplain Ecosystems." *BioScience* 45, no. 3 (1995): 153–58. http://dx.doi.org/10.2307/1312554.

Beckett, D. C., B. W. Green, S. A. Thomas, and A. C. Miller. "Epizoic Invertebrate Communities on Upper Mississippi River Unionid Bivalves." *American Midland Naturalist* 135, no. 1 (1996): 102–14. http://dx.doi.org/10.2307/2426875.

Belim, D. "Illinois River." In *One Hand on the Wheel*, 60–62. Berkeley, CA: Roundhouse, 1999.

Bellrose, F. C. "Lead Poisoning as a Mortality Factor in Waterfowl Populations." *Illinois Natural History Bulletin* 27 (1959): 235–88.

Bellrose, F. C., F. L. Paveglio, and D. W. Steffeck. "Waterfowl Populations and the Changing Environment of the Illinois River Valley." *Illinois Natural History Survey Bulletin* 32, no. 1 (1979): 1–53.

Bernhardt, E. S., M. A. Palmer, J. D. Allan, and 22 others. "Synthesizing U.S. River Restoration Efforts." *Science* 308, no. 5722 (April 29, 2005): 636–37. http://dx.doi.org/10.1126/science.1109769. Medline:15860611.

Bhowmik, N. G. *Physical Impacts of Human Alterations within River Basins: The Case of the Kankakee, Mississippi, and Illinois Rivers.* Long Term Resource Monitoring Program 93-R004. Onalaska, WI: US Geological Survey Environmental Management Technical Center, 1993.

Bhowmik, N. G. *Sediment Sources Analysis for Peoria Lake along the Illinois River.* Long Term Resource Monitoring Program 94-R006. Onalaska, WI: US Geological Survey Environmental Management Technical Center, 1994.

Bhowmik, N. G., and J. R. Adams. "Successional Changes in Habitat Caused by Sedimentation in Navigation Pools." *Hydrobiologia* 176-77, no. 1 (1989): 17–27. http://dx.doi.org/10.1007/BF00026540.

Bhowmik, N. G., and M. Demissie. "Sedimentation in the Illinois River Valley and Backwater Lakes." *Journal of Hydrology* [Amsterdam] 105, no. 1-2 (1989): 187–95. http://dx.doi.org/10.1016/0022-1694(89)90103-0.

Bhowmik, N. G., and R. J. Schicht. *Bank Erosion of the Illinois River*. Illinois Institute of Natural Resources Report of Investigation 92. Urbana: Illinois Institute of Natural Resources, 1980.

Blasing, T. J., and D. Duvick. "Reconstruction of Precipitation History in North American Corn Belt using Tree Rings." *Nature* 307, no. 5947 (1984): 143–45. http://dx.doi .org/10.1038/307143a0.

Blodgett, K. D., R. E. Sparks, S. D. Whitney, and R. Williamson. *Mussel Resources of the Illinois River System: Value to Illinois' Economy and Natural Heritage*. Long Term Resource Monitoring Program 98-R012. Onalaska, WI: US Geological Survey Environmental Management Technical Center, 1998.

Boyer, E. W., R. W. Howarth, J. N. Galloway, F. J. Dentener, P. A. Green, and C. J. Vörösmarty. "Riverine Nitrogen Export from the Continents to the Coasts." *Global Biogeochemical Cycles* 20, no. 1 (2006): GB1S91. http://dx.doi.org/10.1029/2005GB002537.

Changnon, S. A., and J. M. Changnon. "History of the Chicago Diversion and Future Implications." *Journal of Great Lakes Research* 22, no. 1 (1996): 100–118. http://dx.doi.org /10.1016/S0380-1330(96)70940-1.

Changnon, S. A., and M. Demissie. "Detection of Changes in Streamflow and Floods Resulting from Climate Fluctuations and Land Use-Drainage Changes." *Climatic Change* 32, no. 4 (1996): 411–21. http://dx.doi.org/10.1007/BF00140354.

Colten, C. E. "Illinois River Pollution Control, 1900–1970." In *The American Environment: Interpretations of Past Geographies*, ed. L. M. Dilsaver and C. E. Colten, 193–214. Lanham, MD: Rowman and Littlefield, 1992.

Committee on Environment and Natural Resources. *Integrated Assessment of Hypoxia in the Northern Gulf of Mexico*. Washington, DC: National Science and Technology Council, 2000.

Committee on Government Operations. *Stream Channelization: What Federally Financed Draglines and Bulldozers Do to Our Nation's Streams*. Fifth report by the Committee on Government Operations. Washington, DC: US Government Printing Office, 1973.

Covich, A. P., S. C. Fritz, P. J. Lamb, R. D. Marzolf, W. J. Matthews, K. A. Poiani, E. E. Prepas, M. B. Richman, and T. C. Winter. "Potential Effects of Climate Change on Aquatic Ecosystems of the Great Plains of North America." *Hydrological Processes* 11, no. 8 (1997): 993–1021. http://dx.doi.org/10.1002/(SICI)1099-1085(19970630)11:8<993: :AID-HYP515>3.0.CO;2-N.

Critical Trends Assessment Project. *Ecological Resources*, vol. 3: *The Changing Illinois Environment: Critical Trends*. Springfield: Illinois Department of Energy and Natural Resources, 1994.

Critical Trends Assessment Project. *Summary Report: The Changing Illinois Environment; Critical Trends*. Springfield: Illinois Department of Energy and Natural Resources, 1994.

Critical Trends Assessment Project. *Water Resources*, vol. 2: *The Changing Illinois Environment: Critical Trends*. Springfield: Illinois Department of Energy and Natural Resources, 1994.

Darmody, R. G., and J. C. Marlin. "Sediments and Sediment-Derived Soils in Illinois: Pedological and Agronomic Assessment." *Environmental Monitoring and Assessment* 77, no. 2 (July 2002): 209–27. http://dx.doi.org/10.1023/A:1015880004383. Medline:12180657.

DéCamps, H., M. Fortuné, F. Gazelle, and G. Pautou. "Historical Influence of Man on the Riparian Dynamics of a Fluvial Landscape." *Landscape Ecology* 1 (1988): 163–73. http://dx.doi.org/10.1007/BF00162742.

DeLong, M. D. "Upper Mississippi River Basin." In *Rivers of North America*, ed. A. C. Benke and C. E. Cushing, 326–67. Amsterdam: Elsevier Academic Press, 2005. http://dx.doi.org/10.1016/B978-012088253-3/50011-0.

Dettmers, J. M., S. Gutreuter, D. H. Wahl, and D. A. Soluk. "Patterns in Abundance of Fishes in Main Channels of the Upper Mississippi River System." *Canadian Journal of Fisheries and Aquatic Sciences* 58, no. 5 (2001): 933–42. http://dx.doi.org/10.1139/f01-046.

Dettmers, J. M., D. H. Wahl, D. A. Soluk, and S. Gutreuter. "Life in the Fast Lane: Fish and Foodweb Structures in the Main Channel of Large Rivers." *Journal of the North American Benthological Society* 20, no. 2 (2001): 255–65. http://dx.doi.org/10.2307/1468320.

Ebbs, S., J. Talbott, and R. Sankaran. "Cultivation of Garden Vegetables in Peoria Pool Sediments from the Illinois River: A Case Study in Trace Element Accumulation and Dietary Exposures." *Environment International* 32, no. 6 (August 2006): 766–74. http://dx.doi.org/10.1016/j.envint.2006.03.013. Medline:16650471.

Eisler, R. *Atrazine Hazards to Fish, Wildlife, and Invertebrates: A Synoptic Review.* US Fish and Wildlife Service Biological Report 85 (1.18). Washington, DC: US Fish and Wildlife Service, 1989.

Fitzpatrick, F. A., M. W. Diebel, M. A. Harris, T. L. Arnold, M. A. Lutz, and K. D. Richards. "Effects of Urbanization on the Geomorphology, Habitat, Hydrology, and Fish Index of Biotic Integrity of Streams in the Chicago Area, Illinois and Wisconsin." *American Fisheries Society Symposium* 47 (2005): 87–115.

Fitzpatrick, F. A., M. A. Harris, T. L. Arnold, and K. D. Richards. "Urbanization Influences on Aquatic Communities in Northeastern Illinois Streams." *Journal of the American Water Resources Association* 40, no. 2 (2004): 461–75. http://dx.doi.org/10.1111/j.1752-1688.2004.tb01043.x.

Forbes, S. A. "The Biological Survey of a River System: Its Objects, Methods, and Results." *Bulletin, State of Illinois, Division of the Natural History Survey* 17, no. 7 (1928): 277–84.

Forbes, S. A. "The Food of Fishes." *Illinois State Laboratory of Natural History Bulletin* 3, no. 2 (1880): 18–65.

Forbes, S. A. "The Investigation of a River System in the Interest of Its Fisheries." In *Biological Investigations of the Illinois River*, vol. 2. Urbana: Illinois State Laboratory of Natural History, 1910.

Forbes, S. A. "On the Food Relations of Fresh-Water Fishes: A Summary and Discussion." *Illinois State Laboratory of Natural History Bulletin* 2, no. 8 (1988): 475–538.

Forbes, S. A. "On the General and Interior Distribution of Illinois Fishes." *Bulletin of the Illinois State Laboratory of Natural History* 8, no. 36 (1909): 381–437.

Forbes, S. A. "Studies of the Food of Fresh-Water Fishes." *Illinois State Laboratory of Natural History Bulletin* 2, no. 7 (1988): 433–73.

Forbes, S. A., and R. E. Richardson. "Some Recent Changes in Illinois River Biology." *Illinois Natural History Survey Bulletin* 13, no. 6 (1919): 139–56.

Forbes, S. A., and R. E. Richardson. "Studies on the Biology of the Upper Illinois River." *Bulletin of the Illinois State Laboratory of Natural History* 9 (1913): 481–574.

Freeman, M. C., C. M. Pringle, and C. R. Jackson. "Hydrologic Connectivity and the Contribution of Stream Headwaters to Ecological Integrity at Regional Scales." *Journal of the American Water Resources Association* 43, no. 1 (2007): 5–14. http://dx.doi .org/10.1111/j.1752-1688.2007.00002.x.

Frothingham, K. M., B. L. Rhoads, and E. E. Herricks. "A Multiscale Conceptual Framework for Integrated Ecogeomorphological Research to Support Stream Naturalization in the Agricultural Midwest." *Environmental Management* 29, no. 1 (January 2002): 16–33. http://dx.doi.org/10.1007/s00267-001-0038-7. Medline:11740621.

Frothingham, K. M., B. L. Rhoads, and E. E. Herricks. "Stream Geomorphology and Fish Community Structure in Channelized and Meandering Reaches of an Agricultural Stream." In *Geomorphic Processes and Riverine Habitat*, ed. J. M. Dorava, D. R. Montgomery, B. B. Palcsak, and F. A. Fitzpatrick, 105–17. Washington, DC: American Geophysical Union Press, 2001. http://dx.doi.org/10.1029/WS004p0105.

Galloway, J. N., F. J. Dentener, D. G. Capone, E. W. Boyer, R. W. Howarth, S. P. Seitzinger, G. P. Asner, C. C. Cleveland, P. A. Green, E. A. Holland, D. M. Karl, A. F. Michaels, J. H. Porter, A. R. Townsend, and C. J. Vörösmarty. "Nitrogen Cycles: Past, Present, and Future." *Biogeochemistry* 70, no. 2 (2004): 153–226. http://dx.doi.org/10.1007/s10533 -004-0370-0.

Garman, H. "Notes on Illinois Reptiles and Amphibians, Including Several Species Not before Recorded from the Northern States." *Bulletin of the Illinois State Laboratory of Natural History* 3, no. 10 (1890): 185–90.

Garman, H. "A Synopsis of the Reptiles and Amphibians of Illinois." *Bulletin of the Illinois State Laboratory of Natural History* 3, no. 13 (1892): 215–390.

Gillette, R. "Stream Channelization: Conflict between Ditchers, Conservationists." *Science* 176, no. 4037 (May 26, 1972): 890–94. http://dx.doi.org/10.1126/science.176.4037.890. Medline:17829292.

Green, W., and D. J. Nolan. "Late Woodland Peoples in West-Central Illinois." In *Late Woodland Societies: Tradition and Transformation across the Midcontinent*, ed. T. E. Emerson, D. L. McElrath, and A. C. Fortier, 345–72. Lincoln: University of Nebraska Press, 2000.

Hahn, S. S. "Stream Channelization: Effects on Stream Fauna." In *Biota and Biological Principles of the Aquatic Environment*, ed. P. E. Greeson, A43–A49. Geological Survey Circular 848-A. Washington, DC: US Government Printing Office, 1982.

Harris, M. A., B. C. Scudder, F. A. Fitzpatrick, and T. L. Arnold. *Physical, Chemical, and Biological Responses to Urbanization in the Fox and Des Plaines River Basins of Northeastern Illinois and Southeastern Wisconsin*. US Geological Survey (USGS) Scientific Investigations Report 2005-5218. Urbana, IL: USGS, 2005.

Hart, C. A. "On the Entomology of the Illinois River and Adjacent Waters." *Bulletin of the Illinois State Laboratory of Natural History* 4, no. 6 (1895): 149–273.

Heidinger, R. C. "Fishes in the Illinois Portion of the Upper Des Plaines River." *Transactions of the Illinois Academy of Science* 82, no. 1 (1989): 85–96.

Helm, R. B., G. Hewitt, and D. R. Good. "Improving the Illinois." *Water Environment and Technology* 6, no. 6 (1994): 44–46.

Herre, A. W. "An Early Illinois Prairie." *American Botanist* 46 (1940): 39–44.

Hey, D. L. "Nitrogen Farming: Harvesting a Different Crop." *Restoration Ecology* 10, no. 1 (2002): 1–10. http://dx.doi.org/10.1046/j.1526-100X.2002.10100.x.

Hey, D. L., and N. S. Phillipi. "Reinventing a Flood Control Strategy." *Wetlands Initiative* (September 1994): 4–8.

Hooke, R. LeB. "On the History of Humans as Geomorphic Agents." *Geology* 28, no. 9 (2000): 843–46. http://dx.doi.org/10.1130/0091-7613(2000)28<843:OTHOHA>2.0.CO;2.

Hoops, R. "A River of Grain: The Evolution of Commercial Navigation on the Upper Mississippi River." *College of Agricultural and Life Sciences Report* R3584. Madison: University of Wisconsin, 1993.

Howarth, R. W., E. W. Boyer, W. J. Pabich, and J. N. Galloway. "Nitrogen Use in the United States from 1961–2000 and Potential Future Trends." *Ambio* 31, no. 2 (March 2002): 88–96. Medline:12078014.

Illinois Environmental Protection Agency (IEPA). *Illinois Water Quality Report, 1994–1995*, vol. 1: *Illinois' Assessment of Water Resource Conditions.* IEPA/BOW96/06a. Springfield: IEPA, 1996.

Iverson, B. "Silt: A Problem Turned Solution?" *Outdoor Illinois* 8 (2000): 5–7.

Junk, W. J., P. B. Bayley, and R. E. Sparks. "The Flood Pulse Concept in River-Floodplain Systems." *Canadian Special Publication of Fisheries and Aquatic Sciences* 106 (1989): 110–27.

Karr, J. R., L. A. Toth, and D. R. Dudley. "Fish Communities of Midwestern Rivers: A History of Degradation." *BioScience* 35, no. 2 (1985): 90–95. http://dx.doi.org/10.2307/1309845.

Koel, T. M. "Spatial Variation in Fish Species Richness of the Upper Mississippi River System." *Transactions of the American Fisheries Society* 133, no. 4 (2004): 984–1003. http://dx.doi.org/10.1577/T03-089.1.

Koel, T. M., and R. E. Sparks. "Historical Patterns of River Stage and Fish Communities as Criteria for Operations of Dams on the Illinois River." *River Research and Applications* 18, no. 1 (2002): 3–19. http://dx.doi.org/10.1002/rra.630.

Kofoid, C. "The Plankton of the Illinois River, 1894–1899, with Introductory Notes upon the Hydrography of the Illinois River and Its Basin." *Bulletin of the Illinois State Laboratory of Natural History* 6, no. 2 (1903).

Landwehr, K., and B. L. Rhoads. "Depositional Response of a Headwater Stream to Channelization, East Central Illinois, USA." *River Research and Applications* 19, no. 1 (2003): 77–100. http://dx.doi.org/10.1002/rra.699.

Levengood, J. M. "Cadmium and Lead in Tissues of Mallards (*Anas platyrhynchos*) and Wood Ducks (*Aix sponsa*) using the Illinois River (USA)." *Environmental Pollution* 122, no. 2 (2003): 177–81. http://dx.doi.org/10.1016/S0269-7491(02)00298-1. Medline:12531305.

Lowrance, R., R. Todd, J. Fail Jr., O. Hendrickson Jr., R. Leonard, and L. Asmussen. "Riparian Forests as Nutrient Filters in Agricultural Watersheds." *BioScience* 34, no. 6 (1984): 374–77. http://dx.doi.org/10.2307/1309729.

Machesky, M. L., J. A. Slowikowski, R. A. Cahill, W. C. Bogner, J. C. Marlin, T. R. Holm, and R. G. Darmody. "Sediment Quality and Quantity Issues Related to the Restoration of Backwater Lakes along the Illinois River Waterway." *Aquatic Ecosystem Health and Management* 8, no. 1 (2005): 33–40. http://dx.doi.org/10.1080/14634980590914881.

Marlin, J. C., and R. G. Darmody. "Returning the Soil to the Land: The Mud to Parks Project." *Illinois Steward* 14 (2005): 11–18.

Mattingly, R. L., E. E. Herricks, and D. M. Johnston. "Channelization and Levee Construction in Illinois: Review and Implications for Management." *Environmental Management* 17, no. 6 (1993): 781–95. http://dx.doi.org/10.1007/BF02393899.

McClain, M. E., E. W. Boyer, C. L. Dent, S. E. Gergel, N. B. Grimm, P. M. Groffman, S. C. Hart, J. W. Harvey, C. A. Johnston, E. Mayorga, W. H. McDowell, and G. Pinay. "Biogeochemical Hot Spots and Hot Moments at the Interface of Terrestrial and Aquatic Ecosystems." *Ecosystems* [New York] 6, no. 4 (2003): 301–12. http://dx.doi.org/10.1007/s10021-003-0161-9.

Meade, R. H. "Contaminants in the Mississippi River 1987–92." *US Geological Survey Circular* 1133 (1995).

Meyer, J. L., D. L. Strayer, J. B. Wallace, G. S. Helfman, and N. E. Leonard. "The Contribution of Headwater Streams to Biodiversity in River Networks." *Journal of the American Water Resources Association* 43, no. 1 (2007): 86–103. http://dx.doi.org/10.1111/j.1752-1688.2007.00008.x.

Mills, H. B., W. C. Starrett, and F. C. Bellrose. *Man's Effect on the Fish and Wildlife of the Illinois River.* Illinois Natural History Survey Biological Notes 57. Urbana: Illinois Natural History Survey, 1966.

Mitsch, W. J., J. W. Day, J. W. Gilliam, P. M. Groffman, D. L. Hey, G. W. Randall, and N. Wang. "Reducing Nutrient Loads, Especially Nitrate-Nitrogen, to the Surface Water, Ground Water, and the Gulf of Mexico." *Topic 5 Report, NOAA.* Silver Spring, MD: National Oceanic and Atmospheric Admistration, 1999.

Morales, Y., L. J. Weber, A. E. Mynett, and T. J. Newton. "Effects of Substrate and Hydrodynamic Conditions on the Formation of Mussel Beds in a Large River." *Journal of the North American Benthological Society* 25, no. 3 (2006): 664–76. http://dx.doi.org/10.1899/0887-3593(2006)25[664:EOSAHC]2.0.CO;2.

Morrow, W. S. *Anthropogenic Constituents in Shallow Ground Water in the Upper Illinois River Basin.* US Geological Survey (USGS) Water-Resources Investigations Report 02-4293. Urbana, IL: USGS, 2003.

Morrow, W. S. *Volatile Organic Compounds in Ground Water of the Lower Illinois River Basin.* US Geological Survey (USGS) Water-Resources Investigations Report 99-4229. Urbana, IL: USGS, 1999.

Nadeau, T.-L., and M. C. Rains. "Hydrologic Connectivity of Headwaters to Downstream Waters: Introduction to the Featured Collection." *Journal of the American Water Resources Association* 43, no. 1 (2007): 1–4. http://dx.doi.org/10.1111/j.1752-1688.2007.00001.x.

Nelson, J. C., A. Redmond, and R. E. Sparks. "Impacts of Settlement on Floodplain Vegetation at the Confluence of the Illinois and Mississippi Rivers." *Transactions of the Illinois State Academy of Science.* Illinois State Academy of Science 87, no. 3 (1994): 117–33.

Nichols, R. W. "Controlling Soil Erosion in the Illinois River Basin." *Second Conference on the Management of the Illinois River System: The 1990s and Beyond.* University of Illinois Water Resources Center Special Report 18. Urbana-Champaign: Water Resources Center, University of Illinois, 1989.

Nihlgard, B. J., W. T. Swank, and M. J. Mitchell. "Biological Processes and Catchment Studies." In *Biogeochemistry of Small Catchments: A Tool for Environmental Research*, ed. B. Moldan and J. Cerny, 133–61. Chichester: John Wiley and Sons, 1994.

O'Connell, J. C. "Technology and Pollution: Chicago's Water Policy, 1833–1930." PhD diss., University of Chicago, Chicago, 1980.

Page, L. M. "The Crayfishes and Shrimps (Decapoda) of Illinois." *Illinois Natural History Survey Bulletin* 33, no. 4 (1985): 335–448.

Page, L. M., K. S. Cummings, C. A. Mayer, and S. L. Post. *Biologically Significant Illinois Streams: An Evaluation of the Streams of Illinois Based on Aquatic Biodiversity.* Technical Report 1991(4). Champaign: Illinois Natural History Survey, Center for Biodiversity, 1991.

Pegg, M. A., and M. A. McClelland. "Spatial and Temporal Patterns in Fish Communities along the Illinois River." *Ecology Freshwater Fish* 13, no. 2 (2004): 125–35. http://dx.doi.org/10.1111/j.1600-0633.2004.00046.x.

Petersen, C. E. "Water Quality of the West Branch of the DuPage River and Kline Creek, Illinois, as Evaluated Using the Arthropod Fauna and Chemical Measurements." *Great Lakes Entomologist* 24, no. 3 (1991): 127–31.

Peterson, B. J., W. M. Wollheim, P. J. Mulholland, and 12 others. "Control of Nitrogen Export from Watersheds by Headwater Streams." *Science* 292, no. 5514 (April 6, 2001): 86–90. http://dx.doi.org/10.1126/science.1056874. Medline:11292868.

Phipps, R. L., G. P. Johnson, and P. J. Terrio. *Dendrogeomorphic Estimate of Changes in Sedimentation Rate along the Kankakee River near Momence, Illinois.* US Geological Survey (USGS) Water-Resources Investigations Report 94-4190. Washington, DC: USGS, 1995.

Prato, T., and D. Hey. "Economic Analysis of Wetland Restoration along the Illinois River." *Journal of the American Water Resources Association* 42, no. 1 (2006): 125–31. http://dx.doi.org/10.1111/j.1752-1688.2006.tb03828.x.

Rabeni, C. F. "Prairie Legacies—Fish and Aquatic Resources." In *Prairie Conservation: Preserving North America's Most Endangered Ecosystem*, ed. F. B. Samson and F. L. Knopf, 111–24. Washington, DC: Island, 1996.

Raibley, P. T., D. Blodgett, and R. E. Sparks. "Evidence of Grass Carp (*Ctenopharyngodon idella*) Reproduction in the Illinois and Upper Mississippi Rivers." *Journal of Freshwater Ecology* 10, no. 1 (1995): 65–74. http://dx.doi.org/10.1080/02705060.1995.9663418.

Raibley, P. T., T. M. O'Hara, K. S. Irons, K. D. Blodgett, and R. E. Sparks. "Largemouth Bass Size Distributions under Varying Annual Hydrological Regimes in the Illinois River." *Transactions of the American Fisheries Society* 126, no. 5 (1997): 850–56. http://dx.doi.org/10.1577/1548-8659(1997)126<0850:NLBSDU>2.3.CO;2.

Ranalli, A. J., and D. L. Macalady. "The Importance of the Riparian Zone and In-Stream Processes in Nitrate Attenuation in Undisturbed and Agricultural Watersheds: A Review of the Scientific Literature." *Journal of Hydrology* [Amsterdam] 389, no. 3-4 (2010): 406–15. http://dx.doi.org/10.1016/j.jhydrol.2010.05.045.

Retzer, M. E. "Changes in the Diversity of Native Fishes in Seven Basins in Illinois, USA." *American Midland Naturalist* 153, no. 1 (2005): 121–34. http://dx.doi.org/10.1674/0003-0031(2005)153[0121:CITDON]2.0.CO;2.

Rhoads, B. L., and E. E. Herricks. "Naturalization of Headwater Streams in Illinois: Challenges and Possibilities." In *River Channel Restoration: Guiding Principles for Sustainable Projects*, ed. A. Brookes and F. D. Shields, 331–67. Chichester: John Wiley and Sons, 1996.

Rhoads, B. L., J. S. Schwartz, and S. Porter. "Stream Geomorphology, Bank Vegetation, and Three-Dimensional Habitat Hydraulics for Fish in Midwestern Agricultural Streams." *Water Resources Research* 39, no. 8 (2003): ESG 2-1–2-13.

Rhoads, B. L., D. Wilson, M. Urban, and E. E. Herricks. "Interaction between Scientists and Nonscientists in Community-Based Watershed Management: Emergence of the Concept of Stream Naturalization." *Environmental Management* 24, no. 3 (October 1999): 297–308. http://dx.doi.org/10.1007/s002679900234. Medline:10486041.

Richardson, R. E. "The Bottom Fauna of the Middle Illinois River, 1913–1925." *Bulletin, State of Illinois, Division of the Natural History Survey* 17, no. 12 (1928): 387–475.

Richardson, R. E. "The Small Bottom and Shore Fauna of the Middle and Lower Illinois River and Its Connecting Lakes, Chillicothe to Grafton: Its Valuation; Its Sources of Food Supply; and Its Relation to the Fishery." *Illinois Natural History Survey Bulletin* 13, no. 15 (1921): 363–522.

Ruhl, P. M. *Surface-Water-Quality Assessment of the Upper Illinois River Basin in Illinois, Indiana, and Wisconsin: Analysis of Relations between Fish-Community Structure and Environmental Conditions in the Fox, Des Plaines, and Du Page River Basins in Illinois, 1982–84.* US Geological Survey (USGS) Water-Resources Investigations Report 94-4094. Urbana, IL: USGS, 1995.

Salo, J., R. Kalliola, I. Häkkinen, Y. Mäkinen, P. Niemelä, M. Puhakka, and P. D. Coley. "River Dynamics and the Diversity of Amazon Lowland Forest." *Nature* 322, no. 6076 (1986): 254–58. http://dx.doi.org/10.1038/322254a0.

Sanderson, G. C., and F. C. Bellrose. *A Review of the Problem of Lead Poisoning in Waterfowl.* Illinois Natural History Survey, Special Publication 4. Champaign: Illinois Natural History Survey, 1986.

Scarnecchia, D. L. "The Importance of Streamlining in Influencing Fish Community Structure in Channelized and Unchannelized Reaches of a Prairie Stream." *Regulated Rivers: Research and Management* 2, no. 2 (1988): 155–66. http://dx.doi.org/10.1002/rrr.3450020209.

Schlosser, I. J. "Fish Community Structure and Function along Two Habitat Gradients in a Headwater Stream." *Ecological Monographs* 52, no. 4 (1982): 395–414. http://dx.doi.org/10.2307/2937352.

Schoof, R. "Environmental Impact of Channel Modification." *Water Resources Bulletin* 16, no. 4 (1980): 697–701. http://dx.doi.org/10.1111/j.1752-1688.1980.tb02451.x.

Shelford, V. E. "Ways and Means of Measuring the Dangers of Pollution to Fisheries." *Illinois State Natural History Survey Bulletin* 13, no. 2 (1918): 25–42.

Sietman, B. E., S. D. Whitney, D. E. Kelner, K. D. Blodgett, and H. L. Dunn. "Post-Extirpation Recovery of the Freshwater Mussel (Bivalvia: Unionidae) Fauna in the Upper Illinois River." *Journal of Freshwater Ecology* 16, no. 2 (2001): 273–82. http://dx.doi.org/10.1080/02705060.2001.9663813.

Singh, K. P., and G. S. Ramamurthy. "Gradual Climate Change and Resulting Hydrologic Response." In *Conference on Climate and Water*, vol. 1: 476–85. Helsinki: International Association of Hydrological Science, 1989.

Smith, M., and P. Mettler. "The Role of the Flood Pulse in Maintaining *Boltonia decurrens*, a Fugitive Plant Species of the Illinois River Floodplain: A Case History of a Threatened Species." In *Flood Pulsing in Wetlands: Restoring the Natural Hydrological Balance*, ed. B. A. Middleton, 109–44. New York: John Wiley and Sons, 2002.

Sparks, R. E. "Environmental Inventory and Assessment of Navigation Pools 24, 25, and 26, Upper Mississippi and Lower Illinois Rivers: An Electrofishing Survey of the Illinois River." University of Illinois at Urbana-Champaign Water Resources Center Special Report 5, UILU-WRC-77-0005. Urbana-Champaign: Water Resources Center, University of Illinois, 1977.

Sparks, R. E. "The Illinois River-Floodplain System." In *Restoration of Aquatic Ecosystems: Science, Technology, and Public Policy*. Committee on Restoration of Aquatic Ecosystems: Science, Technology, and Public Policy, Water Science and Technology Board, National Research Council, 412–32. Washington, DC: National Academy Press, 1992.

Sparks, R. E. "Need for Ecosystem Management of Large Rivers and Their Floodplains." *BioScience* 45, no. 3 (1995): 168–82. http://dx.doi.org/10.2307/1312556.

Sparks, R. E., P. B. Bayley, S. L. Kohler, and L. L. Osborne. "Disturbance and Recovery of Large Floodplain Rivers." *Environmental Management* 14, no. 5 (1990): 699–709. http://dx.doi.org/10.1007/BF02394719.

Sparks, R. E., and F. S. Dillon. "Illinois River Fingernail Clam Toxicity Study." *Illinois Natural History Survey*, Aquatic Ecology-TR-93/5. Springfield: State of Illinois, 1998.

Sparks, R. E., and W. C. Starrett. "An Electrofishing Survey of the Illinois River, 1959–1974." *Illinois Natural History Survey Bulletin* 31, no. 8 (1975): 317–80.

Starrett, W. C. "A Survey of the Mussels (Unionacea) of the Illinois River: A Polluted Stream." *Illinois Natural History Survey Bulletin* 30, no. 5 (1971): 267–403.

Starrett, W. C., and A. W. Fritz. "A Biological Investigation of the Fishes of Lake Chautauqua, Illinois." *Illinois Natural History Survey Bulletin* 29, no. 1 (1965): 1–104.

Steinauer, E. M., and S. L. Collins. "Prairie Ecology: The Tallgrass Prairie." In *Prairie Conservation: Preserving North America's Most Endangered Ecosystem*, ed. F. B. Samson and F. L. Knopf, 39–52. Washington, DC: Island, 1996.

Steele, E. "A Summer Journey in the West." In *Of Prairie, Woods, and Water: Two Centuries of Chicago Nature Writing*, ed. J. Greenberg, 24. New York: John Taylor, 1841; Chicago: University of Chicago Press, 2008.

Stoeckel, J. A., L. Camlin, K. D. Blodgett, and R. E. Sparks. "Establishment of *Daphnia lumholtzi* (an Exotic Zooplankter) in the Illinois River." *Journal of Freshwater Ecology* 11, no. 3 (1996): 377–79. http://dx.doi.org/10.1080/02705060.1996.9664461.

Stoeckel, J. A., D. W. Schneider, L. A. Soeken, K. D. Blodgett, and R. E. Sparks. "Larval Dynamics of a Riverine Metapopulation: Implications for Zebra Mussel Recruitment, Dispersal, and Control in a Large-River System." *Journal of the North American Benthological Society* 16, no. 3 (1997): 586–601. http://dx.doi.org/10.2307/1468146.

Styles, B. W. "Faunal Exploitation and Resource Selection: Early Late Woodland Subsistence in the Lower Illinois Valley." Evanston, IL: Northwestern University Archaeological Program, 1981.

Sullivan, D. J. *Nutrients and Suspended Solids in Surface Waters of the Upper Illinois River Basin in Illinois, Indiana, and Wisconsin, 1978–97.* US Geological Survey (USGS) Water-Resources Investigations Report 99-4275. Middleton, WI: USGS, 2000.

Sullivan, D. J., T. W. Stinson, J. K. Crawford, and A. R. Schmidt. *Surface-Water-Quality Assessment of the Upper Illinois River Basin in Illinois, Indiana, and Wisconsin: Pesticides and Other Synthetic Organic Compounds in Water, Sediment, and Biota, 1975–90.* US Geological Survey (USGS) Water-Resources Investigations Report 96-4135. Urbana, IL: USGS, 1998.

Tesfamichael, A. A., A. J. Caplan, and J. J. Kaluarachchi. "Risk-Cost-Benefit Analysis of Atrazine in Drinking Water from Agricultural Activities and Policy Implications." *Water Resources Research* 41, W05015 (2005): 13 pp.

Thompson, D. H. "The 'Knothead' Carp of the Illinois River." *Bulletin, State of Illinois, Division of the Natural History Survey* 17, no. 8 (1928): 285–320.

Thompson, J. "Land Drainage and Conflict Resolution in the Lower Valley of the Illinois River, 1890s–1930." In *Sustainable Agriculture in the American Midwest: Lessons from the Past, Prospects for the Future,* ed. G. McIsaac and W. R. Edwards, 77–94. Chicago: University of Illinois Press, 1994.

Tryfonas, A. E., J. K. Tucker, P. E. Brunkow, K. A. Johnson, H. S. Hussein, and Z.-Q. Lin. "Metal Accumulation in Eggs of the Red-Eared Slider (*Trachemys scripta elegans*) in the Lower Illinois River." *Chemosphere* 63, no. 1 (March 2006): 39–48. http://dx.doi.org/10.1016/j.chemosphere.2005.07.080. Medline:16216308.

Tucker, J. K., and E. R. Atwood. "Contiguous Backwater Lakes as Possible Refugia for Unionid Mussels in Areas of Heavy Zebra Mussel (Dreissena polymorpha) Colonization." *Journal of Freshwater Ecology* 10, no. 1 (1995): 43–47. http://dx.doi.org/10.1080/02705060.1995.9663415.

Van Breemen, N., E. W. Boyer, C. L. Goodale, N. A. Jaworski, K. Paustian, S. P. Seitzinger, K. Lajtha, B. Mayer, D. Van Dam, R. W. Howarth, K. L. Nadelhoffer, M. Eve, and G. Billen. "Where Did All the Nitrogen Go? Fate of Nitrogen Inputs to Large Watersheds in the Northeastern U.S.A." *Biogeochemistry* 57, no. 1 (2002): 267–93. http://dx.doi.org/10.1023/A:1015775225913.

Van Nest, J. "Rediscovering This Earth." In *Recreating Hopewell,* ed. D. K. Charles and J. E. Buikstra, 402–26. Gainesville: University Press of Florida, 2006.

Wade, R. J., B. L. Rhoads, J. Rodriguez, M. Daniels, D. Wilson, E. E. Herricks, F. Bombardelli, M. Garcia, and J. Schwartz. "Integrating Science and Technology to Support Stream Naturalization near Chicago, Illinois." *Journal of the American Water Resources Association* 38, no. 4 (2002): 931–44. http://dx.doi.org/10.1111/j.1752-1688.2002.tb05535.x.

Walling, D. E., and B. W. Webb. "Erosion and Sediment Yield: A Global Overview." In *Erosion and Sediment Yield: Global and Regional Perspectives,* 3–19. International Association of Hydrological Science Publication 236. Wallingford, UK: IAHS, 1996.

Warner, K. L. *Analysis of Nutrients, Selected Inorganic Constituents, and Trace Elements in Water from Illinois Community-Supply Wells, 1984–91.* US Geological Survey (USGS) Water-Resources Investigations Report 99-4152. Urbana, IL: USGS, 2000.

Warner, K. L. *Water-Quality Assessment of the Lower Illinois River Basin: Environmental Setting.* US Geological Survey (USGS) Water-Resources Investigations Report 97-4165. Urbana, IL: USGS, 1998.

Warner, K. L., and A. R. Schmidt. *National Water Quality Assessment Program: The Lower Illinois River Basin.* NAWQA Fact Sheet 94-018. Washington, DC: US Geological Survey, 1994.

Webb, D. W. "The Winter Stoneflies of Illinois (Insecta: Plecoptera): 100 Years of Change." *Illinois Natural History Survey Bulletin* 36, no. 5 (2002): 195–274.

GENERAL REFERENCES: BOOKS

Colborn, T., D. Dumanoski, and J. P. Meyers. *Our Stolen Future: How We Are Threatening Our Fertility, Intelligence, and Survival: A Scientific Detective Story.* New York: Dutton, 1996.

Manning, R. *Grassland: The History, Biology, Politics, and Promise of the American Prairie.* New York: Viking, 1995.

Savage, C. *Prairie: A Natural History.* Vancouver: Greystone Books, 2004.

Vileisis, A. *Discovering the Unknown Landscape: A History of America's Wetlands.* Washington, DC: Island, 1997.

Watts, M. T. *Reading the Landscape: An Adventure in Ecology.* New York: Macmillan, 1957.

Index